GREENLAND

ASIA

EUROPE

St.Petersburg

SCOTLAND
Glasgow ENGLAND
London
Galway IRELAND Bremen
Liverpool GERMANY
Brest Frankfurt
Nantes Paris Vienna
Bordeaux Genoa Trieste
Rome

Quebec
Montreal St. John's
Toronto
ago Halifax
mond Boston
New York
Washington AZORES PORTUGAL
Norfolk Lisbon SPAIN
Wilmington BERMUDA Cadiz
Charleston Gibraltar
Savannah MADERA IS. Tangier
St. Augustine CANARY IS. Mogador
Nassau
a
CUBA ST.THOMAS
JAMAICA
CARIBBEAN SEA

Constantinople
TURKEY
MEDITERRANEAN
SEA
Cairo
EGYPT

INDIA

ARABIAN SEA

CEYLON

inwall
City

A T L A N T I C

FERNANDO
DE NORONHA
SOUTH Bahia ASCENCION
AMERICA

AFRICA

O C E A N

I N D I A N

Cape Town

O C E A N

palacios

WHEN THE GUNS ROARED

PHILIP VAN DOREN STERN

WHEN THE GUNS
 ROARED

World Aspects

of the

American Civil War

Doubleday & Company, Inc., Garden City, New York
1965

Library of Congress Catalog Card Number 65-12826

Copyright © 1965 by Philip Van Doren Stern
All Rights Reserved
Printed in the United States of America
First Edition

ACKNOWLEDGMENTS

The author wishes to thank the following institutions and persons: LIBRARY OF CONGRESS: Dr. David C. Mearns, Dr. Percy Powell, NATIONAL ARCHIVES: Forest L. Williams, Elbert L. Huber; SMITHSONIAN INSTITUTION: P. K. Lundeberg; DEPARTMENT OF THE NAVY: Rear Admiral E. M. Eller, Captain F. Kent Loomis, Commander D. D. Overby, Commander Penhard Hendler, H. A. Vadnais, Jr.; U. S. NAVAL ACADEMY: Captain Wade De Weese; U. S. MILITARY ACADEMY: Richard E. Kuehne; DEPARTMENT OF STATE: Carl Bode, Phillips Brooks; DEPARTMENT OF JUSTICE, ADMIRALTY SHIPPING SECTION: Captain Morris G. Duchin; HENRY E. HUNTINGTON LIBRARY: Dr. John E. Pomfret, Dr. Allan Nevins, Mary Isabel Fry, Helen Mangold, Marion Chevalier, Herbert C. Schulz, Carey S. Bliss, Erwin K. Morkisch; RICE UNIVERSITY: Dr. Frank Vandiver; UNIVERSITY OF CALIFORNIA: Dr. Brainerd Dyer, Dr. Jay Monaghan; WHITTIER COLLEGE: James M. Merrill; UNIVERSITY OF ALABAMA: William Stanley Hoole; LOUISIANA STATE MUSEUM: C. E. Frampton; THE CONFEDERATE MUSEUM: India W. Thomas; Eleanor S. Brockenbrough; THE NEW YORK HISTORICAL SOCIETY: James J. Heslin; CHICAGO HISTORICAL SOCIETY: Paul Angle, Mrs. Paul M. Rhymer; GEORGIA HISTORICAL SOCIETY: Walter Hartridge, Lilla M. Hawes; SAVANNAH PUBLIC LIBRARY: Elizabeth Hodge; BROOKLYN PUBLIC LIBRARY: Corinne Shepard, Louise Turpin; NEW YORK PUBLIC LIBRARY: Leon Weidman; MOBILE PUBLIC LIBRARY.

ENGLAND. PUBLIC RECORD OFFICE: E. K. Timings; BRITISH MUSEUM: Frank Francis, C. M. Dodd, B. Schofield; ADMIRALTY: P. W. Kemp; H. M. CUSTOMS AND EXCISE: R. C. Jarvis; UNIVERSITY OF LONDON: J. G. Edwards, Michael Howard; RHODES HOUSE; NATIONAL MARITIME MUSEUM: G. P. B. Naish; CONFEDERATE RESEARCH CLUB: Thomas Green.

FRANCE. ARCHIVES NATIONALES: Jacques Meurgey de Tupigny; BIBLIOTHÈQUE NATIONALE: Julien Cain; BIBLIOTHÈQUE MUNICIPALE DE BORDEAUX. Mlle. Gaston-Cheraud, M. Bruno.

DENMARK. ROYAL NAVAL MUSEUM: Bredo von Munthe af Morgenstierne; SOCIETY FOR NAVAL HISTORY: Captain R. Steen Steensen, A. P. Møller Co., Morten P. Hoogland.

In addition to those listed above, thanks are also due to the following individuals for their helpful cooperation: Miss Marianne M. Laird, Betty Lass, E. B. Long, James F. Mathias, Henry Allen Moe, Mrs. Theodore Douglas Robinson, Colonel William Morrison Robinson, Jr., Archibald Roosevelt, and Miss Frances Leigh Williams.

TABLE OF CONTENTS

ILLUSTRATIONS

INTRODUCTION

After five years and many thousands of miles of traveling, I am bringing this book to a close in London. This seems quite appropriate, for it deals with the effect which the American Civil War had on the rest of the world, and in the 1860s the world was dominated by England. She was so supreme that her Ministers were often arrogant. Fortunately, her Queen was kinder; she could, when necessary, temper their aggressiveness.

England's power was then so great that even the ambitious French Emperor, Napoleon III, had to be content to follow her lead, especially in American affairs. Russia was the only major power that could withstand Britain's influence, and that was because she was far enough away to be out of the mainstream of European politics.

England therefore became the key to the outcome of the war in America. With her help, the South had a chance to succeed, for if Britain openly gave aid, other nations would also. But she was divided about the internal conflict that was dividing her former colony. The British upper classes generally favored the South; working people supported the North, and the middle classes wavered uncertainly in between.

This book therefore deals largely with divided people, divided in America, divided in England, and divided elsewhere. But the Americans and the British had one thing in common—they spoke the same language, the mother tongue which Chaucer had helped to shape and which Shakespeare had brought to perfection. Written in English, also, was the King James version of the Bible which had had so much influence on the phrasing of speeches and state documents in both countries.

The fact that American and British people both spoke the same language helped the North, for it meant that news of the war could be read as soon as it reached England. In other countries, the dispatches had to be translated and were often cut or distorted in the time-consuming process. Since most news came from the North rather than from the South, the Union got more publicity than the Confederacy did. And such publicity, of course, was nearly always favorable, while the South was constantly shown in its worst light. This may seem like a small matter, but it did affect public opinion abroad.

But far more important than a common language was something which bound England and America together more closely than independent nations have ever been bound before. This was an unconscious kinship, an intangible and difficult-to-describe relationship which may best be likened to the subtle interplay of emotions in a large family. In such a group, members may quarrel, but they never lose the sense of belonging to the same clan. Instances of this have often happened when British and Americans came to each others' aid in foreign countries during troubled times. But it is more than a common language that brings them together. They tend to think alike, to believe in the same ideals, and to have the same notions about what is right and wrong. They respect decency, justice, and a fair deal for everyone. They hate tyranny, cruelty, dishonesty, and all forms of chicanery. This, of course, does not mean that all their people live up to these high standards. Both nations have their scoundrels, but they both disapprove of them in the same way. And neither country openly tolerates rascality in high places even though it is sometimes there.

This identity of social—not economic—interest served a good purpose during the war years. Every time England and America came near to open conflict some person or persons in one or both nations managed to solve the difficulty by using the same kind of sensible reasoning that keeps a family together. People could puff and huff, newspapers could cry for blood, and legislators could demand vengeance, but somehow— and always just in time—a father or a mother figure, sometimes in one country, sometimes in the other, would intervene and save the situation. And, most remarkable, this happened when both countries had better cause to dislike each other than they have ever had since.

But enough of England. She was merely the key to the situation during the Civil War. She was important but not all-important. Other countries also played their part. I have attempted to show how the war touched them and how they, in some instances, affected its results. For this war was the first that went around the entire globe and saw shots fired on six of the seven seas. It prepared the way for the greater conflicts of the twentieth century and gave birth to some of the inventions and tactics that were used in them. It was fought at a time when the world was in transition, not only from the outmoded political ideas of the past but also from the narrow provincialism that lack of communication had caused ever since human beings began to live in groups. People every-where were at last beginning to realize that no matter how isolated they seemed to be, they were not alone. Nationalism was strong and was to become still stronger, but some men were farsighted enough to see be-yond their own borders.

A new spirit was abroad, a spirit that was transforming man's thinking about himself and his relationship to other men. This was the revolt against being a mere creature, a voiceless, voteless thing born to remain subordinate to those who had been born to wealth and power. During the past few generations, many agricultural bondservants in Europe had become factory workers, a poor promotion, but in their terms a step upward. And those who could remember their fathers' misery were by nature sympathetic to that most miserable of all nineteenth-century underlings, the American Negro slave.

The war between the North and the South was being fought not merely to keep the Union together, as Lincoln believed, nor to preserve local autonomy, as Jefferson Davis claimed. The far deeper, vastly more potent force that started the conflict and kept it going was the need, the driving need, to make four million chattel slaves into men. Many Europeans understood this better than Americans did. They knew that slavery was a holdover from the past, a dreadful relic that had to be put where it belonged—in a museum along with thumb screws and other instruments of torture that are reminders of man's inhumanity to man.

I have minced no words about slavery in this book and have put aside all the neat socio-economic causes for secession that have been invented to mask the real issue for which the war was fought. After more than 25 years of studying all aspects of that war, I am convinced that human bondage was the basic reason for it. Contemporary European writings, even better than American, show that this is true. At home, there was an attempt to tone down the real meaning of slavery, but no one in Eu-rope hesitated to denounce it. As a result, foreign nations were unwill-ing to back the slaveholding South, although there were occasions when they came near to doing so.

So far as is possible, I have gone to original sources to find out what people were saying then. The world picture was complicated because attitudes constantly kept shifting, and each new dispatch from America altered opinion again. But these were only surface changes; far below them was the irrefutable fact that the great majority of Europeans would not stand for slavery. And because of this deep-seated hatred, they re-fused, in the final showdown, to support the South. Again and again, every effort to make them do so was defeated.

The conflict which was raging openly in America was also being fought in the minds of people in other countries. Freedom from tyranny and want was hungered for everywhere. The manacled slave was a universal symbol, understood even by the illiterate. The true meaning of the Civil War was better appreciated then than it is now when the whole subject has been glossed over and reduced to a few pat formulas. It is time to re-examine the facts and make new appraisals. One way to do so is to look at the conflict—not as Americans have been viewing it for more than a century—but as people in other lands saw it then. They were far away enough from it to judge it impartially, and even though they were not above the battle, they at least were not blinded by its passions.

I have tried to tie together diplomacy, propaganda, espionage, naval affairs, and the many behind-the-scenes actions which affected the outcome of the war. Some of these have been treated separately before, but they have never been put into one book. English diplomacy was done by E. D. Adams; Confederate diplomacy by J. M. Callahan and later by F. L. Owsley; France has only been touched upon. The naval aspect has been described (by me among others), but no one except the Confederate agent, James Dunwoody Bulloch, has written about international espionage during that war. I have found more new material in the Thomas Haines Dudley papers in the Huntington Library than anywhere else, although I did get a lot in Europe.

Much has been written about the battles of the Civil War; too little has been done about its nonmilitary aspects. As a result, people tend to associate it only with cannon fire and the crackle of muskets. There was more to it than infantry fighting. Millions of people living in America never heard a shot. Still more millions in other countries saw nothing but occasional Union or Confederate flags on ships. Yet the war affected them then and still affects us today. To understand its full implications one must try to look beyond the battles to the world involvements of that great human tragedy.

PHILIP VAN DOREN STERN
London, May 9, 1964

I am indebted to the John Simon Guggenheim Memorial Foundation and the Henry E. Huntington Library for grants that helped to make this book possible.

Chapter 1
THE UNHAPPY NEW YEAR

Trouble was brewing in Charleston, "the fountainhead of secession," but the real seat of disaffection was in Washington. There, Congressmen from the South, who had controlled national policy for more than a generation, knew that their hold on the government was broken. The North, generally unwilling to let slavery be extended into the new Territories, had challenged the issue so successfully that the controversy had caused a three-way split in the previously monolithic Democratic Party. This had so disrupted its machinery for winning elections that it lost the contest for the Presidency in November 1860. At that time, the candidate of the new Republican Party, Abraham Lincoln of Illinois, had been voted into office.

Reaction to political defeat was swift. The long-intransigent state of South Carolina seceded from the Union on December 20. Six days later, Major Robert Anderson moved his troops from indefensible shore-based Fort Moultrie to water-surrounded Fort Sumter. Anderson was a Southerner, and his compatriots resented what they considered a breach of faith on his part.

On January 1, 1861, Washington was covered with snow which had fallen two days before with intermittent freezing rain. Snow and ice clung to the public buildings, and the ground was frozen hard. The sun came out during the day to turn unpaved streets into mud.[1] But muddy streets were a familiar problem in Washington; the sprawling young capital was still incomplete, and construction materials, scaffolding, and raw earth were to be seen everywhere. People who came there from European cities looked at the lusty infant with disdain and often concluded that it hardly mattered what happened to so new and untried a nation.

In preparation for the capitol building's new dome, a 130-foot circular hole had been opened through the roof of its central portion. The House and Senate wings were advanced far enough to be usable, but much exterior work had to be done on them, and great slabs of stone, work sheds, and derricks were scattered around the grounds. This symbol of the Republic, like the Republic itself, was in an unfinished condition. But the nation was less than a century old; 82 of the men who had fought in the Revolution were still alive on the first day of 1861.[2]

In the White House, President James Buchanan of Pennsylvania, "a Northern man with Southern principles," was holding a New Year's Day reception.[3] At 11 A.M. the members of the Diplomatic Corps arrived in full court costumes. The 70-year-old bachelor President, with his orphan niece, the statuesque Miss Harriet Lane, acting as hostess, greeted representatives of the various nations. The tense political situation stifled conversation, and the foreign dignitaries confined themselves to a formal *échange de politesses*.

Although Buchanan looked like a naïve child with shabby features and an upstanding tuft of white hair that made him easy to caricature, he had had much diplomatic experience as Minister to Russia in the 1830s, as Secretary of State in the 1840s, and as Minister to England in the 1850s. The years he had spent abroad and in dealing with foreign affairs had taught him nothing about the duplicity of men or nations. Kind, considerate, and trusting, he meant well and believed that others would be as rational and sensible as he himself tried to be. He was a simple, rather good man whom party politics had put into a job that was too big for him. For such a person to be President of the United States at this time was—to say the least—a sad misfortune.

The reception, which was being held in the oval Blue Room, rapidly changed character when the Supreme Court Justices arrived. It soon became a gathering of old men. Chief Justice Roger B. Taney, who had rendered the historic Dred Scott decision, was 84 years old, feeble, and shrunken. Lieutenant General Winfield Scott, who preceded a group of top-ranking Army officers into the sunlit room, was 75, corpulent, short of breath, red of face, and in constant ill health. But he was an able military leader in a nation which now had urgent need of officers with his background and training.

Members of the Cabinet, Senators, Congressmen, and gaily dressed wives of the various officials quickly crowded into the Blue Room. Most of the early arrivals went dutifully on to the adjacent Green Room and then entered the huge East Room. At 12 o'clock, when the public was admitted, the press became so great that many of the first-comers began to leave by way of a temporary wooden bridge leading through a window to the exterior.

Those who remained had little to say. What to do about Fort Sumter was not the only major problem that faced the usually calm and equable President; his administration was also plagued by events that had no direct connection with secession. Paramount among them was the ugly fact that Secretary of War John B. Floyd had resigned under a cloud of suspicion on December 29 because of alleged malfeasance in trust funds held for the Indian tribes. He was also charged with making hurried shipments of Federal arms to Southern states. As a result, the nation was without a Secretary of War at this critical time.

It was also without a Secretary of State, or of the Treasury, for they too had resigned, and it was soon to lose its Secretary of the Interior. These resignations, however, were caused by the controversy over secession. Buchanan was trying to make the best of a bad situation; meanwhile he was counting the days to March 4, when his successor would inherit the problem which he knew was too complicated for him to solve.

In Springfield, Illinois, Buchanan's successor was in the midst of Cabinet making. The year end had been particularly difficult, for all kinds of visitors had insisted on calling on Mr. Lincoln. The most important was Simon Cameron, the slippery Pennsylvania politician who had been promised a post in a pre-election deal. Cameron wanted to be Secretary of the Treasury, but his record of shady financial transactions hardly fitted him to handle public funds. Lincoln finally made him Secretary of War and was to regret it, for he shipped him off a year later to St. Petersburg as Minister to Russia.

In Springfield, the weather on January 1 was unexpectedly bright and balmy with the sun so warm that it was thawing the accumulated ice and snow of late December.[4] The President-elect had moved out of the Governor's office on the 29th and had set up headquarters on the second floor of the Johnson Building across the way from a hotel called the Chenery House.[5] He was waiting now to hear from William H. Seward, whom he had offered the important Cabinet post of Secretary of State on December 8. Since Seward, who had come out second in the Republican Nominating Convention for the Presidency, thought himself a better man than Lincoln, there was some doubt as to whether he would be willing to serve under his successful rival. He delayed making up his mind until December 28, and his letter of acceptance had not yet arrived in Springfield.[6]

Lincoln was spending the holiday at home, where he was plagued by visitors all evening. When one who had had too much to drink showed signs of staying on for the night, Lincoln asked some of his young friends to take the bleary-eyed creature away. Then the President-elect was at last left alone to think about the problems of the new year.

South Carolina, which considered itself an independent republic since its secession from the Union, had sent three Commissioners to Washington to deal with Buchanan over possession of the forts and other Federal property in the state. For once, the vacillating President was firm. He said that Sumter would be defended against attack and angered the Commissioners so much that on January 2 they decided to return home.

The steamer *Star of the West* was sent from New York three days later with men and supplies for Sumter. That night, a group of fourteen Senators from Alabama, Arkansas, Georgia, Louisiana, Mississippi, Texas, and Florida, met in a room in the Capitol to recommend that their states secede and that a convention be held to form a new provisional government in Montgomery, Alabama, not later than February 15. Among those at the conference were Jefferson Davis, Robert Toombs, Judah P. Benjamin, and Stephen P. Mallory, all of whom were soon to be members of the Confederate government. That their recommendations were followed quickly can be seen from the fact that Mississippi seceded on January 9, Florida on January 10, Alabama on January 11, Georgia on January 19, Louisiana on January 26, and Texas on February 1. Only Arkansas delayed, but she too finally left the Union on May 6.

The *Star of the West* was fired upon and turned back on the morning of January 9 when she tried to enter Charleston Harbor. The next day Jefferson Davis made what was supposed to be his farewell speech to the Senate. He used some 15,000 words to unburden his mind and express his regret, but he did not mention the fact that Mississippi was seceding because he had not yet received official word from his state.[7] On the 29th, he and several other Southern Senators formally resigned from Congress; on this occasion, Davis did address the Senate for the last time. Purged of the rhetoric then considered essential, his speech was largely a defense of States' rights, a subject to which the future President of the Confederacy was to devote the rest of his long life.

One after another, Southerners who had served in the national government began leaving Washington to head for Montgomery. The nation, which had been founded by the mutual sacrifice of all its people, was now breaking up along sectional lines.

News of the dissolution of the American Republic spread around the world as swiftly as the means of communication would permit. The telegraph kept the eastern part of the United States informed of events as soon as they happened, but the lines had not yet been extended west of Fort Kearney, Nebraska, and the Pony Express was still carrying news and mail from there to San Francisco. If weather, the temper of the Indian tribes along the lonely route, and the luck, stamina, and horsemanship of the riders were all good, a message could be taken across the 1500-mile gap between the eastern and western ends of the ever-extending transcontinental telegraph lines in the nine days advertised as normal time. But in January 1861, snowstorms in the mountains were delaying transmission so often that it might take twelve to fourteen days for letters or papers to travel from Washington to the West Coast.

This was just about the time needed for news of American affairs to reach England. A complex network of telegraph lines extending eastward from there sped word to all Europe from Liverpool or Southampton, where most of the big ships docked. The huge *Great Eastern* could cross the ocean in nine days—when she ran. And fast ships like the *Adriatic*, which sometimes picked up news at St. John's, Newfoundland, could carry it to the telegraph station in Galway, Ireland, in as little as six days. Such service, however, was unusual, and only two ships a month crossed the ocean in winter.[8]

The transatlantic cable, which had been put into operation on August 4, 1858, had gone out of commission a few days later, probably because of inadequate insulation against the corrosive effect of salt water. Service was not restored until 1866, after the war was over.[9]

What was happening in America was followed with enormous interest in Europe and was given a great deal of space in newspapers there. Far more revealing than the printed news, however, were the private communications arriving from abroad. The British Foreign Office was especially well informed. Hard-working, devoted men, some of them without official connection or payment, wrote long letters to London giving candid accounts of what was going on where they were.

One of the most useful of these correspondents was Robert Bunch, the British consul in Charleston, a city which did much trading with foreign ports. His letters kept the Foreign Office so well-posted about day-to-day events that his home government knew more about the true state of affairs there than Washington did.[10]

Supervising Bunch and other British consuls in America was young Lord Lyons, the Minister whom the Court of St. James's had sent to Washington in 1859. His counterparts, Henri Mercier from Paris, and Baron Edouard de Stoeckl from St. Petersburg, were also in close touch with their governments. These three men, more than any of the other foreign diplomats in Washington, were to be deeply involved in the events of the next four years.

At this time few people in Europe or America thought that growing dissension between the North and the South would result in war. There was much talk about bloodshed, but it was hard to believe that patriots who had fought side by side within the memory of living men to establish their country's independence would now turn on each other. Yet each day brought the hour of armed conflict nearer, and all efforts to preserve peace were proving futile.

Chapter 2

THE HOUSE DIVIDING

President Buchanan continued to do little or nothing because he had only a few weeks to go; as a result, matters steadily got worse. George Templeton Strong, the New York diarist, commented on January 15: "The Old Pennsylvania Fossil is rumored to have relapsed into vaccilation and imbecility. . . . Rumors multiply . . . of an organization in this city intended to give aid and comfort to Southern treason by getting up such disturbances here as will paralyze any movement to strengthen the government by men or money. The programme is (as reported) a nocturnal insurrection by an armed mob, taking possession of the armories . . . breaking into the banks, and sacking the homes of conspicuous Republicans." Then he added: "Treated myself to a 'Maynard Carbine' ($47.50) this afternoon."[1]

The rebellious states were taking over Federal forts and arsenals. A few days after Louisiana seceded, the United States Mint, Sub-Treasury, and Custom House in New Orleans were seized. More than half a million dollars' worth of specie was obtained for the Confederacy in this way.

Even though the South had not yet formed a central government, it was turning to Europe for assistance. On January 15, the *Journal de Havre* reported that Commissioners from the state of South Carolina were in Paris and had already been in conference with Edouard Thouvenel, the French Foreign Minister. Newspapers arriving from Europe showed that businessmen there were becoming aware of the possibilities of profiting from the troubled situation in America. The *Liverpool Post* said on January 23:

> American ships in this port (and, no doubt, in many others), trading with the ports of South Carolina and Georgia, are pre-

paring . . . to sail thither under British colors. The stars and
stripes would, of course, in the present state of feeling, be refused admission, while the British flag will be heartily welcome.
One consequence of this is unprecedented—the British ships
are getting larger freights.

The French were forecasting an increase in the price of cotton; they
also foresaw that the North would be in a better position than the South
to make payments in specie, for the California steamers which brought
gold from the western mines were owned by Northerners. The Paris
Journal des Debats pointed this out on January 22, and predicted that
France would have less to lose than England if civil war broke out, because cotton meant less to the French national economy.

And the London correspondent of the New York *Herald* wrote on
January 19 that if Southerners wanted "to purchase any rifled cannon—
Paixhans, Armstrongs—or war steamers, they must come over with the
'hard tin' and not talk about credit, mortgages on Negroes, cotton plantations, or rice swamps, or national bonds of the state of South Carolina, or any other seceding state. I do not believe the united obligation
of every state south of Virginia and Tennessee, or these included, could,
in the event of secession or civil war, be sold on a European bourse for
twenty per cent, even to as moderate an amount as one or two millions
sterling." He also said that the North, despite its established connections
abroad, would find it difficult to raise money in Europe. Events were to
prove him wrong on the first prediction and right on the second.

In January 1861, the United States Navy had only 42 ships in commission, all but 12 of which were far from home. Three men-of-war were in
the Mediterranean; one was the fast new steamer *Iroquois*, which had
narrowly missed being wrecked during a night run on January 4. She
was now in dry dock in Genoa having her damaged wooden hull repaired. The even newer and far larger but slower *Richmond* was at
Messina, while the old *Susquehanna* was at Naples, ready to leave for
Syria. Word of South Carolina's secession had reached these ships, and
three officers from that state had resigned from service on the *Richmond*
and were on their way home.[2] Enlisted men could not leave the Navy;
they would be charged with desertion if they did—and the penalty for
desertion was death.

Fort Sumter was temporarily forgotten while everyone's attention was
concentrated on Montgomery, where a provisional government for the

seceded states was to be organized. On February 4 people crowded around the State Capitol to watch the ceremonies attending the birth of a new nation of the North American continent. Its President-to-be was not there. Jefferson Davis was at his home in Brierfield, in nearby Mississippi, where he was notified on February 9 that he had been elected to office.

He and his vice-president, wizened little Alexander H. Stephens of Georgia, were inaugurated nine days later. The Confederate States of America now ruled most of the slaveholding areas of the no longer United States. Southerners hurried to Montgomery to offer their services to the new government.

Lincoln left Springfield on February 11 to go to Washington by train. He spent most of the 12th—his 52nd birthday—watching the brown and gray fields of Indiana slip by. He had reason to be reflective, for he had grown up in the southern part of that state, and his mother was buried there. On the 13th, he was in the Governor's office in Columbus, Ohio, when a telegram arrived to inform him that the Electoral College in Washington had officially made him President. Since there had been some doubt whether the customary electoral system would be permitted to work, he must have been relieved to know that all had gone well.

Lincoln continued on his way to Washington, where he arrived on February 23.[3] Again and again he had been asked to speak out on the terrible problem facing the nation, but his speeches along the route purposely evaded the real issues. The anxious people of the nation had no reason to believe that he was anything more than the backwoods politician he seemed to be. They had no way of knowing that he was merely feeling his way and was using great caution not to commit himself to anything.

The President-elect stayed at Willard's Hotel while waiting for the inauguration. All kinds of people called on him; among them was Charles Francis Adams, Congressman from Massachusetts, son and grandson of Presidents. Adams was being considered for appointment as Minister to the Court of St. James's. His good friend Seward was sponsoring him, but Lincoln preferred the New Jersey politician, William L. Dayton, to whom he felt obligated for helping him get elected. And Charles Sumner, the outspoken antislavery Senator from Massachusetts, was also making a bid for the much sought-after post. The innocuous words which Lincoln had spoken while en route to the capital made Adams skeptical about his ability. "Good-natured, kindly, honest, but frivolous and uncertain," he noted in his diary.[4] He was wrong about Lincoln, and Lincoln underestimated the solid virtues of the poker-faced New Englander.

Lincoln found time to have pictures taken by Alexander Gardner at Mathew B. Brady's studio on Pennsylvania Avenue. The photographs show the President-elect seated at a small table with a properly grave expression on his bearded face. When Brady himself had photographed him in New York just a year before, at the time of the Cooper Union speech, the then-obscure Illinois attorney was still smooth-shaven.[5]

On March 1, the President-elect attended a dinner given by the Minister from Bremen.[6] There he first met the suave, very able young British Minister Lord Lyons, who had already predicted that Seward would want to use a threat of war to cover up internal dissention in the often-tense Anglo-American relations of the next four years. Lyons was an excellent diplomat, genuinely interested in preserving peace, and his sound common sense was to be of enormous value.

Two days later, Lincoln made the last of the Cabinet appointments which were to have a direct bearing on international affairs. To everyone's surprise—and especially to the appointee's—he chose 58-year-old Gideon Welles of Connecticut as his Secretary of the Navy. Lincoln had met Welles in Hartford while on a speaking trip in 1860 and had evidently been impressed with him then. The white-bearded, benign-looking Secretary had served as the chief of the Bureau of Provisions and Clothing for the Navy in the 1840s, but that was his only experience with the national government. Charles A. Dana said of him that "there was no noise in the street when he went along," but that "he understood his duty and did it efficiently, continually, and unvaryingly."[7] Welles was to remain in power longer than anyone who had ever been Secretary of the Navy, and he and Seward were the only members of the original Lincoln Cabinet who would still be in office at the end of the war.

The next day, March 4, under circumstances more threatening to a peaceful inauguration than had ever been seen in the history of the young Republic, Abraham Lincoln was sworn into office as President of the United States. Despite all the rumors of violence and assassination that had made Washington uneasy for weeks, the ceremony went smoothly, although it was held under the muzzles of cannon drawn up on Capitol Hill while armed guards were posted along Pennsylvania Avenue and on the roof of the Capitol itself.

Lincoln, still hopeful of holding the South in the Union, concluded his Inaugural Address with the eloquent plea:

We are not enemies but friends. . . . The mystic chords of memory, stretching from every battlefield and every patriot grave to every living heart and hearthstone in the broad land, will yet swell the chorus of the Union.[8]

But the South was deaf to pleas, no matter how eloquent. Not words but bullets were to decide the issue now.

Chapter 3

A NEW NATION, NOT CONCEIVED IN LIBERTY

While Washington had been marking time waiting for the inauguration of a President, the men who had formed a new government in Montgomery quickly went ahead with plans to make it work. In addition to having to organize domestic affairs, prepare against armed attack, and induce several still-unseceded slave states to join the common effort for Southern independence, the leaders who were guiding the nascent Confederacy had to establish connections abroad as early as possible.

Europe was essential to the success of the new nation, for it was only there that the largely agricultural South could obtain manufactured goods, ships, medical supplies, arms, and ammunition. Very few such things were produced in the Confederacy. Without the aid of England and France, it could not fight the kind of war its mechanized Northern adversary could be expected to wage. Not everyone in the South knew this, but its leaders did.

One of the first moves made by the embryonic Montgomery government was to summon Commander Raphael Semmes by telegram on February 14. Semmes, who was then in Washington serving on the Lighthouse Board, answered the call by resigning immediately from the United States Navy. Soon after he arrived in Montgomery, President Davis sent him back to the North to buy matériels of war and hire skilled mechanics to manufacture weapons and ammunition. Communication between the two sections was still open, so he had no difficulty making the journey.

The Confederacy was fortunate in obtaining Semmes' service, for he was not only an experienced naval officer but a resourceful and ingenious raider who would carry the Confederate flag halfway around the world in a bold attempt to destroy Northern shipping.

Fifty-two-year-old Raphael Semmes had begun his education at sea as a midshipman years before the Academy at Annapolis was founded. Long voyages gave him the time to study maritime and international law. Practical experience taught him what one could learn about seamanship. And he was a born commander who could handle an unruly crew and make them work. Like many first-rate leaders he had a high opinion of his own worth and could be caustic when dressing someone down. He was a bit of a dandy, so much so that his men called him "Old Beeswax" because he wore sharply pointed mustaches. But they had no doubt about his courage or his expertness with fighting ships and their guns.

His biggest fault was overconfidence and an all too-evident arrogance that made it hard for him to get on with men of equal or higher rank. The Confederacy did well to send him to sea. He was at his best out there in complete command with no one to criticize his actions or question his judgments—even when they were wrong.

While Semmes was in New York in March, he received instructions to purchase shallow-draft steamers for the Confederacy, but none pleased him, because he erroneously thought he could still afford to be particular. Little actually came of his arms-buying mission, but it showed that the Montgomery government, while still in its formative stage, was already aware of the urgent need for ships and weapons.[1]

During Semmes' absence, a Confederate Navy Department had been organized on February 21. Its Secretary, Stephen R. Mallory, like his Union counterpart, was one of the two Confederate Cabinet members to remain in office throughout the war. Unlike the North's Gideon Welles, however, Mallory had no ships, no guns, and no officers or crews, for there was no Confederate Navy. It is a tribute to Mallory's ability that he was able to build an organization from nothing and have his improvised navy hold off the vastly superior water-borne forces of the North for four long years.

In February 1861, Stephen R. Mallory was 54 years old. The Trinidad-born Secretary had spent most of his life at the tip of Florida in Key West, where the United States Navy was the isolated little town's chief reason for existence. Mallory had been sent to Washington as a Senator in 1851 and had become chairman of the Committee of Naval Affairs in 1857. His experience in that post had given him a good knowledge of recent developments in naval techniques. Like Welles, he was honest, thorough, incorruptible, hardworking, and without the showy qualities characteristic of many of his contemporaries.[2]

While Mallory was creating a navy, Jefferson Davis made his first appointments for service overseas. Davis, who was primarily a military leader, cared little about naval or diplomatic affairs, but he knew that he had to persuade European nations to back the Confederacy. To do this, he chose three men to represent the new nation abroad. They were William Lowndes Yancey, Ambrose Dudley Mann, and Pierre A. Rost. Davis undoubtedly meant well, but he was in a great hurry, and he had a limited number of men suitable for foreign service to choose from. In these first appointments he erred seriously—and soon realized it.

Yancey, although born in the South in 1814, had been brought up in Troy, New York, where his widowed mother had settled after remarrying. Yancey's stepfather was an ardent Abolitionist preacher, and psychological overtones in the rigidly managed household may have alienated the boy against anything that stood for the North. He returned to the South at the age of 18 and rapidly became a power in the political affairs of Alabama. He was a strong believer in States' rights and a persuasive arguer for them. He made frequent appearances in public and was adept at swaying audiences. More than anyone else, he was responsible for the breakup of the Democratic Party at the 1860 Charleston Convention—a move which helped to bring on the war. Today he is almost forgotten, but any true appraisal of the critical period of 1860–61 must take his complicated personality into account. As a foreign emissary who had to deal with some of Europe's shrewdest statesmen, he was an utter failure.[3]

Many Southerners believed that Jefferson Davis sent Yancey out of the country in order to be rid of him. Certainly Davis was not fond of the man. When he wrote his ponderous apologia, *The Rise and Fall of the Confederate Government,* he did not even mention Yancey's name. In fact, this work of more than 1400 pages contains only one short and superficial chapter on foreign affairs. Davis liked to forget failure and ignore those he held responsible for it. It is remarkable that he was able to write so much about a government that went steadily downhill.

He had some reason, perhaps, to think that the second member of the mission, Ambrose Dudley Mann of Virginia, would be more effective, for he had been in foreign service in Central Europe and Assistant Secretary of State in the 1850s. But Davis was not a good judge of character, and was unable to see what a long-winded, futile bumbler Mann was. His correspondence shows that he understood nothing, believed everything that was told him, and could not express clearly whatever ideas he had.[4]

The third Commissioner, Pierre A. Rost, was born in France but had grown up in Louisiana. Davis undoubtedly chose him because of his French background, but he did not foresee the fact that Rost's New Orleans accent would be a drawback in Paris.

Consul Bunch, writing to the British Foreign Office from Charleston, said of Yancey that he was "impulsive, erratic, and hot-headed; a rabid Secessionist [favoring] a revival of the Slave Trade, and a filibuster of the extremest type of manifest destiny." Mann received an even harsher appraisal. Bunch called him "the son of a bankrupt grocer" and said that those who knew him well called him "a mere trading politician possessing no originality of mind and no special merit of any description." Rost was so obscure that Bunch was unable to obtain any information about him beyond the fact that he was "a respectable sugar planter from . . . Louisiana."[5]

These three men in a boat, as ineffectual a trio as ever set out across the seas to win the good will of an entire continent, left Montgomery on March 17 to sail for London. The letter of instruction which Robert Toombs, the Confederacy's first Secretary of State, gave the Commissioners, was quite detailed, but it made no mention of slavery except to state that the new nation had, like most American and European powers, prohibited the African slave trade. It said, however, that the Confederacy "was not prepared at this time to aid the rest of the world in promoting that object."[6]

Accompanying the letter of instruction was a copy of the Constitution of the Confederate States which had been adopted on March 11. This was modeled after the Constitution of the United States—with many modifications. Like the original document, it did not say whether or not a state had the right to secede, but simply ignored that touchy issue. In dealing with slavery, it copied the earlier Constitution by apportioning Representatives and direct taxes "among the several states . . . according to their respective numbers, which shall be determined by adding to the whole number of free persons . . . three-fifths of all slaves." Here it differed from its model in using the word "slaves" instead of the earlier document's evasive "other persons."

Although the new Constitution forbade the importation of Negroes from foreign countries and even from states not belonging to the Confederacy, it said that "no . . . law denying or impairing the right of property in Negro slaves shall be passed."

This was the nub of the matter. The other articles and sections, permitting slaves to be taken from one state or territory to another, or to make sure that they would be returned to their owner when they fled or were removed to another state or territory were all subsidiary to the clause which openly declared that the Confederate States of America was a slaveholding nation.[7]

The Southern press was largely in accord with this as may be seen from the front page of the influential Charleston *Mercury* for February 13, 1861, where a letter from one of its readers was given prominent space:

> Our property in slaves will be established. If it has stood in a Government, more than half of which has been pledged to its destruction, it will surely stand in a Government every member of which will be pledged to its defence. . . . With that perfect economy of resources, that just application of power, that concentration of forces, that security of order which results to slavery from the permanent direction of its best intelligence, there is no other form of human labor that can stand against it, and it will build itself a home and erect for itself at some point within the present limits of the Southern states a structure of imperial power and grandeur—a glorious Confederacy of States that will stand aloft and serene for ages amid the anarchy of democracies that will reel around it.

As if to clarify the Confederacy's position on slavery, its Vice-President, Alexander H. Stephens, in a speech made at Savannah on March 21, declared that "the new Constitution has put at rest forever all the agitating questions relating to our peculiar institutions—African slavery as it exists among us—the proper status of the Negro in our form of civilization. This was the immediate cause of the late rupture and present revolution." He went on to say that Jefferson and his contemporaries had believed that slavery "was wrong in principle, socially, morally, and politically." But, he added, "these ideas were fundamentally wrong. They rest upon the assumption of the equality of races. This was an error."

Then he made a statement that was to circulate around the world and be remembered for generations to come. "Our new government is founded upon exactly the opposite ideas; its foundations are laid, its cornerstone rests, upon the great truth that the Negro is not equal to the white man; that slavery, subordination to the superior race, is his natural and moral condition."[8]

A week later, Alabama's delegate, Robert Hardy Smith, taking his cue from the much-admired Stephens, spoke at Mobile and re-empha-

sized the fact that the Confederacy was to be dedicated to the perpetuation of slavery. He also freely admitted that "we have dissolved the late
Union chiefly because of the Negro quarrel."[9]

Everything said by the fifty delegates to the Montgomery Convention
indicates that they were unanimous in their resolve to make slavery
permanent in the South. Despite all talk of the violation of States'
rights as the major cause for secession, it is clear from what was recorded
in the formative days of the Confederacy that the true reason for the
separation of the Southern states from the Union was the desire to
preserve slavery and all that it meant. Only during later years did the
men who had led the South into defeat and disaster try to justify their
action with high-sounding legalism and pious cant.

The three Confederate Commissioners, carrying a copy of their new
Constitution and soon to be followed by newspapers reporting Stephens'
"cornerstone" speech, were heading into a situation in Europe which
no amount of persuasiveness could overcome. For the one thing, more
than any other, which was to prevent foreign recognition and aid, was
the fact that the Confederacy wanted to keep its slave system intact at a
time when the more civilized nations had outgrown the idea that buying
and selling human beings and forcing them to labor was morally—or
even economically—sound.

Confederate States Seal

Chapter 4
AS ENGLAND SAW IT

In refusing to realize that slavery was on the way out among the advanced nations of the world, the Confederacy was running counter to the times. But it was, of course, to protect the "peculiar institution" in which slave-owners had invested several billion dollars that the Confederacy had seceded from the Union and set up a rival government.

The year 1861 was a particularly unpropitious one for a nation that advocated slavery to expect support from Europe. England had outlawed human bondage in 1833 at an enormous and continuing cost. It is true that the British had not abolished slavery purely for humanitarian reasons; economic changes in the West Indies and at home had made it unprofitable. But she had gotten rid of it and could look down on nations that insisted on perpetuating a system which civilization now deplored. Sweden, Denmark, and France had followed England's example in the 1840s. And in the spring of 1861 Russia was preparing to free her serfs.[1]

Long before this time, the minds of many people in Europe had been turned against slavery by an American book—Harriet Beecher Stowe's *Uncle Tom's Cabin*, which had been published in 1852. Sentimental and emotionally overstrained as the novel was, it had gained enormous readership abroad where it had been even more widely distributed than in the United States. It had gone through edition after edition in nearly every country that had a printing press. There was no denying its power, as William Lowndes Yancey testified on July 3, 1861, when he wrote home to say that "the antislavery sentiment is universal. *Uncle Tom's Cabin* has been read and believed."[2]

Practically no one in Europe favored slavery, but outspoken opposition to it was voiced mostly by the middle and working classes. The old aris-

tocracy was more or less willing to tolerate it in America, particularly if
the disruptive dispute would break up the upstart Republic which had
been challenging its power. Well-to-do businessmen with large investments in shipping and cotton were inclined to favor the South because
it was a major source of their income.

Well-informed Europeans—especially the English—had no illusions
about the reasons for the conflict that was disrupting the United States.
On March 12, the *London News* said:

> The Southern party has enjoyed thirty years' possession of the
> Federal Government—thirty years of domination over the whole
> Union—during which they have altered the laws, undermined
> the Constitution, carved out territory, restricted liberty and
> created license for their own sectional objects and interests. So
> much for the long oppression which has driven them to resist-
> ance. And what outrage roused the reluctant men of peace at
> last? What was the Stamp Act of the present occasion? It was
> the loss of an election, a Constitutional election conducted in a
> regular and orderly way.

Even before war broke out, British opinion was already taking sides.
But the attitude of some noted men was often surprising. It was to be
expected that John Bright, Richard Cobden, Harriet Martineau, John
Morley, Robert Browning, John Stuart Mill, Richard Monckton
Milnes, and Anthony Trollope would refuse to support a cause that had
slavery at its core. Their writings and widely expressed opinions had
indicated that, and they were frankly pro-Northern in what they said and
wrote during the next four years. Others like John Ruskin and Herbert
Spencer were greatly troubled by the war but they tried to remain neutral.[3] Thackeray, then ill and nearing the end of his life, thought that
Americans were so "incurably friendly" that they could not possibly
fight with each other. When they did, he blew hot and cold according
to personal influences, but shortly before he died he helped to raise money
for the starving Lancashire cotton workers and also gave a sizable dona-
tion of his own.[4] T. H. Huxley said that his heart was with the South
and his head with the North. Charles Darwin was all for the North at
the beginning, but events during the war made him lose much of his
original sympathy.

There were many prominent people in England who were intensely
pro-Southern, but few of their names are remembered today. Among
the best known of them were Matthew Arnold, who hated the Philis-
tinism of the North, and Sir Edward Bulwer-Lytton, who had inherited

great family wealth. Tennyson was inclined to favor the South, but he had no strong feelings about it. And Dickens, who had not liked much of what he had seen in America when he was there nearly twenty years before, damned the South for its slavery and the North for its bombast and swagger.[5] Outspokenly pro-Southern, however, were the historians George Grote and Lord Acton.[6]

The titled gentlemen whose backing of one side or the other seemed so important when they were alive are now nearly all forgotten. This also applies to minor politicians like William S. Lindsay and John A. Roebuck who tried to persuade England to back the South. Fear of the growing might of America and the spread of democracy motivated the nobility and its political spokesmen. They saw clearly that the former American colony which had seceded from England might become a rival world power if it succeeded in settling its internal disputes.

But the chief British actors in this wartime drama usually managed to put their nation's welfare above their own class, party, or personal interests. They may not have liked America and its democratic ways, but they were able to deal with it just as they were able to deal with jealous Indian potentates, warring African tribesmen, and their own highly sophisticated counterparts in the chancellories of Europe.

The two men who had most to do with American affairs during the war years were Lord Palmerston, the Prime Minister, and Lord Russell, the head of the Foreign Office. The fact that they were part of a Coalition Government, which could easily be turned out of office, made them wary about taking chances. This, of course, worked for the benefit of the North. Both had been born in the eighteenth century; both brought to their work a lifetime of experience in getting along with the men who ruled the nations of the world; both had held practically every high post in the British Government. After long rivalry, they were now reconciled and were content to spend their old age acting in concert rather than in opposition.

Henry John Temple Palmerston had entered Parliament in 1807 at the age of 23 and had served the British nation almost without interruption ever since. Although he was a liberal in international politics, he was very much the English gentleman of the old school with all the narrow prejudices and intense loyalties of a breed that even then was beginning to die out. He was never reluctant to use the threat of Britain's enormous power to settle a dispute in her favor. Like a twentieth-century American statesman who was also to be noted for his brinkmanship, Palmerston was a dangerous player in the world's most dangerous game.

Richard Cobden once said of him: "Palmerston likes to drive the wheel close to the edge and show how dexterously he can avoid falling over the precipice."[7]

Although he opposed slavery, Palmerston was to be more cordial to the Confederate emissaries than circumstances warranted. Perhaps he was merely obtaining information or getting a firsthand impression of the men who were trying to win England's support. Or perhaps his heart was really on their side, but events were to prevent him from favoring them unduly.

Lord John Russell, the third son of the wealthy Sixth Duke of Bedford, had also entered Parliament at an early age; he was only 21 when he began his public career in 1813. He, too, opposed slavery, but although he did not show any undue predilection for the Confederates, at the start of the war he was even cooler toward the embattled democracy of the North.

Yet there was in him, as there must have been in many sensitive Englishmen, a feeling of guilt for having thrust the "accursed institution of slavery" upon America when it was still a British colony. He was forthrightly honest about this and said: "I cannot but recollect that with our great and glorious institutions, we gave them that curse, and that ours were the hands from which they received that fatal gift of the poisoned garment which was flung around them from the first hour of their establishment. Therefore I do not think it just or seemly . . . that we should reproach them with an evil for the origin of which we ourselves are to blame."[8]

It follows that a man with so fine a sense of honor would exercise much care and industry in handling the vast flood of important papers that came to his desk. His devotion to the most minute details of his work can still be seen in the lengthy comments scrawled in his tiny, almost indecipherable handwriting on nearly every document in the records of the Foreign Office that deal with American affairs during the Civil War.

Although Russell had played a prominent part in getting the Reform Bill of 1832 passed, he had lost much of his belief in democracy. His grandson, Bertrand Russell, who remembers his illustrious ancestor, says that he was "the type of aristocratic reformer whose zeal is derived from the classics, from Demosthenes and Tacitus, rather than from any more recent source. They worshipped a goddess called Liberty, but her features were rather vague." He also says that Lord John, although often

accused of coldness in public life, was warm and affectionate at home—
especially toward a young child, which Bertrand Russell then was.[9]

So far as the United States was concerned, it was fortunate that Russell was in a position to offset Palmerston's hostility, and it was largely
because of his slow but genuine reasonableness that the two nations
never went to war. On at least three occasions they were very near to it.

Russell, as head of the Foreign Office, had more to do with handling
American affairs than anyone else in England. He worked closely with
Lord Lyons, and the astute young diplomat consistently sent him sound
advice. As early as March 30, 1861, Lyons wrote to say that Mercier, the
French Minister in Washington, had shown him a dispatch he was sending to his government urging that the major European powers act together to recognize the Confederacy. In case that was not done, Mercier
wanted to have Lyons and himself authorized to grant recognition if it
suddenly seemed necessary. Lyons informed Mercier that he could not
agree to these proposals. He then told Russell that he thought "the Commissioners from the South should not meet either with a rebuff in London or in Paris or with a cordial or formal reception."[10]

Russell followed his young Minister's advice in his dealings with the
Confederate Commissioners. There emerged from this a crucial bit of
policy making which had two important results: peace was preserved
between England and the United States, and the Confederacy was
doomed to eventual defeat.

During the war years, Russell and his staff had the inconvenience of
having to work in temporary quarters in Pembroke House in Whitehall
Gardens. The Foreign Office had long been established in four ancient
private dwellings in Downing Street, but these were now being pulled
down to be replaced by a new building. A long battle, conducted publicly over the architectural style for the projected office, had finally been
won by Palmerston who insisted that it be done in the Italianate manner
rather than in the Gothic which was then so popular.[11]

Larger quarters were badly needed because the world was growing
larger in population and smaller in the time required to travel around it.
And the Foreign Office had to have more space because its antislavery
department had become very big. Ever since 1807 it had been working
closely with the Navy's African Squadron to control the slave trade. Now
the withdrawal of United States naval vessels from the African coast
patrol was to throw even heavier burdens upon the British Foreign Office and the Admiralty.

Presiding serenely over all the governmental squabbles, large and small, was the Queen, now nearly 42 years old, and her Consort, Albert of Saxe-Coburg-Gotha. They had been happily married for 21 years, and were devoted to their children and domestic life. The throne had lost much of its former power, yet Victoria still had a great deal of authority. An untold story in Anglo-American history is the importance of the Queen's behind-the-scene's actions in preventing war with the United States. Her kindly, well-informed husband sometimes advised her on matters that affected millions of subjects at home and even more in the vast empire on which the sun never set. After his death, his influence upon his devoted widow was so strong that she often did what she thought he would want her to do.

In the early 1860s, Queen Victoria's England was not merely an oddly assorted mixture of old and new—it was a nation in the throes of making itself into something entirely different from what it had been. After centuries of slow development and hardly perceptible change, it had given birth to the Industrial Revolution less than a hundred years before this time. Each decade had witnessed a new form of power come into ever-wider use as steam engines were put to work to supply energy for mines, factories, mills, ships, railroads, and even cumbersome road vehicles. Then electricity made the time-annihilating telegraph an everyday fact. Better methods of agriculture enabled the nation to produce more food. Better medicine, beginning with Jenner's smallpox vaccine at the end of the previous century, was extending the span of Englishmen's lives.

All these things—plus countless others—had helped to increase the population of England and Wales from 8,872,980 in 1801 to 20,205,504 in 1861.[12] Life was becoming better for millions of people whose ancestors had dwelt in numb apathy for generations. And they were flocking from the static countryside into towns and cities where their poverty continued but where they could at least see signs of hope. To those who came from dark, primitive country areas, gaslit streets were a miracle, and running water in the house was a daily blessing. Bad as Victorian living conditions may seem to us, what newcomers found in the crowded sections of the mushrooming cities they settled in was better than anything they or their fathers had ever had. More production brought more wealth to a few, but it also brought useful manufactured articles to many who had never enjoyed such simple luxuries as inexpensive machine-made cloth.

Most of these wide-sweeping changes had come about within the lifetime of people who could remember the harsh days of their youth. They knew from firsthand experience how cruel life can be to the very poor. Less than two decades before, they had seen a murderous famine sweep Ireland when potato crops failed. People died or fled by the millions from the stricken island to reduce its population from 8,196,597 in 1841 to 5,792,025 in 1861.[13] Starvation, misery, and death were still vivid in the minds of Queen Victoria's subjects, but the economy of the nation was improving; more people had more to eat and wear and spend. In his fine study of mid-nineteenth-century England, G. K. Clark calls the period between 1850 and 1875 "the High Noon of Victorianism." But he also points out that this change for the better was very recent:

> It is indeed healthy to reflect how near a neighbour to the eighteenth century was the England of 1850. . . . Most people feel, possibly unconsciously, that somewhere an invisible line crosses history separating our relatively orderly, relatively humane, relatively well-policed society from the wilder, more savage, if more colourful society of the past. . . . Much of life before 1800 . . . was likely to be violent because the forces available to keep order were normally meagre and futile, and as a result smugglers infested the coasts and the counties adjoining the coasts, and highwaymen the roads, while in the towns and in the countryside there was much violent crime and not infrequent rioting. What the law lacked in force, however, it tried to supply in horror by prescribing the death penalty for a long list of offences, some of them trivial, some of them hardly offences at all. The resultant spectacles at Tyburn were much enjoyed by the crowd. For if the habits of many Englishmen were violent, the tastes of still more of them were coarse and their pleasures callous. They delighted in the fighting or the torturing of animals and in the fighting of human beings—violent and damaging forms of wrestling, cudgel play, or prize fighting with the bare fist. Bestial drunkenness was to be found in all classes, and to judge by the accounts in novels and elsewhere, the manners shown towards the unprotected women in the street . . . were often free and menacing, or worse. Meanwhile, as the account of any eighteenth-century town will show, the amount of human misery and degradation that filled the background and showed itself in the streets would surprise anyone who was only familiar with the decent conditions of modern Western Europe.

None of this was new. These things had been part of the ordinary conditions of life in harsh century after harsh cen-

tury; probably there is less to be surprised at in the fact that
they existed than in the fact that a sense of morality coupled
with human ingenuity and good fortune has transformed these
conditions into those of our kinder, much more generally prosperous, world.[14]

Much of the old, however, still remained in 1861. Tyburn was gone,
but men were often hanged in the street in front of Newgate Prison.
This was to go on until 1868 when the last public execution took place.
(The victim was a young Irishman who had tried to blow up a London
prison.) Yet even Newgate's ancient terrors had been ameliorated in
1857 when separate cells replaced the big room where the more hard-
ened prisoners had been able to prey on the weaker inmates without
restraint.[15]

The 1830s had seen many of old England's evils abolished. Cruel
sports involving animals were forbidden, and the pillory was used for the
last time in 1837—the year in which young Victoria became Queen.
That memorable decade, which had also witnessed the end of slavery in
British dominions, had been the time of the Reform Bills, of a new Poor
Law, of some restriction on the labor of young children, of a rise in
trade-unionism, and of a general improvement in the living conditions
of the long-submerged lower part of British society.

The winds of freedom, which had blown across the ocean from England's former colony to fan the fires of the French Revolution, were now
cleansing Victoria's realm. The division between rich and poor was still
marked; labor of all kinds was poorly paid and miserably housed—yet
there were stirrings of hope, and it was slowly beginning to be possible
for a child not to have to follow blindly in his father's footsteps and re-
live his ancestors' wretchedness.

Still strong in their hold upon the political and economic structure
of the England of the 1860s, however, were the representatives of the
ancient aristocracy whose roots of power went deep into the nation's
past. They controlled the Government, the Church, the Army, the Navy,
and owned most of the land. They dominated the press—but not completely. They had huge investments in industry, but they seldom took
an active part in running it.

The day of the autocrat was passing. During the next four years,
while a people's government in America was fighting for its right to
exist, the men who guided Britain's course of action had to listen to
public opinion at home and in other countries as well.

What was happening far away across the Atlantic Ocean was to have

a lasting effect upon the course of civilization. Abraham Lincoln and
the liberal principles for which he stood were to influence the destinies
of long-established nations and those as yet unborn. Alliances and friend-
ships were in the making; policies still undreamed of were being shaped;
posterity was to inherit the results of a Northern victory that was four
years away. The battle being waged in America was far more than the
sectional conflict it then seemed to be. Some men already realized this
and were beginning to speak up for the Union cause. Others, who
wanted to preserve the ancient regime, were openly opposed to it. And
still others, like Lord Russell, who were eager to see the Union dissolved
for their own country's benefit, were slowly and reluctantly to be won
over to support the North. It was a seminal period from which our modern world, in all its complexity, was to emerge. But some few things were
to be settled forever, and one of them was the abolition of slavery. In that
at least, mankind was to take an enormous step forward.

Chapter 5

THE NEW PRESIDENT AND THE STATE DEPARTMENT

After the midday inauguration ceremonies, the Lincolns attended a huge reception and ball during the evening. When the President returned to the White House late that night, he was greeted with a letter from Major Anderson which said bluntly that Fort Sumter's provisions would be exhausted before an expedition could go to its relief.

On the 5th, the President sent his nominations for the Cabinet to the Senate which quickly approved them. The next day, Gideon Welles called to tell him about the condition of the Navy. Then the first Cabinet meeting was held. Foreign affairs first came to Lincoln's attention on March 7 when the Diplomatic Corps, with its members in their national dress, made an official call.

By comparison with the tension that was building up in the United States, Europe was beginning to look very attractive to many people. George Templeton Strong made this entry in his diary on March 12:

> We are a weak, divided, disgraced people, unable to maintain our national existence. We are impotent even to *assert* our national life. The country of George Washington and Andrew Jackson (!!!) is decomposing, and its elements reforming into new and strange combinations. I shall never go abroad. That question is settled. I should be ashamed to show my nose in the meanest corner of Europe. Naples and Florence and Milan, now triumphantly asserting their national life and unity, are entitled to look down on Boston and New York. All my right, title, and interest in the Fourth of July and the American Eagle and the Model Republic can be bought at a low figure. I'm tempted to emigrate, to become a naturalized British subject and spend the rest of my days in some pleasant seaside village

in the southern counties of old Mother England. It's a pity
we ever renounced our allegiance to the British Crown.

The New York diarist, however, was not alone in toying with the idea
that the American Revolution might have been a mistake. Many Southerners also had the same thought; and some of them were seriously proposing that negotiations should be started to rejoin the mother country.

Meanwhile, Secretary of State Seward was beginning his work. His
son Frederick, who was acting as Assistant Secretary of State, was very
much aware of the historic background of the building in which they
had their offices.

> It had a certain stately dignity, enhanced by the remem-
> brance of what had transpired within its gray walls in the
> course of seventy years. Here the foreign relations of the
> United States were conducted for the greater part of the first
> century of the nation. Here were kept the archives and the
> correspondence with all foreign governments, and here were
> prepared the instructions, replies, and treaties which were to
> determine the nation's foreign policy. From here Oliver Ells-
> worth and his colleagues were sent out to make the treaty
> with Talleyrand which averted a threatened war with France.
> . . . Here Madison prepared the instructions to Robert R. Liv-
> ingston, as Minister at Paris, to guide him in negotiating the
> purchase of the great Louisiana Territory. Here Decatur and
> Preble were instructed to break up the piracy of the Barbary
> powers, to release the captives, and make an end of the tribute.
> From here Monroe and Pinckney set out to try to stop the
> impressment of American seamen and the seizure of American
> ships by the British Navy. From here emanated Jefferson's
> proclamation ordering all British men-of-war out of American
> waters. Here Secretary Monroe gave the British Minister his
> passports, and President Madison proclaimed the war with
> England. Here, soon after, came the Russian envoy to offer
> friendly mediation in the conflict, and from here, soon after
> that, Henry Clay and his colleagues went out to effect the
> restoration of peace by the Treaty of Ghent. From here was
> promulgated the celebrated Monroe Doctrine that this con-
> tinent was to be thenceforward free from European dictation.
> Here John Quincy Adams concluded the treaty with Spain for
> the acquisition of Florida. From here went out the recognition
> of the independence of Mexico and the South American repub-
> lics. Here Lafayette was welcomed; and from here Harrison
> bore greetings to Bolivar. . . . Here Webster concluded his

treaty with Lord Ashburton settling all boundary and extradition disputes with Great Britain. And here he made his famous declaration that "Every merchant vessel on the high seas is rightfully considered part of the territory to which it belongs." . . . Here Secretary Buchanan drafted the treaty of peace with Mexico, and from here went out Polk's proclamation of the new treaty of Guadelupe-Hidalgo and the acquisition of California and New Mexico. . . . From here went forth the invitation to Kossuth, then exiled in Turkey, to come to the United States on board an American frigate. Here were framed the instructions and treaty through which Commodore Perry was to open Japan to American commerce. Here Marcy penned his celebrated dispatch in the Koszta case, maintaining the rights of American citizenship. And here President and Queen exchanged congratulations, in the first messages that ever went over the Atlantic cable.[1]

William Howard Russell, who had arrived from London on March 16 as correspondent for *The Times*, described the new Secretary of State:

Mr. Seward is a slight, middle-sized man of feeble build, with the stoop contracted from sedentary habits and application to the desk, and has a peculiar attitude when seated which immediately attracts attention. A well-formed and large head is placed on a long slender neck and projects over the chest in an argumentative kind of way, as if the keen eyes were seeking for an adversary; the mouth is remarkably flexible, large but well-formed, the nose prominent and aquiline, the eyes secret but penetrating, and lively with humor of some kind twinkling about them; the brow bold and broad, but not remarkably elevated; the white hair silvery and fine—a subtle, quick man rejoicing in power, given to perorate and to oracular utterances, fond of badinage, bursting with the importance of state mysteries, and with the dignity of directing the foreign policy of the greatest country—as all Americans think—in the world.[2]

Seward asked for a complete list of the employees—about one hundred—who worked for his Department. An inquiry was quickly made about their background and loyalty to the Union. Seward then immediately "dismissed all except those whose fidelity . . . was undoubted."

Simultaneously with this, he had to settle quickly the appointments to the various American legations abroad. On March 11, he wrote to Lincoln about four candidates the President was sponsoring:

I like Clay for Spain—And am prepared to dispose of the question at once. I like equally Corwin to Mexico—and am also ready—As to Frémont and France—the prestige is good—But I *think* that is all. If as I have heard, he is to be engaged in raising money there for his estates, it would be a serious complication—Besides this, he is by birth and education a South Carolinian, and I am not certain of his being so very decided in the defence of the Union as a minister at Paris ought to be—I would rather send Dayton there—For England I am sure Mr. Adams [is] far above all others adapted to British Court & Society and infinitely more watchful, capable, efficient, reliable [in] every thing—New England is an important point. What better can we do for her? N. Jersey gives us little and that grudgingly—I think Dayton's appointment would be as much too large for her as anything else we are likely to do for New England would be too small for her.[3]

Cassius M. Clay, however, was to be sent to Russia instead of Spain. The picturesque Kentucky Abolitionist, who was as skillful in wielding a bowie knife as he was in handling rough-and-tumble politics, may seem like an odd choice for the St. Petersburg post—and in many ways it was. Actually, Lincoln gave Clay the appointment because he had helped to make him President.

For a Kentuckian to be an ardent and outspoken Abolitionist was remarkable; even more remarkable, though, was the fact that Clay had remained alive long enough to reach the age of 50, for he had been in numerous fights and duels and was always eager to take on a new opponent. When he got to Russia, the people there admired him for his courage and forthright honesty. Since they had no way of telling whether his behavior was typical of his countrymen, they assumed that all Americans were equally crazy. Two Russian noblemen tried to compel the famous fighter to challenge one of them to a duel in which he would be at a disadvantage because they would choose rapiers as weapons—while Clay, of course, had no experience with those delicate blades. When one of the gentlemen slapped the Kentuckian on the cheek with a glove to force the issue, Clay smashed his big fist into the would-be dueler's face and knocked him down. There were no further Russian attempts to test the fierce American's combat ability.[4]

Tom Corwin, Congressman from Ohio, was another of the many outspoken nonconformists who were then prominent in American public life. Although he had recently sponsored an amendment to the Constitu-

tion that would have made it forever impossible to abolish or even re-
strict slavery, he was better known for his opposition to the Mexican
War, which he had considered unjustified. "If I were a Mexican," he
had said in 1847, "I would tell you, 'Have you not room in your own
country to bury your dead men? If you come into mine, we will greet
you with bloody hands and welcome you to hospitable graves.'"[5] These
words had damaged Corwin's political career at home, but the new administration evidently thought they might help him in Mexico.

The idea of making John Charles Frémont Minister to France—or
anywhere else—was quickly discarded, although he had not been born
in South Carolina, as Seward thought, but in Georgia, a fact which might
have hurt him just as much, even though his loyalty was beyond question. The adventurous "Pathfinder," who had helped to open up the
West, was being pushed for the post not only by Lincoln but by influential Horace Greeley of the New York *Tribune*. Yet he was passed over
in favor of innocuous William L. Dayton, whose only qualification
seems to have been his party loyalty. The New Jersey lawyer had been
a Senator, but he had no experience in foreign affairs and could not
speak French. However, ambassadors ignorant of the languages of the
countries to which they are sent seem to be in the American tradition.

The Times correspondent, William H. Russell, saw the State Department in far less romantic terms than young Seward did. To him it
was just another public building:

> A very humble—in fact, dingy—mansion, two stories high,
> and situated at the end of the magnificient line of colonnade
> in white marble called the Treasury. . . . People familiar with
> Downing Street, however, cannot object to the dinginess of
> the bureaux in which the foreign and state affairs of the Ameri-
> can Republic are transacted. . . .
>
> In a moderately sized, but very comfortable apartment sur-
> rounded with book shelves and ornamented with a few en-
> gravings, we found the Secretary of State seated at his table
> enjoying a cigar; he received me with great courtesy and kind-
> ness, and after a time said he would take occasion to present
> me to the President, who was to give audience that day to the
> Minister of the new kingdom of Italy, who had hitherto only
> represented the kingdom of Sardinia. . . .
>
> In a few seconds . . . the Chevalier Bertinatti made his
> appearance in cocked hat, white gloves, diplomatic suit of blue
> and silver lace, sword, sash, and ribbon of the cross of Savoy.
> I thought there was a quiet smile on Mr. Seward's face as he

saw his brilliant companion, who contrasted so strongly with the more than republican simplicity of his own attire. . . .

We . . . set out through a private door leading to the grounds, and within a few seconds entered the hall of the . . . White House, which has very much the air of a portion of a bank or public office, being provided with glass doors and plain heavy chairs and forms. . . . Passing through one of the doors on the left, we entered a handsome spacious room, richly and rather gorgeously furnished. . . .

Soon afterwards there entered with a shambling, loose, irregular, almost unsteady gait, a tall, lank, lean man, considerably over six feet in height, with stooping shoulders, long pendulous arms, terminating in hands of extraordinary dimensions, which, however, were far exceeded in proportion by his feet. He was dressed in an ill-fitting, wrinkled suit of black, which put one in mind of an undertaker's uniform at a funeral; round his neck a rope of black silk was knotted in a large bulb with flying ends projecting beyond the collar of his coat; his turned-down shirt collar disclosed a sinewy muscular yellow neck, and above that, nestling in a great black mass of hair, bristling and compact like a ruff of mourning pins, rose the strange quaint face and head, covered with its thatch of wild republican hair, of President Lincoln. The impression produced by the size of his extremities, and by his flapping and wide projecting ears, may be removed by the appearance of kindliness, sagacity, and the awkward bonhommie of his face; the mouth is absolutely prodigious; the lips, straggling and extending almost from one line of black beard to the other, are only kept in order by two deep furrows from the nostril to the chin; the nose itself— a prominent organ—stands out from the face with an inquiring, anxious air, as though it were sniffing for some good thing in the wind; the eyes dark, full, and deeply set, are penetrating but full of an expression which almost amounts to tenderness; and above them projects the shaggy brow, running into the small hard frontal space, the development of which can scarcely be estimated accurately, owing to the irregular flocks of thick hair carelessly brushed across it. . . .

A person who met Mr. Lincoln in the street would not take him to be what—according to the usages of European society —is called a "gentleman;" and, indeed, since I came to the United States, I have heard more disparaging allusions made by Americans to him on that account than I could have expected among simple republicans, where all should be equals;

but, at the same time, it would not be possible for the most indifferent observer to pass him in the street without notice.

As he advanced through the room, he evidently controlled a desire to shake hands all round with everybody and smiled good-humoredly till he was suddenly brought up by the staid deportment of Mr. Seward, and by the profound diplomatic bows of the Chevalier Bertinatti. Then indeed he suddenly jerked himself back and stood in front of the two Ministers, with his body slightly drooped forward and his hands behind his back, his knees touching and his feet apart. Mr. Seward formally presented the Minister, whereupon the President made a prodigiously violent demonstration of his body in a bow which had almost the effect of a smack in its rapidity and abruptness, and, recovering himself, proceeded to give his utmost attention, whilst the Chevalier, with another bow, read from a paper a long address in presenting the royal letter accrediting him as "Minister Resident." . . .

The Minister forthwith handed his letter to the President, who gave it into the custody of Mr. Seward, and then, dipping his hand into his coat pocket, Mr. Lincoln drew out a sheet of paper from which he read his reply, the most remarkable part of which was his doctrine "that the United States were bound by duty not to interfere with the differences of foreign governments and countries." After some words of compliment, the President shook hands with the Minister, who soon afterwards retired.[6]

Charles Francis Adams had received word on March 19 of his appointment to the Court of St. James's. His grandfather and his father, who had been Presidents of the United States, had represented their country there, and the new Minister was fully aware of all that his appointment meant. He went to Washington to make the necessary arrangements and call on Seward, who took him to Lincoln. Like W. H. Russell, Adams was not favorably impressed by the appearance of the man he met. But far worse was the reception he got. After thanking the President and expressing "hope that the confidence implied in the appointment he had received might not prove to have been misplaced," he waited for a reply.

Lincoln was very casual, almost indifferent. "Very kind of you to say so, Mr. Adams, but you were not my choice," he said. "You are Seward's man."

Then, addressing his Secretary of State with much more animation, he told him that he had just settled the vexing problem of appointing a postmaster for Chicago.[7]

The American Minister to the Court of St. James's never recovered from his astonishment or forgot the incident. But he did not realize that Chicago loomed large in the Middle-Westerner's mind, for it was in his own bailiwick. Lincoln had watched that community grow from a village to the metropolis where he had been nominated for the Presidency. To him, the London he had never seen was far away, and the Court of St. James's was just a place where gentlemen in fancy costumes bowed ceremoniously to one another and talked about European politics in languages he could not understand.

Chapter 6

THE IRREPRESSIBLE SEWARD MEETS HIS MATCH

Born in 1801 in a village in upstate New York, Seward's adult life had been spent in law and politics. He had been Governor of the state and also its Senator, and had taken part in the antislavery movement ever since it had become important enough to be a factor in national affairs. His phrase, which defined the struggle as "an irrepressible conflict," had been famous ever since he first used it in Rochester on October 25, 1858.

Seward was a practical politician who had worked closely with the even more practical Thurlow Weed to keep a firm grip on the New York state electorate, but he also handled cases of public interest without compensation. He was a curious mixture of hard-fisted shrewdness, of idealistic generosity, and—above all—of driving ambition. His defeat at the Chicago Nominating Convention still rankled. He evidently intended to make up for the damage done to his ego then and was all set to take over control of the administration from the naïve and inexperienced Illinois backwoodsman who had been thrust into the Presidency by a combination of political jockeying and the whims of fate.

The situation at Fort Sumter was now rapidly reaching a crisis, for the garrison's food supply was running low. Seward decided to play a bold hand. On April 1, he wrote a series of suggestions which he entitled "Some Thoughts for the President's Consideration." He had the confidential document copied by his devoted son and then had a messenger deliver it to the White House. It was perhaps the most amazing paper ever sent by an American Secretary of State to the head of the Government.

Seward began by saying that "We are at the end of a month's administration and yet without a policy either domestic or foreign." He then suggested a domestic policy which would "change the question before

the public from one upon slavery . . . for a question upon Union or
Disunion." This he would implement by abandoning Sumter (and
blame the loss on the Buchanan administration), but he would defend
the installations on the Gulf and recall the Navy from foreign stations
in order to blockade Southern ports. This was not utterly unreasonable,
but his suggestions for foreign policy must have set Lincoln aback. They
were:

> I would demand explanations from *Spain* and France, cate-
> gorically, at once.
> I would seek explanations from Great Britain and Russia,
> and send agents into *Canada, Mexico* and *Central America* to
> rouse a vigorous continental *spirit of independence* on this con-
> tinent against European intervention.
> And if satisfactory explanations are not received from Spain
> and France,
> Would convene Congress and declare war against them.
> But whatever policy we adopt, there must be an energetic
> prosecution of it.
> For this purpose it must be somebody's business to pursue
> and direct it incessantly. Either the President must do it him-
> self, and be all the while active in it, or devolve it on some mem-
> ber of his Cabinet. Once adopted, debates on it must end, and
> all agree and abide.
> It is not in my especial province, but I neither seek to evade
> nor assume responsibility.[1]

Perhaps it was fortunate for the United States that the impulsive
Secretary of State brought the contest for power between the President
and himself to a showdown as early as he did. Lincoln answered by a
letter which quoted what Seward had said about the President's having
to take action or else allow a member of the Cabinet (i.e. Seward) to do
so. To this Lincoln replied with the gentle firmness that was his customary way of dealing with unreasonable people and said: "If this must
be done, *I* must do it."[2]

And that was that. The Secretary of State had been put in his place.
Oddly enough, Lord Lyons, whose bland British upper-class countenance concealed an unusually perceptive mind, had foreseen just what
Seward would do. In a letter addressed to Lord John Russell on January
7, he had said about the new Secretary:

> With regard to Great Britain, I cannot help fearing that he
> will be a dangerous Foreign Minister. His view of the rela-

tions between the United States and Great Britain has always been that they are a good material to make political capital of. He thinks . . . that they may be safely played with without any risk of bringing on a war. He has even to me avowed his belief that England will never go to war with the United States. . . . The temptation will be great for Lincoln's party, if they be not actually engaged in a civil war, to endeavour to divert the public excitement to a foreign quarrel. I do not think Mr. Seward would contemplate actually going to war with us, but he would be well disposed to play the old game of seeking popularity here by displaying violence towards us. I don't think it will be so good a game for him as it used to be, even supposing we give him an apparent triumph, but I think he is likely to play it.[3]

But Lyons had no illusions about Seward, although he probably underestimated his ability. He once characterized the American Secretary of State as a "Brummagem Palmerston, always talking in a low cunning way to Bunkum."[4]

April 1, which has long been set aside as a day for foolish deeds, was cloudy and cool in Washington. Before it was over, Seward had done something else which was to alienate an important member of the Cabinet. Working with some young naval officers, Seward persuaded Lincoln to authorize sending the warship *Powhatan* to Fort Pickens in Florida when she was expected to go on an expedition to relieve Fort Sumter. Since all knowledge of this was kept from the Secretary of the Navy, Welles was understandably angry when he found out about it.[5]

Events leading to the outbreak of war now followed one another swiftly. On April 12 the guns in Charleston Harbor roared out. Two days later, Major Anderson evacuated Fort Sumter. After that there was no turning back. Both sections prepared for war, and there could be no further thought of a settlement by peaceful means.

Crisis piled upon crisis. On April 15, Lincoln called out 75,000 militia. On April 17, Davis offered letters of marque and reprisal to owners of private ships (as the Confederate Constitution authorized him to do). On April 18 the Harpers Ferry Arsenal was set on fire to keep it from being taken by the Confederates. On April 19, Lincoln ordered the coast to be blockaded from Texas to South Carolina. On April 20, the huge Norfolk Navy Yard fell into the hands of the Confederates before all its ships and weapons could be removed or destroyed. And then, on

April 27, after Virginia had seceded, its coast—and North Carolina's as well—were declared to be blockaded. During part of this time, Washington was isolated from the rest of the country, and soldiers trying to come to its defense were fired upon.

Before that terrible April ended, the United States was no longer united, and its citizens were furiously trying to kill one another. As Thomas Jefferson had predicted in 1820, slavery had become the death knell of the Union. He had also said then:

> I regret that I am now to die in the belief that the useless sacrifice of themselves by the generation of 1776 to acquire self-government and happiness to their country is to be thrown away by the unwise and unworthy passions of their sons, and that my only consolation is to be that I live not to weep over it. If they would but dispassionately weigh the blessings they will throw away, against an abstract principle more likely to be effected by union than by scission, they would pause before they would perpetrate this act of suicide on themselves and of treason against the hopes of the world.[6]

But the wisdom of the past was thrown away, and the passion-blinded nation rushed headlong into violence.

Chapter 7

THE LINEUP IN LONDON

In the spring of 1861 the United States Legation in London was about to undergo a major change. It was soon to move from 24 Portland Place to temporary quarters at No. 7 Duke Street; at the same time, the American Minister, George M. Dallas, was nearing the end of his term of office. Although he was a Pennsylvania Quaker, some people rather unjustly suspected him of being pro-Southern.[1]

Among those who were convinced that Dallas was secretly aiding the South was the secretary of the Legation, 41-year-old Benjamin Moran. This indispensable employee was loyal to the Union; he knew his job well and worked hard at it in his dingy basement quarters where he copied letters by the light of a single candle. His employers praised Moran for his efficiency and industry, but this excellent secretary was "so fawning to his superiors and so insolent to those under him" that even the new Minister, Charles Francis Adams, was to find it "very difficult to act with him."[2] Moran's behavior masked unbounded contempt for nearly everyone he met. Such bitterness had to have an outlet; since the misanthropic secretary could not express himself openly, he poured his venom into his *Journal*. In it he recorded his impressions of his employers and of visitors, great and small, who called at the Legation. Over the years, he filled volume after volume with details of everyday life in the busy office that represented the United States in Great Britain.

Moran was a disappointed literary man who had given up a career as a bookseller and printer to go abroad where he hoped to earn a living from his pen. When he found out that he could not support himself from writing, he got a post as secretary in the Legation and had been there since the beginning of 1857. The unsuccessful author was now turning out daily installments of a masterpiece of shrewd—if outrageously biased—observation. He was never to see his work in print—nor would he have dared to make it public during his lifetime. The Civil War section of his 18-year *Journal* was published in 1948, 73 years after his death.

On Thursday, April 18, Moran noted that Dudley Mann, the first of the Southern envoys to arrive in London, had called at the Legation that morning. "He is an old and very strong friend of Mr. Dallas," he wrote, "and came up under the pretext of paying him a friendly visit. His manner was that of a coward, as he both sneaked in and out. He had a half-hour's conversation in private with Mr. Dallas, but its purport I did not learn. I suspect it was treasonable: and there was great indelicacy in Mr. Dallas' receiving him at all. This man arrived in town on Tuesday and in half an hour was in close chat with Gen'l Campbell, a man holding a position under Mr. Lincoln: and today has been here concocting villainy with our Minister. Dudley Mann is nearly 60 years of age. He is not more than 5 feet 5, is thick, short, and rather heavy. His voice is soft and enunciation slow, with a decided Southern accent. He has a rather good head, but there is not much in him, being like most Southern men, a mere talker."

News of the surrender of Fort Sumter did not reach England until April 26. On the 27th, the other two Confederate Commissioners, Yancey and Rost, landed at Southampton to be greeted with word that war had begun. They immediately sent a telegram to Mann, addressing it to him in care of the United States Legation, which was the only place they could reach him. Moran was incensed when it arrived and noted in his diary: "The unblushing impudence of these scoundrels is in character with their thieving at home! It was truly cool to send their message to the United States Legation for one of their fellow traitors."

With the three Commissioners in England, the Confederate effort to influence European opinion began. Their first move was to seek an interview with Lord John Russell.

News of the breakup of Britain's former colony in America was received in London with much excitement and mixed feelings. The public had been well prepared for something to happen, although few people expected armed conflict. But the roar of cannon in Charleston Harbor meant war even though no one had been killed by the heavy bombardment.

The crisis was debated in the House of Lords on April 29, and the newspapers ran editorials deploring "the calamities which have befallen our kinsmen in America." Mrs. Dallas and her three daughters hastily decided to sail on May 1 in order to get home before Confederate privateers could attack shipping. The *Great Eastern* departed the next day on the second voyage of her career and brought the news of London's reaction to New York in time for it to be printed in the papers on May 13. The huge steamer's deep draught kept her from entering the harbor on May 11 when she arrived off Sandy Hook during an unfavorable tide. There was some talk of chartering the big ship to transport American troops, but nothing came of the idea.

England was so far away from her own civil war between the Roundheads and the Cavaliers in the 1640s that the present generation was without direct experience with such conflict. Yet some of her people were old enough to remember the French Revolutions of 1789 and 1830. The numerous revolts throughout Europe in 1848 were also within recent memory, but the outbreak of violence in America was totally unlike them. Civil war or revolution in Europe nearly always resulted from the attempt of a lower class to throw off the rule of a higher one. In America, however, it was the aristocratic slaveholders who were rebelling against the well-to-do merchants, manufacturers, workmen, and farmers of the North. It was all very confusing to the British; sometimes it was difficult for them to decide just where their sympathies should go.

Nor did the newspapers clarify matters. Mr. Delane's *Times,* the mighty "Thunderer," was definitely pro-Southern. So was Lord Palmerston's mouthpiece, the *Morning Post,* which had more influence than its circulation of only 4500 seemed to warrant. Pro-Southern, too, was the powerful *Standard.* Its circulation of 130,000 was second only to the more or less neutral *Telegraph* with 150,000. Supposedly neutral also was *The Morning Advertiser* which sold 50,000 copies every day. Daily newspapers that favored the North were few and small in circulation. Among them were *The Daily News, The Morning Star,* and some minor journals in Manchester, Birmingham, and Newcastle. *Reynolds' Weekly,* the Liberal penny paper with more than 350,000 readers in the manufacturing areas, was pro-Northern, but it had little influence in London, where the nation's destiny was shaped.[3]

The Confederate Commissioners had high hopes for the immediate success of their mission when they called on Lord John Russell "for an informal interchange of views" on May 3. But they did not know their man. He had written to Lord Lyons a month before that "I shall see the

Southerners when they come, but not officially, and keep them at a proper distance."[4] He was taking no chances with new and still unproved governments. There was plenty of time to find out whether the Confederate States of America was really an independent nation or just an insubstantial dream, an unsuccessful attempt that would soon vanish and no longer be a problem to England.

The Commissioners told Russell how and why Southerners had seceded and had set up their new government, described their ability to defend themselves, promised that the agricultural nation would welcome free trade, and then said that they hoped that Great Britain would "recognize the independence of the Confederate States of America at an early date."[5]

Russell blandly replied that they would surely understand the propriety of his not expressing an opinion upon the matter, and the interview was over. The Commissioners left, feeling encouraged but somewhat baffled by his Lordship, who had been skillfully evasive.

Three days later Russell announced that "the Government had come to the opinion that the Southern Confederacy . . . must be treated as a belligerent."[6] Although this was of far less value to the new nation than full recognition, it at least showed that Britain refused to agree with Seward's uncompromising position that there was no actual war and that the rebellious states were still part of a Union to which they would soon return.

On May 11, the Privy Council met at Whitehall to arrange for a Proclamation of Neutrality to be issued by the Queen. When this went into effect on the 13th, it warned British subjects "against illicit or overt complicity in the Civil War raging in America." This meant that Englishmen could not enlist in the armies or navies of either participant. The Proclamation also forbade Northern as well as Southern warships to equip in a British port.[7]

That England was taking serious notice of the South's claim to be a nation at war was proved by the fact that on May 10 the Admiralty sent letters to British ships enclosing a color picture of the new Confederate flag so captains could recognize it.

All this was a *fait accompli* when the new Minister from the United States arrived in Liverpool on May 13. Dallas and his staff met Adams at Euston Station in London on the following evening. They put him and his family in a hotel where they had reserved rooms, and then went off to try to find Cassius M. Clay. Some time after midnight they finally located him, his family, and a retinue of nine in the lobby of the Westminster Palace Hotel where four cabs loaded with baggage were waiting outside. The American Minister to Russia had been unable to find lodgings.

Moran said that Clay "was walking up and down the magnificent hall like a chafed lion and looked a man to be avoided in the gas light, surrounded as he was by his suite of three tall, sharp-faced Kentuckians. I . . . was surprised to find him a man of some 50 years, 6 feet high, well proportioned, with a fine manly face, and the form of a hero. Oddly enough, he wore a blue dress coat with gilt buttons, and I could not but smile to see an Envoy to Russia in such a costume."[8]

Cassius Clay was often given to melodramatic posturings. John Hay, who had met him at a reception in the White House a few weeks before, said then that the Minister to Russia "wore, with a sublimely unconscious air, three pistols and an Arkansas toothpick and looked like an admirable vignette to 25-cents worth of yellow-covered romance."[9]

On that difficult evening in London, the much-harassed Legation staff managed to establish the Kentuckians in various lodgings. Then they went home to get the office ready for Mr. Adams and arrange for him to be presented to the Queen.

Only some parts of the London to which Charles Francis Adams had come would have seemed at all familiar to his grandfather, John Adams, who had lived on Grosvenor Square from 1785 to 1788 as America's first envoy to Britain. And even Charles' father, John Quincy Adams, who had held the same post much later—from 1815 to 1817—would have had trouble finding his way around the rapidly changing city. London had more than tripled its population since John Adams' time and had spread far out into the surrounding countryside. In 1861, the city of 2,800,000 people was in the midst of sweeping transformations that were making it into a world metropolis.

Many things, of course, were still the same as they had been for centuries. Across the Thames in Southwark were old galleried inns where Chaucer would have felt at home. Sir Christopher Wren's Temple Bar, where the heads of notable prisoners had once been set up as a warning, still separated Fleet Street from the Strand. Hundreds of old buildings, some of them of half-timbered construction, remained in odd corners and neglected areas. But time, the ravages of fire, and the demand for new quarters were all doing away with relics of the past. Many would remain, since no one would ever dare to touch historic places like the Tower or the Abbey.

One of the city's most notable improvements was fairly recent. This was Trafalgar Square, which had been started only a generation before. The Nelson column had been erected there in 1843, but its four bronze lions were not yet in place. The spring-fed fountains, however, were industriously throwing jets of water into the air and drenching standers-by when the wind blew.

Plans were being drawn for the elaborate embankment which was intended to keep London's unruly tidal river within bounds. There had been crudely built flood barriers along the Thames for centuries, but massive stone blocks were now to protect its northern bank and make a pleasant strolling place for future generations.

Reconstruction of the Houses of Parliament, with their tall Clock Tower and even taller Victoria Tower, had just been completed. Westminster Abbey, which represented the England of the past, was overshadowed by the modern and very expensive structures for the House of Lords and the House of Commons. But an Empire that was costing £4,000,000 a year to defend, obviously could afford comfortable accommodations for its legislators.

The Thames, which flows alongside these fine new buildings, was hardly a fitting companion for them. Over the years it had become fouler and fouler, because three million people were pouring their filth into what was no longer a waterway but an open sewer from which the salmon had long since fled. Less sensitive species of fish sometimes ventured into the polluted water, died, and had to be hauled away by the cartload.

London was getting dirtier and uglier every year. Domestic chimneys, tall factory smokestacks, and railway locomotives were poisoning the air with acrid fumes. Soot from soft coal settled on everything and streaked new buildings with black as soon as they were completed. The railroads, which were making London a great city, were also converting it into a far less pleasant place in which to live. Starting with Euston Station in 1838, new terminals were being built in a dozen different sections. Victoria Station had just been opened, and the Metropolitan Railway to connect it to the Great Western at Paddington, was under construction. Parts of this new line were to run underground. Charing Cross Station was also being built. In order to bring trains into it from the south, an iron bridge was being put across the Thames.[10]

In the spring of 1861, the ingenious and somewhat eccentric American, George Francis Train, gave London its first tramways. (He had already constructed one in Birkenhead.) In London he built two lines, one along Bayswater Road from Notting Hill to Marble Arch; the other from

Pimlico to Westminster Abbey. This new method of public transportation did not remain in operation long, because Train made the mistake of elevating his iron tracks a few inches above the ground. An accident, in which a boy was killed, finished London's pioneer tramway, and he had to tear up the rails. It was a pity, for the horse-cars were very popular. And their drivers, dressed in riflemen's uniforms and standing up like Roman charioteers, added a touch of color to the drab city.[11]

London, of course, still had its double-decked omnibuses and other horse-drawn vehicles. Four-wheeled cabs, two-wheeled hansoms, private carriages, carts, and wagons crowded the streets. The city's traffic jams were said to be the worst in the world, but Paris or New York could have contested the claim. All these places—and every other community—were redolent of the odor of manure, for this was the age of the urban animal, and not only horses but oxen—and sometimes even herds of sheep—could be seen on fashionable Park Lane.[12]

Chapter 8

MR. ADAMS BEGINS HIS WORK

Everything was beginning badly for the Adams family. They had been greeted with news of the British Proclamation of Neutrality on their arrival, and even the presentation to the Queen was clouded over, for she was in mourning for her mother, the Duchess of Kent, who had died only two months before. It was a tribute to the United States that Victoria was willing to receive Adams under such circumstances. Since Lord John Russell's brother, the Duke of Bedford, had also just died, Lord Palmerston had to present the American Minister to Her Majesty.

At 3 o'clock on the afternoon of May 16, Mr. Adams, wearing a dress coat and black gloves in respect for the late Duchess of Kent, bowed and presented his Letter of Credence to the Queen. The ceremony was necessarily brief. After it was finished, the new Minister took over the American Legation from his predecessor, who was doubtless glad to be free from further responsibility.

Moran was happy to see Dallas and his family leave. "A more heartless, selfish, coldblooded, and unprincipled set, I never knew," he wrote in his *Journal* that night.[1] But the spiteful secretary was not to find his new employer any easier to deal with. Nevertheless, he was forced to respect the redoubtable Mr. Adams and eventually had to admit that he was the best of the six Ministers he had worked for during his long career at the Legation.[2]

The Adams family consisted of the rather austere Minister, his wife Abigail (whom Moran called "a pleasant intelligent lady"), his daughter Mary, then 15, and his sons Henry, aged 23, and Brooks, who was not yet 13. Mary was too young to play any part in the office life of the Legation, and Brooks was away most of the time at a boarding school in

Twickenham. No one, of course, could foresee that young Henry Adams and his then unpromising and sometimes sickly brother Brooks were to become eminent historians and trenchant commentators on American life and world affairs.

Henry Adams was serving as his father's unofficial and unpaid secretary. In addition to Moran, a 43-year-old Chicago journalist named Charles Lush Wilson, had been sent by the State Department to serve as the Minister's secretary. The three young men never got along, and as time passed their mutual enmity increased. Despite the hostile atmosphere, the work of the Legation was done with remarkable efficiency.

Far more annoying to Adams than the lack of harmony in his office was the constant shifting of location. On May 20 the Legation went into temporary quarters at No. 7 Duke Street, "an obscure locality off Portland Place," about which Moran said, "we consider ourselves fortunate even in getting in there, as it is not everyone who will have us." Then, during the weekend of June 1, they had to move again, this time to No. 17 St. George's Place, which the ever-critical secretary said was "fine looking outside but too small and cranky within."[3]

Moving from one building to another was a nuisance to a Minister who was just starting his work. And Adams also had to find a house for his family. He rented one at No. 52 Grosvenor Square, although he thought it was fearfully expensive. He did not consider it a disadvantage that the house was available for only a few months, because he was already beginning to suspect that his term in office might be short. The way things were going made him believe that he might soon have to go home.

In the midst of all the commotion caused by so much moving, Mr. Adams went on May 18 to pay his first call on Lord John Russell.

By this time, Adams had received Seward's letter of April 24, which was addressed to the American Ministers abroad. This must have weighed upon Adams' mind during the interview, although he did not mention it until the very end of the discussion. It had to do with unfinished international business which the United States now wanted to complete.

In 1856, a European Congress meeting in Paris after the Crimean War had adopted a declaration in which the participating nations agreed that:

1. Privateering is and remains abolished.
2. The neutral flag covers enemy's goods, with the exception of contraband of war.

3. Neutral goods, with the exception of contraband of war, are not liable to capture under an enemy's flag.

4. Blockades, in order to be binding, must be effective; that is to say, maintained by forces strong enough to prevent access to the coast of the enemy.

Other countries throughout the world were then invited to agree to these principles. The United States, which had been exceedingly successful with privateers during the Revolution and the War of 1812, refused to sign the Declaration of Paris when it was given the chance in 1856. Now that the South was issuing letters of marque and reprisal to private shipowners, the North suddenly wanted to become party to an agreement it had rejected only five years before. Seward's letter of April 24 gave a detailed background of the situation and told the Ministers abroad that it was now thought wise "to secure the . . . good offered by the Paris Congress."[4]

At this time, however, privateering seemed less important to Adams than the Queen's Proclamation of Neutrality which had recognized the Confederacy as a belligerent. The United States Minister felt that this had been issued precipitously, and he said so to Russell.

The two men had never met, but in their first session at Pembroke Lodge, Lord John's country home in Richmond Park, they got along quite well. In size and appearance they were a good match, although Lord John was the elder by 15 years. Both were small in stature, both were bald, and their smoothly shaved faces had side whiskers around the edges. Both represented the best traditions of their respective countries. And they probably liked each other's carefully maintained reserve and evident honesty in saying truthfully whatever could be said.[5]

Adams was worried lest the British recognition of the Confederacy as a belligerent might lead to full recognition as an independent nation. Russell said that for the time being his government had no such plan, but he could not, of course, guarantee what it might do in the future.

When Adams returned to the Legation, he said to Moran that he had "told Lord J. that in case there was a disposition . . . to favor the pretended Confederate States, he would have nothing more to do with England." To this remark, "his Lordship [had been] provokingly diplomatic."[6]

According to a letter written on June 10 by Henry to his older brother, Charles Francis Adams, Jr., his father had evidently considered taking extreme measures with England. "Papa's instructions . . . would have justified him in breaking off at once all diplomatic relations with this

Government, and we felt no doubt that . . . the Americans would have
upheld him. But I must confess such a policy appeared to me to be the
extreme of shallowness and folly. In the first place it would have been
a tremendous load for the country. In the second place it would have
been a mere wanton, mad, windmill-hitting, for the sympathies and the
policy of England are undoubtedly with us. . . ."

In the same letter, which covered a number of subjects, young Adams
gave a vivid picture of the class of English people who were most antagonistic to the North:

> Getting into society is a repulsive piece of work here. Sup-
> posing you are invited to a ball. You arrive at eleven o'clock. A
> footman in powder asks your name and announces you. The
> lady or ladies of the house receive you and shake hands. You
> pass on, and there you are. You know not a soul. No one offers
> to introduce you. No one even looks at you with curiosity.
> London society is so vast that the oldest habitués know only
> their own sets and never trouble themselves even to look at
> anyone else. No one knows that you're a stranger. You see
> numbers of men and women just as silent and just as strange
> as yourself. You may go from house to house and from rout to
> rout and never see a face twice. You may labor for weeks
> at making acquaintances and yet go again and again to balls
> where you can't discover a face you ever saw before. And sup-
> posing you are in society, what does it amount to? The state
> dinners are dull, heavy, lifeless affairs. The balls are solemn
> stupid crushes without a scintilla of the gayety of our balls.
> No one enjoys them so far as I can hear. They are matters of
> necessity, of position. People have to entertain. They were
> born to it and it is one of the duties of life. My own wish is
> quietly to slide into the literary set and leave the heavy society,
> which without dancing is a frightful and irredeemable bore.[7]

Just when the United States Minister was congratulating himself for
having treated Russell and his government so tactfully, a dispatch from
Seward dated May 21 arrived at the Legation. It showed the mercurial
Secretary of State at his worst and began with the statement that "this
Government considers that our relations to Europe have reached a crisis."
It then outlined an intransigent policy regarding the blockade, retalia-
tion for possible recognition of the Confederacy, and the reception of
privateers in foreign ports. President Lincoln had seen the document
and had modified some of its more provocative phrases. Seward had

wanted the American Minister to read the ill-tempered paper verbatim to Russell and then warn him that the United States would break off diplomatic relations if the British Government held any further conversations with the Confederate Commissioners. Fortunately, Lincoln had countermanded this to say that Adams was only to use the letter for his own information and not read it to anyone.[8]

Even with these modifications, the document was full of potential trouble. Henry Adams wrote to his brother that it was:

> so arrogant in tone and so extraordinary and unparalleled in its demands that it leaves no doubt . . . that our Government wishes to face a war with all Europe. That is the inevitable result of any attempt to carry out the spirit or the letter of these directions, and such a war is regarded in the dispatch itself as the probable result. . . . Does Seward count on the support of France? It is not likely, for this dispatch applies as much to her as to England. But if he does, he is just as much mistaken as he ever was in his life. Anyone who knows Napoleon knows that he means to stick with England. I cannot tell you how I am shocked and horrified by supposing Seward, a man I've admired and respected beyond most men, guilty of what seems to me so wicked and criminal a course as this. I do not think I exaggerate the danger. I believe that our Government means to have a war with England; I believe that England knows it and is preparing for it; and I believe it will come within two months—if at all.[9]

Charles Francis Adams never found out what was behind the various documents which Seward's fertile mind had turned out, one after the other, from his "Some Thoughts for the President's Consideration" of April 1 to his troublesome dispatch of May 21. Adams died in 1886, a year before Nicolay and Hay published the behind-the-scenes story in *The Century Magazine*. Nor did Adams ever know that the gauche-looking President, whom he had met briefly in the White House under circumstances he recalled only with scorn, had very sensibly toned down Seward's rash words. Adams and Lincoln, working together (although the American Minister did not realize it), had averted war with England. "One war at a time!" Lincoln is said to have protested when he read Seward's dispatch of May 21.

When Adams met with Russell to discuss Seward's letter, he "tried to act up to instructions at the same time that [he] softened as well as [he] could the sharp edges." Russell, as usual, showed no sign of what he was thinking.

Then Adams came to the most difficult part of the difficult interview. He had learned that Russell had seen the Confederate Commissioners again, and he now had to tell Lord John that any further relations, even though unofficial, with "the pseudo-Commissioners could scarcely fail to be viewed . . . as hostile in spirit and to require some corresponding action accordingly."

This was a daring demand to be made by the representative of a nation which had been Britain's colony within the memory of people still alive. Adams must have studied Russell's imperturbable features for an indication of his reaction. But there was no outburst. Lord John merely went over his country's course of action in similar instances and then very quietly said that "he had seen the gentlemen once some time ago, and once more some time since; he had no expectation of seeing them any more."[10]

Adams had won his first victory. And Lord John kept his promise and never saw Yancey, Mann, or Rost again. It took some time for them to realize that they had been checkmated. On July 15, when Yancey and Mann wrote a lengthy letter to their government, they naturally did not admit that they could no longer reach Lord Russell in person, but their somewhat apologetic explanation showed that they were making no progress. They had taken letters of marque and reprisal with them to issue to British shipowners, but they were afraid to use them because they were sure that to do so would offend Her Majesty's Government. They did have complaints, however, about the way the Confederacy was treating them, for they had never received a single dollar to use for secret-service activities, a field in which their adversaries were already active. Things, however, seemed more promising in France, where Rost was at work.[11]

In Washington, the French Minister had suggested to Lyons that their governments act together to break the blockade of Southern ports before it could be firmly established. The time to do this, he said, was in the fall when the newly harvested cotton would be ready to ship. Lyons dutifully forwarded Mercier's idea to the home office where it was quietly shelved.[12]

Chapter 9
EFFORTS TO WIN FRIENDS

Paris, where Rost had gone soon after his arrival in Europe, was then being rebuilt. Ever since 1853, Baron Haussmann had been tearing the city apart, pulling down its old houses, and running wide boulevards through sections which had remained unchanged for centuries. It has been said that he was doing this to make the city defensible against uprisings of its own people and that much of what he destroyed was not fit to live in, but under the ruthless hand of progress, old Paris was disappearing. A good part of Haussmann's work, however, did benefit the rapidly growing metropolis. He installed sewers, improved the water supply, constructed bridges, parks, and public buildings, and made the French capital into the Paris we know today.

As the faithful servant of Emperor Napoleon III, who had made himself all-powerful by a *coup d'état* in December 1851, Haussmann was obviously doing only what his master wanted him to do. Napoleon, for all his many faults, was a forward-looking ruler; under his regime not only Paris but all France was being transformed. He was extending and improving roads and railroads, modernizing ports and docks, and expanding the Army and the Navy. The Suez Canal had been begun, although it was not to be completed until the end of 1869. The Emperor also favored science and technology. Under his encouragement, the brilliant naval architect, Dupuy De Lome, had laid down the keels of four men-of-war which were to be the world's first sea-going ironclads. They were the result of an earlier French invention, the rifled gun, which fired explosive shells that could blast a wooden vessel apart.

When the first French armored ship, the formidable *Gloire*, was launched in 1860, it gave other nations good cause for worry. The British, despite much reactionary protest in their tradition-bound Admiralty, were the first to meet the challenge. They had two ironclads, the *Warrior* and the *Black Prince,* in the water before 1861 was over.

Although there was constant minor friction between the French and the British during these years, Napoleon III was certainly not seeking war. He was content to let England take the lead in most international affairs. He followed her example in the case of the Confederacy, and on June 10 issued a Proclamation of Neutrality closely patterned after the one Queen Victoria had made public less than a month before. Once France had taken a neutral position, the Netherlands followed suit on June 16, Spain on June 17, and Brazil on August 1.[1] The Confederacy was being recognized by many countries as a belligerent but not as a fully independent nation.

When Pierre Rost went to Paris early in May, he obtained an interview with the Duc de Morny, half-brother of the Emperor and a power in the French court. He said that Morny told him that France and England had agreed to stand together in dealing with the Confederacy.[2] (This was confirmed on June 10 when the French Proclamation of Neutrality was issued.) But Morny, according to Rost, also said that full recognition, in his opinion, "was only a matter of time." This was far more encouraging than the British attitude. When the Commissioners wrote to the Confederate State Department on May 21, they qualified Rost's report of Morny's optimism by saying: "We are of the opinion that neither England nor France will recognize the independence of the Confederate States at present, but that England in reality is not averse to a disintegration of the United States, and both of these powers will act favorably toward us upon the first decided [military] success which we may obtain."

Meanwhile, William L. Dayton, the United States Minister to France, had arrived in Paris and had no difficulty in meeting the Emperor. Napoleon III could be taciturn when he did not want to commit himself. He said so little that the new Minister could not determine where he stood on American affairs.

But the ineffectual Dayton did something that was to be of much benefit to his country. As soon as he learned that it was possible to buy favors from some French publications, he wrote to the State Department to propose a practical solution to an awkward problem:

> If a little money were judiciously expended here it would go
> far to put public sentiment right in certain quarters. We can-
> not expect the press to submit as much matter and take as

much interest in American affairs as we could desire without some compensation for the extra service. If a gentleman accustomed to the use of the pen, and especially if he had some acquaintance with the leading men connected with the European press, could be sent over here in the possession, nominally, of a *good* Consulate (the duties of which could be performed by clerks) while his attention could be really directed to the press, it might be of great use in giving a right direction to public sentiment. It is a duty which a public Minister could not, *with propriety,* perform.[3]

As a result of this request, Seward sent the very capable journalist, John Bigelow, to Paris. Bigelow was then 44 years old and a part owner of the pro-administration *New York Evening Post.* He had traveled in Europe and knew many leading people there. Since he would not arrive in Paris until September, the French press had to remain uninformed and uninfluenced about the Northern cause until then.

The South, however, had long been well represented in France by a large but unofficial body of its wealthy citizens who were very much at home there. An American resident of Paris said that the Confederate agents "had the active cooperation of large numbers of Southern men and women. . . . Southern ladies, who formed a brilliant and influential society, vied with each other in their endeavors to enlist in support of their cause everyone connected with the Imperial Court. It was most natural, since they were pleading for their homes and their families. Many of them had fathers, brothers, husbands, and sons fighting for what they regarded as birthrights. Their zeal, their strenuous efforts, and continued labor were not in vain, for the Court was almost entirely gained over to their side. The consequence was that the Emperor was constantly surrounded by those who sympathized with the South. . . . The Emperor was, at times, absolutely beset by these people. According to them, the South was sure of success, and the inability of the Federal Government to carry on the war much longer was a constant theme with them."[4]

The same observer charged that the Southern group in Paris was offering high court officials large quantities of cotton as bribes for them to use their influence on the Emperor to grant full recognition to the Confederacy. Subversion was a powerful force during the Civil War; both the North and the South did not hesitate to use large sums to buy favors. The North had more money, but the South was able to make its limited means go farther.

Of all the Confederate diplomats, the one sent to Mexico was undoubtedly the poorest choice. John T. Pickett was not only a fool in his dealings with a government he despised, he was also unlucky. Everything he said and wrote was quickly reported to that government—and to the Union Minister, Thomas Corwin, as well.

Yet Pickett had been consul in Vera Cruz for some time and was personally acquainted with Mexico's President Juárez. The instructions given to him on May 17 by the Confederate State Department did not help, for they drew a comparison between slavery and peonage and said that the system of forced labor which was common to both countries ought to serve as a tie between them. Benito Juárez was of Indian birth and, although he had never been a peon, he had known poverty in his youth and was trying to improve conditions for the Mexican people. For him to side with the Confederacy because it advocated slavery was unthinkable.

Pickett added a few suggestions of his own to those given to him by the Confederate State Department: "The agent should be furnished with means sufficient . . . to pay for important information . . . and other secret service. A million or so of money judiciously applied would purchase our recognition by the government. The Mexicans are not over-scrupulous, and it is not our mission to mend their morals at this precise period."

Once he got to Mexico, Pickett's behavior quickly alienated the Juárez government. He wavered and blundered, sometimes changing his tactics abruptly, and was incautious enough to use threats of invasion and annexation.[5] He even went so far as to advocate an alliance between the Confederacy and Spain to subjugate and divide Mexico. Since his mail was being opened and read, both Juárez and Corwin knew exactly what he was doing. Then he crowned his career by getting into a fist fight with a Yankee "pill vendor." For this he was thrown into a common jail for a month and had to bribe his way out.[6]

Pickett did his own cause irreparable harm in Mexico. Other Confederate diplomats made mistakes, but at least they did not outrage public opinion.

Mexico was involving Europe in American affairs at this time, largely because British, French, and Spanish investors were in danger of losing the money they had put into that country's bonds. Lord Russell, speaking in the House of Commons on May 12, announced that Sir Charles Wyke had been sent to Mexico to protect British investments there.[7]

Before the year was over, the three nations signed a tripartite agreement for joint action to collect interest on the bonds. They got nowhere, but power-hungry Napoleon III decided to interfere actively in Mexico's internal affairs. He began the series of moves which caused him to send an army there and put Maximilian of Austria on the throne as Emperor in 1864.

Early in May, President Lincoln replied to a letter he had received from the Regent Captains of San Marino, the tiny republic located high in the Apennine Mountains near Rimini, Italy. He thanked them for the honorary citizenship they had conferred on him and then commented on the force of their state's example as the oldest of all republics:

> Although your dominion is small, your state is nevertheless one of the most honored in all history. It has by its experience demonstrated the truth, so full of encouragement to the friends of humanity, that government founded on republican principles is capable of being so administered as to be secure and enduring.
>
> You have kindly adverted to the trial through which this Republic is now passing. It is one of deep import. It involves the question whether a representative republic, extended and aggrandized so much as to be safe against foreign enemies, can save itself from the dangers of domestic faction. I have faith in a good result.
>
> Wishing that your interesting State may endure and flourish forever, and that you may live long and enjoy the confidence and secure the gratitude of your fellow citizens, I pray God to have you in his holy keeping.
>
> Your Good Friend,

Washington, May 7, 1861   ABRAHAM LINCOLN[8]

Chapter 10

ERRORS AND BLUNDERS—SIMPLE AND COMPOUNDED

Washington had much need of a European expert, a man who could speak several languages, who had lived abroad, and who knew how the people there thought and acted. Such a person was at hand.

He was Count Adam Gurowski, an exiled Polish revolutionist who was strongly opposed to slavery and eager to serve the Union cause. He was the kind of applicant who seems impressive in a resumé of his career, for he did speak many languages, and he certainly had lived in Europe for most of his 60 years. He also knew many distinguished people in America; Senator Charles Sumner, Chairman of the important Committee on Foreign Affairs, and Horace Greeley, editor of the New York *Tribune,* among them. Gurowski had even written articles for Greeley's paper. He had also written several books, two of which had the curiously modern sounding titles: *Russia As It Is* and *America and Europe.* In addition to everything else, Gurowski could recite the personal histories of nearly every person in power in Europe and could also reel off intimate disclosures about the various diplomats stationed in Washington.

Such a man was obviously so valuable that he was promptly employed by the State Department where his chief duties were to read foreign newspapers and be on call if information was needed.

But this expert, who seemed to be exactly what the new administration needed, had many serious drawbacks, not the least of which was his personal appearance. He was repulsively ugly, and he emphasized his grotesqueness by dressing in bright colors and wearing a blue veil draped around a big hat to conceal the fact that underneath his thick blue glasses he had only one eye. His voice was shrill, and it ran on endlessly, pouring out a confusing mixture of fact and opinion so fast that most of his listeners could not understand what he was saying. And his

English, which he had learned late in life, was decidedly not good.[1] Although Lincoln was probably responsible for the State Department's hiring Gurowski, he said later that the eccentric Pole was the only one he knew who might attempt to assassinate him. Gurowski, however, was not a killer.

Seward had no reason to like his strange employee, especially after it was reported that Gurowski was saying that he had been given his job to keep the Secretary of State from making a fool of himself. Even Gideon Welles called Gurowski "splenetic and querulous . . . growling and discontented."[2]

Since such a creature was obviously impossible as an employee in a sensitive department, Seward quietly got rid of the brilliant but objectionable expert. That left only William Hunter, the chief clerk, to advise the new head of the State Department. Hunter had worked in the office for years and had memorized much useful precedent. But Gurowski had only contempt for him and said that he did not even know "the red-tape traditions of the department" and was "without any genuine instruction, without ideas." He blamed Hunter for the new administration's first major error in foreign relations—the proclamations of blockade which Lincoln issued on April 19 and 27, 1861. When the correspondence between Lord Lyons and Seward was made public in June, Gurowski wrote that all Hunter knew about a blockade was that

> it was in use during the Mexican War [and] that it almost yearly occurred in South American waters. . . . But that was all . . . this chief clerk knew. Lord Lyons asked for some special precedents or former acts of the American government. The chief [Seward] and his support, the chief clerk, ignored the existence of any. Lord Lyons . . . sent to the department American precedents and authorities. No Minister of Foreign Affairs in Europe, together with his chief clerk, could ever be caught in such a *flagrante delicto* of ignorance. This chief clerk made Mr. Seward make *un pas de clerc,* and this at the start.[3]

All this, of course, had happened before Gurowski went to work in the State Department in June 1861. He was dismissed in September 1862 when Seward was shown his diary. If the published diary was printed without additions or corrections and its entries were actually written when dated, it showed a remarkable knowledge of men and affairs. In April 1861, Gurowski had said:

> How can the Minister of Foreign Affairs [Seward] advise the President to resort to such a measure? Is the Minister of For-

eign Affairs so willing to call in foreign nations by this blockade, thus transforming a purely domestic . . . question into an
international . . . one? . . . The administration ought to know
its rights of sovereignty and to close the ports of entry. Then no
chance would be left to England to meddle.[4]

In this Gurowski was right and the administration was wrong, for a
nation *blockades* an enemy's ports and merely *closes* its own. In issuing
the proclamation of blockade, Lincoln had opened the way for England
and other countries to recognize the Confederacy as a belligerent. The
misuse of the word "blockade" proved to be an expensive and unneces-
sary blunder.

Gurowski wrote to Lincoln "concerning the unavoidable results of his
proclamation in regard to the blockade; [and] explained to him that this
. . . will and forcibly must evoke a counter proclamation from foreign
powers." He also correctly predicted "that the foreign powers will recognize the rebels as belligerents; he, the President, having done it already."
And then he added that "rebel piratical crafts will be recognized as privateers by foreign powers, and as such will be admitted to all ports under
the secesh flag, which will thus enjoy a partial recognition."

He also said he had "learned that Mr. Seward does not believe that
France will follow England. Before long Seward will find it out."[5]

No one, of course, paid any attention to the annoying little foreigner.
But he had analyzed the situation more correctly than anyone else. And
a good many, although by no means all of his predictions, did come true.
Gurowski was not infallible; but he was well-educated in foreign affairs,
and he had excellent sources in circles which no highly placed official
would dare to approach.

Before Gurowski was separated from the State Department in 1862,
he "warned Mr. Seward against making contracts for arms with all kinds
of German agents from New York and from abroad. They will furnish
and bring, at the best, what the German governments throw out as being
of no use at the present moment. All the German governments are at
work to renovate their firearms."[6] This was excellent advice, not only
about Germany but other nations as well. The United States, however,
was already sending agents overseas to purchase arms.

But if the Lincoln administration was wrong about using the word
"blockade," nearly the entire Confederate government and most of the
Southern people were making an even more serious mistake about the
importance of cotton as a long-time factor in world affairs.

The phrase "Cotton is King" had been popularized by a book issued anonymously under that title in 1855. The author later turned out to be, ironically enough, a Northerner from Cincinnati named David Christy.[7] The phrase was seized upon by the South and was quoted so often that its people really began to believe it was true.

In the spring of 1861 cotton might have been used to further the Confederacy's war effort if its government had acted quickly. Instead, it floundered from one blunder to another before doing anything with this tremendously valuable asset. Alexander Stephens, Judah P. Benjamin, and others saw quite clearly that their government should ship as much cotton as possible to Europe before the Northern blockade could become effective. Stored in Europe, the cotton would have been good collateral, and its value would have increased steadily as the world's supply was used up. Every pound of cotton safely landed in Europe was an asset; every pound retained at home was a liability. But very little was sent abroad. Before long, much of the cotton still on the plantations had to be destroyed to prevent it from falling into enemy hands. Naïve belief that "Cotton is King" was the Confederacy's first error. This was a particularly grievous mistake to make in the spring of 1861, for the previous year's cotton crop—the largest ever grown—was glutting the warehouses of Europe. The second error was in doing too little while cotton could still be shipped through the blockade. And these two primary blunders led eventually to the Confederacy's third and most disastrous one—the resort to printing-press currency until inflation drove up prices until they became fantastic while money and bonds eventually became worthless. Brilliant in their military operations and skillful in their handling of naval affairs, the leaders of the Confederacy were children in finance and hardly more than that in dealing with the clever, long-experienced, and utterly ruthless men who were in charge of European diplomacy.

There was, of course, much more to the matter than cotton, for Europe needed the North's wheat just as much as it did the South's cotton—so much so, in fact, that Seward at one time threatened to place an embargo on wheat.[8]

The South's chance to move its cotton abroad did not last long, because the Northern blockade of its major ports soon became more effective. When Sumter surrendered, the Union's Secretary of the Navy called in all available naval vessels. It took months for some of Welles' orders to reach ships in the far parts of the world, and then it took more months for the slow-moving men-of-war to sail back to their home ports. A. T.

Mahan, who was later to write a number of celebrated books on naval affairs, was on board the *Congress* at Montevideo when sailing orders arrived; he did not get to Boston until August, four months after the war had begun. Ships based in the Pacific took even longer to return. But one after the other they came in and were soon ready for blockade work.

Welles did not wait for his men-of-war to arrive; he moved swiftly to build up the blockade fleet by buying commercial vessels, putting guns on them, and sending them out to patrol Southern coasts, stop blockade-runners, and capture or sink privateers.

Confederate privateering was destined to have a short life. In the early days of the war, the South was easily able to persuade private owners to arm their vessels and go searching for Yankee ships and cargoes to seize and sell. The first Confederate letter of marque was granted on May 18 to the *Savannah*, a former Charleston pilot boat. It made its first capture on June 3, and then rashly tried to attack a United States war-ship during the night. When the *Savannah's* officers and crew were brought in to New York, they were charged with piracy—a crime for which the punishment was death.[9] Jefferson Davis promptly threatened to retaliate by doing to Union prisoners whatever was done to the pri-vateersmen. His threat was successful.

Before long the owners of privateers found out that the business was unprofitable because they could not take their prizes into foreign ports to sell them there, while the blockade soon made it impossible to bring them home. By the end of 1861, privateering had almost run its course. A few letters of marque and reprisal were issued after that, but priva-teering had been rendered obsolete by a combination of international law and swift, maneuverable steam power.

Chapter 11

CONFEDERATE AGENTS ABROAD AND
UNION POLICY AT HOME

Although the men sent abroad by the Confederacy to serve as its diplomats were a rather poor lot, the new state was far more successful in its choice of the practical-minded agents who were authorized to purchase arms and ships. They had to work in active competition with similar agents sent to Europe by the United States Government. And the North's ability to pay for what it bought was, of course, infinitely greater than the South's. The new government had to start its career with nothing in its treasury except relatively small amounts of hard currency obtained by seizing the mints and other assets within its borders. It has been estimated that the total amount of gold owned by the Confederacy during its entire history was only $27,000,000.[1] With this, plus whatever it got for the little cotton it was able to ship abroad, it fought a major conflict for four years—a conflict which obviously cost many times more than the real money in its possession. This was possible because of the greed, credulity, and stupidity of foreign bankers, contractors, munitions factories, shipyards, and suppliers who thought that the chance to make large profits was worth the risk. They, and the South's own citizens, financed the war—and lost their money.

Among the very first to go to Europe for the Confederacy was Massachusetts-born Major Caleb Huse, a 30-year-old West Pointer who had been traveling abroad shortly before the war began.[2] He was called to Montgomery early in April and was given orders to go overseas to buy arms. After arriving in Liverpool on May 10, he started to investigate the market for munitions.[3] Although Huse found quality material to be exceedingly scarce, he managed to purchase 10,000 British Enfield rifles for $195,000, a far greater amount of money than he was then able to command. With the help of the Liverpool office of the Southern banking firm of Fraser, Trenholm and Company, who were acting as financial agents for the Confederacy, he was able, after some initial difficulty, to work out satisfactory terms with various sub-contractors for the much-needed infantry weapons.[4] He became friendly enough with Sir William Armstrong to get detailed drawings of the celebrated cannon manufactured by his company. He also met Captain Alexander T. Blakely, maker of equally well-known artillery.[5] Huse preferred the Armstrong gun but was glad to obtain twelve Blakely fieldpieces. He then went on to France and Austria.[6]

Of all the purchasing agents whom the Confederacy sent to Europe, the cleverest, best-informed, and most successful was James Dunwoody Bulloch. This former naval officer, who was born in Georgia in 1823, had been in private mail service for some years. At the beginning of the war, he dutifully returned his ship to her owners in New York and then went to Montgomery to offer his services to the Confederate government. Mallory asked him to go to Europe to buy ships for the navy, a task for which Bulloch was probably better qualified than anyone available. He arrived in Liverpool on June 4 and immediately went to work. Before the month was over, he had made arrangements for the first Confederate cruiser to be built abroad. This was the *Oreto* (later the *Florida*), which was to be ready to go to sea in eight months. During the summer, Bulloch persuaded the owners of the famous Laird yards to begin construction on another commerce-raider which was known temporarily as No. 290, but which became the most celebrated of all Confederate ocean-going ships, the much-feared *Alabama*.[7]

While these two cruisers were being built, Bulloch obtained his government's consent to purchase a fast new cargo steamer named the *Fingal*. He loaded this with the arms that Huse and others had obtained and sailed from Holyhead on October 15 to bring home the first large shipment of war matériel from Europe. These weapons were landed in Savannah and from there were sent by rail to the places where they were most needed. Rifles and guns from the *Fingal* were used to stop McClellan when he began his Peninsular Campaign.[8]

On June 1 two other Confederate agents started out for Europe. These were naval Lieutenant James H. North and Colonel E. C. Anderson. They left Savannah in a yacht renamed the *Camilla*. This was the world-famous *America*, the fast schooner which had won the first cup race against England in 1851.[9]

The Federal Navy's espionage system was functioning well enough by this time to inform Welles of the *Camilla's* departure. He tried desperately to head her off as she crossed the Atlantic, but the former cup winner had no trouble eluding all pursuit and landed the two agents in England to join forces with those already there.

Jealousy showed itself soon after the Confederate agents began to compete for power. On October 9, just before Bulloch left for Savannah on the *Fingal*, he received a letter from Lieutenant North asking that all drawings, specifications, contracts, and cash on hand be turned over to him as the only agent of the Confederate Navy Department who would be in England. Bulloch told North that he was working as a civilian in order to keep the Confederacy's negotiations secret and that he would not think of turning anything over to a known agent of the Navy. He also said that "nearly every farthing thus far sent" to him was already committed for the two commerce-raiders he had ordered.[10]

Semmes was fortunate in not being involved in the petty squabbles in Europe. Being free of any entanglements, he was able to convert a former mail steamer into the cruiser *Sumter* and on June 9 ran her from the Mississippi River into the Gulf, successfully eluding the blockade fleet that was guarding the exits.

The capital of the Confederacy was moved from Montgomery to Richmond late in May. Since Virginia was almost sure to be the target of the first Federal efforts to invade the South, Jefferson Davis wanted to be near the scene of action. Records, employees, and officials were moved north over a period of several weeks. The people of Montgomery were heartbroken at losing the honor of being the capital of the Confederacy, but Davis was a stubborn man who usually got what he wanted. When he arrived in Richmond on May 29, the move was completed, and soldiers from the Southern states were pouring into the new capital to defend it.

On July 4, the Congress of the Northern government met in Washington to approve the use of force to bring the seceded states back into the Union. And on that day, the President of the United States, in his first message to Congress, reviewed what had happened and asked for $400,-000,000 and 400,000 more men for the armed services. The number 400—and multiples of it—was to occur in public documents many times during the next four years. Perhaps it is more than coincidence that $400 was what Lincoln wanted to pay for a slave in his never-to-be-successful scheme for compensated emancipation. And there were 4,000,000 slaves.

In that message, the President defined the cause for which the blood of hundreds of thousands of the nation's citizens was about to be shed:

> This issue embraces more than the fate of these United States. It presents to the whole family of man the question whether a constitutional republic, or a democracy—a government of the people, by the same people—can, or cannot, maintain its territorial integrity against its own domestic foes. It presents the question whether discontented individuals, too few in numbers to control administration according to organic law . . . can . . . arbitrarily, without any pretence, break up their Government and thus practically put an end to free government upon the earth. It forces us to ask: "Is there in all republics this inherent and fatal weakness? Must a government, of necessity, be too *strong* for the liberties of its own people, or too *weak* to maintain its own existence . . . ?"
>
> This is essentially a People's contest. On the side of the Union, it is a struggle for maintaining in the world that form and substance of government whose leading object is to elevate the condition of men—to lift artificial weights from all shoulders—to clear the paths of laudable pursuit for all—to afford all an unfettered start and a fair chance in the race of life. . . .
>
> Our popular government has often been called an experiment. Two points in it our people have already settled—the successful *establishing* and the successful *administering* of it. One still remains—its successful *maintenance* against a formidable [internal] attempt to overthrow it. It is now for them to demonstrate to the world that those who can fairly carry an election can also suppress a rebellion—that ballots are the rightful and peaceful successors of bullets; and that when ballots have fairly and constitutionally decided, there can be no successful appeal back to bullets; that there can be no successful appeal, except to ballots themselves at succeeding elections. Such will be a great lesson of peace; teaching men that what they cannot take by an election neither can they take it by a war.[11]

On that afternoon, the 85th anniversary of the independence of the United States, the President and the aged head of the Army, General Scott, reviewed 20,000 soldiers from 23 New York regiments. Bands blared and flags flew as the long columns marched down Pennsylvania Avenue past the White House.

Chapter 12

THE NEWS OF FIRST MANASSAS REACHES LONDON

Several minor battles had been fought in Missouri and Virginia, but so far there had been much more speech-making, drilling, and parading than actual combat. On May 28, Brigadier General Irvin McDowell had been placed in command of the Union troops in northeastern Virginia and had been trying ever since to make an army out of thousands of eager but largely untrained volunteers. Pressure on him to advance into Virginia and "clean out the rebels" increased as his regiments began to look less like clerks and more like soldiers. Many Northerners were convinced that one good push would topple the Confederacy and end secession. It was a delusion they were to suffer from for some time.

Although McDowell was still uncertain of the fighting ability of his green troops, in mid-July he began moving them toward Confederates encamped near an important railroad junction at Manassas. On Sunday, July 21, the first major battle of the war was fought along the shores of a little creek named Bull Run. Routed Federal troops streamed back in disorder to Washington where men from the various legations and foreign newspapers wrote vivid descriptions of the Union defeat for the information of their home offices.

Prominent among the journalists who went to see the battle was William Howard Russell, correspondent for England's *Times*. He had just completed a tour of the Confederacy, but his long visit there had not won him over to its cause. He still favored the Union on the day he rode out to witness the battle at Bull Run. But what he had to say quickly turned Northern opinion against him. Six days after the Union defeat he wrote to John Bigelow: "It is not true that I commanded the Confederates in person or led off the Federalist centre; neither did I lie on my stomach disguised as Raymond of the [New York] *Times* and kill

Beauregard with a pistol toothpick as he rode insultingly over the battle-field."[1]

But early reaction against Russell was nothing compared to what happened after copies of *The Times* arrived from London. Then the British journalist learned that De Tocqueville had spoken truly when he said that "a stranger who injures American vanity, no matter how justly, may make up his mind to be a martyr."[2]

The Times correspondent became known as "Bull-Run Russell." Epithets were hurled at him in the street, and he received anonymous letters threatening "assassination, tarring, feathering, and the like."[3] When he met Mr. and Mrs. Lincoln one day while they were driving out in their carriage, he found that "the President was not so good-humored, nor Mrs. Lincoln, so affable . . . as usual."

Russell's dispatch to *The Times* gave encouragement to the pro-Southern element in England and made life more difficult for Adams. The United States Legation had moved to new and better quarters at No. 5 Mansfield Street, Portland Place, at the end of July,[4] and it was there, on August 5, that Adams received the depressing accounts of what had happened near Manassas.

When Palmerston, the Prime Minister of England, read the news, he commented:

> The defeat at Bull's Run—or rather at Yankee's Run—proves two things. First, that to bring together many thousand men and put uniforms upon their backs and muskets in their hands is not to make an army: discipline, experienced officers and confidence in the steadiness of their comrades are necessary to make an army fight and stand: secondly, that the Unionist cause is not in the hearts of the mass of the population of the North. The Americans are not cowards: individually they are as reckless of their own lives as of the lives of others . . . and it is not easy to believe that if they had felt they were fighting for a great national interest they would have run away as they did from the battle. . . . The truth is the North are fighting for an idea chiefly entertained by professional politicians, while the South are fighting for what they consider, rightly or wrongly, vital interests.[5]

McDowell was quickly replaced by McClellan, and the North then began to make serious preparations for what might be a protracted conflict, one that conceivably could last several months, or, as a few people were gloomily predicting, even a year or more.

The moment news of Confederate victory at First Manassas reached London, the two Commissioners there went into action. They telegraphed Rost in Paris to come to England at once, and as soon as he joined them they drafted a note to Earl Russell requesting an interview so they could present the Confederacy's case. They had no hope that the British Cabinet would recognize the South's independence so soon, but they thought that the news might induce the British Government to declare the Union blockade ineffective.[6]

Since Russell was away from London, they got no answer for several days. Meanwhile, they wrote to Richmond to state how matters stood. After complaining that they had never had any acknowledgment of the receipt of their dispatches to the Confederate State Department and had no funds to set up a regular method of communicating with it, they made the sad admission: "The commission has not received the least notice or attention, official or social, from any member of the [British] Government since its arrival in England. This is mentioned in no spirit of complaint, but as a fact which the President may or may not deem of any consideration in weighing the conduct of this Government toward the Confederate States."

Then, at the last minute, they added: "Since writing the foregoing, Earl Russell has answered our request for an interview in a note desiring us to 'put in writing any communication they'—the members of the Commission—'wished to make to him.'"

In accordance with Russell's request, the three Commissioners dutifully stated their case in writing, presenting lengthy arguments and urging that England recognize the Confederacy as a government *de facto*.

Russell answered them ten days later, referring in his reply to "the so-styled Confederate States of North America." Then he said curtly that Her Majesty had already declared her intention of preserving a strict neutrality and that "Her Majesty will strictly perform the duties which belong to a neutral. Her Majesty can not undertake to determine by anticipation what may be the issue of the contest, nor can she acknowledge the independence of the nine states which are now combined against the President and Congress of the United States until the fortune of arms or the more peaceful mode of negotiation shall have more clearly determined the respective positions of the two belligerents."[7]

Mr. Adams had won his second victory.

A man who had been helping Dayton in Paris visited the London Legation on June 24. He was Thomas Haines Dudley, a lawyer from Camden, New Jersey, and a friend of Dayton's. He had come to Europe on the advice of his doctor. Moran described him in his *Journal:* "He has a fine head and remarkably intellectual countenance. His hair is dark brown and wavy and sets off his high and broad forehead with great effect, altho' at the same time concealing much of it. He is as intelligent as he looks and talks with great force. . . . I was much gratified to find him a strenuous patriot. He is modest, refined and able: and would make a splendid European representative. I should say he was 42 years of age, has a genteel figure, and is fully 6 feet high."[8]

Moran was correct about Dudley's age, but he neglected to note that he had a beard and that his face was serious to the point of being dour. His remark about Dudley's making "a splendid European representative" was soon to come true, for he was to become the American consul at Liverpool in a few months. And this great port was rapidly developing into a center of Confederate shipbuilding activity.

The Legation was also visited on the same day by Carl Schurz, who was on his way to Madrid to serve as Minister to Spain. Schurz was a young idealist who had had to flee Germany after taking part in the Revolution of 1848. He owed his appointment to Lincoln, with whom he had become friendly during the Presidential Campaign of 1860.

Lincoln had to defend Schurz against Seward, who felt that the young German's revolutionary background might be harmful at a time when the nation needed the good will of foreign governments—even reactionary ones. Lincoln told Seward that Schurz could be trusted to conduct himself discreetly—and "that it was not for the government of this Republic to discriminate against men for having made efforts in behalf of liberty elsewhere—efforts which every good American at heart sympathized; [and] that it might be well for European governments to realize this fact."

Seward yielded, but being overruled by Lincoln made him angry enough to blurt out what he really thought about the President. A Republican Congressman, who called at the State Department to tell Seward that his German-born constituents would be disappointed if he did not honor Schurz with a foreign post, reported that "Mr. Seward jumped up from his chair, paced the floor excitedly, and exclaimed: 'Disappointment! You speak to me of disappointment. To me, who was justly entitled to the Republican nomination for the Presidency, and who had to stand aside and see it given to a little Illinois lawyer!' "[9]

Schurz, who was a professional writer and a good judge of character, recorded his first impressions of the American Minister in London:

He said that he was very glad to see me, in a tone which, no doubt, was intended for kindness. It was certainly courteous. But there was a lack of warmth and a stiffness about it which . . . made me feel as though the temperature of the room had dropped several degrees. Of course, Mr. Adams could have no reason for desiring to chill me, and I concluded that this prim frigidity was purely temperamental and normal. When we began to talk about public business, he did, indeed, not exactly "warm up," but he spoke to me with a communicativeness which touched me as confidential and therefore complimentary. . . .

I left Mr. Adams with the highest impression of his patriotism, of the clearness and exactness of his mind, of the breadth of his knowledge, and his efficiency as a diplomat. . . . He was, in the best sense of the term, a serious and sober man. Indeed, he lacked some of the social qualities which it may be desirable that a diplomat should possess. While he kept up in London an establishment fitting the dignity of his position as the representative of a great republic and performed his social duties with punctilious care, he was not a pleasing after-dinner speaker, nor a shining figure on festive occasions. He lacked the gifts of personal magnetism or sympathetic charm that would draw men to him. Neither had he that vivacity of mind and that racy combativeness which made his father, John Quincy Adams, so formidable a fighter. But his whole mental and moral being commanded so high a respect that every word he uttered had extraordinary weight, and in his diplomatic encounters his antagonists not only feared the reach and exactness of his knowledge and the solidity of his reasoning, but they were also anxious to keep his good opinion of them. He would not trifle with anything, and nobody could trifle with him. His watchfulness was incessant and penetrating without becoming offensive through demonstrative suspiciousness, and his remonstrances commanded the most serious attention without being couched in language of boast or menace.[10]

The fine large building on Mansfield Street which now housed the American Legation was often visited by various people from the State Department as they passed through London on their way to their posts or came to consult with Mr. Adams on official business.

Dayton arrived from France on July 24 to discuss negotiations for the United States to accede to the Declaration of Paris.[11] But this was not going to be easy, for now that Palmerston was in a strong position, he had no desire to do any favors for a nation that had rebelled against Mother England. He delayed matters by saying that he had to make sure that France would agree. Meanwhile, Confederate privateers were legally free to do whatever damage they could.

John Lothrop Motley, the celebrated New England historian who had been appointed American Minister to Austria, visited the London Legation on September 2. Motley's long residence in Europe had brought him many friends there. While in England this time, he went picnicking with Russell and his family in the woods near Pembroke Lodge. Russell, who had just been made an Earl, took him to Balmoral to meet the Prince Consort and be presented to the Queen. This gesture, Motley felt, was intended as a compliment to the United States.[12]

On the heels of Motley came John Bigelow on his way to Paris. Moran called him "a splendid looking man . . . but . . . deserving of a higher post than the one he has."[13] The usually well-informed secretary evidently did not know what the true nature of Bigelow's work was to be while he served nominally as consul.

Bigelow had seen Lincoln just before he sailed from America. He was more favorably impressed with him than Adams had been:

> I observed no sign of weakness in anything the President said, neither did I hear anything that particularly impressed me, which, under the circumstances, was not surprising. What did impress me, however, was what I can only describe as a certain lack of sovereignty. He seemed to me, nor was it in the least strange that he did, like a man utterly unconscious of the place which the President of the United States occupied that day in the history of the human race, and of the vast power for the exercise of which he had become personally responsible. This impression was strengthened by Mr. Lincoln's modest habit of disclaiming knowledge of affairs . . . which, even where it exists, it is as well for a captain as far as possible to conceal from the public. The authority of an executive officer largely consists in what his constituents think it is.[14]

But Bigelow was not impressed by Adams. After dining with him, he wrote: "My respect for Mr. Seward's administration of the State Department has been diminishing. I do not hear of a single first-rate appointment that he has made anywhere. I begin to think less of the merits of my own."

Four days later, when he met Dayton in Paris, he was even more disappointed with his superior officer than he had been with Adams. The

American Minister to France was obviously a political appointee with no training for his work. What he had learned as a successful attorney in New Jersey would not help him deal with the complexities of a French court during the ultrasophisticated Second Empire. Oddly enough, Dayton was personally acquainted with Napoleon III, for he had frequently met him during his brief exile in America, 25 years before.

Dayton and Bigelow were mutually disappointed in each other. The Minister had been told that his consul spoke French well enough to serve as his interpreter. But Bigelow's command of the language was not that good. The energetic consul soon began taking lessons to improve his knowledge of French, and before long was studying German as well. He also traveled around France on several occasions in order to get a better idea of what the people were like.[15] If he was to influence their opinion, he had to understand how they thought.

That was more than Dayton did. To him, his post was a well-earned reward for his political activities at home. He did not even bother to try to learn French, nor did he care how the people thought or felt. He was not a stupid man, but he had grown torpid from lack of exercise, too much smoking, and stuffing himself with good things to eat. His best point of contact with the French was their common appreciation of food. But he was unable to go beyond that to join them in their keen relish for nourishment for the mind.

Back in London, the American Minister there was a far more intellectual type than Dayton was. When Adams was not busy with affairs of state or entertaining distinguished visitors, he liked to roam around the old city. He had a passion for visiting churches, not merely to inspect their architecture, but also to attend their religious ceremonies. Sometimes his young son Brooks accompanied him. Together they would explore the streets, go to the theater, attend auctions of rare coins, or watch the colorful ceremonies the English staged when a noted guest was being officially welcomed.[16]

Oddly enough, Adams did not particularly care for London, but he felt that since he was there he might as well see it. However, he did enjoy taking his family to the country, although it was risky for the Minister to be away from his office even on holidays, for one could never tell what news might arrive on the next ship from America.

Adams knew what the Confederate agents in England were doing, but he was seldom able to thwart them although he never stopped trying. When the blockade-runner *Bermuda* was getting ready to sail in mid-

August, he protested to Russell, who politely answered that his government had no way of detaining the vessel. Lord John admitted, however, that the blockade-runner's cargo was contraband; therefore the Union Navy had the right to seize her if it was lucky enough to catch her.[17] It was not, and the *Bermuda* delivered her war matériel to the Confederacy. By coincidence, word of her arrival at Savannah reached Adams in October, at the very time he learned about the *Fingal's* sailing from Holyhead with another cargo of military supplies.

During the time these blockade-runners were getting ready to go to sea, Adams was concerned about a nasty little problem which the State Department had dumped into his lap. On September 2, a messenger from America had brought him a dispatch bag which Robert Bunch, the British Consul at Charleston, was sending to the Foreign Office. The sealed bag was still unopened but with it were some 200 private letters which had been taken from the man to whom Bunch had entrusted the official pouch for delivery. These letters were from Southerners who wanted to get in touch with people in England and who had no other way of reaching them. The incident was not unusual and would ordinarily have been passed over in discreet silence. But one of the letters described Bunch's activities and contained the significant sentence: "Mr. B., on an oath of secrecy, communicated to me . . . that the first step of recognition was taken."[18]

These were dangerous words. Coming at a time when the United States was still smarting from the wounds inflicted at Bull Run and was indignant about the escape of the blockade-runner *Bermuda,* they were even more trouble-provoking than they might otherwise have been.

Adams read the covering correspondence from the State Department with dismay. It told how the bearer had been arrested in Jersey City just as he was about to sail for England on August 14. An accompanying note instructed the Minister to send the sealed dispatch bag to the Foreign Office, apologize for the delay, and ask whether its contents were in any way treasonable to the United States.[19] Since one of the intercepted private letters showed that the British and French consuls at Charleston had been in official correspondence with the Confederate government on the possibility of its acceding to the Declaration of Paris, Seward felt that Bunch had overstepped his authority and asked that he be recalled.

The next day, Moran took the dispatch bag and the State Department notes to the Foreign Office. Russell's reply to Adams did not arrive until September 13. He admitted that he had told Bunch to get in touch with the Richmond government, but said that he could not recall his man because Bunch had merely obeyed instructions. He assured Adams that the dispatch bag contained no treasonable material. His letter, however, ended on an encouraging note: "Her Majesty's Gov't have not recognized and are not prepared to recognize the so-called Confederate States as a separate and Independent State." As Moran commented, this was "worth more than all the rest."[20]

When Seward learned that the British Government refused to recall Bunch, he canceled the consul's exequatur. Bunch, however, stayed on at Charleston for more than a year. He was still active during that time, but he had to have official papers signed by an assistant.[21]

Chapter 13

THE WAR REACHES OUT

Northerners were kept well-informed of what was happening abroad because the important daily journals regularly printed a great deal of foreign news. The New York *Herald* had correspondents in many countries, and it gave their long, gossipy letters plenty of space.

The *Herald*'s London correspondent, writing on July 25, described the attitude of the well-to-do Englishman toward the war in America:

> The American war continues as great a mystery as ever to the bleared optics of Mr. John Bull. He has so long been accustomed to look at the world through his commercial and manufacturing eyes that he can see nothing . . . but huge granaries with which to replenish his coffers. China is a great tea warehouse; Jamaica, Demerara, Ceylon, Brazil, Java, Mocha, and "Araby the blest" are coffee plantations; your Southern states are his cotton fields, Australia is a sheep pasture, Virginia is his tobacco farm, Carolina sends him his rice, Illinois his breadstuffs, Hudson's Bay his furs, California his gold, Mexico and Peru his silver, and Golconda and Potosi . . . diamonds and precious stones. . . . True, he pays for all these luxuries, but he must have them, and if anything interferes with their production he is in a sad way, and sometimes he gets "riled." I fear he sometimes half forgets the rights of others, and instead of bringing philosophy to his aid . . . quite forgets himself. Then, too, he is so accustomed to have all his wishes obeyed— whether political or commercial—that [he regrets] times are not now as they were in the days when George the Third was king.[1]

The correspondent then went on to say that *The Times* had just published a financial article which was obviously intended to warn its readers not to invest money in the huge war loan which the Lincoln government was trying to float. This newspaper had begun its campaign against the North even before news of the Union's defeat at Bull Run reached London. When its editor, John Thadeus Delane, heard of the Union's humiliating reverse, he intensified his efforts to vilify the Lincoln administration and kept it up for the duration of the war. Delane and his enormously powerful paper were to do more for the South than all the Confederate envoys sent abroad.[2]

The pro-Northern Count de Gasparin, writing from the French point of view, said that "The Times has given the tone . . . to English opinion with respect to America. . . . From the first moment, it maintained, with that capricious abruptness for which it is distinguished, that slavery had nothing to do with the separation of the North and South, that the disruption was final, that it was desirable and right, that the Washington Cabinet was at once insane and criminal in fighting against the Richmond government, that abolition would speedily find its account in Southern independence, that the insurgents had been raised by good right to the character of belligerents."[3]

The Times had one outstanding virtue; it allowed its foreign correspondents to write whatever they wished even when their articles conflicted with the policy of the home office. This was especially true in "Bull-Run" Russell's case, for he had been pro-Northern until he was practically forced to leave the United States. And despite all that had happened, he did not favor the Southern cause even after he returned to England. But The Times continued its attacks upon the Union and never lost a chance to comment unfavorably on anything its political and military leaders did.

The Paris correspondent of the New York Herald, writing on August 2, indicated how things might be expected to go in Mexico. "The trick now," he said, "is to unite Mexico to the Southern states, so that the Northern confederacy and that of the South may be more equalized, and that one may keep the other in check, leaving France and England safe from the annoyance of seeing the American states assuming a power that menaced them."[4]

The only major country in Europe which took a definite stand on the side of the Union was Russia. This was not because that absolute monarchy favored American democracy; it was merely that it was opposed to England and France. The Crimean War of 1853–56 was too recent for Russians to forget, and even though Russia now had a new and more liberal Emperor, Alexander II could hardly be expected to trust the two powers which had helped Turkey defeat his country.

Soon after Cassius Clay arrived in St. Petersburg, he was taken by Prince Mikhailovich Gortchakoff, Russia's Minister of Foreign Affairs, to Peterhoff to be presented to the handsome young Czar on July 14. Clay was impressed by Alexander II, who welcomed the American envoy in excellent English.

The Czar and his Minister had already decided that Russia's policy was to be one of friendliness toward the United States. Prince Gortchakoff sent a long message to Baron de Stoeckl in Washington for him to present to Seward. It read, in part: "The American Union . . . is not simply in our eyes an element essential to the universal political equilibrium; it constitutes, besides, a nation to which our August Master and all Russia have pledged the most friendly interests, for the two countries, placed at the extremities of the two worlds, both in the ascending period of their development, appear called to a natural community of interests and of sympathies, of which they have already given mutual proofs to each other. . . . The American nation may count upon the most cordial sympathy on the part of our August Master during the important crisis which it is passing through."[5]

Lincoln urged Seward to ask Stoeckl to allow the letter to be released to the public. When he gave permission, copies of this statement of Russia's good will were sent to newspapers throughout the world.

When *The Times* printed the letter, Moran noted: "It is amusing to see its illy concealed chagrin at the letter of the Czar. The annoyance arises from the head of an absolute monarchy having been the first to openly address a letter of sympathy to a Constitutional Gov't in its hour of trial, while all Constitutional Gov'ts have held back, and England more determinedly than all the rest. Envy boils over in *The Times* today."[6]

The United States Minister Resident at Belgium, Henry S. Sanford, whom Moran called "that Legation on wheels" and accused of trying to establish a system of espionage in Europe, gave his fellow diplomats some uneasy moments when he went to Italy in September to invite Garibaldi to accept a major generalship in the United States Army.[7] The famous Italian liberator said that he would fight for the Northern cause only if he was given supreme command and the authority to proclaim freedom for all the slaves. These conditions were so far out of line with Northern policy that Sanford had to withdraw his offer.[8]

Garibaldi, however, evidently did not give up the idea of leading an army in the new world, for just a year later he wrote to Theodore Canisius, the American consul at Vienna, that he still hoped "to serve the great American Republic."[9]

Another matter which was troubling the United States legations that summer was the dawning realization that the powerful Reuters news service was beginning to slant its releases in favor of the Confederacy. Reuters used the telegraph to send dispatches all over Europe when they arrived by ship from America. The legation people did not know what was wrong, but a letter made public long after the war explained what was happening. It was written by Dudley Mann to the Confederate State Department on August 3:

> Reuter has entire control of the telegraph in this metropolis for the newspapers of all Europe. I have had two interviews with him during the last week. He is not only willing but anxious to furnish his correspondents everywhere with the latest reliable intelligence from both sides, South as well as North. The modus operandi would be this: That you should employ a strictly trustworthy individual to prepare a short statement of the most important occurrences and transmit it per Cunard steamer to us under cover to "M'Iver, agent Cunard Packets, Queenstown, Ireland." Reuter will give him directions to telegraph the contents to us the moment the steamer touches at that place. If it were deemed important to communicate twice a week, then a dispatch might be sent to "Joseph Sharpe, Southampton, England." . . . We suffer in Europe from the false statements which are furnished in the North for dissemination on this side of the Atlantic. The injury which we sustain can be effectively counteracted in the manner which I have indicated. Both M'Iver and Sharpe are the paid confidential agents of Reuter.[10]

Moran, in his *Journal* for August 26, casts further light on the Reuters matter:

> The German, Reuter, who now supplies the European press with telegraphic reports has evidently been bought up by the rebels, and he systematically prostitutes the monopoly he holds to depreciate the Union. Some time since he offered to furnish his reports to the Gov't, but they were declined, and now he is against us. None of his reports are ever borne out fully by

the details given in the journals; but on the contrary, nine
cases out of ten his reports are proved false, or great exaggera-
tions. But the British Press encourages the deception, and there
is no way to remedy the business but by buying the fellow up.
This I would not do.[11]

Because of their usefulness as waystops for ships bringing goods from
Europe to Southern ports, Bermuda, Nassau, and some of the islands
in the West Indies were provided with agents to serve the Confederacy's
interests there. Chief among them was Charles J. Helm who had been
United States commercial agent at St. Thomas and consul-general at
Havana. On July 22, he was appointed as the Confederacy's special
agent to be in charge of all the islands.[12] Later, when the work of supervising activities in so many places became too much for one person to
handle, other representatives were sent to Nassau and Bermuda.

Most of these men's duties were of a regular commercial nature, involving the handling of cargoes, ships' clearances, and the other numerous small tasks that are part of moving merchandise from one part of
the world to another. Since these islands became more and more important as transfer points when the Federal blockade tightened, the
Confederate agents stationed on them had plenty to do. And they had
to carry on as poorly paid government employees while they watched the
men around them grow rich.[13]

The English were getting uneasy about their possessions in the new
world. Sir Alexander Milne's always powerful British North American
and West Indian fleet was strengthened until it had, by midsummer,
42 ships with 497 guns and 6390 men. In order to reinforce the lightly
held garrisons along the border between Canada and the United States,
the first contingent of British troops was sent out as early as June 1861
in the *Great Eastern*.[14] She was big enough to carry 2144 officers and
men, 373 women and children, and 122 horses. To be chartered as a
transport was fortunate for a ship that was becoming notoriously unlucky. Her luck must have been at its peak during that voyage (which
she made in the record time of eight days and six hours), for she just
missed colliding with the *Arabia* in the fog. And she navigated the St.
Lawrence River all the way to Quebec without mishap.[15]

One reason why the British were worried about Canada was that an
abrupt ending to the war between the North and the South would leave
several hundred thousand well-armed Union troops with nothing to do
—and many people still believed that the war would be short.[16] England

was taking no chances. With a world empire to defend, she had to provide against all possible contingencies.

In turn, of course, the United States also could not afford to take chances. Seward used secret-service funds to hire spies to watch activities along the Canadian border.

As the unhappy summer of 1861 drew to a close, it became evident that the first Confederate mission to Europe was nearing its end. Yancey's health was poor, and he notified Richmond that he wanted to resign. He was discouraged about the possibility of obtaining help from England or France. Early in July, he wrote to a friend that "important as cotton is, it is not King in Europe."[17]

On August 24, Robert M. T. Hunter, who had recently replaced Toombs as the Confederate Secretary of State, notified Mann and Rost that they were to proceed to Spain. On September 23, he modified these instructions and sent Mann to Belgium. He also accepted Yancey's resignation and informed the three men that James M. Mason was to be the new envoy to Great Britain while John Slidell was to go to France.[18]

The first Confederate mission to Europe had lasted only six months. During that time its chief accomplishment was to make European nations aware of the fact that the Confederate States of America existed. Richmond was counting on its two new appointees to do more than that.

Chapter 14

THE *TRENT* AFFAIR

When the first Confederate mission went to Europe in March, its members had been able to cross the Atlantic without difficulty. Since then, the Federal blockade had become effective enough to compel the Richmond government to take extraordinary steps to get Mason and Slidell overseas. At first they were supposed to go on the *Nashville,* a large steamer which had been seized at Charleston at the beginning of the war. Then it was felt that their chances would be better on a smaller, less conspicuous ship, and the *Nashville* went through the blockade without them to start her career as a commerce-raider.

The Confederate Government chartered the small but fast *Theodora* for $5000 to take Mason and Slidell to Nassau or Havana, where they could get a British ship to England.[1] On the night of October 11–12, the *Theodora* ran out of Charleston Harbor, eluded the blockading vessels, and headed for Nassau. On board were Mason and his secretary, Slidell with his family, his secretary, and several others who wanted to go to Europe.[2]

Virginia-born James M. Mason was then 63 years old and had been Chairman of the Senate's Foreign Relations Committee for ten years. As a friend of Jefferson Davis and a prominent exponent of secession, he was a logical choice for a post abroad.[3] He was disliked in the North because he had been largely responsible for the drafting of the much-hated Fugitive Slave Law of 1850.

Although Mason was highly thought of in the South, the opinion of the general public was not always agreed with by the few highly placed people who knew him well. Mrs. James Chesnut, whose husband was serving as an aide to General Beauregard, confided to her *Diary* that "Mr. Mason is a high and mighty Virginian. He brooks no opposition to his will."[4] When she heard that he was to be sent to England, she wrote: "My wildest imagination will not picture Mr. Mason as a diplomat. He will say 'chaw' for 'chew,' and he will call himself 'Jeems,' and he will wear a dress coat to breakfast." Later she said: "It set all the world a laughing when you sent Mr. Mason abroad as a diplomat! The English can't stand chewing tobacco, yet they say that at the lordliest table, Mr. Mason will turn round halfway in his chair and spit in the fire!"[5] Mrs. Chesnut was not alone in feeling about Mason as she did. Moncure Conway, who had known Mason in Virginia, called him "a hard arrogant man" and said that he was the hero of the fire-eating Southerners.[6]

Slidell was believed to have better qualifications for diplomatic work than Mason. Born in New York in 1793, he had settled in New Orleans in 1819 and had become a power in Louisiana politics. He had taken young Judah P. Benjamin into his law office and was now to benefit from his long acquaintance with the brilliant attorney in the Confederate Cabinet. Slidell had been sent to Mexico on a semi-secret mission in 1845. His chances for success there were slight, but he was lucky enough to have his failure forgotten when war broke out between that country and the United States. Like Mason, Slidell had been in Congress. He had also been active in the Charleston Convention in the spring of 1860 when the split-up in the Democratic Party helped to bring on secession and war.

The Cincinnati newspaperman, Murat Halstead, who saw Slidell at the Convention, wrote this vivid portrait of him:

> Seated at a round table on which books, newspapers, and writing materials are scattered about, is a gentleman with long, thin white hair, through which the top of his head blushes like the shell of a boiled lobster. The gentleman has also a cherry-red face, the color being that produced by good health and good living joined to a florid temperament. His features are well cut, and the expression is that of a thoughtful, hard-working, resolute man of the world. He is a New Yorker by birth, but has made a princely fortune at the New Orleans bar. He is not a very eloquent man in the Senate, but his ability is unquestioned; and it is universally known that he is with the present Administration, the power behind the throne, greater than the throne itself. Mr. Buchanan is as wax in his fingers. The name of this gentleman is John Slidell. His special mission here is to see that Stephen A. Douglas is not nominated for the Presidency.[7]

The *Theodora* touched briefly at Nassau and then went on to Cuba where the English mail steamer *Trent* was to sail from Havana on November 7. The Confederate envoys naturally assumed that they could count on being safe on a ship which was under the protection of the all-powerful British flag.

At this time, the U.S.S. *San Jacinto,* a 1500-ton screw steamer, was on her way home after 20 months of patrolling the slave coast of western Africa. Her 63-year-old commander, Captain Charles Wilkes, had headed an exploring expedition to the Antarctic in 1838 and had had a vast tract of that icebound continent named after him. In 1861, his fame was fading, and he had as yet had no opportunity to take part in the war. He was known in the Navy as an able officer, but one who was hard on his men. Fearless, tough, and irascible, Wilkes would take action against the Devil himself if he thought the occasion warranted it. And he disliked the English because one of their naval officers had used some of his material on Antarctica without giving him credit.[8]

When Wilkes heard that Mason and Slidell were in Cuba, he first thought of capturing the ship which had brought them there. By the time he got to Havana, however, the *Theodora* was already on her way back to Charleston. While in port, one of the *San Jacinto's* officers saw Mason in the parlor of the hotel where he was staying.[9] As soon as Wilkes learned that the Confederate envoys could not leave Havana until November 7, when the *Trent* was to sail, he ran over to Key West to try to get other American warships to aid him, but none were in port. He could have obtained advice on international law while in Key West, but he did not ask for it. He had a small library on the subject and thought he was well enough informed to handle any problems without outside help. He sailed for the Old Bahama Channel on the northern coast of Cuba and anchored in the narrowest part at a place where the *Trent* had to pass.[10]

She came in sight on the morning of November 8 and hoisted the English flag when she saw the American warship waiting in the channel. Wilkes ordered his drummers to beat to quarters and launched two boats filled with armed men. It took two shots across the *Trent's* bows to convince her startled captain that Her Majesty's mail steamer was actually being commanded to stop.

Wilkes sent Lieutenant Fairfax to the *Trent* with written orders to arrest the two Confederate envoys and their secretaries and bring them to the *San Jacinto.* He added thoughtfully that if the men's families were with them, Fairfax was "to offer them . . . a passage . . . to the

United States" and to assure them "that all the attention and comforts we can command are tendered them."

Fairfax found the British captain most uncooperative and the Slidell family openly hostile. One of Slidell's daughters protested loudly, and when an unruly wave tossed her against the young lieutenant, it was soon rumored all over Europe and America that she slapped him.

When Mason and Slidell refused to leave the ship unless compelled to do so, Fairfax had some of his subordinates make a show of force by laying their hands on their prisoners' shoulders. Then the Confederates were put into one of the small boats and taken to the *San Jacinto*. The ladies in the party did not see fit to accept Captain Wilkes' kind invitation and remained on board the *Trent*.

The *San Jacinto* arrived at Fort Monroe, Virginia, on November 15 to put the four prisoners ashore. News of their capture went by telegraph to Washington and all the places which could be reached by wire. The victory-hungry North read the newspaper accounts with great glee. People in the South, of course, were outraged. Meantime, Mason and Slidell were sent to Boston to be incarcerated in Fort Warren.[11]

At the British Legation in Washington, where the much-harassed staff was trying to remain calm in the face of what promised to be an international storm, Lord Lyons sent a long dispatch by steamer to the Foreign Office in London. After that, he refused to say anything publicly until he received instructions from home. In a letter to Admiral Milne on November 25, he wrote: "I suppose I am the only man in America who has expressed no opinion whatever on the International Law question or on the course which our Government will take."[12]

Lyons was having a hard time because many high public officials were congratulating Wilkes for what he had done. He was given a banquet in Massachusetts, and Congress awarded him a gold medal.

The *Trent* Affair did not become explosive until news of it reached England. Adams, who was out of town on November 27, when word arrived, hurried back to London. He could learn nothing except what he read in the papers, for the State Department had not sent him any information and did not do so for days.[13] When Russell called upon him for an explanation, he had to admit that he had not yet heard from Washington. Perhaps, he intimated hopefully, the fact that he had not been advised meant that Wilkes had acted without orders.

Reaction in England was not instantaneous, for at first there was some doubt about whether there was any legal ground for protest. The question was very much in the public mind at that time because a United

States warship had entered Falmouth early in November in search of the *Nashville,* which was supposed to be carrying Mason and Slidell. Then the *Nashville* herself arrived in Southampton on November 21 with the captain and crew of the *Harvey Birch* on board. The Confederate raider had captured the Yankee ship only two days before and had burned her almost in sight of the English coast.

It was against the background of the controversy over the *Nashville's* arrival that news of the seizure of Mason and Slidell reached England. When the Law Officers of the Crown gave their opinion that Wilkes had acted wrongly because he did not seize the *Trent* and bring her into an American prize court for adjudication, *The Times* unleashed its fury. Moran commented caustically that "Wilkes did not insult England enough" and said of *The Times'* editors: "There is something positively infernal in the way these assassins are goading the nation on to war. They daily feed the public mind with the most palpable lies and stick at nothing."[14]

Once the Law Officers had stated their views, Russell drew up an ultimatum addressed to the American government. He demanded that the Confederate envoys be released and that an apology as well as reparation be made. At last Russell had Seward in the wrong, and months of pent-up resentment found release in his words. He also wrote detailed instructions for Lyons to follow when he presented the document to Seward. If these demands were not granted within seven days, the British Minister was to leave Washington. Even Gladstone, who certainly did not favor the North, thought that the terms were too strict, but he was overruled by the other members of the Cabinet. He was at Windsor that evening and had a chance to discuss the *Trent* Affair with the royal family. As a result, he was able to persuade the Cabinet to tone down the document's language.[15]

Russell's ultimatum had to be approved by the Queen before it was sent to Washington. It reached Windsor on the last day of November during a particularly trying time, for the Prince Consort was seriously ill. His physicians were slow to diagnose the ailment correctly, but they finally realized that he was dying of typhoid and had only a few days to live.

Early in the morning of December 1, the stricken Prince got up early to read the drafts of the slightly revised ultimatum. He was appalled by the harshness that still remained and wrote a series of suggested modifications.

A note from the Queen accompanied the document when it was returned to Russell:

> The Queen returns these important drafts, which upon the
> whole she approves, but she cannot help feeling that the main
> draft, that for communication to the American Government,
> is somewhat meagre. She should have liked to have seen the
> expression of a hope that the American captain did not act
> under instructions, or, if he did, that he misapprehended them
> —that the United States Government must be fully aware that
> the British Government could not allow its flag to be insulted,
> and the security of her mail communications to be placed in
> jeopardy, and her Majesty's Government are unwilling to be-
> lieve that the United States Government intended wantonly
> to put an insult upon this country, and to add to their many
> distressing complications by forcing a question of dispute upon
> us, and that we are therefore glad to believe that upon a full
> consideration of the circumstances, and of the undoubted
> breach of international law committed, they would spontane-
> ously offer such redress as alone could satisfy this country,
> viz: the restoration of the unfortunate passengers and a suitable
> apology.

Later, Victoria recalled the draft of her letter from the Royal Archives
and wrote on it:

> This draft was the last the beloved Prince ever wrote; he was
> very unwell at the time, and when he brought it in to the
> Queen he said: "I could hardly hold my pen."[16]

Another source of information about Queen Victoria's unceasing efforts to preserve peace is Thurlow Weed, who called on Russell at Pembroke Lodge while the *Trent* Affair was at its height. Weed quickly
realized that his host thought that the North was in the wrong and
stopped discussing the matter with him. When Lady Russell invited him
to view the gardens, she told him that "ladies were not supposed to know
state secrets, but that they had ears." Then, he reported, she went on to
say that "the sympathies of the Queen were with our government; that
Her Majesty remembered the attentions extended to her son, the Prince
of Wales, and would do everything in her power to prevent a war with
America."

Weed said that the Queen's influence helped to preserve peace on at
least three different occasions during the trying years of the Civil War.[17]

John Bigelow also claims to have played a part in keeping peace at this time. He prepared a long statement presenting the case for the United States and with Thurlow Weed's help, got old General Winfield Scott, who was then in Paris, to sign it so it could be released to the French newspapers.[18]

Meanwhile, 8000 British troops were ordered to Canada, arms and munitions for them were loaded on ships, and dispatches were sent to Admiral Milne telling him to prepare the great Atlantic fleet for the possibility of war.[19]

That the British were exceedingly naïve about the difficulty of establishing an effective blockade of the American coast can be seen in an estimate made on December 6 of the number of naval vessels thought adequate to patrol 1260 miles of coast from Portland, Maine, to Port Royal, South Carolina. The Duke of Somerset, head of the Admiralty, confidently said that 60 ships would be enough and put down the exact number needed for each port.[20] Even after it had spent four years building up a patrol fleet of nearly 500 vessels, the Union Navy was never able to blockade all the Southern ports—and it had to contend with only a handful of poorly armed Confederate fighting ships.

The document which the Prince Consort had modified went to America to reach Lord Lyons' desk in Washington at midnight on December 18.[21] News of England's reaction to the seizure of the Confederate envoys from one of her ships had preceded the arrival of Russell's dispatch. When Americans saw how violent British opinion was, stock prices went down and gold went up. Apprehension replaced the wild enthusiasm that had originally greeted Wilkes' action. Word about more British troops and munitions being sent to Canada was particularly disquieting. And it was rumored that one of Her Majesty's warships was on its way from Halifax to pick up the staff of her Washington Legation in case the United States gave an unfavorable answer. What was happening sent a chill into the hearts of those who were old enough to remember what the British had done in 1814 when they invaded Washington and burned the Capitol and the White House.

Lyons waited until December 20 to call on Seward. Then he told the Secretary of State that he was going to leave a copy of the dispatch for him to study before they began their formal discussions of it. Seward, much sobered, was properly grateful. He locked the door of his office, read the document, and began to put his ideas into writing. His draft, he knew, would have to go to the President and the Cabinet for approval.

But he went on composing what, for him, was an exceedingly temperate answer to the British demands.[22]

The reply which Seward wrote that day was remarkably like what Lincoln had told Benson J. Lossing at the time the capture of the Confederate envoys was first announced in Washington. (Lossing was an artist-historian who specialized in writing and illustrating multi-volumed works about the nation's wars.) Impressed by what the President had said, he printed his words: "I fear the traitors will prove to be white elephants. We must stick to American principles concerning the rights of neutrals. We fought Great Britain for insisting . . . on the right to do precisely what Captain Wilkes has done. If Great Britain shall now protest against the act and demands their release, we must give them up, apologize for the act as a violation of our doctrines, and thus forever bind her over to keep the peace in relation to neutrals, and so acknowledge that she has been wrong for sixty years."[23]

When Seward read the rough draft of his lengthy argument at the Cabinet meeting on Christmas Day, it was decided not to make any immediate decision. Lincoln then told Seward that he should continue to prepare his answer. Meanwhile, he said, "I have a mind to try my hand at stating the reasons why they [the prisoners] ought not to be given up. We will compare points on each side."

At the Cabinet meeting the next day, Seward read his completed answer which called for the prisoners to be surrendered to Britain. Approval was unanimous, although some of the members regretted having to let them go. When Seward asked Lincoln what had happened to the argument he was supposed to draft for the other side, the President said: "I found that I could not make an argument that would satisfy my own mind. And that proved to me that you were right."[24]

Lincoln, however, had actually written a reply to Russell but he did not show it to anyone, nor was it seen by the public until long after his death. In it he said that his government had "intended no affront to the British flag or to the British nation." He also made it clear that Wilkes had acted without orders. He offered to submit the matter to arbitration, or if that was not satisfactory, to make reparation provided that the result would become a precedent for deciding any similar cases between Great Britain and the United States.[25]

As soon as news of the administration's decision to release the prisoners was released, the stock market bounced back, the price of gold dropped, and the public, to many people's surprise, seemed relieved rather than angered.

One difficulty remained. Her Majesty's frigate *Rinaldo* was to pick up the prisoners, but no one in the United States Navy was willing to involve himself or his ship in taking the Commissioners to the British vessel. Seward neatly solved the problem by having a hired tug transport them from Fort Warren to Provincetown at the tip of Cape Cod. There, on January 1, 1862, the Confederate envoys were put on board the *Rinaldo*.

Mason and Slidell's sea troubles, however, were not yet over. A terrible storm prevented the *Rinaldo* from reaching Halifax. The captain had to go instead to Bermuda and then to St. Thomas, which, oddly enough, was the Confederate envoy's original destination in the *Trent*. From there, another ship carried them to Southampton where they finally landed on British soil on January 29, 1862.[26]

Chapter 15

THE YEAR 1861

Jefferson Davis delivered his first Annual Message to Congress on November 18; Lincoln's followed on December 3. Both Presidents agreed upon the abundance of the harvests that year; both spoke about relationships with foreign nations, the need for more railroads, financial matters, and various other subjects common to modern governments. They disagreed sharply, however, about the allegiance of the border states, each claiming to have won them to his side. Neither message was in any way eloquent; they were merely summations of how matters stood at the end of the year.

Yet even in Davis' first Annual Message, written at a time when he had most reason to be hopeful for the Confederacy, some petulance crept into his words. In later years, when things got worse, he became still more petulant and avoided commenting on subjects which could not be spoken about encouragingly.

The most notable passage in Lincoln's address dealt with the relationship between capital and labor. In this, he said that "labor is prior to, and independent of, capital. Capital is only the fruit of labor, and could never have existed if labor had not first existed. Labor is the superior of capital and deserves much the higher consideration." The President of a country which employed free labor and paid for its services could speak frankly about it. Jefferson Davis, as the President of a slave economy, refrained from discussing its nature.

Davis rashly predicted that "the Confederate States will exhibit a steadily increasing capacity to furnish their troops with food, clothing, and arms." How this was to be done in an under-industrialized country, he did not explain.

Lincoln just as rashly predicted that if the Union were preserved, people then alive would see a national population of 250,000,000.[1] Both men, of course, were wrong.

At the beginning of the war, the entire population of the country was about 31,000,000 of which the 23 Northern states and seven Territories had some 22,000,000 people while the 11 Confederate states had about 9,000,000.[2]

When the telegraph to the Pacific was completed on October 24, the first message was sent to President Lincoln: "The people of California desire to congratulate you upon the completion of the great work. They believe that it will be the means of strengthening the attachment which binds both the East and West to the Union, and they desire in this— the first message across the continent—to express their loyalty to the Union and their determination to stand by its Government on this, its day of trial."[3]

The picturesque Pony Express was making its final runs. Letters already in the mail had to be delivered, and the last lonely rider reached the western end of the line on November 21. Then the hard-riding young couriers and their hard-pressed horses passed into history to live again only in endless motion picture and television portrayals of their brief but fabulous careers.

Under the pressure of war, the Union Army had changed its supreme commander when McClellan replaced the aged Scott in November. The force had grown from 16,000 men at the time Fort Sumter was fired on to more than 600,000 regulars and volunteers by the end of 1861.[4] And this enormous host needed vast supplies of food, clothing, leather goods, canvas, tinware, and wagons, as well as arms and ammunition. Thousands of horses with all their harness of war were also required. Factories were busy, railroads and ships were overburdened, and the nation's labor force worked long hours to feed Mars' insatiable hunger. Whatever could be obtained abroad was eagerly snapped up to be shipped to America.

The Union Navy had been built up from its original strength of 42 ships in commission to an ever-growing force of 264 ships armed with 2557 guns. And its manpower was increased from 7600 seamen to 28,000 with an additional 12,000 mechanics and laborers at work in government yards and naval stations. Three ironclads were rapidly nearing construction; one of them, the Monitor, was a new kind of fighting ship that lay deep in the water with only its heavily armored revolving turret exposed. In addition to the Navy's wartime duties, it had captured five slave ships during the year.[5] And Nathaniel Gordon, captain of the slave-trader *Erie,* which had been taken in October 1860, was under sentence of death.

A system of strategy, similar to the Anaconda Plan which General Scott had proposed, was being put into effect. It called for blockading all Confederate ports, occupying them one after another, and gaining control of the Mississippi River. In 1861, Union forces had made a beginning by seizing Hatteras, Port Royal, Tybee Island near Savannah, and Ship Island off the coast of Mississippi.

The Union blockade was making it more and more difficult for ships to enter or leave the major Southern ports, but daring blockade-runners, many of them English-built and English-owned, were able to out-maneuver the Union naval patrol and earn enormous profits. Because of a scarcity of food and merchandise and a steady depreciation of currency in the Confederacy, prices kept rising there. Dry goods had doubled in cost, and meat had more than doubled during the first year of the war.[6] England, too, was beginning to feel the effect of the American conflict. Cotton was bringing 25 cents a pound in Liverpool, more than twice what it had cost in 1860. The British were encouraging India, Egypt, Brazil, and the East and West Indies to grow more of the raw material that was needed to keep the Lancashire mills going.

The Confederacy did not make noticeable progress in producing its own war matériel until late in 1861. The long-established Tredegar Iron Works in Richmond were its most important source for heavy armament. And it had also obtained useful weapons-making machinery when it seized the Harpers Ferry Arsenal and the Norfolk Navy Yard. But it was short of gunpowder, which it either had to bring in through the blockade at a high cost or manufacture in plants built especially for the purpose. In October 1861, a start was made to obtain saltpeter in Nashville. Since the South had plenty of sulphur, the only problem was to get it to the new gunpowder mills.[7]

Southern railroads had always been inadequate. They were now going from bad to worse as the available supply of iron decreased. And transportation by ship grew more difficult as the Federal blockade tightened and Union patrol boats and shore batteries along the rivers became more numerous. The South also had trouble obtaining and repairing the steam engines needed for motive power for its factories, railroad locomotives, and ships. Metal was so scarce that public appeals were made for church and plantation bells, and even brass andirons and clock weights.[8]

The Confederate Army, however, was rapidly developing into a large and effective force for a nation which had only about 800,000 white men of military age. Union reports put Confederate strength at 350,000 by the end of 1861.[9] Confederate estimates—there are no dependable records—were less optimistic. The South had few foreign-born people to draw upon for its labor force or its armies. Most emigrants, fearing competition from slavery, had settled in the North, and they continued to do so all through the war. Both the Germans and the Irish helped to swell the ranks of the Union Army. The North, in fact, was so successful in its illegal recruiting efforts in Europe that protests from the countries involved soon began to pour in to Washington.

The Confederate Navy had plenty of experienced officers but it was short of trained seamen. To obtain crews, it often had to press soldiers into service, and its sea-roving commerce-destroyers were manned largely by foreign sailors recruited in overseas ports or from ships captured in various parts of the world.

During the year 1861 the Confederate Navy grew from literally nothing to a small but fairly useful force made up partly of state-owned vessels. More important than its few fighting ships were the new ideas in naval warfare it was developing. Its first underwater mines (then called torpedoes) had been laid, and more were being devised. Proposals for building crude submarines were being considered. The Confederate Navy had already put the little ironclad *Manassas* into action on the Mississippi on October 12. And work was progressing rapidly at Norfolk where the former U.S.S. *Merrimack,* which had been burned and sunk when the navy yard there was abandoned, was being covered with heavy armor and converted into the formidable C.S.S. *Virginia.* Transcending everything else in ultimate value for the Confederate cause, however, were the far-ranging cruisers. The *Nashville,* which had destroyed only one ship (the *Harvey Birch*), was still at Southampton when the year ended. Semmes' far more successful *Sumter,* after having burned seven ships and released another on ransom bond, was on her way to Gibraltar, which was to be her last port. But more cruisers were nearing completion in British yards.

The year 1861 had been one of preparation for war. Now the conflict was to break out in full fury on land and sea, and the contest to win aid and approval from foreign countries was to be intensified.

Chapter 16

THE SEEDS OF CONFLICT ARE PLANTED ABROAD

Overshadowing everything else at the beginning of 1862 was the aftermath of the *Trent* Affair. Lord Lyons, who had "done everything to make the pill as easy to swallow as possible" for the Americans when they had to surrender Mason and Slidell, was soon rewarded by the Queen with the Grand Cross of the Bath.[1] When reliable information that the Confederate envoys were to be released reached London late on the afternoon of January 8, the news was announced during intermission in the theaters that night and was roundly cheered.[2]

But preparations for war, once started, are never easy to stop. British arsenals continued to be busy, and troops kept moving across the ocean to Canada. Seward amazed the British and the world by offering to let the soldiers, with all their arms and ammunition, cross Maine by rail in order to avoid delay in the icebound St. Lawrence. The British high command, taken aback by this wholly unexpected gesture of good will, cautiously refused the offer but finally consented to let the non-warlike supplies go by train. Seward's shrewd move enabled him to emerge from the otherwise humiliating *Trent* Affair with general acclaim. Some 18,-000 British troops were in Canada by the end of spring, but they were no longer considered a threat to the United States.[3]

During the crisis over the *Trent* Affair and for many months afterward, the widely distributed *Illustrated London News* printed article after article intended to impress the world with Britain's armed might. This was hardly necessary, but the excellent wood engravings, which give the details of manufacturing artillery shells, cannon, gun sledges for snow-covered Canada, heavy armor plate for the new ironclads, and cartridges for the much esteemed Enfield rifle, form a useful pictorial record of armament-making methods in the early 1860s.[4]

The Illustrated London News did not run this series as an anti-American gesture, for it had been and continued to be more generous in its attitude toward the United States than most other influential British papers. In its leading editorial on January 18, it expressed openly what had been secretly troubling the consciences of many liberal Englishmen during the *Trent* Affair:

> England allied with a confederation of slaveholding states, the cornerstone of whose constitution is not merely the lawfulness but the expediency of slavery, and the thinly-veiled object of whose policy is the wide extension of slave territory and the speedy revival of the slave trade—England, recognising such a confederation, and thereby imparting to it a vitality and strength which it neither possesses nor deserves, and assisting it to make good its position against the free states of the North, from which, for the sake of perpetuating and extending slavery, it wantonly seceded;—such a position as this would have been for our country a cruel necessity, entailing upon it a humiliation, and exhibiting to the world a scandal for which no military nor naval success could have been accepted as adequate compensation. Thank God, we have escaped the danger.

The Union's position in the British Isles was considerably improved at this time by the arrival in Liverpool of a New Jersey attorney who combined the aggressiveness of a terrier and the tenacity of a bulldog in the performance of his duties as the American consul in that port. This was Thomas Haines Dudley, whose earlier passage through England had been reported by Moran on June 24 when he said that the "modest, refined, and able" lawyer from Camden "would make a splendid European representative."

Dudley got his overseas post as a reward for playing an important part behind the scenes at the 1860 Chicago Republican Convention that nominated Lincoln for the Presidency. His friend and fellow Jerseyite, William L. Dayton, who had retired from the contest for the Presidency in favor of Lincoln, was appointed Minister to France, while Dudley—with some help from Dayton—was made consul at Liverpool.

The new American consul had been born in southern New Jersey in 1819. After a common school education, he had read law in Camden until he was admitted to the bar in 1845. He earned his first legal fee in a case involving a Negro mother and three children who had been kidnaped and taken south as slaves. Dudley disguised himself as a slave trader by wearing a broad-brimmed hat and providing himself with a whip and a pair of pistols. He then went after the captured Negroes and bought them back. He played his role so well and acted so roughly that the terrified mother did not recognize him until they were safely across the Delaware border.

A year later, the 27-year-old lawyer married Emmaline Matlack, who became the mother of several children, three of whom survived infancy.

In 1856, Dudley was nearly killed in a terrible steamboat fire, and his apparently lifeless body was taken from the icy waters of the Delaware River. He was restored to consciousness, but his health was permanently affected. Doctor's orders sent him to Europe at the beginning of the war. While there, he helped his friend Dayton by serving temporarily as the American consul in Paris. He then returned to Camden where he remained until he was appointed to Liverpool.[5]

He arrived in that city to assume his duties as consul on November 22, 1861, just five days before word of the *Trent* Affair startled England. While Dudley was acquainting himself with the work required by his office and was busy searching for living quarters for his family, he received an invitation to attend a dinner at Rochdale at which John Bright was to speak.

This was Dudley's first encounter with the man who was so well known as a liberal and as a friend of the United States that Lincoln kept a photograph of him in the White House. On that evening Bright looked into the future: "In a few years, a very few years, the twenty millions of free men in the North will be thirty millions, or even fifty millions—a population equal to or exceeding that of this kingdom. When that time comes, I pray that it may not be said amongst them that in the darkest hour of their country's trials, England, the land of their fathers, looked on with icy coldness and saw unmoved the perils and calamities of their children."[6]

Deeply moved by John Bright's words, Dudley wrote to him and received in reply a letter which said: "There are two nations in England, the governing class and the millions who toil. The former dislike your Republic, and their [public] organs incessantly misrepresent and slander it. The latter have no ill feeling toward you—but are not altogether unaffected by the statements made to your prejudice."[7]

Most of the Liverpool consulate's business had to do with ships and the sea, and Dudley became interested in protecting the rights of United States sailors who were often the victims of unscrupulous shipping

agents and notorious boardinghouse keepers. Before long, one of the
many agents sent abroad by the Federal Government was apparently
impressed enough with Dudley's honesty and ability to recommend that
he be put in a "position to oversee and direct all the consulates in the
kingdom, exempting that of London." This meant secret-service work, a
field of operations for which the Camden attorney proved to be ideally
suited. Perhaps his sponsor had heard about Dudley's antislavery foray
into the South in 1845.[8]

Dudley began his work of surveillance over Confederate shipping
activities soon after he arrived in Liverpool, for his papers contain a bill
for £2 for one man's services from December 16 to 21, 1861. The bill
was presented by a local detective named Matthew Maguire, a gentleman whose letterhead, printed on lavender paper, read: *"Private Enquiry
and Absconding Debtors Office, 7 Doan Place, Lord Street."*[9] Mr. Maguire played an important (although not always successful or even
honorable) part in Dudley's early secret-service operations. Before December was over, the American consul had run up a bill with him for
more than seventeen pounds.[10] Not all the money the United States
Government handed to professional spies during the next few years was
direct remuneration; a good part of it went for traveling expenses, tele-
grams, tips, "treating," hire of boatmen to explore the waterways, and for
surreptitiously made photographs of suspected ships. But out of much
nonsense and occasional fraud came enough solid information to enable
the American Minister in London to win a diplomatic contest against
some of Britain's shrewdest statesmen.

After having burned the *Harvey Birch* at sea, the Confederate raider
Nashville went into dry dock at Southampton on December 5. The
U.S.S. *Tuscarora* entered that port a month later and began a cat-and-
mouse game with the Confederate ship it had cornered. Moran visited
Southampton and reported in his Journal:

> The *Nashville* was lying at her berth, a sharp little vessel
> of good model with that pirate slave flag of the South at her
> peak. . . . There is something perfectly vile to me about the
> rebel flag, and I never see it without an itching to burn it.
> It lazily flaunted its broad slave-ish lash-like stripes in the wet
> breeze yesterday, as if desirous of being taken as the emblem of
> Southern idleness, listlessness, and slave beating. In the dis-
> tance, like a conscious power maintaining its honest name,

loomed up the *Tuscarora,* with the Stars and Stripes fluttering
in the wind. We got a boat, spread our sail, and were soon
stretching for her. In half an hour we were at her side, and I
looked up at her splendid form with pride. . . . As I reached
her deck and glanced over her heavy armament a smile crept
about my mouth at the thought of the work she would make
of the pirate then lying under British protection within sight,
could she once bring one of her 32's to bear on her. Five minutes would sink her.

Capt. Craven was below and received us cordially. He is a
tall, slender, hardy sailor, and a gentleman. We talked freely
over the objects of his visit and the unmanly course of England
in lending covert material and moral aid to this slave rebellion,
and fire flashed more than once from the captain's eyes. He
told me Capt. Patey had been on board (the Senior Capt. of
the port) and notified him of the necessity of 24 hours elapsing
before he could follow the *Nashville* should she get out first;
but agreed that if Craven saw the *Nashville* making off he
might go, if only a cable's length ahead, and she would be detained the 24 hours. For this purpose Capt. Craven has springs
on his cables, and with fires banked up is ready to leave at a
minute's notice. He is watching day and night and has not been
out of his ship since his arrival. . . .

Before leaving we looked over the vessel. She is as strong
as wood and iron can make her and carries a splendid armament.
There are two 130 lb. shell pivot-guns amidships, and a 12-
pounder rifle gun on the forecastle, besides six 32s. Her crew
consists of about 170 stout, hale men, and they look as if they
would fight![11]

This tense situation, which came right after the *Trent* Affair, kept
England on edge until February 3, when the *Nashville* was ready to
leave. The British, in order to make sure that the Union warship gave
the pursued vessel the required 24-hour headstart, put one of their
frigates alongside the *Tuscarora* to stand guard with steam up and guns
shotted until the *Nashville* would be miles away.[12] Captain Craven
reported to the Secretary of the Navy that "the whole transaction appears . . . to have a strong impress of collusion on the part of the authorities to effect the escape of a privateer." Then, knowing that he had
no chance of overtaking the *Nashville,* Craven headed for Gibraltar
where Semmes' first raider, the *Sumter,* with her boilers out of commission, was being blockaded by several Yankee men-of-war.[13]

Semmes and his dreaded commerce-destroyer, after a brilliant start, had run into bad luck. The officers stationed on Gibraltar had been cordial enough; in fact, Semmes said of them: "The army and navy of Great Britain were with us almost to a man, and many a hearty denunciation have I heard from British military and naval lips of the coldness and selfishness of the Palmerston-Russell government." Semmes noted that Union and Confederate seamen tended to fraternize when they met in port and said that the ships' crews "could probably have been exchanged without much detriment to each others' flag."[14]

But Yankee officialdom was exerting pressure on local merchants. Semmes found it impossible to obtain new boilers and had to have his men patch up the old ones as well as they could. Then no one would sell him coal. He sent two of his officers to Cádiz to try to get some there. When the French steamer they were traveling on stopped in Tangiers, the officers went for a stroll while the ship took on cargo. The United States consul quickly learned of their presence on shore and used his influence on the local officials to have them arrested.

When the consul locked them up in his office for safekeeping, the Confederates tried to bribe his Moorish guards. According to his report: "They offered a valuable gold watch and $100 in gold. This is very tempting to semi-barbarians. They finally offered to secure to them $5,000 to assist them in making their escape. I had to put them in irons. . . . [One of them] got a case knife and sawed off the rivets, and got the irons off and jumped out of the second story of the wall into the house of a Moor and was again arrested and taken back to his room, and the number of guards increased."[15]

The consul then called on the Navy for help. Captain Craven sent the fast clipper-ship *Ino* into Tangiers to take the two prisoners on board. In the city, a crowd of several hundred people attempted to free them from their captors. No Moroccans were involved in this; only English, French, Italian, and Spanish subjects had been recruited in the market place by Confederate sympathizers. The consul therefore had no hesitation in appealing to the Moroccan Government for assistance. He did so dramatically by threatening to "strike the American flag and quit the country."[16] His threat quickly brought out Moorish troops to keep the peace while the commander of the *Ino* had his crew form a double line to hold back the crowd. Then several husky sailors carried the two loudly protesting Confederates to the waiting ship.

After that, a long controversy took place between Acting Volunteer Lieutenant Josiah P. Creesy, who was in command of the *Ino*, and his superior officer, Commander T. Augustus Craven. Creesy was determined to send his two prisoners to the United States, while Craven, who had been reading international law, stated his doubts in a letter:

U.S.S. *Tuscarora*
Off Algeciras, February 27, 1862

Sir: On examination into the laws of neutrality, I find we have no right to detain prisoners in the port of a neutral; the alternative is presented of going to sea or releasing the prisoners and sending them on shore. Under such circumstances, you will therefore release the rebel prisoners you have on board.

Very respectfully, your obedient servant,
T. Augs. Craven
Commander

To this Creesy promptly replied:

U.S. Ship *Ino*
Off Algeciras, February 27, 1862

Sir: I am in receipt of your favor of the above date and note its contents. Without further comments than to say I positively decline to give these men up, and in coming to this conclusion, having no other alternative, shall proceed to sea immediately, where I can carry out my instructions quite as much to the interest of the Government as to be lying here.

Meantime remain, your most obedient servant,
Josiah P. Creesy
Acting Volunteer Lieutenant, Commanding[17]

Creesy boldly sailed west to find an American ship with a captain willing to take the prisoners across the ocean. Off Cádiz, he hailed the *Harvest Home* and put the two Confederates on board. They were landed in Boston and placed in jail there.[18]

When Semmes heard what had happened, he sent angry letters to local officials protesting the treatment his officers had received. The only satisfaction he ever got was to learn that the appointment of the zealous American consul in Tangiers had never been confirmed by the Senate and that the zealous officer was without a job.

Chapter 17

CONFEDERATE PROPAGANDA IN EUROPE

When Mason and Slidell arrived in London on January 29, many Confederate sympathizers called upon them, but the envoys were disappointed to find that a large part of the British public was indifferent or even hostile. Their capture and release had cost England millions of pounds, and their names, from constant circulation, had lost luster. Even the pro-Southern *Times* turned against them and published an editorial charging that they had been enemies of England in their prewar careers. Other papers barely mentioned their arrival. Slidell immediately went to Paris, leaving to Mason the difficult problem of improving relations with Britain.[1]

Three days after his arrival in London, Mason wrote to Richmond: "While the ministry seem to hang fire both as regards the blockade and recognition, the opinion is very prevalent (and in the best-informed quarters) that at an early day after the meeting of Parliament the subject will be introduced into the House of Commons and pressed to a favorable vote."[2] This was the first of many erroneous predictions Mason was to send his government. Most of the Confederate agents sent abroad mingled only with wealthy, highly placed people, and incorrectly assumed that their opinion expressed the views of the entire nation. This had been true enough in the past when a small group of men had been the masters of Europe, but the printing press, the telegraph, and the steam engine were helping to break down the ancient concentration of power. The Confederate envoys, blinded by their devotion to their own outmoded system, were unable to comprehend what was happening. They naïvely believed that the titled gentlemen who sought them out could still tell the ordinary citizen what to think and do.

On February 7, Mason again informed his government that "many members of Parliament warmly in our interest have called on me, including Mr. [William] Lindsay, M.P., for Liverpool . . . who is the largest shipowner in England."[3] Equally friendly was Sir William H. Gregory, another M.P. who had already been helpful to Rost and Yancey.

With this letter, Mason sent to Richmond a copy of a book which was helping the Confederate cause. This was James Spence's *The American Union,* then in its third edition. This remarkable bit of special pleading, in which the author, a Liverpool cotton trader, admitted his bias in favor of the South, also said that he had "carefully avoided the use of figures." He warned his British readers against subscribing to Northern loans because the Federal Government would never be able to pay the huge debts it was incurring. He summed up his argument by emphasizing a fear that was already troubling the British:

> There would be within the Union 500,000 men to disband and cast adrift. . . . There will appear a most formidable danger in suddenly turning loose upon the country half a million armed men, part elated with victory, part embittered with defeat. For some of these employment would be desirable. The conquest of Canada has been twice seriously attempted. . . . The Western states after rescuing the Mississippi, would reassert the inconvenience of leaving the St. Lawrence in the hands of a foreign power. Those who appear to shudder at the idea of such a war may well consider the serious probability that this would result from a triumphant restoration of the Union. . . .
>
> It would appear, therefore, that even were it possible to effect the present object of the North—such a victory would prove in the end more disastrous than defeat. It would probably be followed by a foreign war—free institutions would cease to be practicable—a military hero would take, as a dictator, the seat that Washington filled as father of the country—the former evils incidental to the Union would return with redoubled force—and the prospect of the future would be that of a fresh outbreak at no distant period, to repeat all the present calamities.

The author then concluded by saying: "We express earnestly—be it ever so erroneously—the clear conviction that nothing is more essential to the real welfare of the American people than a termination of the American Union."[4]

There arrived in London, on the same day Mason and Slidell got there, a young man whose services as a propagandist for the Confederacy were to be exceedingly valuable. He was Henry Hotze, who had been born in Zurich, Switzerland, in 1834. Brought to the South at an early age, he grew up in Mobile and became so thoroughly imbued with the idea of white supremacy that at the age of eighteen he translated Count Joseph Arthur de Gobineau's *Essai sur l'Inégalité des Races Humaines* which was then published in Philadelphia. This notorious work, which inspired the rise of Gobineau Societies in Germany, later became one of the influences which shaped the racial notions of Adolf Hitler and the Third Reich.

Despite his advocacy of Gobineau's racist ideas, Hotze was a bright young person, charming in manner, and so able to impress people with his ability that he had been appointed secretary of the American Legation at Brussels in 1858. He soon returned to Mobile where he became a journalist on the *Register*. There he joined the Mobile Cadets and saw enough of military life at the beginning of the war to write a brief account entitled "Three Months in the Confederate Army."[5]

At the end of May 1861, Hotze was made a clerk to the Adjutant General and was stationed in Richmond. On August 31, the Confederate Secretary of War ordered him to go to Europe to carry dispatches and assist the agents who were in charge of purchasing arms and ammunition. He arrived in London on October 4, 1861, but his stay was short, and he was soon back in the South. He sailed from Mobile a few days before Christmas and reached London on January 29. It was at this time that his career as a Confederate propagandist really began.

Before he began his work, he went to Paris to see Slidell. The report he wrote to Richmond about his brief visit shows that he was more candid than most of the other Confederates in Europe. "The French public," he said, "are either wholly indifferent to the events in America or sympathize faintly with the North, partly from sentimental considerations and partly because they see in the power of the United States a counterpoise to that of Great Britain." Then he went on to say that Napoleon III was in grave difficulty because all the parties opposed to him had formed a temporary alliance. The Emperor was in less trouble than Hotze was led to believe. In England, the young journalist was on surer ground.[6]

One of his first tasks there was to ingratiate himself with the editors of Lord Derby's *Herald* and *Standard* and the financial paper, *Money and Market Review.* He also had James Spence's book translated into French and German. And he may have urged Mason to sponsor that gentleman's bid to become the European financial agent for the Confederacy. Spence claimed that he had nearly ruined himself by neglecting his business to work for the Southern cause; he now offered his services— for pay—to the Richmond government.[7]

As soon as Mason and Slidell reached Europe, Yancey sailed for home. When he arrived in New Orleans on March 17, he was very ill. His experiences abroad had disillusioned him, and the state of his health gave everything a gloomy cast. Although he was only 47, the once-vehement fire-eater now seemed to be an old man.

The city's people thronged around him in the huge domed hall of the St. Charles Hotel, asking him to tell them what he had seen in Europe. He said bluntly that the Confederacy had no friends abroad. Europe was antislavery, and the British Government was abolitionist. People in other countries never saw Southern publications, so their opinions were formed by the Northern papers that were sent overseas. It was an error to say that "Cotton is King," for it was not. It was an influential power in commerce but not its dictator. As to the blockade, it was a blessing to the Confederate States, for it was teaching—"nay, compelling— us to depend upon ourselves and to do that for ourselves for which we have hitherto been depending upon others, and they our deadliest foes."[8]

He went on to tell them that Queen Victoria and her late husband were both opposed to the South. "Gladstone we can manage," he said, "but the feeling against slavery in England is so strong that no public man there dares extend a hand to help us. We have got to fight the Washington Government alone. There is no government in Europe that dares help us in a struggle which can be suspected of having for its result, directly or indirectly, the fortification or perpetuation of slavery."[9]

In conclusion he urged support of the Confederate Government. At the very end of his speech he expressed confidence in the final success of the Confederate cause and was cheered by the crowd for his sentiments. But something had gone out of the famous stump orator. He spoke like a man who foresaw his own death and the defeat of his country. He served in the Senate of the Confederacy for a year; then, shortly after Gettysburg, pain became so unbearable that he lost his reason and died in agony, crying out commands to invisible crowds surging around him.[10]

One of the most effective moves of the war was made by the Union when its Naval Board of Strategy planned a series of seizures of Confederate ports. In 1861 Federal forces had occupied Hatteras and Port Royal; early in February 1862 they mounted an attack against Roanoke Island and obtained control of the greater part of the Carolina Sounds. By March they had most of the Florida seaports in their possession. In April, Federal guns blasted the Confederate garrison out of Fort Pulaski and closed the Savannah River to shipping.

All these moves—and the grim fleets of Federal blockaders lying outside every major Southern port—were considered a legitimate part of war because the world was familiar with such methods of fighting. But when the Union tried to block the entrances to Charleston Harbor by sinking obsolete ships loaded with stone in the channels, there was an immediate protest in Europe against this novel way of waging war. Confederate agents stationed abroad took full advantage of the opportunity and were quickly able to report to Richmond that public opinion had been outraged. Lord Russell, laboring under the impression that the sunken ships would put the harbor permanently out of commission, sent two letters of protest to Washington. And the British Foreign Office wrote to the maritime nations of Europe to ask them to state whether they thought that the Yankee stone fleet was "contrary to public law and an outrage on civilization." They were also asked whether the blockade of Confederate ports was effective and binding on neutral powers.[11]

The French Government promptly denounced what the Union had done. So did Prussia, Sardinia, and Austria, while Spain hesitated, and Russia, Sweden, and Holland delayed their replies.

The Confederate Commissioners sent word of this to Richmond and did their best to exploit the situation. Britain's raising the question of the effectiveness of the Union blockade led to other moves which made 1862 a year of international tension.

Oddly enough, the Union's attempt to block the main channel leading to Charleston Harbor soon came to nothing. Wind, tide, and the ever-shifting and uncertain sands off the coast of South Carolina made it impossible to keep sunken hulks in place long enough to plug up the channels. Blockade-runners from England were soon slipping through the Federal fleet again to bring guns and munitions into Charleston.

Hotze succeeded in persuading the Confederate authorities that the best way to overcome the North's extensive press coverage abroad was to publish a newspaper of their own. As its editor, he would then be able to present the war in America from a Southern viewpoint. On May 1, 1862, the first issue of a small-sized journal called *The Index* appeared. It was never to have much circulation, but it was effective in influencing newspaper editors, politicians, businessmen, and others whom the Confederates wanted to win over to their side.

By coincidence the first issue appeared on a day when a great national ceremony was taking place. The new paper began its career by describing what was happening: "The booming of the cannon has just announced to London that the International Exhibition has been opened. The gorgeous ceremonial, the bright sunshine, and the considerable influx of foreign visitors have not excited much enthusiasm. The metropolis is not very gay nor very full. The cotton famine in Lancashire casts gloom upon the season of 1862."[12]

Although it was true that the cotton shortage was hurting the British economy, the Exhibition was of far more interest than Hotze indicated. For propaganda reasons, he probably thought that the cotton problem should be emphasized because everything that made the British resent the prolongation of the war would benefit the Confederacy.

The International Exhibition of 1862, like its predecessor of 1851, was held in Kensington where the main entrance was on Cromwell Road. The new fair got off to a slower start than the previous one. On the opening day, only a few turnstiles were in operation, and many of the exhibits were not yet ready. Packing cases—some of them as yet unopened—stood everywhere, while workmen were still making much noise with their tools. The high price of admission (a sovereign) on the first day was doubtless intended to keep out the poorer classes. It succeeded. No count of the actual attendance was made that day, but the huge courts and halls were far from crowded. More people came after June 2 when the admission price was reduced to a shilling.

But the Exhibition created much talk and got a lot of daily space in the British press. People wanted to see world's products and mankind's latest inventions.[13] Armstrong and Whitworth had their big modern cannon on display, and—fittingly—so did the makers of surgical instruments. These had been so few in number in 1851 that no one had bothered to show them at the Exhibition then. But the Crimean War, Magenta, Solferino, and the conflict in America had created a need for better operating tools, and a fairly impressive array of them could now be seen for the first time.

Another feature of the 1862 Exhibition was 6000 works of art. Britain was represented by eighteenth-century painters like Hogarth, Reynolds,

Gainsborough, and Romney, and by such modern artists as Landseer, Leighton, Millais, and Hunt. Contemporary French paintings were equally conventional. Pictures by Delaroche, Gérôme, Bouguereau, and Meissonier were on the walls. Delacroix was listed in the French catalog, but none of his paintings were shown at the opening.

There was no indication whatever of the revolution in art that was then beginning in France, nor is it likely that anyone in England was aware of its existence. Since the Salon des Refusés was not held until the following year, few people—even in Paris—knew that painting styles were about to undergo a radical change.

Manet's now world-famous "Déjeuner sur l'herbe" with its nude woman and well-dressed men was at that historic salon of 1863. So was Whistler's "The White Girl." Pissarro, Monet, Harpignies, Jongkind, and Fantin-Latour also showed examples of their work. And other young men like Degas, Cézanne, Sisley, and Renoir were busy at this time painting pictures that would soon startle the world.

In England, Victorian stuffiness still prevailed, not only in art but in manners, customs, and ways of thought. The Great International Exhibition of 1862 expressed the taste of the time, and sentimental paintings, realistic sculpture, ornate home furnishings, and gaudy architecture dominated the display. Only the machinery was truly functional. Most functional of all were the big marine engines and the heavy weapons intended for ships of war.[14]

Chapter 18

LINCOLN DEALS WITH INTERNATIONAL AFFAIRS, THE SLAVE TRADE, AND PERSONAL TRAGEDY

Despite the fact that Lincoln had a war in the East, a war in the West, and a war at sea to worry about, the President was never allowed to forget that his country was deeply involved in international affairs. The idea that the United States could remain isolated was fast becoming obsolete. Steam and electricity were beginning to bridge distance and shorten time, thus bringing closer nations that had formerly seemed far apart.

On February 1, 1862, the President wrote a letter of condolence to Queen Victoria for the death of her late husband. This was a matter of routine duty, but the letter he sent three days later was not. It was addressed to the King of Siam, the ruler who was later made famous by the book written about the experiences of a British woman who went to his court to act as governess to the royal children. According to the text of Lincoln's letter, it had taken a year for the communication from His Majesty to travel halfway around the world in the slow ships of the time. The President's letter read:

To His Majesty Somdetch Phra Paramendr Maha Mongut,
    King of Siam,
Great and Good Friend: I have received your Majesty's two letters of the date of February 14th., 1861.

I have also received in good condition the royal gifts which accompanied those letters, namely, a sword of costly materials and exquisite workmanship; a photographic likeness of Your Majesty and of Your Majesty's beloved daughter; and also two elephants' tusks of length and magnitude such as indicate that they could have belonged only to an animal which was a native of Siam.

Your Majesty's letters show an understanding that our laws forbid the President from receiving these rich presents as personal treasures. They are therefore accepted in accordance with Your Majesty's desire as tokens of your good will and friendship for the American People. Congress being now in session at this capital, I have had great pleasure in making known to them this manifestation of Your Majesty's munificence and kind consideration.

Under their directions the gifts will be placed among the archives of the Government, where they will remain perpetually as tokens of mutual esteem and pacific dispositions more honorable to both nations than any trophies of conquest could be.

I appreciate most highly Your Majesty's tender of good offices in forwarding to this Government a stock from which a supply of elephants might be raised on our own soil. This Government would not hesitate to avail itself of so generous an offer if the object were one which could be made practically useful in the present condition of the United States. Our political jurisdiction, however, does not reach a latitude so low as to favor the multiplication of the elephant, and steam on land, as well as on water, has been our best and most efficient agent of transportation in internal commerce.

I shall have occasion at no distant day to transmit to Your Majesty some token of indication of the high sense which this Government entertains of Your Majesty's friendship.

Meantime, wishing for Your Majesty a long and happy life, and for the generous and emulous People of Siam the highest possible prosperity, I commend both to the blessing of Almighty God. Your Good Friend,

ABRAHAM LINCOLN

Washington, February 3, 1862[1]

The King of Siam had written to the President because someone in the Buchanan administration had sent nearly 200 government publications to that country many months before. Impressed by this notice from the head of a large and reportedly powerful nation, the King said that the gift "was received by us in full assembly of the royal princes and nobles of the highest rank, with their insignia of office, as though they were receiving a visit in person from the President of the United States." In Washington the presents from Siam were deposited in a collection of curiosities at the Department of the Interior.[2]

At this time, Lincoln was involved in the only case in which an American citizen was hanged for being involved in the foreign slave trade. On February 2, Ralph Waldo Emerson was at the White House while the President "argued to Senator [Charles] Sumner the whole case of Gordon, the slave trader, point by point, and added that he was not quite satisfied yet and meant to refresh his memory by looking again at the evidence." Emerson said that Lincoln was a "frank, sincere, and well-meaning man," and that his carefully reasoned argument about the Gordon case showed great conscientiousness.[3]

Nathaniel Gordon, a young sea captain from Portland, Maine, had been in command of the *Erie* when his ship was stopped on August 8, 1860, near the mouth of the Congo River with 897 slaves whom he expected to take across the Atlantic. They were put ashore at Monrovia while Gordon was brought to New York to be tried under the slave-trading act of 1800 and for piracy as well. In his first trial in June 1861, the jurors were deadlocked; a second trial in November brought conviction. He was sentenced to be hanged on February 7, 1862.

Although there was no doubt of Gordon's guilt, many kind-hearted citizens felt that the penalty of death was too severe, especially since it had never been inflicted for such a crime. They brought the case to the President's attention with a request that the sentence be reduced to life imprisonment. Lincoln, who was already under criticism for being too ready to grant pardons, struggled with his conscience and then refused to alter the sentence, although he did give the prisoner a two-week reprieve.[4]

During the night before the day set for the execution, Gordon took poison, but a stomach pump restored him to life. Then he was given enough brandy to keep him from being aware of what was happening.

The New York *Herald* describes the fate of the pale-faced, dark-eyed little man whose life was taken as inadequate expiation for the deaths of thousands of helpless Negroes who had perished during the notorious Middle Passage:

> At twenty minutes past twelve o'clock a procession was formed in the corridor of the prison, and, the word being given, the cortege moved in solemn silence to the gallows. . . . All eyes were fixed upon the condemned, who tottered to the scaffold like a man half dead with fear or stupified with liquor. . . . The feebleness of the culprit, the agony with which he viewed the preparations which had been made for his execution, the solemn and careworn appearance of the marshal and his depu-

ties, the presence of the military drawn up in line, all contributed to render the scene a most impressive and painful one.
When the culprit reached the gallows and took up his position
immediately under the fatal noose, there was a pause of a few
seconds, but all was as still as death. The work of adjusting the
rope was quickly performed; for it was evident that Gordon
could not stand long; but hardly had the task been completed
when he showed evident signs of fainting. The cap was quickly
drawn over the culprit's face, and the marshal was about to
give the signal to the executioner, when Gordon staggered,
and would have fallen to the ground had he not been caught
by one of the deputies. In another moment, however, he was
straightened up, the signal was given . . . and the body of
Gordon was dangling in the air.[5]

During the time between February 4, the day on which Lincoln signed
the document setting a new date for Gordon's execution, and the day
on which the slave trader was hanged, the President encountered death
in his own family. His sons Willie and Tad were stricken with fever,
and on February 20 Willie died. The Executive Mansion became a house
of mourning; fears were expressed for Mrs. Lincoln's sanity, while the
President retreated deeper into the somber state of melancholy that had
often characterized his youth.

This month, however, was a time of public rejoicing for the Northern
cause. Fort Henry was captured on February 6; just ten days later Fort
Donelson also capitulated when a new general named Ulysses S. Grant
achieved fame by demanding "unconditional surrender" as the only
terms he would accept.

On February 19, a strange-looking and novel armored vessel named
the *Monitor* went through her trial runs in New York Harbor. No one
paid much attention to the insignificant little fighting ship because she
lay so low in the water that she could hardly be seen. Only a revolving
turret with two heavy guns stood up above iron decks that were nearly
awash.[6] But the *Monitor* had a rendezvous with the equally new Confederate ironclad *Virginia* at Hampton Roads, a rendezvous which
would make naval history.

The hanging of Nathaniel Gordon did not discourage the foreign slave
trade. It was far too profitable for that, and war in America meant that
nearly all the United States patrol vessels had been removed from the
African coast. It seemed like a field day for the slavers, because British

warships had no right to stop suspected American vessels. Spain, Portugal, and Brazil had given the British permission to search and seize slave ships using their flags, but they were relatively small nations which did not have to demonstrate their power, so they could gracefully allow the British to act for them on the African patrol. But the United States had stationed its own warships there for decades, and it was going to be difficult for a growing nation, even though plagued by an internal war, to grant the British Navy the right to stop ships displaying the American flag. The fact that British men-of-war had been far more effective than American in overhauling and arresting slave ships did not make Washington feel any better about the matter.

But the United States needed help if the slave trade was to be kept under control at its point of origin. Negotiations with the British were begun without letting the American public know what was happening. A treaty allowing British warships to stop and search suspicious-looking ships carrying the American flag was drawn up and ratified. At the request of the United States, a ten-year term was placed upon it. When it was brought before the Senate, that august body met behind closed doors. Both Senate and House passed it quickly and without discussion as though it were something shameful.[7]

By mid-1862, prices for captive Negroes in Africa declined to the point where it was no longer profitable to bring them to the noisome barracoons that had been a scandal to the civilized world. Stockades rotted in the jungles, and manacles and leg-irons rusted in the rains. Victory against slavery had been achieved on the African front before it had been won at home.

In Washington, Radical Republicans in the Government and Abolitionists everywhere wanted to get rid of slavery as quickly as possible, but the President, who favored gradual rather than immediate emancipation, was trying to persuade his associates to adopt a plan to compensate plantation owners for the loss of their slaves. Lincoln had a keen sense of property value, and he realized that under existing American law, slaves were property in the same sense that horses and cattle were.[8]

He called for a Cabinet meeting on March 5, at which his proposal was discussed, but there are no records of what was said. The next day he sent a message to Congress calling for a joint resolution to cooperate with any state that would try to abolish slavery gradually. Lincoln knew that the war was costing, in terms of dollars alone, far more than it would take to buy all the slaves from their masters and set them free.

Britain's compensated emancipation had been exceedingly successful, and even though its eventual cost was higher than had been anticipated, the total bill was small compared to the purely monetary expense of fighting a major war.

In his message to Congress of March 6, 1862, Lincoln said:

> In the mere financial, or pecuniary view, any member of Congress, with the census tables and Treasury reports before him, can readily see for himself how very soon the current expenditures of this war would purchase at fair valuation all the slaves in any named state. . . .
>
> The proposition now made, though an offer only, I hope it may be esteemed no offence to ask whether the pecuniary consideration tendered would not be of more value to the states and private persons concerned than are the institution and property in it, in the present aspect of affairs.[9]

Throughout the war Lincoln never stopped trying to persuade Congress and the public to accept his plan for compensated emancipation, but emotion ruled the nation, and the price for freeing the slaves had to be paid with blood, as John Brown had predicted when he went to the gallows.

Blood was shed at Pea Ridge in Arkansas early in March and even more copiously a month later at Shiloh in Tennessee. Neither battle won ground for either side, nor did they settle anything. The spring foliage was stained with red, and the shattered bodies of thousands of men were put into their graves. The war continued, and General McClellan prepared to send a huge army against Richmond by marching up the peninsula between the York and James Rivers.

Chapter 19

"CONFEDERATE AFFAIRS ARE IN A BLUE WAY"

Except for losses on the field, the North had not yet been hurt much by the war. The soldiers were having a hard time, but civilians were fairly well off. Some of them were beginning to be prosperous as they benefited from the armed forces' insatiable need for all kinds of goods.

In the South, however, conditions were bad even at home. On January 9, 1862, J. B. Jones, the Rebel War Clerk, noted in his diary that in Richmond: "Butter is selling for 50 cts. per pound, bacon 25 cts., beef has risen from 13 to 30 cts., wood is selling for $8 per cord, but flour is abundant and cheap enough to keep us from starving." These prices, which were brought about by inflation rather than genuine scarcity, were to grow steadily worse.

On February 11, Mrs. Chesnut wrote: "Confederate affairs are in a blue way. Roanoke taken, Fort Henry on the Tennessee open to them, and we fear for the Mississippi River too. We have evacuated Romney —wherever that is. New armies and new fleets are swarming and threatening everywhere. We ought to have as good a conceit of ourselves as they have of us, and to be willing to do as much to save ourselves from a nauseous Union with them as they are willing to do by way of revengeful coercion in forcing us back. England's eye is scornful and scoffing as she turns it on our miseries. I have nervous chills every day. Bad news is killing me." And on the 16th she added: "Awful newspapers today. Fort Donelson they call a drawn battle. You know that means that we have lost it! That is nothing—they (the Yankees) are being reinforced everywhere! Where are ours to come from, unless they wait and let us grow some."

The Confederate States of America, which had been operating under a provisional government since February 1861, was now ready to "usher into existence" a more permanent form of nationhood. On February 22, 1862 (Washington's Birthday), the highest officials of the Southern Confederacy met in the Capitol at Richmond to inaugurate Jefferson Davis as President. Weather usually favored the Confederate cause, but this time it did not; rain poured down on the city, drenching the people who had come to witness the ceremony, and compelling Davis to seek shelter under a hastily erected stand while he took the oath of office.

The weather was not the only bad thing that day. News of the surrender of Fort Henry had already been received, and word of Fort Donelson's fall had reached the War Department. Davis is believed to have suppressed the facts about the second surrender until the inauguration was over. Jones said that the reception at the President's house that night was "lugubrious," although it was well attended.[1]

At the other end of the Confederacy, the Committee of Safety in New Orleans reported to Davis on February 26 that the Navy Department there was in a deplorable condition and owed $600,000 or $800,000 to suppliers. For months a sign had been hanging over the paymaster's office marked "No Funds."[2]

The Union Navy was making plans to capture the city, and David Farragut, who was to be in charge of the operation, had already arrived at Ship Island in the Gulf of Mexico. The two massive forts guarding the way up the Mississippi River had been strengthened, but New Orleans was highly vulnerable, as events were soon to prove.

The Confederacy had one brief burst of hope in the midst of all this gloom, when the C.S.S. *Virginia,* the huge ironclad which had been built on the burned-out hulk of the former U.S.S. *Merrimack,* came out of Norfolk on March 8 to attack the Union warships lying near Fort Monroe. Within an amazingly short time the seemingly invulnerable iron-sheathed vessel destroyed the wooden men-of-war *Cumberland* and *Congress* with much loss of life. The armored *Virginia* emerged from the conflict almost unscathed although shot after shot had struck her.

The Confederates were jubilant, but their rejoicing was short-lived. The Union ironclad *Monitor* had been towed from New York to Hampton Roads, and when the *Virginia* came out again the next day to finish the destruction of the Yankee wooden fleet, the little "cheese-box on a raft," as she was derisively called, was waiting for her. A historic five-hour engagement took place in which the two ironclads fired at each other with negligible results. Neither was seriously damaged, and the battle was practically a draw, but it demonstrated to the world the fact that wooden fighting ships could not stand up against armored vessels. In May, when the Confederates had to abandon Norfolk, they set the wooden interior of the *Virginia* on fire. She was blown to pieces by the intense heat that ignited her powder magazines.

The Confederacy had another brief moment of encouragement when the *Nashville,* which had arrived from England late in February, left Beaufort a few weeks later to run through the Federal fleet and successfully reach Georgetown, South Carolina, where she was converted into a blockade runner.

In the spring of 1862, despite minor triumphs, the Confederacy was hard pressed. While Richmond was being threatened by McClellan's army, J. B. Jones, the Rebel War Clerk, noted that when the passport office was moved to Ninth and Broad Street, "In the long basement room underneath were a thousand garments of dead soldiers, taken from the hospitals and the battlefield, and exhaling a most disagreeable . . . odor."[3]

A nation that had to strip uniforms from the corpses of its soldiers to provide the living with clothes was in a poor position to stand off repeated attacks by a well-fed and well-clothed adversary. Nevertheless, the Confederacy fought on, making up for its deficiencies in matériel by ingenuity, added effort, and the ability of its generals and men in the ranks.

But things continued to go against the South. When Mrs. Chesnut first heard that conscription was to be introduced in order to fill up the thinning regiments, she wrote: "Conscription means that we are in a tight place. This war was a volunteer business. Tomorrow conscription begins—the last resort."[4] Less than two months later she said: "The best and the bravest went first. Now the lag-lasts do not want to be conscripted. As officers they would gladly face the music, but the few that are left are old, or middle-aged, and nothing remains to them but the ranks. They hoped to reap where others had sowed, to win where they did not work. Without a murmur they sent their sons, but they grumbled when asked for money, though they gave it. Kill a man's wife (or son) and he may brook it, but keep your hands out of his breeches' pocket. Their own sacred skins they respect, but there was not a regular shrinking until sacred property was touched. This never-to-be-too-much-abused Council wants to take their Negroes and send them to work at the forts; hence these tears. How long before they will lay violent hands on Negroes and put them in the army? The only question now; could they be induced to stand fire, fighting on our side? The Council is in bitter earnest, anxious to fortify the outpost, to prepare for the worst; and the few remaining big braves, the stay-at-homes, thought talk was to do it. Negroes were to stay and work, while they overlooked them. Now they are ready to cut the Council's throats because the Negroes are to be forced into the army."[5]

Late in April, the Confederacy suffered a major set-back when Farragut's fleet captured New Orleans. The South then lost its largest city and the lower Mississippi River. At the same time McClellan kept moving his huge army up the Peninsula toward Richmond.

General Benjamin F. Butler, who was in command of the Union troops occupying New Orleans, tried to bring its recalcitrant citizens to heel by issuing his celebrated "Woman Order" on May 15. It read:

> General Order No. 28
>
> As the officers and soldiers of the United States have been subject to repeated insults from the women (calling themselves ladies) of New Orleans, in return for the most scrupulous non-interference and courtesy on our part, it is ordered that hereafter when any female shall, by word, gesture, or movement, insult or show contempt for any officer or soldier of the United States, she shall be regarded and held liable to be treated as a woman of the town plying her avocation.[6]

The order immediately attracted worldwide attention and did great damage to the Union cause. The French were especially bitter about Butler's threatened treatment of well-born ladies who dared to show how they felt about their conquerors. In England, Lord Palmerston got up in the House of Commons to denounce the Union commander: "I am quite prepared to say that I think no man could have read the proclamation . . . without a feeling of the deepest indignation—a proclamation to which I do not scruple to attach the epithet infamous. Sir, an Englishman must blush to think that such an act has been committed by one belonging to the Anglo-Saxon race. If it had come from some barbarous race that was not within the pale of civilization, one might have regretted it, but that such an order should have been promulgated by a soldier—by one who had raised himself to the rank of general, is a subject undoubtedly of not less astonishment than pain."[7]

Palmerston also sent a letter of protest to Charles Francis Adams. Moran, who watched the incident grow into an affair that threatened to disturb the peace between nations, describes the daily exchange of messages from his vantage point inside the United States Legation:

> A serious correspondence has just taken place between Lord Palmerston and Mr. Adams which is destined to become his-

torical. His Lordship, with that impudence that only an Englishman can be guilty of, wrote a private and confidential note to Mr. Adams on the 11th Inst., [June] about Gen'l Butler's late order at New Orleans in which he said he could not "express adequately the disgust which must be excited in the mind of every honorable man" at that regulation "of a general guilty of so infamous an act as to deliberately hand over the female inhabitants of a conquered city to the unbridled license of an unrestrained soldiery."

Mr. Adams replied on the 12th refusing to recognize the note, unless he was assured it was official, and expressing surprise at such an unusual proceeding on the part of the Prime Minister, instead of the Minister of Foreign Affairs, with whom Foreign Ministers carry on their correspondence on matters connected with the duties of their mission.

To this Ld. Palmerston rejoined on the 15th by saying his note was official.

In the interview, Mr. Adams saw Lord Russell and stated the case to him. He was much offended and said Ld. Palmerston had exceeded the bounds of good behavior—a thing he had often done of late, and had no business to write such a note.

Mr. Adams renewed the subject on the 16th and after commenting on the nature of his Lordship's letter, said that "the Government he represented would visit with just indignation upon its servants abroad their tame submission to receive under the seal of privacy any indignity which it might be the disposition of the servants of any sovereign, however exalted, to offer to it in that form."

Palmerston with his usual insolence answered this in a sophistical strain on the 19th, and on the 20th Mr. Adams closed the affair by a note in which he said he would decline while here to receive such communications from him. This severe reprimand had its intended effect, and his Lordship has remained silent under it. The incident placed Mr. Adams in a very critical position, and for a few days we considered things so serious as to strongly anticipate a sudden rupture of all intercourse. Fortunately, Mr. Adams' decision saved such a result.

A more impudent proceeding than that of Palmerston in this case cannot be discovered in the whole range of political life. Knowing the brutality of his own officers and soldiers, he readily imagined ours of the same stamp, and insolently presumed to lecture Mr. Adams on a thing which was not his business. His ill-manners were properly rebuked. American soldiers, he will find out, are not beasts, altho' English soldiers are; and he will also learn that it is only a debased mind that would construe Gen'l Butler's order as he has done.[8]

This seemingly trivial bit of international acrimony broke off social communication between the Palmerstons and the Adams family. The American Minister made it clear that in the future any communications from the British Government would have to come from Earl Russell. Nothing was gained from this unseemly display of two aging men's petulance, and Anglo-American relations suffered because of it. Adams, as a Massachusetts fellow-citizen of Ben Butler's, should have known better than to try to defend that political general's injudicious actions. According to Butler, the "Woman Order" executed itself. He said that "No arrests were ever made under it or because of it. All the ladies in New Orleans forebore to insult our troops because they didn't want to be deemed common women, and all the common women forebore to insult our troops because they wanted to be deemed ladies."[9]

But effective as it was, the famous order made the general who issued it infamous. Southerners fastened the name "Beast" on Butler, who had the misfortune to have a gross-looking face with a wickedly drooping eye.

The teapot tempest over the "Woman Order" turned part of British public opinion against the North and roused pro-Confederate politicians to try to persuade the House of Commons to recognize the Confederacy. They also began to call for international mediation to end the war in America. This was particularly annoying to the Federal Government because it had steadfastly insisted that its armed forces were not fighting a war but were merely carrying out a police action.

Young Henry Adams regretted the break between his father and Lord Palmerston because it deprived him of invitations to Cambridge House. He had no use for the trouble-making Prime Minister, but both his mother and he were fond of gentle Lady Palmerston. He describes what he thought would be his last visit to "the best diplomatic house in London:"

He gave his name as usual at the foot of the staircase and was rather disturbed to hear it shouted up as "Mr. Handrew Hadams!" He tried to correct it, and the footman shouted more loudly: "Mr. Hanthony Hadams." With some temper he repeated the correction and was finally announced as "Mr. Halexander Hadams," and under this name made his bow for the last time to Lord Palmerston who certainly knew no better.

Far down the staircase one heard Lord Palmerston's laugh as he stood at the door receiving his guests, talking probably to one of his henchmen, Delane [of *The Times*], Borthwick, or Hayward, who were sure to be near. The laugh was singular, mechanical, wooden, and did not seem to disturb his features. "Ha! . . . Ha! . . . Ha!" Each was a slow, deliberate ejaculation, and all were in the same tone, as though he meant to say: "Yes! Yes! Yes!" by way of assurance. It was a laugh of 1810 and the Congress of Vienna. Adams would have much liked to stop a moment and ask whether William Pitt and the Duke of Wellington had laughed so; but young men attached to foreign Ministers asked no questions at all of Palmerston, and their chiefs asked as few as possible. One made the usual bow and received the usual glance of civility; then passed on to Lady Palmerston, who was always kind in manner, but who wasted no remarks; and . . . then went through the diplomatic corps . . . finally dropping into the hands of some literary accident as strange there as one's self.[10]

Fortunately the breach between the Adams family and the Palmerstons was at least partially healed in March 1863 when they began to see each other again.[11] Henry Adams, however, never lost his dislike—and distrust—of old Lord Pam.

Chapter 20

THE FRENCH MINISTER VISITS RICHMOND

Europe was running out of cotton in the spring of 1862, and the shortage was to get worse. Not only England, but France, where the making of cotton textiles was a fairly important industry, was affected. Meanwhile, Napoleon III was becoming more and more interested in Mexico. After April 9, when England and Spain withdrew from the tripartite occupation of that nearly helpless country, the ambitious Emperor had the field to himself. He also had good reason to believe that no one in America would obstruct his efforts. Richmond did not support the Monroe Doctrine, and trouble at home was almost sure to keep the Washington government from interfering with his plans for Mexico.

April was a crucial month for Franco-American relations. The French Minister, Henri Mercier, apparently acting without instructions from Paris, told Seward that it was a pity he could not visit Richmond to see how matters stood there.[1] Seward immediately suggested that he go and offered to give him the necessary pass. The American Secretary of State believed that the Confederacy would soon have to surrender, but Mercier, who favored the South, did not agree. Seward thought that a short stay in Richmond might convince Mercier that the Confederacy's chances for survival were poor.

Since policy required that France act with England on American affairs, Mercier consulted Lord Lyons about his projected visit. Lyons, suspecting that the journey to the Confederate capital might be a prelude to a single-handed French move to back the South in order to obtain cotton—and he was also well-informed about the Emperor's hopes for Mexico—could hardly be expected to favor the visit. But he consented because he wanted to preserve solidarity on American affairs between his country and France.

Mercier went to Norfolk on the *Gassendi* and then proceeded overland to Richmond. Northern newspapers were led to believe that his
visit was merely to safeguard French-owned tobacco stored in Southern
warehouses. The New York *Herald*,[2] which evidently did not know
that Mercier was pro-Confederate, misquoted him by saying that he
regarded "the capture of the rebel capital a foregone conclusion."

He arrived in Richmond on April 16 and called on the newly appointed Secretary of State, Judah P. Benjamin. The New Orleans attorney, who had an excellent knowledge of the French language and
customs, was far better able to deal with Mercier than any Union government officials had been. The two men, of course, had known each
other in Washington when Benjamin had represented Louisiana in the
Senate.

Judah P. Benjamin, who has been called the mystery man of the Confederacy, was one of the shrewdest members of Jefferson Davis' Cabinet.
Born in St. Thomas in 1811 of Portuguese-Jewish parents, he had been
brought up in Charleston and had gone to Yale.[3] At that university, he
met his first set-back when he was charged with petty thievery. The
accusations may have been invented by some of his fellow students, but
this dreadful ending to his brilliant college career left ineradicable scars
on the young Benjamin. He went to New Orleans, where he became a
remarkably successful lawyer. In that city he met his second major personal disaster in 1833 when he married Marie Augustine Natalie St.
Martin de la Caze, the beautiful daughter of French plantation owners
who had been driven out of Santo Domingo during the slave revolts.[4]
Benjamin was to remain in love with his wife as long as he lived, but
she was self-indulgent, superficial, wildly extravagant—and a nympho-
maniac who finally deserted him for a German officer with whom she
ran off to Paris. Nevertheless, the infatuated husband continued to send
money to her and often sought her out in later years when he was in
Europe.[5]

Natalie was Benjamin's only weakness. After she left him, he tried
to make up for her loss by working day and night. His ever-ready smile
and invariably suave manner, which masked whatever he actually
thought or felt, often made people misjudge him. He became quite
popular in New Orleans and Washington society. His popularity, however, disappeared rapidly when he became a member of the Confederate
Cabinet, first as Attorney General and then as Secretary of War. The
series of military disasters in the spring of 1862 made it impossible for
Benjamin's good friend, Jefferson Davis, to retain him in that post. Davis
appointed him Secretary of State in March 1862 when the permanent

government of the Confederacy was formed. Benjamin was well-suited for handling international affairs, but he was so bitterly hated by certain parts of Southern society that nothing he did could please them.

There is no doubt, though, that he charmed Mercier when the French Minister came to Richmond. Benjamin wrote to Slidell that Mercier told him that "he considered the capture of all our cities within reach of the water as a matter of certainty, that it was purely a question of weight of metal, and that as the North had undoubtedly a vast superiority of resources in iron and other materials for gunboats and artillery, he did not deem it possible for us to save any of our cities, and he asked me to say frankly what I thought would be the course of our Government in such an event."[6]

When the French Minister returned to Washington he told Lyons what Benjamin had said. Lyons promptly informed Earl Russell that Mercier was "persuaded that the confidence and the resolution of the Confederates are increased rather than diminished by recent events. If they are worsted anywhere they will still not surrender. They will destroy their stores of cotton and tobacco, and all other property which they cannot remove. They will retire into the interior of their country and defy the North to follow them. They will endure any privations and sufferings rather than be again united to the North. Their unanimity and devotion to the cause are wonderful. They are not carrying on a war in the usual manner for dominion as the North is; they consider themselves to be fighting for their homes and their liberty, and are making and are ready to make any sacrifices."[7]

Lyons also said that Seward, after hearing Mercier's report of conditions in Richmond, came to the conclusion "that the Confederates were about to make a last effort: that they had their last armies in the field; and that their last resources were brought into action." Lyons commented that "I suppose the truth lies somewhere between M. Mercier's views of the prospects of the South and Mr. Seward's."

Lyons also told Seward that President Lincoln was to dine with Mercier and the captain of the Gassendi and then visit the French warship. The episode nearly ended in disaster. Lincoln, always willing to oblige and keenly aware of the need to keep friendly relations with France, was rowed out to the Gassendi, which had been anchored in the Potomac near the Washington Navy Yard. Young Frederick Seward, who accompanied the President, described the occasion:

> [The Gassendi] lay with her bows pointing out into the stream, so we approached under her stern. She was gay with bunting in

honor of her distinguished guest. Her crew were beat to quarters, and her commander and officers in full uniform were at the gangway to welcome him. Presentations followed, drums rolled and bugles sounded, while the Stars and Stripes were unfurled at the top of the mainmast.

Champagne and a brief conversation in the captain's cabin came next; then a walk up and down her decks to look at her armament and equipment. Though the surroundings were all new to Mr. Lincoln, he bore himself with his usual quiet, homely, unpretentious dignity on such occasions, and chatted affably with some of the officers who spoke English. The visit over, we were escorted to the side ladder and reembarked in our barge.

As Mr. Lincoln took his seat in the stern he said: "Suppose we row around her bows. I should like to look at her build and rig from that direction." Captain Dahlgren, of course, shifted his helm accordingly. The French officers doubtless had not heard or understood the President's remark and supposed we were pulling off astern in the ordinary way.

We had hardly reached her bow, when, on looking up, I saw the officer of the deck pacing the bridge, watch in hand and counting off the seconds, "*Un, deux, trois,*" and then immediately followed the flash and deafening roar of a cannon, apparently just over our heads. Another followed, then another and another in rapid succession. We were enveloped in smoke and literally under fire from the frigate's broadside. Captain Dahlgren sprang to his feet, his face aflame with indignation as he shouted: "Pull like the devil, boys! Pull like hell!"

They obeyed with a will, and a few sturdy strokes took us out of danger. After he had resumed his seat and calmed down, I said in a low voice: "Of course those guns were not shotted, and we were below their range?"

He answered, gritting his teeth, "Yes, but to think of exposing the President to the danger of having his head taken off by a wad!"[8]

Mercier's visit to Richmond puzzled statesmen in Europe largely because they could not believe that it was actually unauthorized. The Confederate envoys abroad tried to figure out ways to turn it to their own advantage, but they were so confused by speculative talk that they did not know what action to take. They had to sit by, paralyzed by their own uncertainty, until the opportunity was lost.[9]

The Emperor was annoyed that Mercier had acted without instructions, but he had no intention of letting what had happened interfere with his plans for Mexico. In the mid-nineteenth century it was by no means certain that republican forms of government would endure. Napoleon III had overthrown one such government in France by seizing power in 1851. The United States was struggling against armed insurrection, and he felt sure that the breach between the North and the South would never be repaired. While war between the two sections continued, he had a good chance to oust Benito Juárez and replace democracy in Mexico with a monarchy. Like the Confederates, the Emperor was trying to turn the clock back.

During the time Mercier was in Richmond, an effort was made in Parliament to have the British Government act jointly with France and other European nations to attempt to end the war in America by mediation. This move was backed by Confederate sympathizers and those who hoped that such a peace settlement would weaken the United States as a power by dividing it into two separate nations. But at this time, McClellan's march up the Peninsula toward Richmond seemed likely to succeed, and the British Government was unwilling to take action. Lyons wrote to Russell on May 16, correctly predicting that McClellan would get near Richmond and then not be able to occupy the city. At the end of the month, when Joseph Johnston was seriously wounded and command of the Confederate armies in Virginia was taken over by a still-untried officer named Robert E. Lee, nobody could foresee that the new general would be responsible for one Confederate victory after another. Lee successfully held off McClellan and saved Richmond, but by this time both England and France were hesitant about granting recognition to the South. The Confederate envoys were discouraged and said so when they wrote to Richmond.

Lyons' health was bad, and he wanted to avoid having to spend another hot summer in Washington, which the British, who live in a cool climate, have always considered a tropical city. Before sailing for England on four months' leave, Lyons wrote to Russell on June 9 to sum up the situation in America:

> There are three things to which we must not blind ourselves:
> 1. That we have a very small chance of getting cotton from this country for a long time to come.
> 2. That there is no Union feeling in the South.
> 3. That the war has become one of separation or subjugation.[10]

Chapter 21

THE UNION CONSOLIDATES ITS POSITION IN EUROPE

Cassius Clay found living in St. Petersburg difficult because costs were impossibly high for a man of moderate means. When he hinted that he might like to return home, Lincoln quickly granted his wish. The President had been waiting for just such a chance, because he wanted to replace him with Secretary of War Simon Cameron who had turned out to be as bad at his job as had been predicted. There were charges of corruption, not directed at the head of the huge and costly Department, but, as is so often the case in American politics, at Cameron's friends, who were said to be enriching themselves at public expense.

On January 11, 1862, Lincoln replaced Cameron with Edwin M. Stanton, and then nominated Cameron as Minister to Russia. After a four-day debate, the Senate reluctantly confirmed the nomination by a vote of 28 to 14. When Clay learned about Cameron's appointment, he said caustically that it was "a parachute to let him down gently."[1]

Cameron and his Chargé d'Affaires, the popular author Bayard Taylor, did not reach Russia until June; by that time Clay had changed his mind and wanted to remain at his post. But Washington denied his request to stay on.

When Cameron said that he expected to be in Russia only a short while, Clay returned to the United States where he had been given a commission as a major general of volunteers. His military career, however, was brief and inglorious. He soon asked Lincoln to reappoint him to his former post when Cameron was ready to leave.[2]

During a visit to London in May, John Bigelow heard that Cameron, who was then on his way to Russia, was in Scotland trying to trace his ancestry back to the celebrated Cameron known as Lochiel. Bigelow also met "Bull Run" Russell of *The Times* and found him in bad health. Russell's wife said that he had left the United States because he was afraid of being assassinated there. Bigelow attributed the famous correspondent's illness to his unhappy experiences in America.[3]

By the end of June, when it became evident that McClellan was not going to take Richmond and that the new Confederate commander, Robert E. Lee, was more than a match for him, there was talk not only of mediation but of actual intervention by the European powers. On June 25, Seward wrote to Bigelow:

> The American people . . . are being wrought up by the European press to the point of meeting a European invasion. It seems to them as if such an invasion gains favor in Europe just in proportion that excuses for it are removed. . . .
>
> I do not write or even talk just now about Mexican affairs. I think it prudent to watch and wait. *Between you and myself alone, I have a belief that the European state, whichever one it may be, that commits itself to intervention anywhere in North America, will sooner or later fetch up in the arms of a native of an oriental country not especially distinguished for amiability of manners or temper.* . . .
>
> Propositions and debates about mediation and recognition do not tend to make our people amiable. If the debates are kept up abroad, we shall have a navy that will be worthy of a great maritime power. *It might perhaps be well if it were known in Europe that we are no longer alarmed by demonstrations of interference.*[4]

This veiled hint about possible assistance from Russia has long been a matter for conjecture because there is no record of it in government archives. Bigelow believed that the offer was genuine but that it was never put into writing. In a footnote in his *Retrospections*, published in 1909, he said: "Flirtations between nationalities, as between the sexes, are not apt to be proclaimed from the housetops, nor even made matters of record."[5]

The Bigelow-Seward correspondence for this period is of especial interest. On June 27, Bigelow wrote:

> I am in receipt of some intelligence this morning of almost too horrible a character to be credited, but which comes through such sources as to leave me in no doubt as to my duty in reporting it to you.
>
> Mr. Duncan, a lawyer of New Orleans, formerly from

Kentucky and one who went reluctantly into the Rebellion, is now in Paris. In the course of his conversation yesterday at dinner with a friend of mine . . . he said that there was a plan on foot to have a simultaneous assassination of all Unionists in the slave states. As a preliminary to this atrocity, the Unionists were to have their suspicions disarmed as much as possible by professions of loyalty on the part of the rebels. They expected that an apparently cordial acquiescence in the Federal rule would soon lead to a reduction in the Federal garrison and meantime that the conspirators might gradually get the confidence of the Unionists and possess themselves as far as possible of such information as would be necessary for the success of their scheme.[6]

In his reply, Seward, who was to be the victim of an attempted assassination at the time Lincoln was killed, said:

There is no doubt that from a period anterior to the breaking out of the insurrection, plots and conspiracies for purposes of assassination have been frequently formed and organized. And it is not unlikely that such a one as has been reported to you is now in agitation among the insurgents. If it be so, it need furnish no ground for anxiety. *Assassination is not an American practice or habit, and one so vicious and so desperate cannot be engrafted into our political system.*

This conviction of mine has steadily gained strength since the Civil War began. Every day's experience confirms it. The President, during the heated season, occupies a country house near the Soldiers' Home, two or three miles from the city. He goes to and from that place on horseback, night and morning, unguarded. I go there unattended at all hours, by daylight and moonlight, by starlight, and without any light.[7]

Ironically enough, a hidden sniper narrowly missed Lincoln in August 1864 as he drove through the woods near the Soldiers' Home. And John Wilkes Booth made an abortive effort to capture him there a few days before he fired the fatal shot in Ford's Theatre in 1865.[8] These were only a few of the numerous attempts which were to be made on the lives of American Presidents during the next century.

The Federal Government was encouraging influential men to go to Europe on unofficial missions to try to further its cause there in financial, political, and religious circles. In November 1861, Thurlow Weed, Seward's friend and adviser, departed for France and England. So did the

Protestant Episcopal Bishop of Ohio, Charles P. McIlvaine, and the
Roman Catholic Archbishop of New York, John Joseph Hughes. Old
General Winfield Scott, who had just retired from active duty after
more than fifty years of service, was on the ship that carried Weed
abroad. Except for General Scott, who returned to Washington as soon
as he heard about the *Trent* Affair, the unofficial emissaries did their
best to convince leaders in Europe that the Northern cause was not only
just but that it would surely prevail.

Weed, who was a practical politician and a successful businessman,
spent the spring of 1862 getting in touch with governmental and commercial leaders in Europe.[9] Young Henry Adams, whose background had
made him despise the kind of men Weed dealt with, was nevertheless
enormously impressed by the unofficial emissary's activities:

> Thurlow Weed was a complete American education in him-
> self. His mind was naturally strong and beautifully balanced;
> his temper never seemed ruffled; his manners were carefully
> perfect in the style of benevolent simplicity, the tradition of
> Benjamin Franklin. He was the model of political management
> and patient address; but the trait that excited enthusiasm . . .
> was his faculty of irresistibly conquering confidence. Of all
> flowers in the garden of education, confidence was becoming
> the rarest; but before Mr. Weed went away, young Adams
> followed him about not only obediently—for obedience had
> long since become a blind instinct—but rather with sympathy
> and affection, much like a little dog.
>
> The sympathy was not due only to Mr. Weed's skill of man-
> agement, although Adams never met another such master, or
> any one who approached him; nor was the confidence due to
> any display of professions, either moral or social, by Mr. Weed.
> The trait that astounded and confounded cynicism was his
> apparent unselfishness. Never, in any man who wielded such
> power, did Adams meet anything like it. The effect of power
> and publicity on all men is the aggravation of self, a sort of
> tumor that ends by killing the victim's sympathies; a diseased
> appetite, like a passion for drink or perverted tastes; one can
> scarcely use expressions too strong to describe the violence of
> egotism it stimulates; and Thurlow Weed was one of the ex-
> ceptions; a rare immune. He thought apparently not of him-
> self, but of the person he was talking with. He held himself
> naturally in the background. He was not jealous. He grasped
> power, but not office. He distributed offices by handfuls with-

out caring to take them. He had the instinct of empire; he gave, but he did not receive.[10]

Henry Adams, whose family knew Seward well, felt that one dangerous situation after another was slowly educating the Secretary of State for his difficult job. Sending so astute a man as Weed to Europe, he thought, was evidence of Seward's growing skill.

In Liverpool, the obscure American consul, Thomas H. Dudley, was busy piecing together bits of evidence which he and his spies were gathering about Confederate activities in that and other British ports. He sent these dutifully to London, but so far no one had paid much attention to what he was doing. In February his reports took on sudden significance. By this time, the ship which the Confederate agent, James D. Bulloch, was having built in the yards of W. C. Miller and Sons, was already in the water and was being fitted out. Bulloch was still on the high seas, returning from his successful blockade-running voyage to Savannah on the *Fingal,* but he was due to arrive in Liverpool early in March. The mysterious vessel that Dudley was so concerned about was temporarily called the *Oreto;* it was said that she was intended for a private shipping company in Palermo. Few people believed this story because anyone could see that she was pierced for guns even though none had been put on board.

On February 24, Dudley received a note from one of his paid operatives which turned suspicion into certainty. It came from a Mersey River pilot and read: "I have received orders this evening to be in readiness for taking the Gun Boat out Night or Day, but to keep it strictly Secret. There is no doubt of her being for the Confed. G'mt."[11]

Chapter 22

THE *FLORIDA* AND THE *ALABAMA* START THEIR CAREERS

James Dunwoody Bulloch knew his business. He not only knew how to get gunboats built in a foreign shipyard; he also learned how to deal with the intricacies of British law. One of his first moves was to retain the services of F. S. Hull as his Liverpool solicitor, and that gentleman, whom Bulloch called "a prudent, cautious, conscientious advisor and . . . a watchful and safe mentor," told him exactly what to do.[1]

Under the British Foreign Enlistment Act of 1819, as interpreted by the ingenious Mr. Hull, it was permissible to build any kind of ship in Her Majesty's dominions even though it was obviously intended for warlike purposes. But such a vessel could not be armed in Britain or loaded with ammunition or the equipment needed to make it into a commerce-raider. One could, however, buy matériel of war in England and send it elsewhere to arm the ship. Everything was very simple so long as one stayed within the law. British shipbuilders and munitions makers got the business; the Confederates got a new, powerful cruiser, and officials of Her Majesty's Government could look Mr. Adams in the face and say coolly that no law had been broken.

On March 4, a British customs collector with the memorable name of J. Mudie Searcher went on board the *Oreto*, which was under construction in Liverpool, examined her carefully, and made out an affidavit in which he listed in detail all the food, drink, and tobacco on the ship. He left the space marked "guns" blank which meant that none were on board. The fact that the sides of the ship were pierced for four cannon was not his business, so he ignored it in his report. His superiors bore him out by adding: "She had no gunpowder or even a signal gun, and no colors save Marryatt's code of signals and a British ensign, nor any goods on board except the stores."[2] Since Bulloch had employed an English captain to take the ship to her alleged destination in Palermo, Italy, it was only natural that the unarmed *Oreto* should sail under a British flag.

Bulloch arrived in Liverpool on March 10 accompanied by several Confederate naval officers. He moved to No. 2 Marine Terrace, Waterloo, a few miles down the Mersey, where his wife had found a small house. Then he went to work.

He inspected the finished *Oreto* (now briefly named the *Manassas*), visited the Laird yards across the river at Birkenhead where his next cruiser, known only by her yard number 290, was under construction. He then appointed John Low, who had been with him on the *Fingal*, to be in charge of the *Oreto* until her British captain was able to take her across the Atlantic to Nassau, where he was to turn her over to John Newland Maffitt. The announced destination, Palermo, had, of course, been a blind.

Since the *Oreto* could not legally be armed in Britain, her guns and munitions were to be shipped separately to Nassau. The weapons would be transferred to the *Oreto* somewhere in the Bahamas where there were plenty of isolated cays suitable for a rendezvous.

After two careful inspections by British Customs House officials,[3] who still wanted to make sure that no weapons were on board, the *Oreto* sailed from Liverpool on March 22 and arrived at Nassau after a passage of 37 days. There Maffitt took command. He soon ran into trouble with the British authorities, who were being urged by the United States consul to stop the potential raider from going to sea. They seized her on June 17 and held her until early August when she was at last allowed to sail. The arms intended for her had been put on board the schooner *Prince Albert*, which met the *Oreto* at Green Cay, 60 miles south of Nassau. Two United States warships were searching the area for the Confederate ships, but they could not locate them.[4]

Under the hot August sun, four 7-inch rifled cannon were moved to the *Oreto* and mounted in place. Then it was discovered that much of the equipment needed to operate the guns was missing. Maffitt was in the embarrassing position of being in command of an armed cruiser which could not properly aim and fire her weapons. Still worse was the fact that yellow fever was on board. One man died two days before the ship was ready to leave Green Cay.

On August 17, the Confederate flag was run up, and the new commerce-destroyer was christened the *Florida*, a name that was to become the terror of the Atlantic shipping lanes. As she moved out to sea and headed west, the crew were so ill that they could hardly man the ship. She entered Cardenas, Cuba, two days later, in search of medical assistance. From August 22 to 29, Maffitt himself was incapacitated by the dreaded fever. Then he came out of his delirium to find that his beloved stepson Laurens was spewing up the black vomit which marks the fatal end of the disease. The young boy and four others died the next day.

They buried their dead and went on to Havana, where they found a pilot who could take them into Mobile, the nearest Confederate port large enough to have the ordnance matériel they needed.

On September 4, when they approached Fort Morgan at the entrance to Mobile Bay, they found three Union blockade ships waiting for them. Maffitt was still so weak from fever that he had to be carried up to the deck. He ordered most of the men to go below and then prepared to run past the warships without being able to fire back at them.

Shot and shell poured into the *Florida* as she moved up the narrow channel leading to the fort. A shell took off one man's head; nine others were wounded. The ship was badly damaged, but Maffitt was able to bring her in. He remained in Mobile for the rest of the year, recruiting a crew, and waiting for repairs to be completed.

The fact that the *Florida* had been able to sail from Liverpool with so little trouble made the Federal authorities in England redouble their efforts to prevent any more Confederate ships from being built there. Dudley's network of spies was effective in finding out what was going on in the dockyards of England and Scotland, although he had to employ sailors along the waterfront, workmen in the shipyards, and private detectives like Maguire to obtain such information. Some of these people were of the sort that would hardly make a favorable impression on a British official. As a result, Dudley found it difficult to persuade anyone in power to take action. It was obvious that the Confederates were building a navy in England to harass American commerce, but neither Dudley nor Adams could convince the British that this was really so—even after the *Florida* had gone to sea. Dudley knew perfectly well that Bulloch's second cruiser, the 290th ship to be built in the Laird yards, was intended to be a Confederate commerce-raider, but no matter how many sworn affidavits he presented to Samuel Price Edwards, Her Majesty's Collector of the Port, that skeptical officer always muttered "Not sufficient evidence."[5]

Work on the 290 progressed steadily after the *Florida* had left on March 22. On May 15 she was launched and temporarily christened the

Enrica. On June 14 the new ship, still unarmed, of course, made a satisfactory trial run and then dutifully returned to her base. During the next month the final work was rushed toward completion as she lay in the water.

Word of the *Florida's* escape from Liverpool and her arrival and detention in Nassau soon reached Washington. On July 12, Seward, who had been informed about the 290 nearing completion in the Laird yard, wrote to Adams to tell him that a move was under way to authorize the United States Government to issue letters of marque and reprisal to induce owners to arm their ships and send them out against the Confederate commerce-raiders.[6] Congress actually passed such a law in March 1863, but nothing ever came of it. Private shipowners were not going to put their cargo vessels and mercantile crews up against Confederate cruisers manned by sailors who had been trained by professional naval officers.

But Seward's letter must have been disturbing to Adams who was in the midst of an aggravating mixup over the 290 just then. Dudley, who had been unable to prevent the *Florida* from getting away, was determined to stop the 290. He had been gathering affidavits and piling up evidence against the ship which everyone in Liverpool and Birkenhead knew was intended to be a Confederate cruiser. Like the *Florida,* she was pierced for guns, and there was no disguising her warlike appearance. But Price Edwards, the Collector of the Port, remained obdurate.

In June a Southern boy named Robinson had come ashore from a blockade-runner and was induced to take lodgings—of all places—at Matthew Maguire's house. The wily detective quickly found out from the lad that he had heard the blockade-runner's officers talk about a cruiser being constructed for the Confederacy by the Lairds. They said that a man named Bulloch was in charge of the operation and that the money for it came from the well-known Southern banking firm, Fraser, Trenholm and Company, which handled the Confederate Government's accounts.[7]

Dudley went to London to consult Adams. The consul had wanted to keep the affair on a local level by continuing to deal with the immovable Price Edwards, but Adams wisely overruled him and had him prepare more evidence for presentation to Earl Russell. He sent this to the Foreign Office on June 23 with a covering letter, asking that the 290 be prevented from leaving port.

Russell was impressed enough to send the dossier to the Officers of the Crown and the Lords Commissioners of the Treasury. The Crown

Officers felt that there might be a case against the ship under the Foreign Enlistment Act. But the Lords of the Treasury, who were in charge of—and kept informed by—the Customs Office, sent Russell the report of their man in Liverpool who, of course, was Price Edwards. He scoffed at the idea that anything was wrong.[8]

More time was lost, especially since Earl Russell listened to the Board of Customs. On July 4 he sent Adams their report, which recommended that the American consul present his evidence to the Collector at Liverpool—again Price Edwards.

Dudley now had to deal with Edwards once more. Meanwhile, the 290 was put into Birkenhead's Great Float, stocked with provisions, and loaded with coal. The Board of Customs then ruled that there still did not seem to be enough proof to justify seizing her.

Adams now employed the services of Robert P. Collier, a barrister whose name meant a great deal in the highest official circles. When Collier gave his opinion on July 16, he said he believed that what was happening was in violation of the Foreign Enlistment Act and that the ship should be seized by the British Government.

Dudley immediately asked A. F. Squarey, of the Liverpool law firm of Duncan, Squarey, and Blackmore to handle the local details of the case. More affidavits were prepared and presented to the Collector of the Port on July 21, but Price Edwards remained unimpressed.

Dudley and Squarey hurried to London two days later to see Adams. As might have been expected, the Board of Customs rejected their new evidence. Collier examined the latest affidavits and again gave the opinion—in even stronger terms—that the ship should be seized.

On being shown Collier's statement, the secretary of the Lords of the Treasury evidently began to feel so uneasy that he wrote to the Foreign Office to find out whether Earl Russell might want to get an opinion from the Queen's Law Officers. For British mid-nineteenth-century officialdom matters now began to move reasonably fast. Dudley and Squarey returned to Liverpool in order to be on the spot if the ship tried to depart.

On Saturday, July 26, the entire dossier was sent to the home of Sir John D. Harding, the Queen's Advocate. What no one knew was that this gentleman had just had a nervous breakdown and had gone insane. His terrified wife told no one about his condition and ignored the papers from the Foreign Office.

In Liverpool, on the same day, William Passmore, a seaman who had already provided Dudley with an affidavit, now testified that in

Birkenhead that afternoon, "he met the seamen, say 30 in number, coming down Canning Street from the ship [the 290], playing 'Dixies Land' on a fife, concertina, and a cornopean and they all took the 4:30 Woodside boat to Liverpool. They still kept playing 'Dixies Land' on the ferry boat. Went up to one of the men and asked him when he thought the ship would be going out. He told me that their bed clothes . . . were on board and that the boatswain had told those who intended to go in her to hold themselves in readiness for early next week."[9]

Since nothing is done on Sunday in London, no one noticed that Sir John Harding had paid no attention to the urgent problem stated in the papers sent to him. When the documents were finally asked for, his wife wrapped them up in a brown paper parcel and returned them to the Foreign Office. The Confederates are believed to have had an opportunity to examine the top-secret material while it was on its way there.

Moran had another version of the leak. In December 1865—when the war was over—he showed Adams "what purported to be a copy of a short note signed by V. Buckley and addressed to Mr. [Caleb] Huse, the rebel agent, warning him that what he called his 'protégé' was in danger." Victor Buckley was a young clerk in the Foreign Office.[10]

Bulloch and his friends would never reveal how they found out about the British Government's plans, but there is no doubt that they learned enough to make it imperative for the 290 to leave immediately.[11]

On Monday, Squarey wrote to the secretary of the Commissioners of Customs in London calling for prompt action because he had good reason to believe that the Confederate cruiser would sail the next day. The secretary answered by return mail, saying that in the absence of instruction: "the Board are unable to give any directions."[12]

As had been predicted, the 290 was in the river on Tuesday morning, dressed with flags, and made to look as if she were going on a pleasure trip. Bulloch had invited a party of ladies and gentlemen (including John Laird and his daughter) to accompany the ship down the river for another "trial run." A steam tug was alongside to go with her.

During this demonstration an average speed of 12.8 knots was attained. After lunch Bulloch told his guests that the ship was to remain out all night and politely invited them to return to Liverpool with him in the tug. Since this seemed reasonable enough, everyone agreed.[13]

On Tuesday morning, Bulloch arrived at the landing-stage to meet the 35 or 40 men who were to go on the ship. Unfortunately for Bulloch, they were not alone. The local prostitutes who had been the sailors' temporary companions in port were with them. When Bulloch told the shipping master that the women could not go to the ship, he was informed that it was "a case of all or none," for they would not leave until they got the men's first month's advance pay.[14]

Everyone piled into the tug and went down the river. It was raining, and there was nothing to eat. When they reached the ship at 4 P.M., the sailors and their hungry females had to be fed, thus wasting more precious time. It was midnight before the women were paid off, put on the tug, and sent back to Liverpool. And just before Bulloch had left the landing-stage earlier in the day, he had been given a telegram informing him that the U.S.S. *Tuscarora* had left Southampton and was believed to be on the way to intercept the 290. Bulloch also knew there was a good chance that the British Government might order his ship to be stopped. There were enough men-of-war in the Liverpool area to blow the Confederate vessel out of the water. Besides, she had no arms and could not even put up a show of resistance.

On the evening of Monday, July 28, when the 290 was already under orders to go down the river the next morning, the other two Law Officers decided to act without Harding. Their opinion, at last arrived at, called for seizing the Confederate ship. This reached the Foreign Office on Tuesday when the 290 was beginning her "trial" run. The document was delivered to the Treasury on Wednesday, July 30; the next day, orders were telegraphed to Liverpool to stop her. By this time, the 290 was in the Irish Sea. She was still in coastal waters on July 31 and could have been overtaken if any of Her Majesty's numerous warships had been sent after her. But none was, and she reached the Atlantic Ocean.

At the time when the 290 was leaving Liverpool, Dudley made desperate efforts to see Price Edwards in order to make a last-minute appeal to hold up the ship's sailing. Only the Collector of the Port had the authority to do this. At this crucial time, Edwards could not be found.

While the 290 was cruising along the north coast of Ireland on the late afternoon of Wednesday, July 30, Bulloch had himself put ashore near the Giant's Causeway; the ship then headed toward the Azores, where she was to be armed. Originally, Bulloch was supposed to command her. But he was needed in Europe to supervise the construction of ironclads for the Confederates, so Raphael Semmes was to have the fine new ship. His now-useless *Sumter,* with her engines out of commission and several Federal warships standing guard over her, had been abandoned at Gibraltar. Semmes arrived in Liverpool on August 8 and went with Bulloch on the *Bahama* to join the 290 at the rendezvous in the Azores. The

Agrippina had already sailed from London with guns and equipment to arm the cruiser.

How did the 290, soon to become world-famous as the C.S.S. *Alabama,* get away? The accident of Harding's mental breakdown, the bumbling of British officialdom, and the law's delays all helped to make her escape possible, but she could have been stopped if someone in authority in Liverpool had insisted that the highly suspicious ship delay her departure until the matter was settled.

Moran, who had the instincts of a good detective, spotted the probable culprit immediately. Writing in his *Journal* on August 2, only a few days after the *Alabama* had vanished, he said: "Indifference and connivance characterized the entire proceedings of H.M.'s officers in this matter, and Edwards, the Collector at L'pool, has aided her escape by falsehood and almost perjury." On September 3, he wrote to Dudley, saying that Edwards "must be a great scamp."[15] And there the affair rested until January 17, 1867.

On that day a small printed circular was privately distributed among a few people in Liverpool.[16] There had already been talk in town, for it was public knowledge that the local cotton brokers, Titherington, Gill, and Company, had sued Edwards for reneging on an order he had placed with them for purchasing cotton for his account. He had denied under oath that he had ever placed such an order, but the brokers were able to prove that he had. They won their case, and Edwards was arrested for perjury. It was then, acting under advice of counsel, that he prepared the printed circular in which he admitted his guilt. The case against him was dropped, but Edwards was a marked man after that. Bulloch, who had remained in England, met him and reported that "he appeared much broken in health and greatly depressed in spirits."

Dudley, too, was still in Liverpool. He persuaded William Titherington, a partner in the firm of cotton brokers which had brought suit against the former Collector of the Port, to sign an affidavit on January 24, 1872. This was even more damning to Edwards than the admission of perjury he had printed five years before. In it, Titherington stated under oath that Edwards, whom he had known well during the American Civil War, had been "a very warm sympathizer with the Confederates and their cause."

After the escape of the *Alabama,* some of the local papers had blamed Edwards for letting the ship get away. When Titherington questioned him about this, "he replied in his flippant style . . . with a significant shrug of his shoulder, 'My dear boy, how could I prevent it, for I was out of the way at the very top of the pool when she sailed.'"

Titherington said that he understood this remark to indicate that the Collector of the Port "was purposely out of the way at the time of the sailing of the *Alabama*. I thought that the place . . . he was at the time of sailing was a place where no one would ever think of looking for him."

The broker also said that Edwards had been speculating in cotton as early as 1862, and that "his dealings were large and in the end did not prove profitable." He had, of course, everything to gain by prolonging the war in America and favoring the Confederate cause. He was dismissed from his post after the perjury scandal, and, as Bulloch noted, rapidly went downhill after that.

Titherington was not the only person in Liverpool to tell Dudley about the doubtful character of the man who had been Her Majesty's Collector of the Port when the *Alabama* escaped. A Mr. George Warren wrote on January 22, 1871, that "I was thoroughly convinced that he [Edwards] was unreasonably insensible to the circumstantial evidence which I knew to be tendered to him respecting the *Alabama*. He was a thoroughly bad man and only escaped perjury by confessing it."[17]

It could not be proved that Price Edwards had been paid for absenting himself from his post on that crucial day. He may not have been; his greed for making a profit in cotton speculation was enough to motivate him. And the greed that dominated him finally ruined him. But what he had done was to cost his country several million pounds.

Chapter 23

GLADSTONE SPEAKS OUT OF TURN

All through the summer and well into the autumn of 1862 several attempts were made in Europe to bring about an end to the war in America
by mediation, or, failing that, by intervention. The state papers of half
a dozen nations are filled with references to these efforts. England and
France were primarily involved, sometimes with one taking the lead;
sometimes the other. Napoleon III often proposed such a move, but
shortly after September 14, when England received news of the South's
victory at the Second Battle of Bull Run, Palmerston suggested to Russell that this might be the time "to recommend an arrangement upon
the basis of separation."[1] In reply, Russell went even further and said
that no matter whether Lee had destroyed the Union Army or not, "England should recognize the Southern States as an independent state."

Before either of these elderly statesmen, who still recalled the battle
of Waterloo, could start to move the ponderous government machinery
into action, word arrived on September 30 that the Union Army had
turned Lee back at Antietam. Earl Russell quickly changed his mind
about recognizing the Richmond government, but the Chancellor of the
Exchequer, William E. Gladstone, was indiscreet enough to voice his
personal opinions. What he said did not come well from a man who had
been born in Liverpool in 1809 of a family which had made a fortune
from slave labor in the West Indies. So extensive were the Gladstones'
slaveholdings that in 1833 they were paid more than £75,000 as compensation when the British Government set their 1609 Negroes free.[2]

Gladstone was a very intelligent, well-educated, and usually good-
intentioned man who had helped to maintain peace during the *Trent*
Affair, but he could, on occasion, act stupidly. One of those occasions
came on October 7, when he spoke at a banquet held in his honor at

Newcastle. What he said was inspired by the many Cabinet discussions about ending the war in America, but the Chancellor jumped to hasty conclusions without waiting for his colleagues to agree on the kind of action to be taken. Yet his diary shows that he had had plenty of time for reflection. Nevertheless, he rashly went ahead to utter words he was later to regret. At Newcastle that day, they seemed to be enormously important, for people naturally believed that he was expressing the views of the Cabinet.

He said—and in public with reporters present to notify the press: "We may have our own opinions about slavery; we may be for or against the South; but there is no doubt that Jefferson Davis and the other leaders of the South have made an army; they are making, it appears, a navy; and they have made what is more than either, they have made a nation."[3]

His words created a great stir. Orders for cotton were canceled because traders suspected that the war might end suddenly and glut the market with the American fiber. Not only businessmen but diplomats were startled. Adams wrote in his diary the next day that "if Gladstone be any exponent at all of the views of the Cabinet, then my term here is likely to be very short."

Moran was more forthright in his *Journal*: "Mr. Gladstone, as Chancellor of the Exchequer, makes an insulting attack upon us, and it is applauded. But an insult in England is no insult at all if directed against foreigners."[4]

Ten days later, Adams informed Seward that after discussing the matter with several liberal British statesmen, it became apparent "that Mr. Gladstone had been expressing his individual opinions . . . whilst his course was regarded by several of his colleagues as transcending the line of policy formerly agreed upon."[5]

The Confederate envoys in Europe were naturally pleased with Gladstone's statement. Dudley Mann wrote to Benjamin: "This clearly foreshadows our early recognition . . . The assertion produced a profound sensation . . . and such is the importance attached to it that it has been telegraphed all over Europe."[6]

John Bright was not surprised by the Chancellor's speech. He told Dudley: "Gladstone . . . comes of a family long connected with slavery and is now the Minister in a country where aristocracy rules and by which a republic is necessarily hated . . . Don't be unhappy about English opinion . . . It is what you *do* in America and not what people *think* here that will decide the contest."[7]

Russell wrote to Gladstone a few days after the Newcastle speech to reprove him in the gentle manner which the men who then ruled England reserved for their colleagues: "You must allow me to say that I think you went beyond the latitude which all speakers must be allowed when you said that Jeff. Davis had made a nation. Recognition would seem to follow, and for that step I think the Cabinet is not prepared."8

The Cabinet, with good sense and customary British caution, continued to refrain from making a decision about which side to back in the American war until it could be certain which was going to win. Gladstone's Newcastle speech was better remembered for its well-balanced phrases than for its premature advocacy of recognition for a country that had not yet proved its right to nationhood. Actually, it benefited the North, for the controversy it aroused ended all thought of British proposals for mediation.

More than a generation later, in July 1896, the too-readily outspoken Chancellor admitted that he had been wrong. "An undoubted error," Gladstone confessed, "the most singular and palpable, [and] I may add the least excusable of them all, especially since it was committed . . . when I had outlived half a century . . . That my opinion was founded upon a false estimation of the facts was the very least part of my fault. I did not perceive the gross impropriety of such an utterance from a Cabinet Minister of a power allied in blood and language and bound to loyal neutrality . . . My offence was indeed only a mistake, but one of incredible grossness, and with such consequences of offence and alarm attached to it that my failing to perceive them exposed me to very severe blame. It illustrates vividly that incapacity which my mind so long retained, and perhaps still exhibits, an incapacity of viewing subjects all round . . . and thereby knowing when to be silent and when to speak."9

This was an honorable amend, but no words spoken so late could make up for damage done 34 years before.

Henry Adams, who was still young enough to be shocked by duplicity in high places, studied the Gladstone outburst for years, gathering evidence in an effort to find out the real truth. He summarized his findings in the chapter entitled "Political Morality" in his *Education* and came to the disquieting conclusion that "the cat's paw theory offered no safer clue than the frank, old-fashioned, honest theory of villainy. Neither the one nor the other was reasonable." He ended by saying that the answer was obscure and that "every student would . . . [have to] answer for himself alone."10

According to Brooks Adams, writing nearly 50 years later about this crucial period in Anglo-American affairs, October 1862 was a historic turning point in the relationship between the ruling class in the mother country and the people in her former colony. He pinpoints the time by saying that "the English aristocracy had collapsed with the repulse of Lee at Antietam. By a subtle instinct all Europe and America became conscious of a change of status. It was the United States now which pressed upon England, not England on the United States." After this date, he said, his father did not hesitate to put on pressure, "even verging on coercion."[11]

October 7 was an inopportune day for Gladstone to have made his unauthorized speech, for news had just arrived in England that Lincoln had made the first step toward putting an end to slavery.

The idea of emancipation had been in Lincoln's mind for some time, and he had already drawn up a draft of a proclamation which he had read to the Cabinet on July 22. He was disappointed to find that some of its members thought its release would be premature. Then the Union defeat at Second Manassas made him postpone taking further action until a more favorable time. On August 22 he wrote to Horace Greeley a statement which left no doubt that he was still more interested in preserving the Union than in freeing the slaves:

> My paramount object in this struggle is to save the Union, and it is *not* either to save or to destroy slavery. If I could save the Union without freeing *any* slave, I would do it, and if I could save it by freeing *all* the slaves I would do it; and if I could save it by freeing some and leaving others alone I would also do that.[12]

This, however, did not mean that Lincoln had given up the thought of emancipation. The exigencies of the war and the force of public pressure were driving him toward it. He waited for a victory and found one at Antietam even though McClellan did not follow it up to make it decisive. The battle was fought on September 17, and on the evening of that day and over the weekend following it, Lincoln prepared a draft of what was to be known as the Preliminary Emancipation Proclamation. He read it to the Cabinet on Monday, September 22. After a long discussion, it was given to Seward to release to the press the next day.[13]

It was a military measure, taken to further the progress of the war, and it was not to go into effect until January 1, 1863. Even though it affected only the slaves in areas in rebellion against the United States, it declared them to be "thence forward and forever free." Its impact upon public opinion in other countries was eventually to be great. It became a useful tool of diplomacy, for it showed a world which had outgrown slavery that the United States was at last initiating action against the peculiar institution which for so long had been its shame.

Seward had copies of the Emancipation Proclamation printed and sent to diplomatic posts abroad. Its text was also reproduced in full in the important American newspapers which normally circulated overseas. It got a mixed reception in foreign countries at first. Palmerston said that the document could not be treated seriously and called it "trash."[14] *The Times* accused Lincoln of attempting to stir up slave revolts.[15]

But the British working class ignored the fulminations of the government's spokesmen and held meetings throughout the country to discuss the real meaning of the Proclamation. The people who attended these gatherings often drew up and signed elaborately engrossed documents which were sent to Lincoln to express approval of what he had done.

In France the same sort of division took place between the Emperor's controlled press and the common people. Other European nations were more generally favorable. Even Spain refrained from criticism although the government was fearful about what Lincoln's action might do to the slaves in Cuba. Germany and Switzerland were more unreservedly approving. Russian reaction was exceedingly mixed.[16]

John Hope Franklin, in his book on the Proclamation, sums up its effect abroad by saying: "The initial European reaction . . . could give the government in Washington little comfort. Some Europeans were sympathetic to the Confederacy and reacted unfavorably to this latest gambit by Lincoln. Others, more neutral, doubted that it could have any significant effect or had grave doubts about the legality of the move. Even many who were deeply committed to the Union cause were disappointed because it was 'coldly indifferent' to the moral and humanitarian aspects of slavery. Only gradually, as Union victories gave support to the Proclamation, did its effect on European attitudes become clear."[17]

Large numbers of British workingmen had emigrated to the Northern states before and during the war. Their letters were arriving at their former homes to give confidential, man-to-man appraisals of slavery, the Union cause, and the Emancipation Proclamation. Thousands of these unsolicited, highly effective propaganda messages were being read throughout the British Isles by their senders' families and friends.[18] No formal subsidized campaign could have been half so convincing. The laboring classes, more than ever, were swinging toward the Northern side because it was advocating freedom. Since very few European immigrants had settled in the South, the Confederacy had no similar willing, unpaid propagandists to sponsor its cause overseas.

John Bright, who was an inspired propagandist, wrote to Charles Sumner to urge the American people not merely to contribute money for the relief of the out-of-work Lancashire cotton operatives but to send them something tangible. As a result of his suggestion, ships laden with food began to sail to Liverpool.[19]

Chapter 24

MORE COUNTRIES BECOME INVOLVED

In April 1862, Robert H. Pruyn, the new American Minister Resident, arrived in Japan to replace Townsend Harris, who had been highly successful in his dealings with that still feudal country. Harris was lucky in leaving when he did, for his successor was to have an even harder time than he had.

Anti-foreign sentiment was rising in Japan. The nation had been closed to the world until 1853 when Commodore Matthew C. Perry, in command of four American naval vessels, entered Yedo Bay (now Tokyo Bay) and was able to negotiate a treaty with the Japanese Government that was signed the next year. After this, several other nations sent diplomats and businessmen into the newly opened country. Many Japanese, who were strongly traditionalist, viewed the newcomers with alarm.[1]

Distrust turned into violence when the interpreter of the American Legation was murdered in the streets on a dark and rainy night. The Japanese offered to pay $10,000 to the dead man's family, but money, as Harris pointed out, was not the question.

In July the British Legation was attacked by 14 men, some of whom later admitted that they hoped to bring on a war that would drive the hated foreigners out of the country and let the Japanese return to their ancient ways.[2]

Then, on June 26, 1862, shortly after Pruyn arrived, the British Legation, although heavily guarded by the Japanese, was again invaded at night by a killer—or killers—who slew two of Her Majesty's soldiers.

On September 15, four civilians, one of them a woman, were attacked while riding on a road near Kanawaga.[3] They were assaulted because they failed to dismount to show their respect for a Japanese lord who was passing by. One of the riders was so badly hurt that he fell from his horse and was quickly dispatched by spears and swords. When the British demanded £110,000 as indemnity, the controversy served only to intensify Japanese hatred of outsiders. They then attempted to put an end to all dealings with foreigners.[4]

During these disturbances, which took place at a time when Anglo-American relations at home were rapidly worsening, the British and American Legations in Japan were brought closer together by the need for mutual defense. The correspondence between the representatives of the two countries show that they were then on the best of terms. They also worked closely with the Dutch and the French who were stationed in Japan. One Dutch, three French, and four British men-of-war were in port at this time, but the nearest United States naval vessel, the *Wyoming*, was in Hong Kong. Pruyn wrote to her captain, requesting that he bring his ship to Japan, where a display of American strength was needed.[5]

Pruyn was an upstate New York attorney who had been educated at Rutgers College. Since he had served as Judge Advocate General of the New York State forces for some years, he was often addressed as "General" although he had no military training. Commissioned by the Lincoln Administration in October 1861, he had no diplomatic experience or knowledge of dealing with foreign governments. Yet he did so well in his new post that it has been said that "if Perry opened the gates of Japan, and Harris threw them wide open, then Robert H. Pruyn is entitled to no little credit for preventing their being closed again."[6]

Pruyn acted wisely when an American bark was wrecked on a sand bank about 100 miles north of Yokohama. The French Minister offered to send a gunboat to protect the survivors, for it had been the custom to put the victims of a shipwreck in cages and send them to Nagasaki for deportation in a foreign vessel. But Pruyn refused the well-meant offer and had the American consul go to the scene of the wreck in a Japanese warship. He found that the shipwrecked sailors had been treated with great kindness and were in excellent health. In his report, the consul said that what the Japanese had done was a "demonstration of the rapid advance this remarkable people and government are making towards a full emancipation from exclusiveness which is to place them speedily in the front rank of nations."[7]

Since more and more civilians in America were becoming soldiers, and men in both armies were being killed or wounded, a shortage of labor naturally developed. On August 8, 1862, Seward sent a circular to diplomatic and consular officers which described the North's prosperity and the high wages being offered. It authorized American representatives abroad "to make these truths known in any quarter and in any way which may lead to the migration of persons to this country."[8] Not only the Federal Government but several transatlantic steamship companies were interested in increasing emigration to America. And the War Department, of course, was not sorry to see large numbers of healthy young foreigners come flocking in. Early in the war it had sent recruiting agents abroad. They had been particularly successful in Ireland, because its long-starved people welcomed any chance to move to a place where living wages were paid even though military service was the price required. Since Irish and German regiments had already been formed by enlisting volunteers who had already settled in the North, it was easy to persuade the newcomers to enroll in units in which they would feel at home with their fellow countrymen.

The bounty system, which made it possible for unscrupulous men to earn big profits by procuring large numbers of recruits, also helped to swell the ranks with newly arrived immigrants. Before long, Earl Russell was complaining to Adams about the enlistment of British subjects.[9] The early recruiting agents, however, had already been withdrawn by this time, perhaps because they were no longer needed.

Even the Confederacy, which had found it difficult to persuade Europeans to come to a country where they had to compete with slave labor, was able to get plenty of aliens for its armies. Whole regiments of foreign-born soldiers were formed, mostly of Irish or German origin, but there were English, French, Polish, Italian, Spanish, and Mexican recruits as well. Company I of the Tenth Louisiana Regiment was outstanding in that it had men from 15 countries on its rolls.[10]

Both the Union and Confederate Army had numbers of European officers who came to America to act as observers and learn what they could about tactics, field operations, and the effect of new weapons on methods of attack and defense. Some of the things they found out were to be put to use a few years later in the Franco-Prussian War. Even the First World War was to be a continuation of the stalemated trench fighting around Petersburg and Richmond in 1864 and 1865.

The Confederate Navy also needed foreign manpower, for it had hardly any common seamen and had to recruit them in the ports from which its ships sailed. Since British law forbade enlistment in another nation's service, this involved extra risks which had to be compensated for by extra pay. By offering that inducement Confederate ships had no trouble getting crews.

As time went on, more and more people from more and more countries were caught up in the currents generated by the war between the American North and the American South. Its international involvements foreshadowed the great world conflicts that were to come a few generations later.

On the ever-changing front lines, men from the same country must often have faced each other across the sights of their guns, and, unless they had enlisted only for money, they probably wondered why they had crossed the ocean to shoot a fellow countryman who was equally alien to this strange land. But the God of Battles is indifferent to national origins, and the guns mowed them down, foreigner and American alike, to be flung into a common grave.

Chapter 25

BUILDING THE CONFEDERATE NAVY IN EUROPE

The 290 took on the arms and ammunition which had been brought to the Azores by her supply vessel. Then, at noon on Sunday, August 24, she got up steam and moved away from shore toward the open sea. When she was four or five miles out—beyond the marine league—she fired her starboard bow gun, hauled down the English ensign, and ran up the Confederate flag, while the ship's band played "Dixie." She was then commissioned as a Confederate cruiser and named the *Alabama*.[1]

The Laird yard, which had built her, had already started work on two ironclads that were to cause Dudley, Adams, and the British much trouble. They were far more formidable than the wooden *Alabama*, for they were not only armored but had two iron-plated revolving turrets to carry their guns. And each one was provided with a sharp, metal underwater ram that could sink a wooden-hulled ship.

As the *Alabama* ran westward across the Atlantic, capturing and burning Yankee commercial vessels as she went, everyone who had been concerned in trying to stop her from leaving Liverpool soon realized what a destructive force had been let loose. American officials abroad and at home were dumfounded when reports of one capture after another came in. In London even Earl Russell had some qualms about the ship his countrymen had built and turned over to the Confederates. He confessed these to Lord Lyons who had returned to his post in Washington late in October.

But it was too late now to do anything about the *Alabama*. She was responsible only to Richmond, and communications from the Confederate government there took many weeks to reach Semmes. He enjoyed being his own master, although he did not like destroying unarmed ships. He did what he had to do and was considerate of his prisoners, especially the female ones. When his unwanted guests became too numerous, Semmes put them on a captured vessel and sent them to the nearest port. There they promptly forgot whatever good treatment they had received and told sensational stories about the blood-thirsty pirate who was the terror of the seas.

Gideon Welles sent out ship after ship to overtake and destroy the Confederate raider, but they never caught her although she had several close escapes. All sorts of strange plans were conceived to trap the *Alabama,* but nothing came of them, and the white-sailed raider roamed the ocean as free as the homeless water birds that sometimes followed her.

Dudley was quickly informed of what the *Alabama* was doing. On September 6 the Liverpool *Courier* printed a long piece sent in by "a gentleman on board." It told about the raider's escape and gave details about her fitting out and commissioning in the Azores. On October 4, Dudley clipped another news item listing a dozen ships the Confederate cruiser had destroyed.

Dudley also saw the local movement to support the Confederacy take on new organizational effectiveness at this time. On October 10 he cut out and preserved a newspaper account of a meeting held by the Liverpool Southern Association at which the members said that Gladstone's Newcastle speech had "paved the way for recognizing the Southern States as a separate nationality."[2]

The American consul intensified his efforts to keep an even closer watch over Confederate activities in England. One that took a great deal of work was keeping track of the numerous blockade-runners which were constantly entering and departing from British ports. Sometimes Dudley's spies made mistakes and wasted time watching a vessel that proved to be innocent.

Dudley kept himself so well posted about the building of the two ironclad rams in the Laird yards that he was almost as familiar with their progress as Bulloch was. The consul never had any difficulty collecting evidence. But presenting a case airtight enough to convince skeptical British officials was another matter. It almost seemed as if they had learned nothing from the escape of the *Alabama.*

Bulloch might have enjoyed the success the *Alabama* was having (and he knew, of course, that the *Florida* was rapidly being repaired in Mobile) if the Richmond government had left their very capable naval agent alone. But governments nearly always think that if one man is doing a good job, two men will do a still better one. Yet it hardly ever works out that way, and in this instance it certainly did not.

The Confederate Government was sending one of its very best men abroad. Matthew Fontaine Maury was not only a distinguished scientist who had achieved world fame as a pioneer oceanographer; he was also a professional naval officer who had begun his career as a midshipman on an American man-of-war. After 14 years of active service he was crippled in a stagecoach accident that prevented him from continuing as an officer of the deck. Confinement to work in the Naval Observatory at Washington made him into a first-rate scientist. He knew mathematics, navigation, ocean currents, meteorology, and anything that had to do with theory far better than Bulloch did, but he lacked that practical man's experience with commercial ships.

Maury, a Virginian born and bred, had sacrificed his career in the United States Navy to follow his native state into war. In the early days of the conflict, he had proposed to Mallory that a fleet of 100 inexpensive, quickly built steam launches be constructed and armed with rifled cannon. Work on these precursors of the modern PT boats was actually started, but the funds allotted to the project were transferred to building large ironclads after the success of the C.S.S. *Virginia* at Hampton Roads showed the effectiveness of the big armored ship.

Maury was put to work to develop underwater mines (then called torpedoes) for the Confederacy. Just as Semmes did not like to burn ships, Maury hated blowing them up with their crews unaware of the fact that a lethal device was about to be exploded under them. Both men, however, like all military experts, did not hesitate to do their duty.

After founding a Confederate torpedo bureau, for which he invented the first electrically exploded mine to be used in wartime, Maury was ordered to go to Europe for secret-service work. His forthrightness had made him many powerful enemies in the Confederacy (Davis and Mallory among them), and it was said that the brilliant but crotchety naval innovator was being sent abroad in order to get rid of him. He sailed from Charleston early in October 1862.[3]

On the same vessel was a young Confederate midshipman, James Morris Morgan. The captain of the steamer that was to take them to England had been in the coastal trade and had no knowledge of blue-water navigation, although he was reluctant to admit it. Six days out, when he could not find Bermuda, he called on Maury for help. That night the celebrated scientist took observations of the stars, charted a course, and told the captain that he should be in sight of the lighthouse at Port Hamilton by 2 A.M. It was 2:05 when the lookout spotted the signal.[4]

Maury was received with great deference by the British in Bermuda and in England and had access to highly placed government officials. His name meant something even to the press, so his letters defending the Southern cause were published in *The Times*. Maury could have been very useful to the Confederacy if his efforts had been confined to doing the sort of work he was best fitted for. But he had been sent to England to purchase ships that could be converted into cruisers. Much as Maury knew about naval affairs, he was like a child compared with Bulloch at this kind of task. It took him months to find a 550-ton iron-screw steamer in Glasgow. Launched under the name *Japan* and then renamed the *Georgia*, Maury's cruiser turned out to be more of a liability than an asset.

Early in the war the Secretary of the Confederate Navy ordered Lieutenant James H. North to go abroad to have two ironclads built, one in England and one in France. Mallory estimated that each ship would cost about $1,000,000.[5]

North arrived in England in July 1861, found no money available for his use, and was unable to do anything except make a general survey of the situation until April 1862, when he informed Mallory that he could get a 3000-ton ironclad built at the Thompson yards in Glasgow for the amount agreed upon. Elaborate specifications were drawn up and the contract was signed on May 21. The ironclad was to be 270 feet long and was to cost $910,000, which did not include armaments, munitions, stores, steward's furnishings, or charts and instruments.[6]

North gave Bulloch a good deal of trouble on several occasions. When he was offered command of the *Florida*, he refused to take it unless the ship could be armed in port, which was obviously impossible. Then he offered to turn over the construction details of his ironclad if he could have the *Alabama*. When she was given to Semmes, North was openly disappointed.

Clarence Yonge, a Confederate paymaster who became an informer, characterized the sometimes difficult officer in a statement written for Bulloch: "Lt. North . . . is not scrupulously neat in personal appearance. . . . His manner of speaking is slow and easy. His walk and everything about him indicate an indolent . . . disposition."[7]

Correspondence between Bulloch and North shows that the latter could be exceedingly petty. Bulloch, who was purposely working as a civilian to avoid detection, was evidently excluded from the little naval clique that wanted to assert its power. He wrote on July 10 to North that "there seems to have been a strange feeling among the majority of naval officers who have been in England that my position in the service was incompatible with their own dignity and that I must therefore be regarded as one to be left alone. This gives me no concern beyond the detriment such a state of feeling may prove to the public service, but you and myself are of an age to be above the display of childish jealousies and offishness, and I propose that we . . . not avoid each other's glance as was the case this morning."[8]

North, Bulloch, and Maury were only some of the many Confederate agents who were trying to buy ships in Europe. They were often at cross-purposes, and their desire to outdo each other raised prices, delayed construction, and confused foreign shipbuilders. Their multiplicity finally made it necessary to put a single financial officer in charge of disbursing Confederate purchasing funds abroad. This was done on October 28, when Benjamin wrote from Richmond to appoint James Spence, the Liverpool cotton broker, as financial agent for Europe. But Spence was unable to bring order to the tangled accounts. Not until September 1863 was a competent man (Colin McRae) given the job. By then it was too late. Confederate funds in Europe were exhausted at this time, and Confederate commercial credit was beginning to be impaired.[9]

The failure of the British attempt to end the war in America by mediation or intervention discouraged the Confederate Commissioners, but they still hoped that France would continue its efforts. After a long personal interview with the Emperor on July 20, Slidell felt that he could be depended on to favor the South. By mid-October he believed that France was ready to act and that recognition could soon be expected. Then, on the seventeenth, a crisis in the French Cabinet over Italy compelled Thouvenel to resign. Drouyn de Lhuys, whom Slidell did not know, became the French Foreign Minister. Again the Confederate Commissioner had to wait for further developments.[10]

They came quickly, for it was during the last few weeks of 1862 that France seemed most friendly to the Confederate Government. Late in September, Slidell wrote to Benjamin: "I was much and agreeably surprised last week by a visit from the head of an extensive banking house of Paris, who came to know if I had authority . . . to borrow money for my Government."[11] On October 26, the Confederate envoy was received by the new French Foreign Minister, and two days later was again allowed to see the Emperor. There was more talk of mediation, and Napoleon III showed Slidell a letter from the King of the Belgians which indicated that Leopold was also in favor of putting "an end to the bloody war" that was desolating America.[12]

But of far greater importance was what the Emperor casually let drop about the possibility of building ships in France for the Confederate Navy. Slidell said cautiously that "if the Emperor would give only some kind of verbal assurance that his police would not observe too closely when we wished to put on board guns and men we would gladly avail ourselves of it."[13]

Napoleon III replied: "Why could you not have them built as if for the Italian Government? I do not think it would be difficult, but will consult the Minister of Marine about it." Since it was well known that the French autocrat did not have to consult his ministers but merely tell them what he had decided, Slidell naturally had every reason to believe that this was an open invitation to have warships built in France.

He wrote to Benjamin about the conversation that same day and—this seemed to be his moment now—also wrote him another and more formal communication setting forth the terms of the loan which "the extensive banking house," Emile Erlanger & Co., proposed to make to Richmond. It was to be for £5,000,000 sterling and was to have cotton as its collateral.[14]

At this time Bulloch was having much doubt about being able to get the two Laird rams out of England. Doubtless the encouragement Slidell was receiving in France inspired Bulloch to write to Mallory on November 7: "I have decided upon the means of getting the first of these ships clear of British jurisdiction in a manner not to infringe Her Majesty's neutrality proclamation, but the attempt will be attended with difficulty and will require to be conducted with such caution and secrecy that I fear to mention the plan."[15]

It was not long after this that Bulloch was able to arrange for the transfer of the two Laird rams to the Bravay Brothers in Paris. Their company was to take title to the ironclads and then turn them over to the Confederacy after they had left England.

Word of Confederate shipbuilding activities soon began to leak out in France. As early as August 21, Bigelow noted in his diary that "Prince Polignac was saying about town that three iron-cased ships were soon to sail to attack New York." This, of course, referred to the Laird rams and perhaps to the armored warship which Lieutenant North was having built in Scotland.

Bigelow heard all sorts of rumors, some of which were brought to him deliberately. Three days later, when Sanford came from Belgium to visit Paris, he told the consul that there was "some thought of giving Dayton a judgeship or otherwise disposing of him to make place for a live Minister here." Bigelow had no ambitions for the post although he was very well qualified for it. He went quietly about his work, constantly buying scholarly books, especially those dealing with late seventeenth-century France, for he was becoming interested in writing a life of Fénelon.

1. & 2. Lord Lyons, the British Minister to Washington; M. Mercier, the French
Minister to Washington

Harper's Weekly, February 22, 1862

3. & 4. James M. Mason, John Slidell, the Confederate Commissioners to England and France

The Illustrated London News, December 14, 1861

5. John Bull as painted by himself

"England sells . . . the component parts of Ships-of-War (the Pirate *Alabama*) to all comers." — *London Times*.

Harper's Weekly,
December 6, 1862

6. "John Bull and Louis Napoleon descry upon the horizon a cloud about the size (and shape) of two Big Men's hands, and are frightened nearly out of their boots by the phenomenon."

Harper's Weekly,
November 21, 1863

7. An American caricature of "Bull-Run" Russell

Harper's Weekly, February 15, 1862

8. Charles Francis Adams, American Minister to England

9. Thomas Haines Dudley, American consul at Liverpool

Chapter 26

THE UNION HAS ITS TROUBLES TOO

Lincoln had promised himself that if his dilatory general, George Brinton McClellan, did not follow up his victory over Lee at Antietam and let the Confederate commander escape beyond the Blue Ridge Mountains, he would terminate his connection with the Army of the Potomac. On November 5, Lee safely reached Culpepper Court House, and the exasperated President replaced McClellan with Ambrose E. Burnside. It was an unhappy choice, as events of the next few weeks were to prove.

When the Emancipation Proclamation had been made public after Antietam, antislavery people in the North began to feel more friendly to the President. Prominent among them was Harriet Beecher Stowe, whose *Uncle Tom's Cabin* had so stirred the women of England when it was published there in 1852 that 562,848 of them signed a document entitled "The Affectionate and Christian Address of Many Thousands of Women of Great Britain and Ireland to their Sisters, the Women of the United States of America." This was an impassioned appeal for American women to put an end to slavery. The weighty manuscript had been bound in 26 large volumes which were presented to Mrs. Stowe and had been gathering dust for nearly ten years. That redoubtable propagandist now resolved to make use of the fact that the affectionate and Christian women of England were tolerating the building of a Confederate Navy in British shipyards and were not protesting when their government showed signs of granting recognition to the slaveholding South. Mrs. Stowe arranged to have her stirring reply published in *The Atlantic Monthly*. In order to make certain that the Emancipation Proclamation was surely going into effect on January 1 as scheduled, she went to Washington to visit her soldier son and call on the President. The world-famous novelist had no difficulty in getting into the White

House. Lincoln, who had never met her, received her graciously and said: "So this is the little lady who made this big war!"

The tribute to the power of her book pleased Mrs. Stowe. She told the President about the article she wanted to write and got his approval. He also assured her that the Emancipation Proclamation would be issued on New Year's Day.

She returned to her hotel and on Thanksgiving Day finished the most effective attack on slavery she had written since *Uncle Tom's Cabin*. Published in the *Atlantic* and widely reprinted abroad, it was a factor in shaping foreign opinion. *Uncle Tom* and its author were still a force in world affairs.[1]

On December 1, in his second Annual Message to Congress, Lincoln reviewed foreign affairs, departed slightly from the truth by saying "we have attempted no propagandism," and reported that he favored "the project for connecting the United States with Europe by an Atlantic telegraph and a similar project to extend the telegraph from San Francisco to connect by a Pacific telegraph with the line which is being extended across the Russian empire." He also discussed the problems facing the Treasury in wartime, when vast expenditures had to be made. The seemingly staggering sum of $570,841,700.25 had been spent during the fiscal year ending June 30, 1862, but this had been more than offset by receipts of $583,885,247.06. After the first year of active warfare, the United States was more than 13 million dollars ahead.

The President said that progress had been made toward the idea of building a railroad to the Pacific Coast, and that the nation's canals were to be enlarged and improved. He also reported that a Department of Agriculture had been organized during the year.

Lincoln then proposed an amendment to the Constitution which would provide for compensated emancipation. This was his favorite scheme for dealing with slavery. In the long and carefully reasoned argument presented to support his proposal, he erred in being too optimistic about population growth. Although he said that he still favored colonization for the liberated Negroes, he pointed out that even if they remained in the country their presence would not disturb the labor supply, for they had been here before as slaves; as freedmen, they would be doing the same work. But he was wrong when he predicted that they would remain contentedly in the South. He had no way of knowing, of course, what living conditions for them would be like in the postwar years. In conclusion he emphasized the fact that his proposed plan would "shorten the war and thus lessen its expenditure of money and blood."

But his much-cherished idea was never to be put into effect, and the war had to go on for more than two years, destroying human lives and property until it came to an end that was to prolong conflict between the states for a long time to come.

That Lincoln was a modern leader who was fully aware of the novel problems that faced him and his contemporaries is attested to in his eloquent closing passage:

> The dogmas of the quiet past are inadequate to the stormy present. The occasion is piled high with difficulty, and we must rise with the occasion. As our case is new, so must we think anew—and act anew. We must disenthrall ourselves, and then we shall save our country.
>
> Fellow-citizens, we cannot escape history. We of this Congress and this administration will be remembered in spite of ourselves. No personal significance, or insignificance, can spare one or another of us. The fiery trial through which we pass will light us down, in honor or dishonor, to the latest generation. . . . In giving freedom to the slave, we assure freedom to the free—honorable alike in what we give and what we preserve. We shall nobly save, or meanly lose, the last best hope of earth.[2]

The prairie lawyer had come a long way from the vernacular of his youth.

On December 13, Ambrose Burnside, the new commander of the Army of the Potomac ordered an attack against the Confederates' almost impregnable positions above the town of Fredericksburg, halfway between Washington and Richmond. It was a hopeless and insane venture. The ground in front of the Confederates' trenches turned blue with the uniforms of Union soldiers who were mowed down by the thousands as wave after wave of them were sent in to meet certain death. Burnside wanted the survivors to renew the attack on the fourteenth, but his officers persuaded him not to throw more men away. The Federal Army withdrew on the fifteenth, and the senseless Battle of Fredericksburg— and the career of another incapable Union commander—was over.

The nation—and Congress—reacted swiftly to the third great military failure that year. A caucus of Republican Senators met on the sixteenth to find a civilian scapegoat. (It was obvious that General Burnside's days were numbered, so there was no need to bother about him.) Led by Charles Sumner, Chairman of the Foreign Relations Committee, the attack was concentrated on Seward. The Secretary of State, of course, had had nothing to do with the defeat of the Union Army, but the Senators needed a prominent victim. Seward would do nicely, for he had many enemies.

As soon as he heard of what was happening, Seward and his son tendered their resignations to the President. Lincoln's astute maneuvering during the next few days shows that he had become a master of men who could operate on a national scale. And he was shrewd enough to know that the Senate's malice was really directed at himself. "They want to get rid of me," he confided to Browning.[3]

At a Cabinet meeting, Secretary of the Treasury Chase also offered his resignation, which he had prepared in writing. Since Chase was the man the anti-Seward faction was most likely to sponsor, Lincoln immediately saw a way out of the difficulty. All he needed was to have the resignation in hand. Welles, who was present, tells the story:

" 'Where is it?' said the President quickly, his eye lighting up a moment.

" 'I brought it with me,' said Chase, taking the paper from his pocket. 'I wrote it this morning.'

" 'Let me have it,' said the President, reaching his long arm and fingers toward C., who held on, seemingly reluctant to part with the letter, which was sealed, and which he apparently hesitated to surrender. Something further he wished to say, but the President was eager and did not perceive it, but took and hastily opened the letter.

" 'This,' said he . . . with a triumphal laugh, 'cuts the Gordian knot . . . I can dispose of this subject now.' "[4]

That same day Lincoln wrote a joint letter to Seward and Chase, saying that it would be against the public interest for them to resign; he therefore requested them to stay on.[5] The President was now firmly at the helm, the rebellious Senators had been put in their places, the Cabinet was intact, and the ship of state could maintain a steady course.

No official explanation of what had happened was sent to American diplomats abroad, but their friends wrote to inform them in varying degrees of accuracy about the narrow escape the State Department had had from being disrupted in the middle of a major war.[6] Lyons and Russell exchanged letters saying how glad they were that Seward was to remain in office.[7] He had at last won their respect.

When John Bright spoke at Birmingham on December 18, he summed up the English liberals' case against the Confederacy and its British supporters by saying: "I blame men who are eager to admit into the family of nations a State which offers itself to us, based on a principle . . . more odious and more blasphemous than was ever heretofore dreamed of. . . . The leaders of this revolt propose this monstrous thing —that, over a territory forty times as large as England, the blight and curse of slavery shall be forever perpetuated.

"I cannot believe . . . that such a fate will befall that fair land. . . . I have another and far brighter vision. . . . I see one vast confederation . . . and I see one people and one language, and one law, and one faith, and, over all that wide continent, the home of freedom, and a refuge for the oppressed of every race and of every clime."[8]

Ben Butler's military occupation of New Orleans was an endless source of trouble, not only to the Confederates, but also to other people in the conquered city. Among them was the Dutch consul, Amedée Couturié, who was called upon by one of Butler's officers shortly after the Union Army moved in.

Acting on a tip that a large sum of money of questionable ownership was to be found in the consulate, a search was made of the premises, and the keys of the vault were forcibly taken from Couturié, who was roughly handled in the process. More than $800,000 was removed from the vault, the consulate's papers were seized, and everything was placed in the United States Mint for safekeeping.[9]

The Netherlands Minister in Washington promptly protested to Seward. The money, he explained, had been deposited in the consulate by a local Dutch firm to whom it rightfully belonged. They demanded that it be returned and due apology made to all concerned, especially the consul, whose authority had been violated.

Negotiations and investigations dragged on all summer. Then Butler was replaced by a Union officer whose rule over the occupied city was expected to be somewhat milder. All the evidence presented to Seward indicated that the Netherlands consulate in New Orleans had indeed been unlawfully invaded and its chief officer treated badly. There was nothing for the Secretary of State to do but order the money to be returned and apologies made.

It was an unhappy affair which did not help the relations of the United States with a country which had long been one of its best friends. There was another brief flare-up a few days later when over-zealous draft officers in Philadelphia tried an attempt to enroll the local Dutch consul for military service although representatives of foreign governments were exempt. This, however, was a far less serious matter than the one in New Orleans and was soon settled.[10]

When the ousted general left his post in New Orleans on December 23, Jefferson Davis, who was still incensed at Butler for his "Woman Order" and for executing a man who had torn down and destroyed a United States flag displayed on the New Orleans Mint, pronounced the Union commander to be a felon "deserving of capital punishment" and ordered him to be treated "as an outlaw and common enemy of mankind." If taken by the Confederates, "the officer in command of the capturing force [was] to cause him to be immediately executed by hanging." He also said that "all commanding officers in the command of said Benjamin F. Butler be declared not entitled to be considered as soldiers engaged in honorable warfare but as robbers and criminals, deserving of death; and each of them be, whenever captured, reserved for execution."[11]

A few days later, a Charleston man publicly offered a reward of $10,000 "for the capture and delivery of the said Benjamin F. Butler, dead or alive." And a woman wrote to the Charleston *Courier* proposing "to spin the thread and make the cord to execute the order of our noble President, when old Butler is caught. . . . My daughter asks that she may be allowed to adjust it around his neck."[12]

Thus did violence breed more violence, and soldiers, government officials, and civilians, male and female alike, demanded blood for blood. The ideals on which the nation had been founded were forgotten, while lynch law was replacing the right to a fair trial that had been guaranteed by the Constitution.

In Richmond, the Rebel War Clerk, Jones, who only a few days before had said that "we are out of humor with England now and court a French alliance" noted on Christmas Day that turkeys were selling at $11 each in depreciated Confederate currency, while shoes brought $25 a pair. This, however, did not mean that the South was yet undergoing serious shortages. It was simply that monetary inflation was getting worse. In Charleston sugar was a dollar a pound, butter a dollar and a half, while shoes cost nine dollars more than they did in Richmond. But a dinner given at this time by General Roswell S. Ripley to some French officers in Charleston was so sumptuous that Lord Lyons' biographer reproduced the elaborate menu in full. It included salmon, turtle soup, oysters, fillet of beef, capon, mutton, turkey, sweetbreads, duck, quail, snipe, venison, ham, all kinds of vegetables, relishes, pastry, and dessert. Highly placed Confederates and their foreign guests were still eating well.[13]

Even before the Emancipation Proclamation was put into effect on the first day of 1863, people in England began to hold meetings to discuss it. There was a big one in London and another in Manchester on the last day of the old year. The workingmen of the industrial city of Manchester drew up an address to the President of the United States honoring him for the move he was to make the next day. The document was transmitted quickly to America, where it made such a strong impression upon Lincoln that he replied to it at length on January 19. He closed his letter by saying:

> I know and deeply deplore the sufferings which the workingmen at Manchester and in all Europe are called to endure in this crisis. It has been often and studiously represented that the attempt to overthrow this government, which was built upon the foundation of human rights, and to substitute for it one which should rest exclusively on the basis of human slavery, was likely to obtain the favor of Europe. Through the actions of our disloyal citizens, the workingmen of Europe have been subjected to a severe trial for the purpose of forcing their sanction to that attempt. Under these circumstances, I cannot but regard your decisive utterance upon the question as an instance of sublime Christian heroism which has not been surpassed in any age or in any country. It is, indeed, an energetic and reinspiring assurance of the inherent power of truth and of the ultimate and universal triumph of justice, humanity, and freedom. I do not doubt that the sentiments you have expressed will be sustained by your great nation, and, on the other hand, I have no hesitation in assuring you that they will excite admiration, esteem, and the most reciprocal feelings of friendship among the American people. I hail this interchange of sentiment, therefore, as an augury that, whatever else may happen, whatever misfortune may befall your country or my own, the peace and friendship which now exist between the two nations will be, as it shall be my desire to make them, perpetual.[14]

Chapter 27

THE YEAR 1862

By the end of 1862 it was evident to the world that the Confederacy, although it had fewer people and resources than the North, was holding out very well. A handful of extraordinary men were making this possible. Chief among them was Robert E. Lee, who had welded the poorly equipped and underprovisioned Army of Northern Virginia into a formidable fighting force. Lee kept the Confederacy alive; his victories gave the Southern people heart and enabled them to go on against odds that became even greater. And what the South was doing on the battlefield made the nations of Europe believe that the Confederacy might become an independent country in fact as well as in name. Only two things caused them to delay granting recognition: one was fear that the North might eventually prevail; the other was that fatal flaw in the Confederacy itself—slavery.

Despite the fact that his army was defending slavery, Lee had always opposed the institution. But most Southerners, especially since they had gone to war over it, were insistent that slavery be preserved. Davis and Alexander Stephens, although kind, well-meaning men, firmly believed that the Negro must be kept in bondage. So did the elderly, conservative state representatives who sat in the Confederate Congress and shaped its policies. They were a quarrelsome, cantankerous lot who sometimes resorted to physical violence on the floor of the House or the Senate.[1]

There was no keeping the South's attitude toward slavery secret. Its people's opinions on the subject appeared in print too often for that, and the printed word was circulated all over the civilized world in the 1860s. This hurt the South's chances for success so much that it was like trying to win a war with a big, manacled black man strapped to its back.

Proposals had been made to put Negroes into both the Northern and Southern armies as fighting troops, but much as this was talked about, few officers as yet really wanted to employ them for combat. Perhaps it was a matter of trust—or distrust. Even the Union Army was slow to recruit the blacks and train them for active fighting. It had used them unofficially as early as October 1861 at Hilton Head, but the President himself opposed enlisting them and did not change his mind until the Emancipation Proclamation was put into effect. The Union Navy was far in advance of the Army, for Welles had issued an order on September 25, 1861, authorizing the enrollment of Negro sailors. But at the end of 1862, when manpower shortages were developing in both armies, new efforts were about to be made to let the Negroes fight as well as dig, wash, cook, clean, and carry.[2]

Civil War military statistics are notoriously unreliable, but one has to depend upon what is available. According to T. L. Livermore's study, the Union Army had 918,121 men under arms in December 1862 while the Confederate Army had only 466,622. In one year, the Federal forces, which had numbered 527,804 at the end of 1861, had added almost as many men as there were in the entire Confederate Army.[3]

The discrepancy between the two navies was even greater. By December 1, 1862, Gideon Welles had built the Federal fleet up to 427 ships armed with 3268 guns and manned by 28,000 seamen. Mallory had created a navy out of nothing, but he still had fewer than 30 armed vessels, nearly all on inland waters, with a total of 2700 men.[4]

In December 1862, the *Alabama* was the only Confederate warship operating on the high seas. Since making her first capture on September 5, she had taken 28 Yankee commercial vessels and had burned all but seven of them. On the last day of the year, she was approaching the coast of Texas. In Mobile, the *Florida*, with her war damage repaired and with her crew brought up to nearly full strength, was about to try to break out of that heavily blockaded port.

The entire coast of the Confederacy from Virginia to the Mexican border was under a blockade which by this time had become fairly effective although hundreds of little inlets and rivers were unguarded because they were too numerous to be worth patrolling. They would remain this way throughout the war, but only small sailing vessels could venture into their shallow waters. The Union Navy had captured 390 blockade-runners during the first 11 months of the year. Many others, however, still managed to get through.

And one by one, Confederate seacoast points of strategic value had been taken. Roanoke Island, Beaufort, Fernandina, St. Augustine, New Bern, Fort Pulaski, New Orleans, Norfolk, and Galveston were occupied by Federal forces during the first half of 1862.

Under the circumstances, it is hard for a modern observer to understand why the people of the Confederacy were willing to continue a struggle against such uneven odds. But the odds had been against them from the start. They were stubborn, defiant, and often unreasonable in their thinking. Ignorance of the true situation often led them to believe that things were better than they actually were. And, there was always the seemingly invincible Lee to give them hope. The people inside the Confederacy may have misjudged their prospects at the end of 1862, but there were at least a few apparently valid reasons why they clung to the belief that the South would win.

More inexplicable is the thinking of the diplomats and businessmen of Europe who had no emotional involvements to color their views. They were still willing to extend credit to an unrecognized country which had no assets except cotton—and it could not send enough of that through the blockade to matter. The blindness of ordinarily hard-headed Europeans in 1862—and even in 1863—is one of the curiosities of history. Only their desire to come to the aid of the planter aristocracy can explain the strange aberration that was to cost them a good part of their investment capital. They did, of course, hope to make a profit, but they did not display much financial judgment in calculating the risk.

Patriarchal-looking Gideon Welles was not sorry to see the old year go. After attending a Cabinet meeting that dealt with minor changes in the Emancipation Proclamation, which was to be issued next day, he wrote in his diary:

> The year closes less favorably than I had hoped and expected, yet some progress has been made. It is not to be denied, however, that the national ailment seems more chronic. The disease is deep-seated. Energetic measures are necessary, and I hope that we may have them. None of us appear to do enough, and yet I am surprised that we have done so much. We have had some misfortunes, and a lurking malevolence exists towards us among nations that could not have been anticipated. Worse than this, the envenomed, relentless, and unpatriotic spirit of party paralyzes and weakens the hand of the Government and country.[5]

Chapter 28
THE CONFEDERATE SEESAW

The year that began with the Emancipation Proclamation marks the turning point of the war. Before 1863, all had been preparation and trial; now the conflict was to reach its climax, and the men who had thus far only been in training were to become—so far as they were able—experts at their work. This applied to the soldier in the field, the sailor on deck, the statesman at home, the diplomat abroad, and the spy no matter where he was. Some, of course, had learned nothing and would continue to stand stupidly still, unaffected by experience, the counsel of others, or anything within themselves.

The hundred days between the Preliminary Emancipation Proclamation and its release in final form were over. For 100 days the Confederate Government had had an opportunity to devise some way of meeting this new threat to the age-old status of slavery. But it had done nothing except fulminate, expostulate, and denounce. Yet the more knowledgeable Southern leaders clearly foresaw that Lincoln's war measure would be a powerful propaganda weapon—especially overseas.[1]

On January 5 an unknown Northern propagandist released a forged address purporting to have been made by Jefferson Davis. In this, the Confederate President was supposed to have said that the slaves freed by the Emancipation Proclamation would be used in the Union Army and Navy, "the inevitable tendency of which will be to inaugurate a Servile War." As a compensatory measure, the rather clumsy forgery declared that "on and after February 22, 1863 [Washington's Birthday], all free Negroes within the limits of the Southern Confederacy shall be placed on the slave status, and shall be deemed to be chattels, they and their issue forever." Negroes captured in free states were also to become slaves. The document ended with a statement that "the proper condition of the Negro is slavery or a complete subjection to the white man" and then predicted that the old Union would be restored with slavery "nationally declared to be the proper condition of all of African descent."[2]

This spurious bit of propaganda came stillborn from the press and had such limited circulation that copies of it are scarce. If it had reached Davis' attention, he could easily have denounced it for the fraud that it was. Actually there was no need to issue it, for only a week later the Confederate President came out with statements that were almost as harsh as those which had falsely been put into his mouth. What he said appears in his message to Congress of January 12. (This is the counterpart of Lincoln's Annual Message of December 1, 1862.) Davis had the advantage of being able to compose his address after Lee had repulsed Burnside at Fredericksburg and the prospect for further Southern victories appeared to be good. He also had had time to observe the initial reaction to the Emancipation Proclamation.

At no moment in his career as President of the Confederacy did Davis have a better opportunity to inspire his Congress and his people with words that would give them heart. But his 20-page address is mostly filled with excuses, complaints, and threats. After beginning with a review of historical events that had affected Anglo-American relationships since 1778, he launched into a diatribe against the Northern states and then attacked England and France for adopting a policy of neutrality "in which less than justice has been rendered to this people . . . and undue advantage conferred on the aggressors in a wicked war." He also charged European powers with issuing "orders prohibiting either party from bringing prizes into their ports," a move which he said adversely affected the South and favored the North.

He went on to state that the "monstrous pretension" of the Union to have established an effective blockade was meekly observed by neutral Europe despite the fact that many steamers were continually arriving and departing.

He accused the Northern armies of committing "every conceivable atrocity" and then proposed a countermeasure:

> We may well leave it to the instincts of that common humanity which a beneficent Creator has implanted in the breasts of our fellowmen of all countries to pass judgement on a measure by which several millions of human beings of an inferior race, peaceful and contented laborers in their sphere, are doomed to extermination, while at the same time they are encouraged

to a general assassination of their masters by the insidious recommendation "to abstain from violence unless in necessary self-defense." Our own detestation of those who have attempted the most execrable measure recorded in the history of guilty man is tempered by profound contempt for the impotent rage which it discloses. So far as regards the action of this Government on such criminals as may attempt its execution, I confine myself to informing you that I shall, unless in your wisdom you deem some other course more expedient, deliver to the several State authorities all commissioned officers of the United States that may hereafter be captured by our forces in any of the States embraced in the proclamation, that they may be dealt with in accordance with the laws of those States providing for the punishment of criminals engaged in exciting servile insurrection.

Fortunately, the Confederate War Department and its soldiers in the field paid no attention to the President's threat to Union commissioned officers. This was one of the many instances in which Davis' ideas were so far away from his people's thinking that they were never put into effect. What he said obviously came from his hatred of Ben Butler and his attempt the month before to strike back at the general, who in his mind, symbolized the worst qualities of the North.

The rest of Davis' address dealt with financial matters and summarized reports from the War Department, the Navy, and other branches of the government. It ended with a statement which was partly true but which did not tell the whole truth:

> From our own foundries and laboratories, from our own armories and workshops, we derive in a great measure the warlike material, the ordnance and ordnance stores which are expended so profusely. . . . Cotton and woolen fabrics, shoes and harness, wagons and gun carriages are produced in daily increasing quantities by the factories springing into existence.[3]

The people of the Confederacy, after reading their President's reassuring statement about the domestic production of war matériel, must have wondered where the factories and mills were located, for it was not likely that one was in their neighborhood. A few existed, but very few. And the soldiers, who had to capture arms and ammunition and plunder corpses for uniforms and shoes, may even have been a bit skeptical about the promises coming from Richmond. Most of the equipment actually issued to them was plainly of foreign origin.

Before departing from the Arcas Islands, where the *Alabama* had spent
Christmas, some of her officers prepared a souvenir of their visit. Her
Master's Mate described it in his private log: "In anticipation of news
being received of Lincoln's proclamation, a tombstone, consisting of a
board about four feet in length and two in breadth, was sent on shore
and placed in the most prominent position the largest island afforded.
In black letters on a white ground was the following: 'In memory of
Abraham Lincoln, President of the late United States, who died of nigger
on the brain, 1st January, 1863.'—'290.' Upon a piece of paper, protected
from the weather, was written in Spanish the following: 'Will the
finder kindly favour me by forwarding this tablet to the United States'
Consul at the first port he touches at.' "[4]

Semmes had a chance to do more serious damage than this to the
North when he approached Galveston, which had been lost to the Fed-
erals and then recaptured by Southern forces. Five Union Navy ships
were now besieging the city and firing shells at it. When their commander saw the *Alabama,* he sent the U.S.S. *Hatteras* out to investigate.

The *Hatteras* was a sorry-looking warship, for she was a former side-
wheel excursion steamer pressed into service because of the emergency.
She was as big as the *Alabama,* but she had only one engine, and she
was much less heavily armed.[5]

It was night by the time she got within hailing distance of the Confederate raider. At first Semmes pretended that his ship was British, but
before opening fire he announced her true origin. Despite the broadside
that raked the *Hatteras,* her captain ran in until he was close enough for
musket and pistol shots to be exchanged. Then two shells set the steamer
on fire while another put her engine out of commission. She had to
remain motionless while the *Alabama* withdrew beyond the range of
her inadequate guns. Two men had been killed and five wounded. Since
the fire was progressing rapidly, water was entering the hold, and the
ship was beginning to sink, there was nothing to do but surrender. When
all the living were taken off, she went down, and the first high-seas battle
of the Civil War was over. It had lasted just 13 minutes.[6]

A boat, which the *Hatteras* had sent out before the firing began,
reached the Federal fleet with word of the disaster. News of the *Alabama's* victory over a Union naval vessel spread throughout the world to
increase already apprehensive American shipowners' fears of the famous
raider. The flight from the flag became a panic as they transferred one
vessel after another to foreign ownership.

At 2 A.M. on the stormy night of January 16, 1863, Maffitt ran the *Florida* out of Mobile Bay and by skillful seamanship managed to evade the seven blockading vessels that were waiting for him. Not a shot was fired as he hurried past the anchored ships. His presence was finally detected, and a chase was made, but he soon shook off his pursuers and was off to the West Indies to begin a career of capture and destruction that was to rival Semmes' record.[7]

The anger caused by the steady flow of reports of the damage done to American shipping by the *Alabama* and the *Florida* was building up to an explosive force that could readily have led to a war between the United States and England. The British, however, seem to have been largely unaware of this although Russell's notes sometimes indicate that he was a bit uncomfortable about the increasing tension between the two nations. Her Majesty's Government protected itself against unpleasant reality by a simple device which Adams' son Charles described: "While the statute law of the realm was being turned into a manifest farce, everything was done gravely and in an orderly way."[8]

But this genteel method of putting off a crucial moment by refusing to recognize that it might be at hand could not continue to work indefinitely. What was happening in Birkenhead could be ignored, denied, or brushed aside, but not forever.

The two armored rams being built there in the Laird yards were the object of much suspicion, particularly when they neared completion in the spring of 1863. Every iron plate that was put in place to armor them was bringing the inevitable crisis nearer. But several diversions temporarily distracted the public's attention from them. One was the capture and publication of Confederate Government correspondence being sent from Richmond to London.

When a United States Minister or consul sent information to Washington, he could be reasonably sure that it would reach its destination safely. The Confederates had no such assurance because Union naval vessels continually patrolled the sea lanes near the coast and often stopped ships (especially those that looked like blockade-runners) to search them for contraband material. While doing this, they sometimes intercepted Confederate messages of prime importance.

When one such haul was made in January, Seward sent copies of the highly confidential correspondence to Adams in London to use there as he saw fit. Much of it was merely a résumé of events in the field to bring the Confederate Commissioners up to date on what was happening at home. Of far greater interest were documents which said that:

1. The French had been making inquiries about the possibility of Texas separating itself from the Confederacy and resuming its former independence.
2. That Secretary of State Benjamin thought Commissioner James M. Mason's correspondence with Earl Russell showed that he had been treated "with scant courtesy" and that "a principal cause of the dislike and hatred towards England . . . is the offensive arrogance of some of its public men." (Russell must have read this with mixed feelings when he examined copies of the captured documents which Adams sent to him early in February.)
3. That James Spence had been made the financial agent of the Confederacy in England and that he was authorized to deal with Fraser, Trenholm & Co., "its depositaries under the law." Also that $2,500,000 in gold and silver coin was on hand in Richmond for "payment of articles purchased in England."
4. That George Sanders, who had once been a friend of several leading European revolutionists and who was to be mixed up in plots and counter-plots all his life, was authorized to place contracts for the building of six ironclads in Europe. (The intercepted documents had been taken from his son, Reid Sanders.)[9]

These and other morsels of almost equally important inside information about the secret activities of the Confederate Government were published in American newspapers and were also distributed in Europe.[10] Oddly enough, they seem to have had little effect upon the thinking of the British officials who were concerned with the Foreign Enlistment Act and the building of ships in Great Britain for the Confederate Navy. By this time, their minds had evidently been made up and nothing could change them. The evidence, again and again, had been irrefutable, but so far no one in the Government would believe it. Adams' only hope was Russell, a man with whom he was often exasperated but with whom he felt an odd kinship.

Russell was unpredictable in major affairs of state but in minor matters he would often abide by the letter of the law. When the British consul at Mobile, James Magee, transgressed the law, Russell moved quickly.

Magee had been involved in an effort to send specie to England to pay British subjects some £40,000 sterling due them in London as interest on Alabama state bonds. When H.M.S. *Vesuvius* wanted to enter Mobile Bay in November 1862, the commander of the United States blockading squadron saw no reason why the British warship should not go up to the dock at Mobile and take the kegs of specie on board.

As soon as word of what was happening reached Lord Lyons in Washington, he frantically tried to stop the shipment, but by this time the *Vesuvius* had sailed away with her precious cargo. Lyons explained to Russell: "I really could not answer for the peace if, in addition to the irritation about the *Alabama,* should come the fury which would be excited if it were shown that our men-of-war had carried Confederate gold through the blockade."

As soon as he learned the facts, Russell instantly dismissed Magee from Her Majesty's service and gave orders to the Admiralty "to forbid any similar shipment from Confederate ports."[11]

When Russell notified Adams of what he had done, everyone in the American Legation was delighted. Moran wrote: "This is the first time during the war that malpractices of British officers have been condemned by the Gov't here. I hope it is the beginning of decent behavior in such matters."[12]

Since the *Alabama* and the *Florida* were far away at sea, Adams could do nothing about them, but it was his duty to prevent any more commerce-raiders from going into action. Dudley had told him that a new Glasgow-built ship named the *Georgiana* was in Liverpool being loaded with cargo and that he feared she would soon join the other Confederate cruisers. The usual routine with the Customs House began. Price Edwards again denied that the ship could be made into a commerce-raider although he cheerfully admitted that the nature of her cargo indicated that she was a blockade-runner.[13] Moran noted in his Journal: "The Collector of Customs at Liverpool connives openly and flagrantly at the preparation and departure of these pirates. When proof is brought to him of the character of these ships he impudently meets it with a flat, unsupported denial and absolutely assists the corsairs to leave."[14]

The British refused to do anything, and the *Georgiana* sailed on January 21. Her career was brief and inglorious. While trying to slip past the blockade to enter Charleston Harbor on March 19, she ran aground, was disabled by shells from a Union gunboat, and was then set on fire by her crew before they abandoned her.[15] Adams and Dudley must have smiled wryly when news of her fate reached London.

Chapter 29

THE ERLANGER COTTON LOAN
ATTRACTS EUROPEAN CAPITAL

While the men in charge of the Confederacy's finances were busy making arrangements for a European bond issue which would use cotton stored in the Southern states as collateral, Adams, Dudley, and other Union officials in England were trying to find out who really owned the two formidable rams in the Laird yards. When it was said that they were intended for the Chinese Government, the American Legation in London attempted to obtain a description of the flags which would be used by that country's naval forces.[1] No one there had ever seen a Chinese ensign or even a picture of one. This was only the beginning of a paper chase that was to lead to France, Egypt, Turkey, and Denmark as Bulloch named one supposed owner after another in order to hide the true ownership of the rams.

While this fruitless search was being made, the Legation people were cheered up to see that not only British working-class but also British middle-class opinion was beginning to line itself up on the side of the Union. On January 30 a meeting in London's huge Exeter Hall was so well attended that many had to be turned away to stand in the streets and hold outdoor meetings of their own. The speakers in Exeter Hall were not particularly well known, so it was not their names that drew such crowds. People came to express their support of the Northern cause. When Mrs. Stowe's *Reply* to the women of England was read, the audience cheered.[2]

The Illustrated London News ended its long report on the meeting by saying that "whatever the result as regards North and South—the permanent rupture or reunion of the states—it is impossible to doubt that the Divine hand is so fashioning things as to destroy slavery." The keynote at Exeter Hall, it also said, was "Emancipation and Union."[3] *The Times,* in order to disparage the largely middle-class gathering, said that both the speakers and the audience were "nobodies."[4] But these nobodies were now becoming somebodies and were beginning to make themselves heard in England. Before long their voices would drown out the old, cracked, feeble tones of the relics of the ancient regime.

Adding to the sudden popularity of the North was the arrival of relief ships bringing food from America for the starving cotton operatives.[5] Started by John Bright's suggestion, they came in from Philadelphia loaded with edible cargoes which were so welcome that port pilotage and dock dues were remitted, and the heavily laden vessels were towed up the Mersey free of charge. Thousands of people visited the waterfront to see the good-will ships and watch their freight being discharged.[6] "The pettiest details in connection with a vessel on such an errand are of interest and invested with a dignity which the doings of no mere trading-ship, were she laden with gold and precious stones instead of with bread and pork, could command," said *The Illustrated London News,* which also printed several pictures of this demonstration of international amity.[7]

The Relief Committee of the Manchester Society of Friends presented the captain of the *Achilles* with a gold chronometer for himself and an engrossed address for him to take home to the Philadelphia Quakers who had sponsored the mission.[8] On Dudley, who was responsible for everything that had to do with American shipping, fell the task of handling the details of receiving the food and seeing that it was properly distributed.

Dudley was swamped with work at this time. He not only had to worry about the growing menace of the Laird rams, but also about a new ship named the *Alexandra* which was being built with Fraser, Trenholm and Company's own funds as a gift to the Confederate Government. She was launched in Liverpool on March 7, while Dudley was doing his best to gather evidence to be used against her. Still another ship with which Fraser Trenholm were connected was the *Japan-Virginia* that was now nearly ready to leave Scotland under the final name *Georgia.* This was the cruiser which Maury had ordered. She was soon to be under the command of his cousin, Lieutenant William L. Maury.

In the midst of all these demands on Dudley's attention came letters from Gideon Welles advising him that two distinguished Americans, John Murray Forbes and William Henry Aspinwall, were on their way to Liverpool on what was obviously some sort of important secret mission which Welles did not describe. He merely asked that Dudley give them his assistance; they would explain what they wanted.[9]

While waiting for them, Dudley notified the American Legation in London that a shipment of 90 boxes containing $250,000 belonging to the Confederacy was on its way from Liverpool. It was thought the specie might have some connection with the European cotton loan, for which the subscription books were to open on March 19.[10]

The Erlanger Cotton Loan had been in the making since October 1862. The French banking house sent representatives to Richmond, and the final negotiations began there in mid-January. Benjamin, who was probably the one person in the Confederate capital best qualified to deal with the sophisticated European financiers, wrote to Slidell that "the terms were so onerous that we could not assent to them, nor would it have been possible to obtain the sanction of Congress." Benjamin saw what the proposed loan really was—a contract for obtaining cotton. Under the terms offered, the subscribers would have had the right to buy cotton for 3⅔ pence a pound or less than $30 a bale. Since this was far below the current price and likely to be even more of a bargain when that scarce commodity rose higher in the future, the first Erlanger proposal was rejected. But a compromise was agreed upon, and a revised contract was drawn up. Benjamin said of it: "By this new arrangement we agreed to take only $15,000,000 instead of $25,000,000; to issue 7 per cent bonds instead of eights; and we are to receive 77 per cent instead of 70, while the deferred payments are so arranged that after allowing commission and discount we shall receive 70 per cent net. This will give us about $33.60 per bale of 400 pounds. . . . The profits by the takers of this loan will be enormous."[11]

It was a poor deal for the Confederacy, and no one knew it better than Benjamin, but he was willing to agree to it for the political purposes he hoped it would have. Chief among them was recognition of the Confederacy.

Other financial arrangements which had been in the making in England pending the completion of the Erlanger loan were held up. Payments to suppliers of ships and munitions were not made, and creditors who were owed large sums began to demand their money—or at least a part of it.[12]

When the subscription books for the Erlanger loan were opened on March 19 in Paris, London, Liverpool, Frankfort, and Amsterdam, it was so heavily oversubscribed that the bonds commanded a premium of

4½ to 5 per cent before nightfall of the first day. Mason wrote jubilantly to Benjamin about "the decided and brilliant success of the Confederate loan." He also exclaimed "that Cotton is King at last."[13]

It seemed to all concerned that the loan was a great success, but as time quickly proved, it was a success only for the Erlangers. Everyone else did badly. The profit-blinded investors wrongly believed that the bonds gave them an absolute right to cotton as collateral even if the Confederates lost the war. But the Federal Government was certainly not going to allow this, nor was the South able to let the investors obtain their collateral. Actually, much of the cotton was destroyed during the final days of the war.

Slidell, however, did better than most. His daughter Matilda married Erlanger's son and became a baroness.[14]

The Erlanger bonds almost immediately developed a tendency to decline in value. The Confederates suspected that the market was being deliberately depressed by Union stockbrokers acting under government direction, but they were never able to prove their charges. (The promoters of highly speculative securities can never believe that their printed paper will sink to its true level of its own accord; according to them, manipulators are always forcing it down.)

That the Erlanger bonds should be depreciating early in April, only a few weeks after they were issued, threatened to ruin Confederate credit. By the terms under which the bonds had been sold, another payment of 15 per cent was due on April 24, and if the bonds went down too much by then, subscribers would simply abandon the 15 per cent they had already paid. In order to prevent this, it was hurriedly agreed in Paris (under the circumstances it was impossible to ask Richmond for authorization) to have Erlanger and Company buy in bonds offered on the market in order to sustain their price. This, of course, had to be done with Confederate funds—part of the money just raised by the loan.[15]

This cannibalistic scheme began on April 8 and succeeded in propping up the sagging prices of the bonds for a while. Mason wrote to Richmond to point out that even if a million pounds went down the drain in this way, "the effect will only be to reduce the loan by that amount."[16]

It did. Before the salvaging operation was over, more than £1,500,000 had been paid out, much to the Erlangers' profit.[17] It has been esti-

10. John Laird, whose shipyard built the *Alabama*

The Illustrated London News

11. James Dunwoody Bulloch, Confederate naval agent in Europe

12. The *Alabama* meets the *Kearsarge* in
battle off the coast of Cherbourg,
France, on June 19, 1864
The Illustrated London News

BY ORDER OF THE UNITED STATES CONSUL AT LIVERPOOL.

TO BE SOLD BY AUCTION,

ON THURSDAY, the 22nd MARCH, 1866,

AT ONE O'CLOCK,

AT THE BROKERS' SALE-ROOM,

WALMER BUILDINGS, WATER STREET,

THE SCREW-STEAMER

SHENANDOAH,

(Late the Sea King,) 1,018 tons gross, 790 tons net Register.

Built by Messrs. A. Stephen and Sons, Glasgow, in 1863, on the composite principle; she has all iron frames, beams, stringers, keelsons, &c.; is planked with East India teak, and appears in Lloyd's classed 18 years A 1; she has engines of 140-horse power, tubular boilers, and lifting screw. This vessel was built specially for the China trade, for which she is admirably adapted; she is well found in sea-going stores, and has just lately had a new complete suit of sails, and is otherwise in splendid order and ready for immediate employment; she is sheathed with yellow metal. Dimensions:—Length, 220 feet, breadth, 32.5 feet; depth, 20.5 feet.

LYING IN THE BIRKENHEAD FLOAT.

For orders to view the Ship, and further particulars, apply to

C. W. KELLOCK & CO., Brokers for the Sale of Ships,

Walmer Buildings, Water Street, Liverpool.

INVENTORY.

(detailed ship's inventory list: Anchors, Cables, Boats, Sails, Masts, Carpenter's & Boatswain's Stores, Cooper's Stores, Shiplandler's Stores, Cabin Stores, Cook's Stores)

14. An auction poster

13. The Old Rip of the "Shenandoah"

Captain Waddell (as Rip Van Winkle): "Law! Mr. Pilot, you don't say so! The war in America over these eight months? Dear! dear; who'd ever a' thought it!"

mated that the net receipts of the £3,000,000 loan were only £1,283,-930 for the Confederacy.[18]

Yet this sum, reduced as it was, helped Huse, Bulloch, and other Confederate agents make enough payments to keep the stream of much-needed supplies flowing to Southern shores. And bad as the Erlanger deal seemed to be, it was pure profit to the Confederacy.

The Erlanger bonds continued to be bought and sold in European markets throughout the rest of the war. Their price, if charted daily, would be an accurate reflection of the Confederate's prospects for success, for they rose after each Southern victory and sagged after a Northern one.

Chapter 30

THE FORBES-ASPINWALL MISSION

Until the spring of 1863 the South had been far more active than the North in sending propagandists, purchasing agents, and financial experts abroad. Now the Federal Government, with its vast resources and long-established connections, began sending specialists to Europe. In typically American fashion, it was thought that large sums of money, liberally expended, might accomplish miracles. Perhaps one could even buy up the ships intended for the Confederate Navy. It was only a matter of outbidding the original purchasers, for it was thought that the British shipbuilders would surely accept a larger offer.

This novel scheme seems to have been devised simultaneously by two men who were widely separated in location and background. One was Freeman H. Morse, who had become the American consul at London at the beginning of the war. The other was John Murray Forbes, a wealthy Boston merchant and shipowner. Both wrote to Washington late in 1862 outlining a plan to paralyze Confederate activity in Europe by using money as a weapon. No matter what ships like the dangerous Laird rams cost, they would be worth the price if the South could be stopped from getting them. And once in possession of the Union, their guns could, of course, be turned against Confederate ports. Northern ingenuity and gold would thus dethrone the Cotton King.[1]

Morse, who was 3000 miles away from Washington, was in no position to follow up his original proposal. But Forbes was. He interested Welles and Chase in it and was soon invited to meet them in New York to discuss the project further. His friend William H. Aspinwall, another self-made shipping millionaire, was also to be there.

Forbes and Aspinwall were representative specimens of the men who were rapidly rising to positions of wealth and power during the period before the war. They were far less ruthless than their successors who knifed their way up during the more competitive postwar years. Circumstances in those early days were easier. It was possible to amass a fortune then without robbing others and openly damning public opinion.

Forbes was one of the nineteenth-century American businessmen who had received their training in China. His influential Perkins uncles sent him to Canton where the fabulously powerful local merchant Houqua befriended him and taught him the intricacies of dealing with his people. Money came easily to those who were engaged in trade with the Orient then, and Forbes returned to Boston at the age of 24 with enough capital to enable him to make highly profitable investments in land, railroad building, and shipping. He and his brother Robert, who had been in China with him and had also founded his fortune there, became known as experts and innovators in the rapidly expanding American shipping trade.

Aspinwall had grown up in the same trade and had become wealthy from it. His New York firm did business all over the world and had especially strong connections in South and Central America. At the time of the California gold rush, he resigned active management of the New York house to turn his attention to the Isthmus of Panama which was the key to quick transportation between the Atlantic states and the West Coast. He built a railroad across the narrow strip of land in order to move men and merchandise from one ocean to another. Its eastern terminal was named after him, and the port of Aspinwall (now Colón) became famous.[2]

Both men were rich enough not to have to care about money. Both were ardent Unionists opposed to slavery, and both, of course, had a common interest in promoting and defending American shipping. Their country's sea trade was under heavy attack, for the damage done by the *Alabama* and the *Florida* was making owners transfer their ships to foreign flags. The Laird rams now threatened to be an even greater menace, and there were well-founded reports that the Confederates were building more armed ships in Europe.

At the meeting with Welles and Chase in the Fifth Avenue Hotel on Sunday, March 15, Forbes and Aspinwall were asked to go abroad on a secret mission for the United States Government. They were to have Treasury credits for £1,000,000 and were to try to persuade Baring Brothers, the United States financial agents in England, to lend £1,000,000 sterling, using as security $10,000,000 in 5–20 bonds which they were to take with them. Aspinwall had to wait for the bonds to be printed, but Forbes was to leave on March 18. Both men were given wide powers of discretion and advised to depend heavily on Dudley and Morse for information and advice.[3] They were to leave Adams alone, because it was felt that he should not be mixed up in their secret operations. He was apparently instructed about this, for he later told Forbes that he wanted to know only what was absolutely necessary about the mission because it might not be the sort that "a diplomat would care to indorse."[4]

Forbes spent some time in Liverpool being briefed by Dudley on the background of the building of Confederate ships in England. He had arrived on March 29 in the midst of exciting events which were crowding each other so fast that it must have been difficult for the newcomer to grasp their full significance. The country was still buzzing with talk about the success of the Erlanger loan; Dudley was busy trying to have Fraser, Trenholm's ship, the *Alexandra,* seized by the British; news about the *Japan-Virginia-Georgia* was coming in from Greenock where she was getting ready to sail; a young American named George Temple Chapman, who had some knowledge of naval shipbuilding, was being considered by Dudley for employment as a spy, and another young man who had been Semmes' paymaster on the *Alabama,* had become disillusioned about the Confederate Navy and now wanted to tell all he knew about its operations in England. This was Clarence Yonge, a 29-year-old Southerner whose background was described by Moran when he met him at the Legation in London. "Yonge," wrote Moran in his *Journal,* "is a man of talent . . . still, he is a slippery fellow. It appears that he was dismissed [from the *Alabama*] at Port Royal for marrying a Negro there, brought her to L'pool where he deserted her, and that it was from her Dudley got the papers [regarding the *Alabama*]."[5]

And there had been a great stir in the House of Commons on March 27 when John Laird of Birkenhead got up to reply to John Bright. After pointing out that the North had obtained large quantities of weapons from England whereas the South had got only "two ships, unarmed [and] unfit for any purpose of warfare, for they procured their armaments somewhere else," Laird concluded by declaring that "to talk about freedom in a land like the Northern States of America is an absurdity" and that he "would rather be handed down to posterity as the builder of a dozen *Alabamas* than as the man who applies himself deliberately to set class against class, and to cry up the institutions of another country which, when they come to be tested, are of no value whatever, and which reduce the very name of liberty to an utter absurdity."

The fact that this hostile speech was greeted with cheers was even more depressing to the little group of Northerners in England than the import of its words. And it was followed by a defense by Palmerston of the Government's actions—or lack of them—in the escape of the *Alabama*. Russell, however, admitted to Adams that the cases of the *Florida* and the *Alabama* were a scandal.[6]

The week after these speeches in the House of Commons marked a new low spot in Anglo-American relations—and it was at this time that Forbes arrived in a country with which it was felt that his own might soon be at war.

Liverpool was a new world for Forbes, with intrigue and double dealing as widespread as that which he had known in his youth in the treaty ports of China. In Liverpool, however, conspiracy was operating on a much larger scale than it had in the Orient, and so far as Forbes was concerned, it struck closer to home.

The shipping magnate was greatly impressed by young Chapman, who had just visited the Laird yards and had written a report about the two rams being built there.[7] He said that the ironclads would be completed in four months. Forbes offered to reimburse Dudley for £100 to finance further investigations by the new spy.[8]

He then went on to London to call on Morse and Adams. Soon after his arrival, he set up a system of coded telegraphs so Dudley and he could communicate with each other in secrecy. He also went to Baring Brothers to see Joshua Bates whom he knew and with whom he could discuss the details of the loan which would be needed as soon as Aspinwall arrived with the Treasury bonds.[9]

Forbes quickly came to the conclusion that the letters of marque and reprisal authorized by Congress on March 3 should not be used because of the difficulties they might bring with other nations.[10] He also felt that Charles Wilkes, of *Trent* Affair fame, should be sent to some part of the world where he would no longer be an irritant to the British. Word just received that Wilkes had seized the British steamer *Peterhoff* while it was on its way from London to Matamoros was causing so much anger in England that even Cobden complained about the troublesome naval officer.[11] Evidence of Forbes' power in Washington is shown by the fact that Welles transferred Wilkes to a less sensitive area when he received a letter from Forbes about him.[12]

Since Forbes and Adams were not supposed to confide in each other, the newcomer could not have learned about the disturbing message Russell addressed to the American Minister on April 2. Its final sentence showed how determined British policy was to protect British business: "Except on the ground of any proved violation of the Foreign Enlistment Act, Her Majesty's Government cannot interfere with commercial dealings between British subjects and the so-called Confederate States, whether the subject of these dealings be money [like the Erlanger loan] or contraband goods, or even ships adapted for warlike purposes."[13]

Events, however, soon took a sudden turn. Dudley's protests about the *Alexandra,* which had been filed with the Foreign Office by Adams on March 30, produced unexpected results. The British Government took action and seized the ship on April 5.[14]

The jubilation of the Americans was quickly sobered by the realization that this was only the first move in what would undoubtedly be a long-drawn-out law case of the kind Dickens had immortalized in *Bleak House* only ten years before. But the seizure of the *Alexandra* was a blow to the Confederates. Hotze wrote to Benjamin that it "proves undoubtedly a strong desire to propitiate our enemies." The young journalist had evidently had good legal advice, for he explained that by selecting the unusual process of "exchequering" in this case, the British Government had rendered itself liable to heavy damages.[15]

When Aspinwall arrived in Liverpool he had with him several trunks containing the $10,000,000 worth of Federal bonds that were to finance the mission. He had also brought Captain Robert H. Pearson, who had commanded the *Oregon,* the second steamer to be put in commission by the Howland-Aspinwall Pacific Mail Steamship Company on the West Coast. Pearson had suppressed a mutiny on his ship in 1849 and was known to be an iron-fisted captain of the old school. Aspinwall wanted his expert opinion about what was going on in British shipyards. The captain remained in the Liverpool area for a few days with Aspinwall's son while Aspinwall himself took the bonds to London to deposit them in Baring's vaults.[16]

The steamer that had brought the Aspinwall party from America had also carried a choice bit of information which appeared in *The Times* on April 7:

> The private commercial advices today from New York contain the important statement that two well-known merchants, one from Boston and one from New York, have been commissioned by the Washington Government to proceed to London on financial business. The former sailed from Boston by the steamer which arrived last week, and the latter was to sail in . . . the

Australasian. It was understood that they are instructed to dispose of £2,000,000 of six per cent bonds, with which they are furnished, and that they also have authority to negotiate a further sum of £10,000,000. . . . The Commissioners in question are expected, it is also said, to employ part of the £2,000,-000 of which they are positively to dispose by buying up "the gunboats now building in England for the rebels," a device which seems to have excited great admiration and confidence among the mercantile community of New York.[17]

This early exposure of what was intended to be a secret mission required a drastic change of plan. Dudley and Morse, who fortunately had not been mentioned in *The Times* article, would now have to do most of the behind-the-scenes work. Forbes and Aspinwall remained in London for a while to handle financial matters. Being on the ground soon made them change their minds about the feasibility of purchasing the Laird rams. They wrote a joint letter to Welles on April 18, saying that "to offer to buy the ironclads without success would only be to stimulate the builders to greater activity and even to building new ones in the expectation of finding a market for them from one party or the other."[18]

At the same time they wrote to Chase that they had obtained a six-months' loan of nearly £600,000 from the Barings, using $4,000,000 of the bonds as collateral. Since the loan was conditional upon letters of marque not being used against British vessels, it put an end to the efforts to send out privateers from the Northern states.[19]

On April 20 there arrived at the Legation a third civilian from America who was to play a part in the financial tug-of-war that was going on in Europe. This was Robert J. Walker, a truly picturesque figure whose life had been a continual series of adventures. Born in Pennsylvania, he had married the granddaughter of Benjamin Franklin and had gone to Natchez to speculate in land and slaves. After making a fortune and learning the ways of the South, he had been sent to the Senate for two terms and had been active there in the move to annex Texas. Unlike most men of his background, he did not believe in slavery even though he had owned many Negro bondsmen. He freed them all in 1839. In 1845 he became Polk's Secretary of the Treasury and established a reputation for himself in money matters. In 1857 he was appointed Governor of Kansas Territory and was in that violence-ridden area during the struggle between the settlers from the North and the proslavery men from Missouri. He broke with the South once and for all during the controversy over the Lecompton constitution and resigned shortly thereafter.

Chase had sent him to Europe to work with the others already there. And Walker had the advantage of knowing Earl Russell, who had entertained him on a previous visit. Moran described the redoubtable newcomer to the Legation: "He is a very small person, not being more than 5 feet 3 inches high; but he has a good head and a well-cultivated mind. He is one of the best talkers I ever knew. He is an odd-looking fellow about 60 years of age, is most slovenly in his dress, has thin hair which has been dyed almost black, and is evidently very proud of himself. . . . He will publish some letters here exposing the whole Mississippi repudiation [of state bonds] and Davis' connection with it."[20]

Walker was out to destroy European confidence in the Confederacy's credit. The fact that he himself had had more to do with bond repudiation than Davis had during depression days in the South was evidently considered irrelevant in propaganda work.

Moran was meeting a number of interesting people at this time. Cassius Clay was in London again on his way back to Russia. While seeing Clay off to Paris, Moran met the young American artist James McNeill Whistler who was going on the same boat train. Moran was shocked to find that Whistler was living openly with a mistress whom he described as "an Irish girl with the golden tresses of Venus and deep blue eyes as large as those of Juno." But his disapproval—and perhaps envy—of the informal sex arrangement did not prevent Moran from paying tribute to Whistler's paintings which he called "remarkable . . . [and] full of vagary and . . . genius."[21]

Mason gleefully reported the exposure of the Forbes-Aspinwall mission in a letter to Benjamin.[22] But he was not, of course, aware of its success in obtaining funds in England without fuss or publicity. The Erlanger bonds were constantly slipping in value and had to be supported in the unstable market for them whereas the money which the Barings had advanced upon the credit of the United States Government was only a token of what was to come. Before the war was over, Europeans had purchased $250,000,000 worth of Federal securities. And since they were acquired at exceedingly favorable discounts, their buyers eventually made a handsome profit.

The little group of Union agents was joined by a fourth when William M. Evarts arrived. He had been sent as an expert on maritime law

who could advise Adams on legal matters. The Confederate propaganda
machine quickly went to work to discredit him. A letter from a New
York correspondent appeared in the pro-Southern London *Standard*
charging that eight more "delegates" were on the way and that Adams
was to be nothing more than their mouthpiece. Evarts, the letter said,
was Seward's man, sent because the Secretary of State had lost all confidence in Adams whose "stupidity" had created bad feeling in England
toward the Northern cause.[23] Adams remarked mildly on seeing this
that "I doubt whether any Minister has ever had so much of this kind
of thing to contend with."[24]

When Evarts came to the Legation on May 1, the ever-observant
Moran said that "he is a thin Cassius-faced man, with a good forehead,
fine thoughtful eyes, and pleasing manners; in person not unlike Mr.
Seward."[25]

With Evarts on the scene, the mission had its full complement of
personnel, but the exposure of its intentions hampered the activities
of its leaders. Forbes provided Dudley with money for espionage, in one
case sending him one half of a £100 note with the other half in a separate letter for safety's sake. He also kept Dudley informed about what
he heard in London. And he came to the conclusion that while the Confederates "may mean mischief they mean also to exaggerate it in order
to hurry us into a war with England."[26]

With adequate secret-service funds available, Dudley now made Liverpool a center of activity. Word of liberal government spending evidently
reached John Bright, for he wrote to Dudley to suggest that Washington
finance ocean passage for 50,000 Lancashire men and so make labor
scarcer and dearer for their employees.[27]

Since the two consuls evidently had things well in hand, Aspinwall
and Forbes went to the Continent. And at this time Welles was getting
cold feet about using Navy money for secret-service work abroad. He
politely suggested that Forbes and Aspinwall confine themselves to the
State Department which had special funds for that purpose.[28]

Forbes traveled up the Rhine by steamer and then stopped in Amsterdam, Brussels, and Paris on his way back to London. When he rejoined
Aspinwall they agreed that the time was not ripe yet to try to dispose
of any more 5–20 bonds. The market was not ready for them and would
not be until a series of Northern victories convinced Europeans that
the South could never win.[29] May was particularly inopportune for

this because news of Lee's smashing defeat of Hooker at Chancellorsville had arrived in London.

During Forbes' final days in England he thought up a grandiose scheme
for punishing Europe for its misdeeds:

> One project which we thought of at this time might have
> turned into great results if the Mexicans had had any Minister
> or recognized agent in London. They were at open war with
> France, and it occurred to us that if they would do towards
> France exactly what the rebel cruisers were doing against us,
> we should bring the European powers to a realizing sense of
> their misdeeds towards us. We discussed the question and
> thought of lending to Mexico a few thousand dollars out of our
> resources to enable them to fit out cruisers in English ports to
> go into the Channel and destroy French ships and to return to
> British ports to coal and recruit and get ready for other depreda-
> tions; in fact repeating what was being done in British neutral
> ports against the United States. If some morning a Mexican
> cruiser had put into Plymouth after destroying a lot of French
> ships, the replies of the British Foreign Secretary to a powerful,
> warlike nation like France would have been very different from
> what they were saying to us, hampered as we were with our in-
> ternal war; and, if they had treated France as they did us, war
> would have been the consequence in about twenty-four hours.
> But there was no Mexican Minister or agent, and we could do
> nothing.[30]

The two men sailed for home on the *Great Eastern* at the end of June
and arrived in New York on July 12 just as the draft riots were breaking
out there. Forbes had three trunks containing $6,000,000 in unused
bonds which he had to take to the Brevoort Hotel through streets that
were already dangerous. He was fortunate in obtaining the services of
an Irish cab driver, a former soldier who had met him during a visit to
his regiment at Port Royal.

Forbes—and the bonds—remained in the city until the street fighting
quieted down at the end of the week. Then he went to Washington to
make his report and return the bonds.[31] The expedition had cost amazingly little, and although the mission could hardly be called a success, it
did accomplish certain things. Chief among them was bolstering up secret-service activities in England. Forbes urged Seward to supply the
two consuls with enough money to make their espionage efforts truly
effective. Many of the future developments in preventing more Con-

federate shipbuilding in British yards came from the Forbes-Aspinwall visit which told the State Department what was going on and what to watch out for. The mission was also helpful in keeping peace between England and America, although international tensions were to build up almost to the breaking point in September.

Chapter 31

MR. ADAMS THREATENS WAR

Bigelow informed Seward on June 12 that a telegraph operator (whom he was paying for information) had told him that nearly 175,000 soldiers were suddenly being mobilized in France. He was under the misapprehension that they were intended for use against Germany, but he soon realized that they had been called up because things were going badly in Mexico.[1] Benito Juárez, whom the French Emperor had despised as a powerless peasant, was beginning to show unexpected strength. Greater force was going to be needed to bring Mexico under control, and Napoleon III began to realize that he must have a personal representative in that rebellious country. He needed a man of high rank and impressive stature; perhaps such a leader could be found in the courts of Europe.

Even though the South had lost Stonewall Jackson at Chancellorsville, Lee's decisive victory over Hooker enhanced the Confederacy in the eyes of the world. And when Lee started to move toward Maryland and Pennsylvania, it was evident to every military observer in Europe that this might be a successful operation against an important area of the North. As Lee drove on, there was much talk about Baltimore and Washington being taken; the Lincoln government might even be driven from the nation's capital.

In June events seemed to be favoring the Confederates. On the 22nd, when the case of the *Alexandra* came up for trial, the court ruled against Her Majesty's Government. The verdict surprised everyone in the British bar and angered the American Legation. Since the courts were adjourning for the summer, any appeal would have to wait until they reopened in the autumn. Meanwhile, Confederates and their sympathizers could be happy that this important decision had favored them.[2]

Undoubtedly tied in with the expected victory of Lee's northward marching army was a carefully planned move in Parliament. If the Southern forces were strong enough to conquer the Northern army on its own ground, recognition of the Richmond government would ride in on a wave of enthusiasm. Chosen to guide this motion through the House of Commons was John Arthur Roebuck, who was so diminutive in stature that he had been caricatured in *Punch* as "Don Roebucco, the smallest man in the House." He was vehement in speech and bold in whatever he undertook. In 1862 he had made himself unpopular with the working class because he declared that its men were spendthrifts and wife-beaters. Henry Adams said that the fiery little statesman was "regarded by all parties . . . as rather more than three-quarters mad."[3] Perhaps the fact that Roebuck, who was born in India, had been educated in Canada, gave him more than an ordinary interest in American affairs.

Late in June, Slidell and then Roebuck and William S. Lindsay had interviews with Napoleon III, who led them to believe that France was ready to take positive steps to urge England to acknowledge the Confederacy. Encouraged by this, and with Mason and Slidell pressing him on, Roebuck got up in the House of Commons on June 30 to make a motion that the Queen "enter into negotiations with the great powers of Europe for the purpose of obtaining their cooperation in the recognition of the independence of the Confederate States of America."

A long, wordy debate followed during which Roebuck's motion got little support. Gladstone, amazingly enough, was opposed to it. Even Palmerston helped delay matters. And delay was welcomed because everyone wanted to see how Lee's invasion of Pennsylvania would turn out.[4]

On July 13, before it was known whether Lee had succeeded or not, Roebuck "very reluctantly" withdrew his motion.[5] Three days later, London learned that Lee had met with defeat at Gettysburg. Following this, came word that Vicksburg and the Port Hudson had been surrendered. With the loss of the last two, the entire Mississippi River was in Union hands.

Confederate bonds fell in value, and Confederate prestige also dropped. From now on it was going to be difficult for any European to understand why the Confederacy should continue to fight.

J. B. Jones, writing about Richmond reaction in his diary, shows that Southerners were exceedingly gloomy during the rainy month of July.

All kinds of rumors were springing up. One was that Texas had put itself under the protection of France. The Confederate states beyond the Mississippi were now isolated, and it was not inconceivable that Texas might make such a move. The rumor, however, turned out to be false.[6]

On July 19 Seward wrote a long letter to Adams summarizing the North's strength after the victories at Gettysburg, Vicksburg, and Port Hudson:

> Our naval force is steadily and rapidly increasing. The Navy has already in actual service 54,000 men. New, better, and more effective steamships, ironclads, as well as others, are coming from the docks; and we do not distrust our ability to defend ourselves in our harbors and on the high seas, even if we must unhappily be precipitated through injustice in Europe into a foreign war. The fall of Vicksburg releases a large naval force for effective service, while the free navigation of the Mississippi, now immediately expected, will restore to us our accustomed facilities for foreign conflict. The same great event relieves the army of General Grant, which numbers 100,000 men, from the labors and fatigues of a siege and gives us movable columns for uncompleted purposes of the war. . . . The army . . . is still strong and effective. It will now be re-enforced, easily and cheerfully, by the people with an addition of 300,000.[7]

Since Federal armed forces were so powerful, Seward thought they could be used as a threat to make Europe behave. If England found it difficult to put a stop to Confederate shipbuilding under her Foreign Enlistment Act, she should "amend the existing statute." And if she was unwilling to change the law, then he felt that "the United States must bring into employment such private armed forces as the mercantile marine shall afford."[8] Seward was reluctant to give up the idea of using letters of marque although nearly everyone else was convinced that Union privateers were impractical. And the Forbes-Aspinwall mission had promised the British that they would not be used.

The British had good reason to be worried about privateers. Correspondence in the Foreign Office shows that they had heard that even if the United States did not issue letters of marque, Japan might do so, in which case American ships could go there to be commissioned to operate under her flag. Since there were 46 British vessels of various kinds in Japanese waters at this time, Her Majesty's Government was naturally concerned about their safety.

Dudley was keeping a sharp watch on the Laird yards in Birkenhead and was fully aware of what was happening when the first of the two ironclad rams was launched there on July 4. Three days later he had his evidence ready. Among the men who provided affidavits were Clarence Yonge and George Chapman.[9] Yonge was to be a detriment to the Federal case, for he had the kind of background that would antagonize the august gentlemen who represented British law. Nevertheless, he had served on the *Alabama* and knew a great deal about Confederate shipbuilding activities. But the men of law seldom believed him even when he spoke the truth.

That the two rams could be exceedingly dangerous was fully realized by everyone. Bulloch had told Richmond that they could be used to destroy the Union blockading fleet at Wilmington, then ascend the Potomac to make Washington untenable, after which they could attack Philadelphia and go on to bombard the important navy yard at Portsmouth, New Hampshire. He also thought that even though they were a bit large for operating in the Mississippi River, they might, with smaller vessels to help them turn, drive the Yankees out of New Orleans and then go upstream to force the Union fleet to abandon Vicksburg and Port Hudson.[10]

Seward had the same thought, and his notions of what the seemingly invincible Laird rams might do curiously parallel Bulloch's plans for them. He wrote to Adams that "the new vessels which the Lairds are preparing must . . . be expected to enter Portland, Boston, New York or . . . attempt to break the blockade at Charleston or ascend the Mississippi to New Orleans."[11]

This gives an idea of the importance of the two ironclads which Dudley somehow had to prevent from sailing. The next few weeks were to bring the controversy over them to a point where the United States and England would again be close to war.

Adams sent Dudley's evidence about the rams to Russell, but it was an awkward time for him to receive it. The British Government had lost the first round in the *Alexandra* case, and Bulloch had been clever enough to transfer the ownership of the Laird rams to Bravay in France. Price Edwards, the Collector of Customs at Liverpool, had already gone on record as saying that the rams were not intended for the Confederates but for a French firm which had contracted for them.[12]

But when things were at their very blackest for Adams and Dudley, the situation suddenly changed. Bravay announced that he was acting as an agent for Egypt which he now said was the real owner of the rams. When the Foreign Office asked the British consul at Cairo to investigate this, he reported that it was not true.[13] Russell then telegraphed the British Ambassador in Paris on August 22 to find out whether the ironclads were intended for the French Government. When he learned that they were not, he requested information about the background of the Bravay brothers. This took time. Meanwhile, Dudley learned that the first ram might soon go out on a trial run.[14] Everyone involved remembered how the *Alabama* had escaped during such a test. Dudley filed protest after protest with Price Edwards, but the Collector of Customs, as usual, did nothing.[15]

To add to the tension, the much-dreaded *Florida* arrived in British waters. Her machinery and her captain's health were in such poor condition that John Newland Maffitt wanted to be relieved of command. He burned two Yankee ships as he approached the coast, secretly put a messenger to Slidell ashore in Ireland, and then entered the harbor at Brest on August 23. Word of his arrival there was immediately telegraphed to England and made public.[16]

Also publicized in Europe at this time were the amazing exploits of a young Confederate naval officer, Lieutenant Charles W. Read, who had persuaded Maffitt to let him take a small captured brig and run along the New England coast to terrorize American shipping. Read had transferred himself and his crew from ship to ship as he captured them, so it had been impossible for the Union Navy to track him down. He had finally come to grief in Portland, Maine, when he entered the harbor, seized a revenue cutter, and was then overtaken by several steamers during a dead calm when there was no wind for his sails. The British press applauded him for his daring and romantic courage, but the Legation people thought that what he had done was simply an extension of the English-built *Florida's* attacks on American commerce.[17]

When Adams returned from Scotland on September 3, he had to deal quickly with the problem of the Laird rams. On hand was a long letter from Seward written on July 30 in which the Secretary of State said "we are drifting . . . towards a war with Great Britain." The letter went on to marshal a case against England and said that if the two countries became enemies the responsibility would rest on the British.[18]

Knowing that Seward would back him up convinced Adams that the time had come to take a strong stand against England's lackadaisical attitude about letting the Confederates build ships and buy arms in their

country. Letters written by him and Russell during the first few days of
September show the development of a possible international crisis:

> September 1. *Russell to the Home Office:* "So much suspicion
> attaches to the ironclad vessels at Birkenhead that if sufficient
> evidence can be obtained to lead to the belief that they are
> intended for the Confederate States of America . . . the ves-
> sels ought to be detained until further examination can be
> made."[19]
>
> September 1. *Russell to Adams:* "H.M. Gov't are advised that
> the information contained in the depositions is in a great
> measure mere hearsay evidence and generally it is not such
> as to show the intent or purpose necessary to make the build-
> ing or fitting out of these vessels illegal under the Foreign
> Enlistment Act. . . . Her Majesty's Government are ad-
> vised that they cannot interfere in any way."[20]
>
> September 3. *Russell to Palmerston:* "The conduct of the gen-
> tlemen who have contracted for the two ironclads at Birken-
> head is so very suspicious that I thought it necessary to direct
> that they should be detained. The Solicitor General has been
> consulted and concurs in the measure as one of policy though
> not of strict law. We shall thus test the law, and if we have to
> pay damages, we have satisfied the opinions which prevails
> here as well as in America that that kind of neutral hostility
> should not be allowed to go on without some attempt to stop
> it."[21]
>
> September 3. *Adams to Russell:* "I feel it is my painful duty to
> make known to your lordship . . . the grave nature of the
> situation in which both countries must be placed in the event
> of an act of aggression against the . . . United States by
> either of these formidable vessels [the Laird rams]."[22]
>
> September 4. *Russell to Adams:* "The matter is under the serv-
> ices and anxious consideration of Her Majesty's Govern-
> ment."[23]
>
> September 4. *Adams to Russell:* "Begging your Lordship's per-
> mission to record . . . this last solemn protest against the
> commission of such an act of hostility against a friendly na-
> tion. . . ."[24]

Adams, of course, had no way of knowing that on September 3 Russell
had notified the Lords Commissioners of the Treasury to direct the Customs authorities at Liverpool to stop the Laird rams "as soon as there was
reason to believe that they were actually about to put to sea." And Rus-

sell's letter of September 4 (quoted above) did not reach Adams until late on September 5. Since he was uninformed about Russell's intentions, Adams wrote to him early in the day on September 5, using a phrase that has echoed down the years: "It would be superfluous in me to point out to your Lordship that this is war."

Fortunately for the peace of the world, this threatening message reached Russell when he knew that he had already removed Adams' reasons for writing it. The very practical British Secretary of Foreign Affairs had found a way out of the difficulty. His solution would be expensive, but it was worth the cost. On September 14 he wrote to the Duke of Somerset, First Lord of the Admiralty:

> It is of the utmost importance and urgency that the ironclads building at Birkenhead should not go to America to break the blockade. They belong to Monsieur Bravay of Paris. If you will offer to buy them on the part of the Admiralty you will get money's worth if he accepts your offer; and if he does not, it will be presumptive proof that they are already bought by the Confederates.[25]

This letter shows that Russell was still laboring under the misapprehension that the rams might really belong to Bravay. The Bravay name had been given to the government by the Lairds on September 4. The builders still wanted to send the first ship on a trial run and may even have believed that the transfer of title to Bravay was legitimate. They said nothing, however, about their dealings with Bulloch.

The whole episode shows that British naval intelligence in the 1860s was still in a primitive state. That the Admiralty should have known so little about what was going on in the Laird yards is surprising because its big ironclad *Agincourt* was under construction there, and its representatives were regular visitors.[26]

The Admiralty sent a naval officer to Paris to try to purchase the rams, but the Bravay brothers refused to consider an offer until the ironclads were completed and safely delivered to a French port. This was so far in the future that the officer broke off negotiations. The moment he left, one of the Bravays rushed to Slidell to tell him that the British Admiralty wanted to buy the rams.[27]

When questioned further, the Bravays still insisted that the rams were to go to Egypt, and after it was proved that this could not be true, they mentioned Turkey, Italy, Austria, and Denmark as possible customers.

Henry Wilding, Dudley's British-born vice-consul, had an interesting encounter with Price Edwards on September 14 when he gave him a letter from his superior. This said that the more nearly completed Laird ram had been taking on coal during the night and would go out that day "on a pretended trial trip" from which she would never return. Dudley, who did not yet know what steps the British Government was taking, requested Edwards to stop her.

The Collector asked Wilding: "Do you believe what is stated in this letter?" Wilding said that he did.

"She will never reach the Confederates," Edwards told him.

Wilding said he was glad to hear that. But if she did, he warned the Collector, "the consequences would be fearful," not because the United States was threatening England but because people would then be convinced that England would do anything she could to harm the United States.

Edwards terminated the brief interview by saying again that the Laird rams would never reach the Confederates. "They are for a totally different destination," he added mysteriously.[28]

By this time, the British Government was convinced that the rams were intended for the Confederates even though final and positive proof was still lacking. The two ironclads were seized on October 9 while investigations were still under way.

The Illustrated London News published a full-page engraving of the two ships on November 28. It showed them lying in the Mersey in unfinished condition with the H.M.S. *Majestic* moored between them. They had been given the names *El Tousson* and *El Mounassir* in order to make the story of their Egyptian ownership seem more credible.

The popular weekly paper said forthrightly that it was generally believed that the rams were intended for the Confederates. But they were of no use to anyone while they remained in the river accumulating rust. Bulloch had given up all hope for them and had been spending most of his time in France where the chances of having ships built seemed better than in England.[29]

Chapter 32

THE CONFEDERATES ORDER SHIPS IN FRANCE

Although the French Proclamation of Neutrality was stricter than the British, Slidell and Bulloch knew perfectly well that what mattered was not the law but the Emperor's wishes. And Napoleon III had practically invited the Confederates to use French shipyards.[1]

At first Bulloch had been a bit hesitant about doing so because he had so much money tied up in construction in England. But as early as February 3, 1863, he had to tell Mallory that he thought the British would prevent ironclads from leaving because it was obvious that they were designed to be fighting ships. In the same letter he suggested that naval vessels be built in France.[2]

Emile Erlanger, who was well thought of by Confederates while his European cotton loan was being negotiated, had a friend named M. L. Arman, a shipbuilder with yards at Bordeaux. Slidell, who had been advocating the building of ships in France for some time, asked Arman to go to England in March to see Bulloch.[3]

Arman, whose yards had built ironclads for the French Navy, was an influential industrialist. He was deputy for the Gironde in the Corps Legislatif, and he had access to the Emperor. In fact he had already been in touch with him to make sure that the project would meet with royal approval. As a cover story, it was to be said that the ships were to be used in trade between San Francisco and the Orient.

Richmond was delighted with the *Alabama* and the *Florida* and wanted more ships like them. While negotiations to build them were under way with the French, the Erlanger bonds came on the market, and the initial demand for them was so great that it seemed as though it would be easy to raise large sums of money for the Confederacy.

Bulloch went to Bordeaux, where he was impressed by the size and efficiency of Arman's establishment. He placed an order for four wooden corvettes to be delivered complete with sails, gear, and 12 or 14 rifled cannon mounted in place on each. This was far different from England where British law required the ships to leave the country without arms. And the French were so open in their dealings that Arman applied to the Minister of Marine for permission to go ahead and promptly got it.

Bulloch, of course, was fully aware of the fact that the French Emperor was not permitting such a transaction out of the goodness of his heart. Since Napoleon III was interested in Mexico, it was to his advantage to keep the United States divided. He could afford to encourage the Confederates to build their navy in France—or so it seemed in the spring of 1863 when the South was winning all the victories and Gettysburg was still only an obscure country town.

Once the order was placed, Arman found that his yard was too busy with work to complete all four of the corvettes in ten months, so he subcontracted two of them to M. J. Voruz at Nantes.

On May 6 Mallory wrote to Bulloch that the Confederate Congress had appropriated £2,000,000 for building ironclads in France. And they had to be shallow enough in draft to go up the Mississippi River.

Since the new Confederate financial agent, Colin McRae, had just arrived in Europe, Bulloch consulted him about getting the necessary funds. Because no money was in sight except the cash received from the Erlanger loan—and that was dwindling rapidly—it was decided to go ahead with the construction of only two armored ships, the contract for which was placed with Arman on July 16.

Mallory was so eager to obtain ironclads that he wrote again to Bulloch suggesting that he offer to buy some completed ones from the French Navy. Bulloch had the good sense to realize that this was impossible and said so in carefully phrased diplomatic language. But work on all his six French ships was going ahead nicely, and it looked as though the Confederacy would have them early in 1864.[4]

John Bigelow's life as the American consul in Paris had been relatively quiet. He had spent some time writing a book for Hachette entitled "Les États-Unis D'Amérique en 1863. Since then he had kept up his contacts with French journalists, but there was so little to do that he thought of resigning and wrote to Seward in May asking to be relieved of his duties, saying that he thought he "could render more service in a private than in a public capacity." Seward, of course, refused to let him leave. Bigelow toured Switzerland and the French Alps in July and after returning to Paris was called upon by Henry Ward Beecher. The popular Brooklyn minister was in Europe for a holiday, but he was often asked to address public meetings in behalf of the Northern cause. The observant consul said of his celebrated visitor: "He is conscientious and means to do right, but it is evident that his facility of expression has been a temptation to him to speak and write before he has fully reflected." This was a weakness of the Beecher family, a weakness of which sister Harriet was equally guilty.

When Sanford came to Paris in August, the diplomat from Brussels, who seemed to relish participating in secret-service activities, told Bigelow that Belgian newspapers (which were beyond the reach of the French Emperor's tight censorship) were printing stories about Confederate ships being built in France. Bigelow listened and decided that the would-be spy master was trying to beat Dayton "on his own ground and unseat him as Minister and get into his place."

A week after the *Florida* arrived in Brest on August 23, a French shipping operator who had had his chartered vessel diverted from her course along the coast of Brazil when Maffitt ordered her captain to take prisoners into Pernambuco, came to the Legation with a plan to detain the Confederate raider by bringing a suit for damages. He wanted money for legal expenses and thought that the Americans might be willing to finance him.

Bigelow undertook the long and wearisome train journey to Brest in order to investigate the situation. He went out in a sailboat to get a close look at the famous Confederate ship as she lay at anchor in the harbor. He examined her with great curiosity and saw Maffitt himself as he stood talking to several French boatmen who apparently had some dealings with the cruiser. Bigelow thought that "the Captain looked pale and haggard, the effect probably of yellow fever."[5]

After Bigelow returned to Paris, the idea of backing the Frenchman's suit was discarded as impractical. But this brief introduction to espionage and international intrigue was only a beginning for him. The restless consul soon found himself deeply involved in a major operation.

On September 10 a stranger, a "Frenchman of the Gascon type, small of stature, with glittering black eyes, and thick, coarse, jet-black hair which had appropriated to itself most of his forehead," came to his office.[6]

The stranger, whom Bigelow referred to only as Mr. X, began by asking if he knew that the Confederates were building warships in

France. The consul said he had heard such rumors, but they seemed to be without foundation. The visitor then began to give the American consul convincing details about the ships under construction in Bordeaux and Nantes. When Bigelow said that they could not be built without government approval, his visitor told him that official permission had been given and that he could prove it.

Bigelow said: "What you state is of grave importance to my government if it can be substantiated. What kind of proof can you furnish?"

"Original documents." Mr. X then produced some papers which showed that he was telling the truth. He offered to leave the documents with Bigelow until Saturday when he would bring more.

Bigelow then asked how much he wanted for this information and was told 20,000 francs, a rather large sum for those days. After some haggling, he got his mysterious visitor down to 15,000 francs. Then, while waiting for Mr. X to return on Saturday, he consulted Dayton in order to make sure that the United States Government would approve the deal and reimburse him for the money he had to advance out of his own pocket.[7] Bigelow knew that he was at last on the trail of something important. He had good reason to be glad he had improved his knowledge of French, for Mr. X spoke only that language, and Dayton had sent him to Bigelow because he could not understand him. The man turned out to be a confidential clerk in Voruz's office.[8]

On Saturday, Mr. X returned and proceeded to hand Bigelow one remarkable document after another. They were the key to Confederate shipbuilding in France. Among them were:

1. A note (in Arman's handwriting) addressed to Voruz which acknowledged a check from Bulloch for 720,000 francs as first payment on two corvettes. It also revealed the fact that Erlanger was getting a commission on the deal. This document alone, Bigelow said, was worth the price asked for the entire lot.
2. Erlanger's guarantee of the first two of five payments. He was to retain a commission out of these.
3. A letter from Bulloch to Voruz about getting cannon for the ships.
4. Arman's request to the French Minister of Marine for permission to build and arm the four corvettes together with a favorable reply. With these was Slidell's approval of the contract.

5. Information about the cost of the ships and their armaments
as well as reports on the progress of their construction.[9]

After consulting further with Dayton and sending copies of the documents to Seward, Bigelow decided to seek French legal advice. He called
on Antoine Berryer, who was known to be opposed to the Emperor.
After some discussion, Bigelow asked the noted lawyer to prepare a
lengthy brief summarizing the whole affair. While this was in work,
Bigelow continued to get more useful data from Mr. X. Everything was
going very well now for the Union men stationed in Europe. The Laird
rams had been stopped in England, and so much had been learned about
Bulloch's plans that it seemed unlikely that he would ever be allowed
to get his ships out of France.

Richmond was evidently aware that something was going wrong—in
England at least—for Benjamin wrote to Mason on August 4 that he
should consider his mission at an end and withdraw from London.[10]
Despite Richmond's uneasiness, however, it is evident that the officials
there did not really know how matters stood abroad. On September 29,
Mallory sent a letter to Captain Samuel Barron, then on his way to
Liverpool, which shows that the Confederate Government was still entertaining great hopes for the ironclads under construction in Europe.
It said: "The plan for manning the ships off Wilmington is determined
upon, and the men will be kept in readiness there. A sufficient number
of reliable men to bring the vessels over must be engaged. . . . The
blockade of Wilmington may thus be raised, and then, with full crews,
circumstances will determine where and how to strike next."[11]

It was a nicely thought-out plan. Circumstances, however, were being
determined in Europe and not in America. On October 20, Bulloch
wrote to Mallory that he hoped Napoleon III would have his government make an official demand to England to turn the Laird rams over
to Bravay in Paris. He said nothing about the ships being built in
France.[12] But information regarding the protests Dayton had made to
the French Government soon reached Slidell. He did not report to Richmond until he was able to find out just what had happened. Then, on
November 19, he gave Benjamin a complete account of the way Voruz's
confidential correspondence had been sold to Bigelow.[13]

Bulloch wrote to Mallory on November 25 to explain his need for
funds, listing the ships under construction in France among others. The
next day he wrote again, saying that everything was progressing satisfactorily in Bordeaux and Nantes. In this letter he mentioned the fact

that United States officials knew about the vessels being built there. But he said: "I do not anticipate any interference until the ships are ready for sea, and hope from what I now learn that even then the vessels will be allowed to go away unarmed."[14] He went on to speak bitterly about the way United States agents in Europe were resorting to bribery. Despite his apparent optimism, Bulloch was candid enough to say that what really mattered would be the state of affairs at home when the ships were completed. He predicted that if the Confederate cause was doing well then "the local authorities will be instructed not to be too inquisitive, and the escape of the ships will be connived at. But if . . . the Federal cause prospers, the affairs of the Confederate ships will be turned over to the responsible Ministers of the Empire who will justify their claim to American gratitude by strict enforcement of the neutrality of France." He added that he would permit nothing to delay progress in constructing the ships, and when they were ready every effort would be made "to get them to sea in the manner least calculated to compromise the French authorities if they choose only to be judiciously blind."[15]

Right after Bulloch wrote this forthright statement of how matters stood in France, everything there suddenly changed. The Foreign Minister, Drouyn de Lhuys, told Arman and Voruz that they would not be permitted to proceed with their work on the Confederate ships unless they made a *bona fide* sale of them to some other government.

Satisfying as this first victory was to Bigelow, he was not content to let things rest. His French attorney, Berryer, had completed his brief. Since ordinary legal methods were too slow to prevent the Confederate ships from sailing if the Emperor should change his very changeable mind, some other way had to be found to make use of Berryer's able presentation of the case. Best of all would be to have his brief published, but, as Bigelow soon found out, having material printed that was hostile to the government was not easy. Meanwhile he financed the publication of a brochure by Henri Moreau that was a good summation of Franco-American relations during the war. Since Moreau, who was a friend of Berryer's and the editor of *La Revue Contemporaine*, was a well-respected writer, people would listen to what he had to say. In his brochure, Moreau reminded his readers that France and America were bound together by historical ties, surveyed slavery and the war, and covered other interesting but harmless political topics. Then, starting on page 129, he gave the people of France their first report of what was going on in Bordeaux and Nantes.[16] But it was a short account that simply brought the matter to public attention. Bigelow paid for printing 1650 copies of the pamphlet and circulated them "in all the best places with great care."[17]

It was going to take time to get Berryer's detailed coverage of the case published. Bigelow tried one method after another, only to find himself blocked by the French Government or met by polite silence.

Chapter 33
THE *ALABAMA* GOES TO THE FAR EAST

1863 was the *Alabama's* triumphal year. After sinking the *Hatteras* off the coast of Texas, Semmes headed for Jamaica to put his prisoners ashore. Then the Confederate raider sailed through the West Indies, capturing many Yankee vessels. The *Florida* was also cruising these waters. Both ships reached Fernando de Noronha, off the coast of Brazil, early in May but not in time to meet. On May 13 the *Alabama* encountered W. L. Maury's *Georgia* in Bahia, Brazil. The officers from the two commerce-raiders went ashore to see the city and visit the country around it.

After leaving Bahia both vessels sailed south along the coast of Brazil and then started across the Atlantic for Cape Town. Semmes nearly got the Confederacy into a war with England when he overtook one of Her Majesty's battleships at night and tried to stop her. Shots were exchanged, but the ships recognized each other for what they were before any damage was done.[1]

The *Alabama* reached South Africa first, arriving late in July. When the *Georgia* came in on August 16, it missed making contact with Semmes although he remained in the area for nearly two months. He and his ship got a great deal of attention in the local press. The *Alabama* and her personnel were sketched and photographed so often that their pictures were published in newspapers throughout the world.

Semmes had often said that he was compelled to burn Yankee ships at sea because he could not take them into foreign ports to dispose of them as prizes. When he captured the *Sea Bride* near Cape Town, he sold her to local merchants for £3500 in gold. They disguised her to look like a Dutch vessel so they could send her to another port.[2]

When the U.S.S. *Vanderbilt*, which was twice as big and much better armed than the *Alabama,* arrived in South African waters to search for Confederate ships, Semmes decided that it was advisable to proceed to the Far East. He would have to go alone because Maury was not well, and the *Georgia* was proving to be inefficient as a cruiser. While Semmes headed east, Maury started back to Europe.[3]

As early as January 26, some stray bit of information—or perhaps just a hunch—had made Gideon Welles send the U.S.S. *Wyoming* to the Far East in case Semmes decided to go there. Thus it was the possibility of the *Alabama's* being in the Orient that brought the *Wyoming* to this part of the world.[4] Robert Pruyn, the American Minister Resident in Japan, was glad to see the American gunboat enter Yokohama Harbor on May 11. Life was becoming more and more dangerous for foreigners as he found out two weeks later when the Legation building burned down. Pruyn preferred to believe that the fire was accidental although some people said it had been started deliberately.

By the end of the month things became so bad that a Japanese friend urged Pruyn to leave Yedo, because a murder had just been committed in the street near the burned-out Legation. The American Minister and his staff took a steamer to Yokohama where they would be protected by the guns of the *Wyoming.*[5]

The American steamer *Pembroke,* which was on her way from Yokohama to Shanghai, noticed that a Japanese-owned European-built ship kept working toward her during the evening of June 25 while she was anchored near the eastern entrance to the Straits of Shimonoseki. At 1:00 A.M. this strangely behaving vessel came near enough to fire a dozen shots at the American steamer. Another ship then came out of the darkness, but by this time the *Pembroke* had steam up and was able to get away.

During the next two weeks other foreign ships were shot at. When word of this reached Yokohama, the *Wyoming's* commander, David McDougal, ordered his gunboat to get under way at dawn on July 13. It took him three days to reach the Straits of Shimonoseki. The *Wyoming* ran in as soon as it was light and was met with fire from six shore batteries and three Japanese ships. A lively engagement took place in the narrow waters during which a number of shots struck the American gunboat, killing four men and wounding seven others. But she succeeded in sending two 11-inch shells into the boiler room of one of the Japanese ships, damaged the other two, and landed some effective shots on the shore batteries. The *Wyoming* then steamed out of the straits and returned to Yokohama. McDougal waited there for the U.S.S. *Jamestown* to arrive from Nagasaki.[6]

What happened in the Straits of Shimonoseki concerned every nation that wanted to trade with Japan. Two American ships would not be enough to make the kind of demonstration that was needed, and the United States, with her Navy tied up in a war at home, could not send more. It would take many months to gather an international fleet that would be powerful enough to open up the vital passageway.

Semmes left the Cape of Good Hope on September 24 and began crossing the wide expanse of the Indian Ocean bound for the Straits of Sunda between Java and Sumatra. Sea traffic was concentrated there because American ships trading with the Orient used this route. The *Alabama's* arrival in the Far East would be a surprise to them.

Semmes approached the Straits of Sunda late in October and stopped an English bark from which he learned that the *Wyoming* was nearby, undoubtedly searching for the Confederate raider. Since the *Alabama* was a fair match for the Union warship, Semmes decided to seek her out and give battle. He cruised around the strait for days but never found her. But he did meet several Yankee ships which he destroyed. It was so misty that the *Wyoming* might easily have missed seeing the flames or the tall columns of smoke rising from the burning vessels. Semmes allowed the prisoners from the captured ships to take their boats and row ashore.[7]

After more cruising around, the *Alabama* reached the island of Puolo Condore on December 2. Since it was supposed to be uninhabited, Semmes toyed with the idea of taking possession of it for the Confederate States of America in order to give the South an outpost in the East. But he found a small armed vessel, rigged like a junk, and flying French colors, anchored near the head of the harbor. France had occupied the island and had stationed some 60 or 70 soldiers there.

The French were cordial enough, so Semmes remained in the sheltered waters for some days to make essential repairs. His men amused themselves watching the monkeys on shore and catching huge lizards and 3-foot bats. It was a pleasant interlude which lasted until December 15 when the *Alabama* headed south and began her long return voyage. Since his ship needed mechanical work and new copper for her hull, Semmes went to Singapore, which was the nearest port equipped to do major repairs.[8]

When the *Alabama* entered Singapore Harbor on December 21,

Semmes was informed that the *Wyoming* had been ordered to leave there at the beginning of the month because her captain had forcibly tried to take a letter addressed to Semmes away from a native boatman.

The *Alabama* stayed long enough to get coal and give Semmes a chance to visit the picturesque city. He describes what he saw there:

> There are from 80,000 to 100,000 Chinese on Singapore Island, nearly all of them in the city; from 12,000 to 15,000 Malays, and about 1,500 Europeans. . . . The business is almost exclusively in the hands of the Chinese, who are also the artisans and laborers of the place. The streets are thronged with foot passengers and vehicles, among which are prominent the ox, or rather the buffalo cart, and the hacks for hire, of which latter there are 900 licensed. The canal is filled with country boats, of excellent model, and the warehouses are crammed with goods. Money seems to be abundant and things dear. They are just finishing a tasteful Gothic church with a tall spire, which is a notable landmark as you approach the town. . . . The moving multitude in the streets comprises every variety of the human race, every shade of color, and every variety of dress, among which are prominent the gay tartans and fancy jackets of the Mohammedan, Hindu, etc. Almost all the artisans and laborers were naked, except a cloth or a pair of short trousers tucked about the waist. The finest dressed part of the population was decidedly the jet blacks, with their white flowing mantles and spotless turbans.
>
> The upper class of Chinese merchants are exceedingly polite and seem intelligent. I visited the establishment of Whampoa & Co. Whampoa was about the middle size, stout, and with a large, well-developed head. I was told that his profits some years amounted to £40,000 or £50,000. He was sitting in a small, dingy, ill-lighted little office on the ground floor, and had before him a Chinese calculating machine, over the numerous small balls of which, strung on wires, he was running his hands for amusement, as a gambler will sometimes do with his checks. At the suggestion of the gentleman who was with me, I requested him to multiply four places of figures by three places—naming the figures—and the operation was done about as rapidly as I could write down the result.
>
> The workshops all front upon the streets, and these busy, half-naked creatures may be seen working away as industriously as so many beavers all day long, seeming never to tire of their

ceaseless toil. I saw but one female in the street, and she of the lower class, amid all this busy population.

A few miles beyond the town the whole island is a jungle, in which abounds the ferocious Bengal tiger. It is said that one man and a half per day is the average destruction of human life by these animals. Visited opium-preparation shop. It pays an enormous license.[9]

Some two score American ships were tied up or anchored in Singapore Harbor because they were afraid to venture out while the notorious Confederate raider was in the vicinity. Semmes remained at Singapore only three days and, except for the desertion of some of his crew, gave no reason for so short a stay in a port where he had expected to have his engines overhauled. But his sail-master, Henry William Allcot, told Dudley eight years later what had happened there. According to him, some 500 crewmen from the American ships confined to the harbor armed themselves and started out in small boats to seize the *Alabama*. This concerted attempt was stopped by the local authorities who threatened to use the guns in the shore batteries against the attackers.[10]

After leaving Singapore, the *Alabama* headed up the Strait of Malacca with heavy rain accompanying her for the entire run. But bad weather did not prevent Semmes from making several more captures. Destroying Yankee ships was his business, and with grim determination he did what he had to do. He reached the exit of the strait on the last day of 1863 and started crossing the Bay of Bengal, bound for India so he could get rid of prisoners by putting them ashore.[11]

Chapter 34

THE INTERNATIONAL CHESS GAME

Whatever faults Seward may have had—and he had many—he was passionately devoted to his work, and he learned a great deal from day-to-day experience. Like Lincoln, he grew up to fit his job.

He collected portraits of the leading men and women of the countries with which his department had dealings and kept the pictures on the walls of his office. When he showed them to visitors, he would say: "These are my tormentors." The people they portrayed, according to his nephew, were:

> Queen Victoria, the Emperor and Empress of the French, the King and Queen of Prussia, Queen Isabella of Spain, King Victor Emanuel of Italy, King Leopold of Belgium, the Emperor Alexander and Empress of Russia, Francis Joseph and the Empress of Austria, Pope Pius IX, Sultan Abdul-Aziz, Ismail Pacha of Egypt, King Charles of Sweden, King Christian of Denmark, the President of Switzerland, Dom Pedro of Brazil, King William of Holland, King Louis of Portugal, King Kamehameha of Hawaii, the Emperor of China, and the Tycoon of Japan, President Mitre of the Argentine Republic, Presidents Juarez of Mexico, Perez of Chili, Mosquera of Colombia, Mora of Costa Rica, Moreno of Ecuador, Geffrard of Hayti, Benson of Liberia, Martinez of Nicaragua, Lopez of Paraguay, San Roman of Peru, together with Earl Russell, M. Thouvenel, Drouyn de l'Huys, Rogier, Cavour, Ricasoli, Bulow, Bismarck, Gortschakoff, Ali Pacha, Calderon, Antonelli, Prince Kung, and other Ministers of Foreign Affairs.[1]

During the summer of 1863 the astute Secretary of State invited some of the members of the Diplomatic Corps to tour New York State.

Since Washington is so hot at that time of the year that the British Foreign Office pays its representatives stationed there the special salary rate for service in the tropics, the men were doubtless glad to go to upper New York. The War Department provided a private car for the distinguished guests so they could travel in style. And Seward was clever enough to let them decide where they wanted to go and what they wanted to see. They went to New York City, up the Hudson River to Albany, Schenectady, Utica, Rome, Syracuse, Cooperstown, and Auburn, where their host's residence was located. They got an enthusiastic public reception everywhere, and in Auburn were put up in the homes of Seward's friends and neighbors. Then they went on to Rochester, Buffalo, and Niagara Falls. As they traveled they had a chance to see the bountiful agriculture and industrial prosperity of the North. More than two years of major warfare had not impaired the ability of the United States to produce. This was something for foreign diplomats to consider. And Seward was a charming host who gained added respect in the eyes of his guests.

While they were in Utica they visited nearby Trenton Falls, which was then a great attraction. And there, on a picturesque ledge of rocks below the rushing waters, they were photographed. The miracle of the silver image preserves their faces and costumes. Among the figures are Seward, Lord Lyons, Mercier, and Baron de Stoeckl.

During the journey through New York State, Seward had a chance to spend some time with Lyons and converse with him freely. The American Secretary of State said one day that improving relations between England and America was important, and he had a suggestion to make. He told Lyons that the Prince of Wales' tour of the United States before the war had helped the two nations understand each other better and then proposed that the United States should make a similar gesture of good will to England. This, however, was not easy because the President could not leave the country in the midst of a war, and America had no princes. Would Lyons be kind enough to give the idea some thought?

The shrewd young diplomat instantly sensed what was in Seward's mind and wrote to Russell about the awkward problems involved:

> The only conjecture I can make is that he thinks of going to England himself. He may possibly want to be absent for some reason connected with the Presidential contest [of 1864]. . . . It is . . . generally considered to be an advantage to a candidate to be out of the country during the canvass. I cannot see

any good which his going to England could effect with regard
to public opinion. If he considered himself as returning the
Prince of Wales's visit, the absurdity of the notion would alone
prevent its being offensive. The majority of the Americans
would probably be by no means pleased if he met with a brilliant reception. He has besides, so much more vanity, personal
and national, than tact, that he seldom makes a favourable impression at first. When one comes really to know him one is surprised to find much to esteem and even to like in him. It is
however hardly worthwhile to say more on the subject, for it is
a mere conjecture of mine that he was thinking of going to
England when he spoke to me. It might however be of advantage for me to know whether you would wish to encourage the
idea.

Russell cheerfully agreed with his young Minister's appraisal of the
situation:

Upon considering Mr. Seward's hints to you of doing something here as an equivalent or a return for the Prince of
Wales's visit to the United States, I do not see my way to anything satisfactory. These visits of Great Personages seldom
have more than a transient effect; they form no real and solid
relation of friendship between nations, though if undertaken at
a fortunate moment, they serve to bring out and demonstrate a
friendship already existing.

The visit of the Prince of Wales was thus fortunately well
timed; but if Mr. Seward or any conspicuous statesman of the
United States were to visit this country now he would find us all
divided. The Government would show him every attention and
civility: the Anti-Slavery party would probably make great show
of sympathy by addresses and public receptions. But the party
who press for recognition of the South would hold aloof, and in
some unmistakable manner prove that there is a great deal of
sympathy with the South in this country.

In these circumstances I do not think that any such mark of
friendship as Mr. Seward suggests would be likely to produce
the good effect of which he is desirous.[2]

While Baron de Stoeckl, the Russian Minister, was traveling with
Seward in August he must have known that his country's fleet was then
on its way to the United States. In 1863, and for many years afterward,
Americans believed that this visit was a good-will gesture intended to
show the world that imperialist Russia was lending support to the liberal

government of the United States. The Russians let their hosts believe
that this was true—and there was a certain amount of truth in it.[3] The
Czar's government had consistently refused to deal with the Confederacy,
so much so, in fact, that Lucius Q. C. Lamar, whom the South had appointed to be its Commissioner to Russia, never filled his post.[4] And
Russia was certainly the only major power which had been at all friendly
to the United States. People in New York in September and in San
Francisco in October therefore apparently had every right to rejoice when
they saw the Czar's warships enter their harbors.

In New York, a grand reception was given to the visitors on October
1. It began with an elaborate parade down Broadway where Russian
and American flags were displayed. Tiffany and Company decorated the
front of their building with a huge Russian banner and strips of blue
bunting which ran from the roof to the sidewalk. The officers from the
fleet were driven in open carriages past cheering throngs of New Yorkers.

This celebration was followed on November 5 by a great Russian Ball
at the Academy of Music which was attended by leading society people.
It was an occasion for female finery which a *Herald* reporter described
as being worn by "ladies in silks and satins of pink, pearl, white blue,
of all the possible varieties following up the shade from indigo till it
melted into white; silks of green, crimson, purple, and yellow; silks
ornamented and silks plain. And silks were not all, for there were ladies
in velvet and ladies in lace, ladies in cloaks, in furs, in shawls, and in
hoods, ladies in head-dresses, and ladies with their glorious little heads
left alone with their own beautiful hair. Every lady had diamonds on."

The affair was such an important one that Harper's *Weekly* ran many
pages of illustrations by Winslow Homer to show the dancing ladies and
their gallant Russian partners. Then there was a feast prepared by Del-
monico in which 12,000 oysters, 1200 game birds, 250 turkeys, 400
chickens, 1000 pounds of tenderloin, and 3500 bottles of wine were
consumed. The Russian guests from the fleet, the reporter said, were
worn out by the expressions of friendship and affection extended to
them.

San Francisco, which was, of course, much smaller than the great
eastern metropolis, also did its best to entertain its visitors from Russia.
And the Czar's sailors showed their gratitude by helping to put out one
of the western city's frequent fires. The commander of the fleet helped
again when it was rumored that the *Alabama* had crossed the Pacific
and was going to attack the gold-rich city. Admiral Popov said that the
people of San Francisco could depend upon the Russian ships to defend

them if Semmes dared to enter the bay. His declaration, however, was unofficial, and he was later reprimanded for it by Stoeckl. Russian diplomacy required that the United States be treated as a single country without a separate North or South, and the Russian Navy had no right to meddle in the internal affairs of another nation.

In the spring, the two Russian fleets returned to their home waters. Their stay in America had been a great propaganda success which had made England and France revise their thinking about the United States. When the ships arrived in New York, Gideon Welles wrote in his diary on September 23: "The Russian fleet . . . are not to be confined in the Baltic by a northern winter. In sending them to this country at this time there is something significant. What will be its effect on France . . . we shall learn in due time. . . . God bless the Russians."

But all Americans were not completely misled about the real purpose of the Russian fleets coming to their shores. Harper's *Weekly,* which in its issue of October 17, had advocated an alliance with Russia because it was a great continental power like the United States and could someday be expected to rank with it because it would have "100,000,000 educated, intelligent people," came out a week later with a remarkably frank editorial: "England and France are the quasi enemies of this country and of Russia. England and France have recognized the belligerent rights of the rebels, and . . . Russia has not. . . . Americans understand that the sympathy of France in our Revolution was not from love of us but from hatred of England. They know, as Washington long ago told them, that romantic friendship between nations is not to be expected."[5]

Charles Sumner also refused to be deceived about the Russians' motives. But it was not until shortly after the beginning of the First World War that the true reasons for the Russian fleets' visit to America were revealed. Then Frank A. Golder, who had a good knowledge of the language, was permitted to examine the records of the Ministry of Marine and articles in the *Morskoi Sbornik* (naval collection) while making investigations in Russian archives for the Carnegie Institution of Washington. From what he found he was able to show that:

1. The Russian fleet was very weak; its ships were wooden ones primarily built for sail although equipped with auxiliary steam engines. And their guns were all smooth-bore.
2. In case of war with England and France, its fleet could not attack their powerful navies, but its ships, if properly dis-

posed, could prey upon their commerce and bombard colonies that were poorly defended.

3. If the fleet remained at home it would be blockaded.

4. The Poles had been restless for several years, and on January 15, 1863, a number of their leaders were jailed by Russian police. This led to insurrection and diplomatic intervention by England, France, and Austria. There was a good chance that war might result.

5. On July 26 the Atlantic fleet was ordered to sail for New York and stay there, if permitted. If war broke out, as then seemed likely, it could sally out to attack British and French commercial vessels. The Pacific fleet was instructed to go to an American port, and Admiral Popov chose San Francisco because he had been there and could be sure of a friendly reception. Some of the Russian warships were in such poor condition that they had to be left behind; others made the trip but were so badly outfitted that the crews suffered.

6. During the winter of 1863–64 the two fleets were in ice-free waters. And during that time, the war scare in Europe died down. In April the ships were called home.

Golder concluded by saying: "Russia had not in mind to help us but did render us distinct service; the United States was not conscious that it was contributing in any way to Russia's welfare and yet seems to have saved her from humiliation and perhaps war."[6]

In 1930, E. A. Adamov, a Russian scholar who was apparently unaware of the existence of Golder's pioneer work, had access to the documents his predecessor had seen and also to the archives made public after the Revolution of 1917. He published some of the evidence in full. He also showed that rumors about sealed instructions ordering the admirals of the fleets to come to the assistance of the United States if it was attacked by England and France were not true. Adamov felt that the squadrons had not been sent to America to save them from an enemy (a passive move) but "to put them in the most favorable position for the opening of warlike activities with the maximum of energy and productivity against England and France" (a potentially aggressive move).[7]

The Russian visit was one more nail in the coffin of the ailing Confederacy, for it ended the last chance of European intervention. And it was now practically impossible for the South to be recognized as an independent nation although its leaders never gave up hope or ceased to make active efforts to gain that status. The threat of a possible alliance between the United States and Russia even acted as a postwar deterrent to France when it was trying to keep its puppet Emperor Maximilian on the Mexican throne.

Pope Pius IX had written letters to the Catholic Archbishops of New York and New Orleans in which he expressed his concern over the sanguinary war in America and urged them to take every possible step to try to bring hostilities to a close.[8] His words to his representatives in the North and the South favored neither side, but when they were published, Richmond had Dudley Mann go to Rome to deliver a message from Davis which thanked the Pope for what he had said and assured him that the Confederacy devoutly wanted peace.[9]

Mann called on Cardinal Antonelli, the Papal Secretary of State, on November 11. Antonelli told him how greatly he admired the way the Confederacy had withstood the repeated attacks of the North and said that Jefferson Davis' name "would rank with those of the most illustrious statesmen of modern times."[10] Mann informed him that the Lincoln Administration could never have carried on the war for so long if it had not been for the 100,000 Catholic Irishmen brought across the ocean to be enlisted in the Union Army.[11]

Antonelli promised to arrange an audience for him with the Pope.

When this took place two days later, Mann presented the letter from Davis, which had to be translated by the Confederate Commissioner's secretary. While it was being read, the Pope was obviously affected. He asked whether Davis and Mann were Catholics and was told that they were not. Then he said that the Lincoln Administration had created "an impression abroad that they were fighting for the abolition of slavery." Would it not be wise for the Confederacy "to consent to gradual emancipation?"[12]

The slavery issue, which had dogged the Confederate Commissioners in every court in Europe, was now being held against them in the Vatican. Mann tried to explain that the central government of the Confederacy had no control over the matter and that only the individual states could decide it. He also gave His Holiness some information about the benefits of slavery. Freedom would convert "the well-cared-for civilized Negro into a semibarbarian." Slaves captured by the enemy were in worse condition than when they had been on the plantation, and they often wanted "to return to their old homes."

Mann went on to talk about the poor Irish and German Catholic recruits who were tempted to enlist in the Union Army by the offer of high bounties and were then "invariably placed in the most exposed

points of danger in the battlefield" where they were slaughtered. Without these foreign recruits, Mann said, "the North would most likely
have broken down months ago in the absurd attempt to overpower the
South."

According to Mann, the Pope readily believed everything he told
him, even that Northern ministers were openly advocating "greek fire
for the families and cities of the rebels and hell fire for their chiefs."

At the end of the interview, the Pope promised to write a letter to
President Davis which the Confederacy could publish. Mann retired
from the audience chamber and sent an exultant report to Benjamin:

> Thus terminated one among the most remarkable conferences
> that ever a foreign representative had with a potentate of the
> earth. And such a potentate! A potentate who wields the con-
> sciences of 175,000,000 of the civilized race, and who is adored
> by that immense number as the vice regent of Almighty God in
> this sublunary sphere.
>
> How strikingly majestic the conduct of the government of
> the Pontifical States in its bearing toward me when contrasted
> with the sneaking subterfuges to which some of the govern-
> ments of western Europe have had recourse in order to evade
> intercourse with our Commissioners. Here I was openly re-
> ceived by appointment at court in accordance with established
> usages and customs and treated from beginning to end with a
> consideration which might be envied by the envoy of the oldest
> member of the family of nations. The audience was of forty
> minutes duration, an unusually long one.[13]

The Pope wrote his promised letter to Davis on December 3, but it
was disappointingly vague, so vague in fact that it merely deplored war
and said that His Holiness would pray for peace to be restored "upon
all the people of America."[14] Yet the befuddled Commissioner wrote to
Benjamin that because it was addressed "to the Illustrious and Honorable
Jefferson Davis, President of the Confederate States of America," that
nation was "acknowledged, by as high an authority as this world contains, to be an independent power of the earth."

The Commissioner who had long been grasping frantically at straws
now thought he had obtained a great prize. "I congratulate you," he told
Benjamin hysterically, "I congratulate the President, I congratulate his
Cabinet, I congratulate all my true-hearted countrymen and country-
women upon this benign event."[15]

He wrote again from London a few weeks later to say that "in all intelligent British circles our recognition by the sovereign Pontiff is considered as formal and complete."[16] But Britain, no matter how intelligent, was not impressed by the Pope's generalized hopes for peace. Nor was Catholic France.

And the realistic Benjamin's reply would have deflated any self-esteem less puncture-proof than Mann's. The fact that the Pope had addressed his letter to Davis as President of the Confederate States of America was, he said, only "a formula of politeness to his correspondent, not a political recognition of a fact."[17]

Chapter 35

THE SOUTH BREAKS WITH ENGLAND

By the autumn of 1863, when the results of Gettysburg, Vicksburg, and Port Hudson were known, it should have been evident that the South could not win. This seems clear now, but it was not clear then. So long as Confederate armies were active in the field it was hard to believe that the war was already lost. Too much hope was placed on General Lee's ability to win battles when the odds were against him. No one could know then, of course, that Gettysburg was the last major offensive the Army of Northern Virginia was ever to make. It still had to do much fighting, but except for one brief and disastrous offensive at Fort Stedman a few days before it had to surrender, Lee's superb fighting machine was now reduced to purely defensive action. And very few people knew that the general's health was bad. Even Lee himself did not realize how poor it was. He had had a heart attack just before Chancellorsville, but medicine was still so primitive then that his doctors were unable to diagnose his malady.

Jefferson Davis, because of his background as a West Point graduate and professional Army officer, was partly to blame for the Confederacy's concentration on land warfare. While the armies struggled, and the wounded poured into the cities, few Southerners could see beyond what was happening around them. The Federal blockade of Confederate ports was becoming tighter, and the possibility of getting Confederate ships in Europe was rapidly dwindling. But the South's eyes were fastened on its armies. When Bragg won a victory at Chickamauga in September, Confederate hopes rose again. The fact that this was offset by a Union victory at Chattanooga in November was largely ignored. And most Southerners underrated Western generals like Grant, Sherman, and Sheridan. All three, however, helped to win the victory at Chattanooga.

In his message to the Confederate Congress of December 7, 1863, Jefferson Davis said more about the Post Office than he did about the Navy. He gave many pages to Foreign Affairs, but what he had to say was not encouraging. After reviewing them from the beginning of the war, he launched into a long complaint against England. He accused Russell of favoring the North, blamed him for not trying to break the Union blockade, and said that he had recalled Mason from England when it became "apparent by the declarations of the British Ministers in the debates of the British Parliament in July that Her Majesty's Government was determined to persist indefinitely in a course of policy which under professions of neutrality had become subservient to the designs of our enemy."[1]

Davis couched in abstract terms what many Southerners were saying more forthrightly. Nor was the Confederacy's unfavorable opinion of England limited to private conversation; it was openly expressed in Congress and in newspaper editorials. England's refusal to grant recognition and her seizure of Confederate ships had made her name anathema in the South.[2] She was no better liked, of course, in the North.

The Confederacy showed its animosity toward England not only in words but also in deeds. There was much resentment against British consuls because they operated in the South under old exequaturs issued by the United States Government, and England had made no effort to have this situation changed. When the consuls tried to keep men of dubious British origin out of military service, resentment against them increased. And Lord Lyons' dismissal of the British consul at Mobile for permitting specie owed to English bondholders to be shipped on one of Her Majesty's men-of-war angered Southerners because they felt that Britain's Minister to the Northern government had been exercising unwarranted power on Confederate territory. There were other such incidents, all tending to make the consuls unpopular in the South.[3]

As the need for soldiers for the Confederacy's depleted armies became more urgent, the feeling against the British officials grew worse. In July the consul in Savannah wrote to the governor of Georgia that he was afraid that British subjects in the Confederate Army who were captured in battle might "be treated as rebels and traitors and not as prisoners of war." This was an unfortunate choice of words. The exchange of letters that followed made the consul even more disliked, especially when the governor published the correspondence. More trouble with other consuls was brought to light, and newspapers throughout the South became bitter. Soon they were calling for the expulsion of all British consuls.[4]

Matters came to a head early in October when Jefferson Davis was away from Richmond visiting his western armies. This left Secretary of State Benjamin without supervision at a crucial time. Benjamin called a Cabinet meeting on October 7 at which he found its members "unhesitating and unanimous in the conclusion that the British consular agents should be at once expelled from the Confederacy."[5]

This grave step—a slap in the face at England—was accordingly taken. Davis, who was far more interested in discussing military affairs with his generals than in worrying about diplomatic matters, telegraphed his approval. Benjamin notified Slidell in France that the British Empire had been put in its place.[6]

Harper's *Weekly* expressed the Northern reaction to the dismissal of the British consuls in its October 31 issue:

> Jeff Davis has taken umbrage at the action of the British Consuls in reference to foreigners enlisted in the army of the rebel service, and has dismissed them all from the Confederacy. The Southern papers rejoice greatly at this event. Some of them attribute the dismissal of her Britannic Majesty's representatives to a broader reason—namely, the treatment which Mr. Mason received at the Court of St. James, which required his withdrawal from the diplomatic mission by order of Mr. Davis. Intense disgust of the late action of the British Government toward the Confederacy . . . is manifested in the tone of all the Southern journals, and a firmer confidence in the friendly interference of France is exhibited.

Much of the South's disillusionment with England stemmed, of course, from the fact that the British were evidently not going to let any more Confederate naval ships leave their ports. The situation became worse in December when Her Majesty's Government seized the *Pampero* which was being built at Glasgow. And there was much doubt that Lieutenant North's ironclad, also under construction there, would ever be allowed to depart. A discarded British naval vessel named the *Victor,* which Matthew Fontaine Maury had bought, managed to get to Calais where she was renamed the *Rappahannock.* But the French never let her go to sea, which was perhaps just as well, for she was a poor ship in such miserable condition that she could not have been an effective cruiser.

Mason, after being ordered by Richmond to abandon his post in London, had gone to Paris. Benjamin wrote to him on November 13 to say that his services were too valuable to be dispensed with and appointed him to be a sort of Commissioner-at-large. Mason, who knew no French, did not care for Paris. He called the city a Babel and never went to the theater or the opera because he could not understand what was being said. But perhaps something more than the strangeness of a different environment was affecting him, for he told his wife: "I have not the heart or spirit to gaze after new things, or else I am getting too old for new excitements."[7] Failure, too, may have been the reason for his low spirits. It was evident now that his mission to England had accomplished nothing.

Barron wrote to Mallory on December 15 that the French Government "is as friendly to us as the Government of Great Britain is hostile."[8] But Bulloch, who had much greater experience than Barron in dealing with Europeans, had already told Mallory on November 26 that he was afraid things were not going well for the Confederacy in France.[9]

England was saddened at the end of 1863 by the loss of one of her greatest writers, William Makepeace Thackeray. He and Dickens had only recently been reconciled after a long and senseless quarrel. They met again only a few days before the long-ailing man died in his sleep on the day before Christmas.

But Thackeray's death was the only unhappy event to mar the year-end holidays at a time when the British Empire was nearing the height of its power. Minor wars in countries like New Zealand, Mexico, Poland, Japan, Santo Domingo, China, and along the frontiers of India were regarded as normal, while the major war in America was something to be deplored but not to be unduly worried about. Despite the North's ever-growing fleet, the British Navy was still larger and stronger so far as ocean-going ships were concerned. Several big ironclads had been built during the year, and the huge Armstrong 600-pound cannon was showing how the newest British guns could penetrate heavy armor.[10] If it had not been for the continued distress among the Lancashire cotton operatives, England could have been having one of her merriest Christmases. Fortunately, some cotton was arriving from various countries. If this could be encouraged and still further increased, the British Isles might be made independent of America. Even wheat could be had from other sources by paying a little more for it. The future looked bright for the Empire, and if the United States could be kept permanently divided, the two mutually hostile sections, like Kilkenny cats, would be too busy trying to harm each other ever to attain enough power to rival the mother country.

As the year drew to a close in Richmond, there was much talk about the need for a dictator to take over the Confederate Government from Jefferson Davis and run it with an iron hand. The Lynchburg *Virginian* openly advocated such a move and suggested that General Lee be made the despot.[11] It was obvious that the editor who nominated Lee had never met him, for the Confederate commander's greatest weakness as a soldier was his kindness, his consideration for others, and his never-failing courtesy.

In Washington, Lincoln summed up the year for the North in his Annual Message to Congress. Few nations, in the midst of a war, have ever been in such good condition as the United States was at this time. The President said that the people were bearing their burdens cheerfully, that crops were good, and that relations with other countries were improved. The war was progressing well. A thousand ships had been captured since the blockade began. The Navy now had 585 vessels, 75 of which were armored, and there were 35,000 men in service against about 6000 in the Confederate Navy. (The President did not mention the strength of the Army, but it had 860,737 men against the Confederacy's 481,160.)[12] He also said that 100,000 former slaves were now in the services with about half of them actually bearing arms. Most important of all, was the President's Proclamation of Amnesty and Reconstruction appended to the Message, because it looked forward to the end of the war and tried to deal with what must come afterward. For the present, anyone who had been in rebellion (with certain specified exceptions) could take an oath to support the Constitution and be granted a full pardon.[13]

Lincoln's year-end message to Congress, in sharp contrast to Davis', breathed confidence and hope. Seward, to make sure that Americans stationed abroad were acquainted with both documents, distributed copies of them with his circular of December 15.[14]

The day after Seward sent out this circular, Lincoln granted one of the most remarkable pardons of his much-pardoning career. A 20-year-old British subject named Alfred Rubery had been arrested in San Francisco nine months before as one of three leaders in an attempt to outfit the schooner *J. M. Chapman* as a Confederate privateer. There was no doubt of the young man's guilt. He and his companions had a letter of marque from Richmond; they intended to capture a steam vessel and use it as a cruiser; they would then attack California gold ships after which they planned to go on to the coast of Peru, the China Seas, and the Indian Ocean. But the ambitious plotters were caught before they sailed, and all the evidence on board was used against them. At their trial it was brought out that they had intended to seize the forts in San Francisco Bay and urge the people of California to revolt against the Union and join the Confederacy. The court found all three guilty and sentenced them to 10 years in jail and a fine of $10,000 each.[15]

But young Rubery was no ordinary prisoner; he came from a good family in Birmingham, who had John Bright request Senator Charles Sumner to bring the case before the President. When Lincoln let the lad go free, he said that because Rubery was "of the immature age of twenty years, and his pardon is desired by John Bright," he was granting it under condition that the prisoner leave the country within 30 days. Perhaps as a result of this leniency, Rubery's two companions were also released after taking the oath of amnesty.[16]

The same month saw another privateering case with international repercussions. This was the seizure of the steamer *Chesapeake* while en route from New York to Portland by 15 Confederates pretending to be ordinary passengers. The ship was taken to the Bay of Fundy where a Union warship found her. Her captors hurried ashore, and the steamer was then towed out of Canadian waters. A second Union gunboat came up with a captain who felt that international law was being violated. The *Chesapeake* was therefore returned to Nova Scotia where she became involved in a lawsuit in which the Confederacy tried to claim the vessel.[17] But the claim was so flimsy that even the special commissioner sent to Nova Scotia to try to obtain the ship felt that the case was "very doubtful both in law and morals." He wrote to Benjamin advising that it be dropped.[18]

Chapter 36

THE CONFEDERACY RUNS INTO TROUBLE

The year 1864 began inauspiciously for the Confederates when John Slidell was made an object of public ridicule in Paris on New Year's Day. Bigelow thought the incident was important enough to report it to Seward:

> Slidell had a fracas yesterday with some Yankee boys on the Champs-Elysées, which is in all mouths this morning. They had been out sailing their boats in the Bois de Boulogne. Coming back, they met him and made the Union flags on their boats as conspicuous as possible when he passed. Afterwards one of them fired a popgun, which struck him in the back—the boy says by accident. Slidell turned, collared the boy, and raised his umbrella to strike him. The boy followed the example of Joseph in the hands of Potiphar's wife and left nothing but his coat in the arms of the Commissioner, who bore it off not knowing what else to do with it, while the boy left him to his embarrassment.[1]

George Eustis, Jr., Slidell's secretary, described the affair somewhat differently. According to him, the boys were not children with sailboats but were students from the Lycée Condorcet who carried a banner with the inscription "Down with Slidell, the slavedriver" and a caricature of him dragging a chained slave. They had also composed a song said to be "of a most vituperative character." Slidell was warned about the planned attack, but he refused to listen to his secretary's suggestion that he call the police and insisted on going out to face the boys.[2]

Something more serious occurred a few days later. Although Hotze and Mason had both enthusiastically endorsed James Spence's book, *The*

American Union, as a good British defense of the South's right to secede,
they evidently had not bothered to read it carefully. Hotze had had it
translated into French and German, and Mason had sent a copy of it to
Jefferson Davis. Such distinguished sponsorship had induced a Richmond
publisher to bring out an American edition in 1863. By this time Spence
had been made the Confederate financial agent in England and was often
speaking in public in and around Liverpool in support of the Southern
cause.[3]

Spence, who knew how to deal with his own countrymen, realized
that it was impossible to make British people accept slavery. Some of his
listeners at pro-Confederate meetings evidently reported to Hotze that he
was not following the standard Confederate line. Hotze wrote to Benjamin on November 21, 1863, saying that Spence was making "unnecessarily large concessions to the antislavery prejudice."[4] When this letter
reached Richmond, Benjamin replied on January 9 to thank Hotze for
drawing the matter to his attention. With his reply he enclosed a copy of
a note addressed to Spence dismissing him from his post because of what
he had said about slavery.[5] Someone, possibly Benjamin himself, had
evidently examined *The American Union* and had found this outspoken
passage:

> In fact, slavery, like other wrongs, reacts on the wrongdoer.
> Taking the most temperate view . . . it remains an evil in an
> economical sense, an outrage on humanity in a moral one. It is
> a gross anachronism, a thing of two thousand years ago, the
> brute force of dark ages obtruding into the midst of the nine-
> teenth century. No reasoning, no statistics, no profit, no phi-
> losophy can reconcile us to what our instinct repels. After all
> the arguments have been poured into the ear, there is something
> in the heart that spurns them. We make no declaration that all
> men are born equal, but a conviction—innate, irresistible—tells
> us with a voice none can stifle that a man is a man and not a
> chattel. Remove from slavery . . . all romance and exaggera-
> tion in order that we may deal with it wisely and calmly, it re-
> mains a foul blot from which all must desire to purge the
> annals of the age.[6]

The expression "foul blot," became popular in England after Spence's
book was published. But that phrase was not all that proved to be troublesome. His entire fourth chapter, which dealt with slavery, contained
many other statements distasteful to Southern plantation owners. Yet
the book had gone through four editions in England, two in foreign lan-

guages, and one in Richmond itself at a time when printer's ink and paper had become exceedingly scarce. Amazingly enough, this controversial chapter had remained unchanged in all these editions. And Spence was still making similar remarks when he spoke in public. Naturally, the well meaning but unconforming Confederate employee had to go.

The issue of slavery was hampering the South's propaganda efforts in Europe so much that the various clubs, associations, and societies organized to influence British opinion did not remain active very long. The dismissal of Spence, who had been helpful in forming such groups, practically put an end to them. Hotze's *Index,* which had always covered their meetings in detail, did not mention a single one from April to August, 1864. In some cases they did not go out of existence but merely stopped functioning.[7]

By February 1864 the very word "slavery" had become so offensive in England that Hotze had to come to its defense in *The Index.* He attempted to show that in America the slave system was very different from what it had ever been anywhere else. The South, he said, had "consistently and conscientiously been the friend and benefactor" of the Negroes.[8] But *The Index* had a small circulation, and its editor was trying to argue his case in unemotional terms. Nothing he could do would even slightly change the practicably indelible impression already made upon the British mind by Mrs. Stowe's widely read *Uncle Tom's Cabin.* She had written fiction, exaggerated much, and had not even tried to present her material fairly, but she had created a picture of slavery in dramatic and emotional language that made her novel unforgettable. Uncle Tom, Eva, and Simon Legree were serving as effective propaganda agents for the Union. Their appeal could not be counteracted by a journalist whose writings appeared in a seldom-read newspaper openly dedicated to the defense of the Confederate cause. The differences between the North and the South were beginning to be judged on a moral basis. The Emancipation Proclamation was at last having an effect.

When Grant was made the head of all the Union Armies on March 7, 1864, and began mounting a massive campaign that was intended to sweep down to Richmond and capture or drive out the Confederate Government, the end seemed near. Perhaps the best gauge of what people thought of the South's chances for success was the fluctuating rate of the Confederate dollar. It began to depreciate rapidly after Gettysburg until it reached a new low in February 1864. In May and June, while Lee was

successfully holding off one attack after another as Grant hurled huge
masses of men and metal against him in the series of battles from Wil-
derness to Cold Harbor, the value of the Confederate dollar began to
increase. It rose to a temporary peak in June and early July when it
looked as if Early might capture Washington. His raid failed on July 12,
and Southern currency then started down again. After that it fell steadily.[9] By this time it was evident that the South could not indefinitely
withstand the pressure being brought against it. When a Confederate
soldier was slain, he could not be replaced; when a freight car carrying
supplies on a Southern railroad was destroyed, there was no possibility
of getting another, for men and matériel were becoming scarce.

Barron wrote a long letter to Mallory on February 15, 1864, giving a
candid appraisal of Confederate naval affairs in Europe. He was able to
express himself freely because his message was being taken to Richmond
by William L. Maury, whose ill health had compelled him to relinquish
command of the *Georgia*. The contents of this letter and its important
enclosures from Bulloch, North, and Sinclair were memorized by Maury
so he could repeat the information verbally if he had to destroy the documents en route.

Mallory now learned that practically all the attempts to build Confederate ships in Europe had failed or were failing. The correspondence
gave ominous details. Not in order of their relative importance but as
Barron and the other agents listed them, they were:

1. Lieutenant North's ironclad, which was being built in Glasgow, had been sold to Denmark. There would be no financial
   loss, but title to the ship had already been transferred.
2. The two Laird rams which the British had seized and were
   standing guard over were also to be sold. So were the two
   rams under construction in Bordeaux. Again there would be
   no monetary loss, but the ships were to go to other nations.
3. The *Pampero*, seized by the British the previous November,
   was in the exchequer court. Barron thought that she might
   escape legal forfeiture but admitted that if she did it would
   "require great skill and dexterity of management in order to
   get possession of her."
4. The Confederate agents had "abandoned hope of ever getting an ironclad from any European port during . . . the
   present friendly relations between the United States and
   these Governments. . . . and would therefore . . . recom-

mend that no other engagements for the construction of ironclads be entered into."

5. The four wooden corvettes in Bordeaux and Nantes would
   be completed, but they would have to be removed from
   France to be armed and equipped. Since the difficulties of
   getting them out would be very great, it was better to count
   on obtaining only two of them.

6. The agents all complained about Adams' watchfulness and
   lavish expenditure of money. Bulloch was bitter about the
   spies his adversaries were employing. North said that they
   had forced him to leave Glasgow. The agents also felt that
   Earl Russell was favoring the Union and that British pressure was making Napoleon III go back on his word about
   having Confederate ships built in France.

7. Bulloch, as usual, made the most intelligent and constructive
   suggestions. It was essential, he said, to have some Confederate commerce-raiders operating because they were keeping
   Yankee vessels off the seas. He also had a plan for the Confederacy to "take the blockade-running business into its own
   hands." The Government-owned steamers could be armed
   when in port and sent out as a squadron to attack the Union
   fleet when practicable.[10]

At this point in the Confederacy's career it can be said that the new nation was kept going by two men—Robert E. Lee and James Dunwoody
Bulloch. No one but Lee could have stood up against Grant's hammer-
ing blows in the Wilderness-Cold Harbor Campaign. No one but Bulloch could have kept the discouraged Confederate agents in Europe en-
heartened enough to continue their work. Mason, Slidell, and Mann
had accomplished nothing in their careers abroad. Maury had been a
failure as a buyer of ships. So had North and Sinclair. Huse and Hotze
were doing useful work, but they were not operating on a policy-making
level. Barron and McRae were, but they lacked Bulloch's strength and
ingenuity. Semmes was a brilliant sea captain, but he had nothing to do
with Confederate naval plans. Mallory, at headquarters in Richmond,
was an able administrator and a clever innovator, but most of his time
was taken up by the war on interior waters, and he was isolated—except
for occasional contacts—from what was happening abroad. It was on the
ocean and in the chancellories of Europe that the fate of the Confederacy
was largely to be decided. The Union blockade, the loss of one seaport
after another, and the withholding of recognition by foreign countries

did more to defeat the South than anything its armies could ever do to offset these crippling blows.

Both Lee and Bulloch were destined to lose because they had backed a losing cause. Lee was already a world figure who was to become even more famous. He had the good fortune to be working in the open, while Bulloch had to operate behind the scenes. Lee was handsome in his general's uniform, worshiped by the thousands of Southern soldiers and civilians who saw him; Bulloch, dressed in drab street clothes, was not a romantic figure, and his existence was known only to a small group. Lee remained in Virginia after Appomattox to win even more enduring celebrity and much-deserved approbation for what he did as president of Washington College; Bulloch stayed on in Liverpool and was forgotten.

That Bulloch's influence on the conduct of the war was great may be seen by the fact that his suggestion that the Confederate Government operate its own blockade-runners was quickly put into effect. And it was he who obtained the last two sea-going Confederate naval vessels, both of which were in operation for some time after Appomattox. Bulloch was worth more to the South than a regiment of minor military officers whose names are much better known than his. Jefferson Davis, whose chief contribution to the war was a ponderous mass of turgid prose, is remembered while Bulloch, the secret operator, the ingenious planner, the good technician, the astute businessman, the honest administrator of huge funds, the man who was responsible for the most effective moves his government made beyond its borders, remains almost unknown.

Commander William Maury arrived in Richmond on April 3 with the depressing news of the stalemate that was paralyzing Confederate naval affairs in Europe. When Mallory wrote to Barron and Bulloch, he naturally expressed his disappointment, but in order to keep the war going, he suggested that efforts be made to strike at Northern fisheries and coastal trade. This was to be done not by single ships but by squadrons which would separate after each attack. He explained the idea by saying, "Such a system of alternate united and separate action—naval light infantry tactics—has never been adopted upon the sea, simply because under sail it would be impracticable; since the application of steam to warships, the opportunity has never been offered. Let us be the first to put it to good account."[11]

Mallory's ideas were to have an important effect upon Confederate naval strategy on the high seas during the next twelve months, but only a few ships would be available, and Appomattox was only a year away.

Bulloch's suggestion that the Confederate Government operate its own blockade-runners reached Richmond on April 3. Two months before this date, the Confederate Congress had passed an act prohibiting luxuries from being imported.[12] At the same time it had also stopped the export of Southern-grown raw materials except under government regulations. Under this new arrangement, the Confederate Government was to have the right to use one-half of every blockade-runner's freight capacity on both inward and outward voyages. These rulings caused the number of foreign ships entering Confederate ports to drop. As a result, enforcement of the measures had to be unofficially relaxed. Trade picked up again, but this did not help the government obtain the kind of material it needed. It was far more profitable to carry "brandies, wines, and flimsy gewgaws" that brought high prices than it was to transport such unprofitable but essential supplies as lead, chemicals, or army blankets.[13]

The idea of the Confederacy owning blockade-runners was not new, for Bulloch had bought the *Fingal* in 1861 for that purpose. When he took the ship into Savannah himself, he brought in what was probably the most valuable cargo of war matériel ever to enter the South. In October 1863 he had purchased another blockade-runner for his government. This was the *Coquette* which was needed to transport marine engines and ordnance stores to Wilmington.

In the late spring of 1864, Richmond told McRae and Bulloch to acquire suitable ships for the government to use as blockade-runners. In order to obtain them quickly, Bulloch bought four paddle-wheel steamers that were already in an advanced state of construction. They were given single-syllable animal names: *Owl, Bat, Stag,* and *Deer.* Ten other vessels were to be built to more exacting specifications.[14]

The project started badly when the *Bat* was captured while attempting to run in to Wilmington. But the others brought in weapons and supplies and took out cotton, thus putting the Confederate Government into the shipping business late in 1864.

Chapter 37

"THE CONFEDERACY'S ONLY FOREIGN WAR"

Something happened just outside Charleston Harbor on the night of January 17, 1864, which was of enormous importance to the future of naval warfare and its effect upon the world, but so little notice was taken of the incident that Gideon Welles did not even mention it in his diary, although he was sent a full report of what had happened.[1] The U.S.S. *Housatonic*, a steam sloop-of-war which had been launched late in 1861 at a cost of nearly a quarter of a million dollars, was sunk by a torpedo exploded under her stern. Only five men were lost because she went down in shallow water, and most of the crew were able to save themselves by climbing into the rigging. Another Union man-of-war had been damaged by somewhat similar means during the previous October, but the *Housatonic* was the first ship ever to be sunk by a truly submersible vessel. The crude, hand-propelled Confederate *H. L. Hunley*, which did the sinking, went down herself with all her crew.[2]

The episode attracted little attention at the time because practically no one understood its real significance. Fifty years later, when German submarines began their destructive work, everyone was shocked by the deadly efficiency of undersea vessels that could strike without being seen. During the four years of the First World War, German U-boats sank nearly 6000 ships, and the unrestricted phase of their operation brought America into the world-wide conflict in 1917. Everything that has happened in submarine warfare from 1914 to the present day, with its globe-circling, atomic-powered undersea missile-launchers, stems from that dark night in 1864 when the *Housatonic* was the first of thousands of ships that were to be sent to the bottom by an enemy operating below the surface.

On the other side of the world the *Alabama* was sailing toward Ceylon and the western coast of India. On the way, Semmes stopped a British ship which was carrying Moslem pilgrims from Singapore to the Red Sea port of Jedda from which they could travel overland to Mecca. They had heard that the *Alabama* kept black giants on board who ate the prisoners. They had also heard about the Mormons in Salt Lake City who, like themselves, believed in having many wives. The boarding-officer solemnly assured them that the black giants had found their Yankee prisoners too lean and tough to eat. He also said that his friends at home each had three or four dozen wives.[3]

The *Alabama* sailed on; Semmes landed his prisoners near Cochin on the Indian coast and then headed for Africa. Without thinking of what his prediction would mean to the South if it ever came true, he said that cotton production in India was an assured success and that "the time is not far distant when Yankee spindles and looms will be spinning and weaving India cotton for the supply of their own people."[4] Fortunately for those who grew cotton in his own South, the brilliant navigator was wrong. He was wrong about many other things when he departed from what he knew—ships and the sea—and expressed his opinions on politics or economics.

Early in February the *Alabama* reached the volcanic Comoro Islands between the northern tip of Madagascar and the east coast of Africa and anchored at Johanna, a small Moslem community. Semmes was pleased to learn that the inhabitants had heard of him and his ship. English vessels that stopped there had spread word of his fame.

He remained in port for a week to give his crew shore leave. When the thirsty sailors found out that it was impossible to buy liquor on the Mohammedan island they did not bother to return after their first visit.

Slavery flourished there. Female slaves could be bought for 20 dollars, while those who had just been imported from Africa could be had for half as much. This was about a hundredth of their value in the South before the war.

From Johanna the *Alabama* returned to Cape Town and arrived there on March 20 after having been away for nearly six months.[5] Semmes was greatly put out to find that the British authorities had seized the *Tuscaloosa,* a captured ship which he had armed and manned to serve as a cruiser. England was evidently turning against the Confederacy. He thought Lord Russell was to blame. While at Cape Town, Semmes also had a chance to read some American papers. "The news was not encouraging," he wrote. The Southern people were being pressed and were losing ground while the blockade of their coasts was becoming tighter. "Our finances were rapidly deteriorating," he added, "and a general demoralization . . . seemed to be spreading. From the whole review of the situation, I was very apprehensive that the cruises of the *Alabama* were drawing to a close."[6]

He left Cape Town on March 25 and headed for St. Helena and the east coast of Brazil. Yankee ships openly registered as such were still rare in the Atlantic although that ocean had been free from Confederate cruisers during most of the winter.[7] The *Alabama* was now back in familiar waters; the *Florida* had sailed from Brest on February 10, and the *Georgia* had left Cherbourg a few days later to meet the *Rappahannock* at a rendezvous at sea. But the French authorities in Calais would not permit the latter ship to leave, and they continued to make things unpleasant for her. Like the British, they too were apparently becoming hostile to the Confederacy.

The *Georgia*, under a new commander, because W. M. Maury had gone home ill, waited for several weeks off the Atlantic coast of Morocco near Mogador for the *Rappahannock*, but she, of course, never appeared. Occasional trade with the Moors who came out to the anchored ship gave the captain and the crew the idea that they would be pleasant to deal with.

One day, when crewmen had rowed an elderly native back to the beach after he had swum out to the ship and collapsed from exhaustion, the captain permitted some of his men to go ashore to stretch their legs. As evidence of their friendly intentions, he told them not to carry arms. One of the men in the boat was young James Morris Morgan who had crossed the ocean with Matthew Fontaine Maury. He described what happened soon after they landed:

> At the foot of the cliffs, some forty yards from the water, there was a growth of dwarf bushes. Suddenly we were separated and surrounded by hundreds of Moors armed with spears and old-fashioned guns of extraordinary length whose barrels were banded with silver at intervals of a foot or two apart. The Moors were shaking their guns and brandishing their spears while yelling like fiends, and all the time a seemingly endless stream of the black demons poured out from the bushes. I tried to see what had become of my companions, but could only discern a surging, struggling mass of Moors in every direction. One gigantic fellow seized me from behind and whirled me around

until I faced the sea, and while others struck me with their hands, my particular giant preferred to use his feet, and he kicked me until I was almost up to my neck in the water. From my sensations I should judge that the sole of that Moor's foot without further roughening would have served very well for a blacksmith's rasp. Our unarmed boat-keepers gamely waited for us, and when I climbed into the boat I found my companions, who had been similarly treated, already there—safe but very wet, and looking very foolish.[8]

When they returned to the *Georgia*, they told the captain about their rude reception. Since no one was injured, they were inclined to treat the whole matter as a joke, but hot-blooded young Lieutenant Evans, who was in command of a ship of his own for the first time, was determined to punish the Moors. He ordered the drummer to beat to quarters and had the guns cast loose to fire shells at the astonished natives on the beach. They immediately disappeared, probably into cave dwellings. The Confederates never found out whether any were hurt or killed.

The next day a tremendous storm struck the coast. The *Georgia* began to drag her anchor and steadily drifted toward the shore. When the Moors saw the ship being driven nearer and nearer, they came out to dance delightedly on the beach and wait for the hated vessel to be dashed on the rocks. But the engineer got steam up in time for the engine to take the strain off the two anchor cables. Then, just when it seemed that they were safe, the badly designed engines' wooden cogs broke. For two hours, while repairs were being made, it was touch and go. During that time the Moors waited hopefully to kill the Confederates or perhaps sell them into slavery, as was their custom. Finally the engines began to operate again. The anchors were weighed, and the *Georgia* steamed away from the dangerous coast. Morgan called the encounter "the Confederacy's only foreign war."

The *Georgia* headed north to enter the Garonne River and anchor in the port of Bordeaux. The French ordered her to leave within 24 hours, but she remained under various pretexts. Then the United States warships *Niagara* and *Sacramento* came up and bottled her in the river. But she escaped one dark night and arrived in Liverpool where she was ordered to be put out of commission and sold.[9] The Confederacy lost another cruiser, but the *Georgia* had never been a good one. She was so slow—and perhaps unlucky—that she had captured only nine ships, five of which she allowed to proceed under bond.[10]

Only two Confederate commerce-raiders were now at sea—the *Alabama* and the *Florida*. Another ship which was to operate during the summer as an armed cruiser was then being used as a blockade-runner under the name *Atlanta*. Renamed the *Tallahassee* when she was made into a raider, she played a part in Mallory's plans to terrorize the Northern coastal states in 1864.[11]

While the *Florida* was cruising between the West Indies and the Bermudas, the *Alabama* was running north along the coast of Brazil where she was finding relatively few ships that could legitimately be destroyed because most of them were of foreign register.[12] On April 23, she captured the guano-carrier *Rockingham* which was fair prey. After taking stores and prisoners off, Semmes used her for a target so his gunners could get some practice. During the firing of the cannon, it was noticed that the powder had lost much of its effectiveness. Long cruising in moist tropical waters had caused it to deteriorate.[13]

Semmes burned the riddled hull and went on to capture the *Tycoon* five days later. Although the *Alabama* was to overtake 19 more vessels, they all proved to be of foreign origin and had to be let go. The *Tycoon* was the last ship Semmes was to destroy. She was set on fire shortly after dark, and she burned brightly before she went down off the coast of Brazil.[14]

The *Alabama* kept going north. At the end of May, when she passed the Azores where she had been commissioned less than two years before, she was an old, tired ship with copper peeling off her bottom and with water rising in her hull. Her decks leaked badly, and her engines needed repair. She sailed on until June 10 when she was put under steam in the English Channel. Semmes was suffering from a cold and fever and was glad to pick up a British pilot near the Lizard. The next morning a French pilot took the ship into Cherbourg. It was the *Alabama's* last port.[15]

Chapter 38

THE LAIRD RAMS
BECOME AN ISSUE IN PARLIAMENT

The Laird rams had been stopped by the British Government in the autumn of 1863 and were kept anchored in the Mersey in an unfinished
condition with one of Her Majesty's men-of-war stationed near them.
Perhaps by oversight, perhaps on purpose, Seward had the correspondence concerning them included in the published report of the State Department at the end of the year. When the bulky volume which contained
"Papers Relating to Foreign Affairs: Great Britain, 1863," reached London,[1] many Englishmen eagerly went through it, while newspapers
published long excerpts. Most interesting of all was Seward's letter to
Adams of July 11, 1863, in which the Secretary of State had told his
man in London to take a strong stand even if it led to armed conflict.
When readers saw the published documents, they naturally assumed that
this letter had induced Adams to say to Russell on September 5: "It would
be superfluous in me to point out to your Lordship that this is war." But
the average reader could not know the whole truth, for the exchange of
letters early in September had been so rapid and complicated that even
Russell and Adams had difficulty in recalling the exact order of their being sent and received. Actually, Russell had already ordered the Laird
rams to be detained by the time Adams' war threat reached him. Consequently, the statement of September 5 was less explosive than it seemed
when it was printed without explanation.

Both men must have taken it for granted that their confidential letters
were safely filed away in their government's archives. But Seward had
now made the American correspondence public. And Adams had never
told Russell about Seward's bellicose instructions of July 11.

The material published in the American Diplomatic correspondence became a controversial issue when the new session of Parliament opened on February 4, 1864. The leader of Russell's Tory opponents was 65-year-old Edward Geoffrey Smith-Stanley, the 14th Earl of Derby. He was no defender of slavery and had been active in the movement for the relief of the starving cotton operatives in Lancashire. But the very fact that he came from that area meant that he had a more than ordinary interest in the Laird rams, for the father of the men who built them had been elected in 1861 to the House of Commons on the Conservative ticket. Obviously Derby had to protect the interests of his neighbor and fellow-Tory, John Laird.

Derby was fully able to lead the attack on Russell. He was an aggressive sportsman who was fond of shooting and of his famous racing stable. His boisterous manners in the field, however, quieted down in the library. He was a good scholar, a master of several languages, and so well versed in Greek that he had recently completed a new translation of the Iliad. Perhaps long involvement in the Homeric wars had made him more than ordinarily pugnacious. Or perhaps it was the painful gout that was beginning to afflict him. People noted that his temper was becoming testier.[2]

At the opening of Parliament, Derby, who had seen but not read the controversial American volume, began by referring to a newspaper reprint of Seward's trouble-making letter of July 11. He quoted it indirectly by saying that the Federal Government had threatened to take the law into its own hands and have its cruisers follow British-built Confederate ships (like the *Alabama*) into British waters to destroy them there unless the sale of such vessels to Richmond was stopped.[3]

Then he said: "I hope the noble Earl will be able to show that he has answered that dispatch in a manner which will put an end to such monstrous demands." He also said that early in September Russell had taken "the strong step of seizing the so-called Confederate rams in the Mersey" and pointed out that he had done so after Seward's threatening dispatch of July 11 had been received in London. Derby took it for granted that Adams had shown Russell this important letter. Russell, of course, had not seen it because Adams had carefully kept it away from him.

Since what Derby had said about America was only a part of a long attack covering many other points about British Foreign Policy, Russell was able to make a general reply and delay answering the charges dealing with Seward's threats and his own orders to detain the Laird rams.

In the House of Lords on February 9, Derby repeated the question.[4]

Russell requested that his reply be put over for two days and admitted that on the first occasion he had not remembered seeing Seward's dispatch but had since found out that Adams had never let him see it. As to the detention of the Laird rams, he objected to producing correspondence about them because the case was about to be brought before a court of law.[5]

Two days later, Derby was at it again. This time he expanded his question to make it cover much more ground. He had been studying the documents in "the very thick volume" from the United States, and he quoted from them extensively. Now that he had seen the American side of the story, he wanted to examine the English version. What had Russell done to meet these threats and insults? He read some of the correspondence which had been published in Washington and drew from it the conclusion that it was "a great triumph to the diplomacy of the United States, and that the British Government had given in to intimidation and menace." This was a serious accusation; perhaps, he suggested, Earl Russell could refute it by producing all the correspondence. The British side should be laid before Parliament and published.[6]

In reply, Russell told about the difficulties he had had in tracing the true ownership of the Laird rams because they seemingly had been transferred to a French firm and then to Egypt. The complicated matter was still under investigation. Under the circumstances, it would be prejudicial to the case to produce the papers.[7]

The two noble Lords were wrangling again on February 15 and getting nowhere. On February 23, members of the House of Commons brought the subject to debate in order to demand that the British papers be produced. By coincidence, this debate followed a long discussion of public executions, for an immense crowd had gathered at Newgate Prison on the previous day to watch the hanging of five foreigners who had committed a particularly vicious crime on a British ship. What the members had to say indicated that some of them were beginning to feel that executions should be carried out behind prison walls and not made public spectacles. Even the effectiveness of capital punishment as a deterrent to crime was being questioned.[8]

The debate about the Laird rams began with a detailed summary of their background so the members could understand what was involved. But the evidence was slanted so as to make it seem that Russell had detained the rams only because Adams threatened war. Not only the papers dealing with the British side, but all the letters between the Government and the Lairds were asked for. It was also brought out that the govern-

ment was trying to purchase the two ironclads—something very few
people had yet heard.[9]

When the new Attorney General, Sir Roundell Palmer, rose to defend
the Government, he read a passage from a document which he said had
"been made public as the Report of the Secretary of the Confederate
Navy to his own Congress." According to this, Mallory had summed up
Confederate shipbuilding in England and France by saying:

> In accordance with the order of the President, early in the pres-
> ent year I despatched several agents to England and France
> with orders to contract for eight ironclad vessels suitable for
> ocean service and calculated to resist the ordinary armament of
> the wooden vessels of the enemy. These ships were to be pro-
> vided with rams, and designed expressly to break the blockade of
> such of their ports as were not blockaded by the ironclad *Moni-
> tors* of the enemy. Five of these vessels were contracted for in
> England and three in France. Due precautions were taken
> against contravening the laws of England in the construction
> and equipment of these vessels. Three have been completed;
> but, owing to the unfriendly construction of her Neutrality
> Laws, the Government of England stationed several war vessels
> at the mouth of the Mersey and prevented their departure from
> England. Subsequently they were seized by the British Govern-
> ment.[10]

The Attorney General then said that in this document "we seem to
have information from headquarters of a character perfectly unquestion-
able . . . that these ships were being built in violation of our laws and
for the purpose of being used in the belligerent service of the Confederate States."

After the debate had continued for some time, Sir Hugh Cairns, whom
Palmer called a "zealous advocate of Messrs. Laird," suddenly launched a
surprise attack on the Attorney General by denouncing the quoted statement from Mallory's report as a forgery.[11] Unfortunately for Palmer,
this was true, and it was not only a forgery but one which had already
been exposed by M. F. Maury in a letter he had sent earlier in the month
to the London *Standard* and *The Times*:

> Soon after the commencement of the American war the Yan-
> kees resorted to the trick of getting up facsimiles of Richmond
> papers in type, paper, and size; of copying their advertisements;
> and then filling up with reading matter of Northern manufac-
> ture. These papers were then put into the mails, received,

copied from, and circulated without suspicion as Southern "utterances."

The English press is now the victim of another "trick" of the same sort. A document, copied from the Northern papers is now going the rounds of the continental and English press, which purports to be the official report of Mr. Mallory, the Confederate Secretary of the Navy, to the Congress in Richmond.

It is a take-in, it bears internal evidence of a hoax, and I know many of its statements to be false. Please, therefore, assure your readers that no such document has ever been uttered by the Secretary of the Confederate Navy, and so help me to "nail to the counter" this spurious thing.[12]

Maury was correct in saying that internal evidence showed that the document had been written by someone not fully informed about all the facts. It was wrong about the number of ironclads ordered; none had been completed; and the British Government had not stationed "several war vessels at the mouth of the Mersey" to stop the two Laird rams— one standing close guard over them was enough. A number of Confederates in Europe were in a position to detect the forgery. Maury exposed it because what he said was most likely to get printed and be believed.

That the British Government's Attorney General had been careless enough to use the supposed Mallory statement without checking its authenticity was inexcusable, for Maury's exposure had been published widely throughout Europe. Seward, however, had been equally careless because he had sent American legations newspapers containing the false statement. Dayton gave a copy of it to Drouyn de Lhuys, and then, when he saw Maury's denunciation, wrote to Seward on February 5 enclosing a clipping of what Maury had said.[13] When Seward replied on February 25, he defended what he had done by saying that the supposed Mallory report had circulated at home for two months without being disavowed by the Confederates. He ended by remarking that "the merely unauthorized denial of its genuineness by M. F. Maury in London is deemed unworthy of consideration."[14]

But Seward was wrong—as he often was. Both Hotze and Bulloch wrote to Mallory after the House of Commons debate suggesting that he make "an authoritative denial of the authenticity of the report." Actually, Mallory had already done so. On March 10 he had provided Benjamin, as the Secretary of State, with a letter denouncing the report as "a paltry forgery . . . from beginning to end."[15]

In England, Russell asked Adams to find out the truth about the matter. When the European legations received a letter from Seward dated March 21, the real story could be told. The editor of the New York *Sun* had deliberately concocted the pretended Confederate naval report in order to "create the impression that he had means of communicating with the insurgent capital superior to those of his professional brethren."[16] Thus did yellow journalism, even in that early stage of its fungoid growth, push aside all responsibility for sticking to the truth even when its spuriously manufactured documents might disturb the peace of the world.

The debate in the House of Commons on February 23 involved far more than Sir Roundell Palmer's using a known forgery in an attempt to substantiate the Government's case. Many important things came out, not the least of which was the fact that Russell had told Adams on March 27, 1863, that "the cases of the *Alabama* and *Oreto* [*Florida*] were a scandal."[17] Sir Hugh Cairns made much of that phrase and also strongly emphasized the fact that Russell had ordered the Laird rams to be detained before he had conclusive evidence about their Confederate ownership. In his summation he said: "The seizure of these vessels . . . raises constitutional questions of as great importance . . . as were ever brought before this House. . . . I charge the Government . . . with having done . . . on their own confession, what was illegal and unconstitutional, without law, without justification, and without excuse."[18]

But the case against the Government was quietly punctured when Thomas Baring, the head of the house that handled the United States' financial affairs in England, got up to speak "as an humble member of the mercantile community." He said that fitting out privateers and warships to fight in the war in America would not benefit British commerce. And if England ever became involved in a war, the precedent would go against her. Then he said forthrightly that the opposition was acting tamely by merely moving for the papers to be made public. "Why do they not at once move a vote of censure on the Government?" he demanded. He concluded by thanking Russell and his advisers for their conduct although he still thought they were "open to grave censure for not having prevented the departure of the *Alabama*."[19]

The Government had not done well that day, but when the opposition's question was put to have all the correspondence on the Laird rams made public, the motion was lost by a vote of 178 to 153.[20] Russell's actions were thus tacitly approved, and his party could breathe easier.

The Lairds, perhaps with some idea of substantiating the Tory case, printed a pamphlet containing the Government's letters to them.

More than a generation later, Brooks Adams, who had been a child in 1864, wrote a long article on the seizure of the Laird rams. He was in a good position to do so, for he had access to his father's papers. According to him, February 23 was an important day in British history. On that day, he said, "the aristocracy . . . quietly and . . . voluntarily abdicated . . . Not daring to raise the blockade with the British Navy, because of fear of British democracy, the aristocracy undertook to build and deliver a navy to the South. They built the ships, but when it came to delivering them, they flinched before the North, even though to effect a delivery they had prostituted their judges and degraded their courts . . . The action of the House marked the rise of new social classes, the advent of a new ruling class."[21]

This is an oversimplification of an exceedingly complicated matter, for it does not take into account such economic factors as the shipbuilders' and munition makers' desire for profits or the natural tendency of men to keep a government in power rather than ruthlessly turn it out of office (and the Conservatives at that time did not have qualified personnel to replace the existing setup). But it was true that the old aristocracy were losing power to the rising middle classes, and their failure to challenge the Liberals on February 23, when the Liberals were exceedingly vulnerable, was an indication of their growing weakness. The issue that troubled the House that day may seem trivial, but it was a turning point in the long battle for power.

The British Government, now sustained in its actions by the vote in Parliament, wanted to make sure the Confederacy did not get possession of the Laird rams. The simplest way to settle the problem was to buy the two ironclads for its own use, as had already been rumored. It had to pay a good price for them—£220,000, but for that sum, agreed to on May 20, Her Majesty's Navy acquired its first ships designed to have revolving gun turrets. Under the names *Wivern* and *Scorpion,* the former Laird rams had long and useful careers.

Of the total amount paid for the two vessels which had caused so much trouble to several governments and which had nearly brought on a war, the Lairds got £29,000 while the rest went to the Bravays who deducted their commission and then turned over the balance to the Confederates.[22] It was this fund, together with what was received from the sale of Lieutenant North's ironclad in Glasgow and the ships under construction in France, that kept the Confederate agents in Europe going. The money thus obtained enabled them to buy blockade-runners and the two ships which were to carry the Stars and Bars upon the seas after all the land forces of the South had been surrendered.

Chapter 39

FRANCE MAKES MAXIMILIAN EMPEROR OF MEXICO

John Lothrop Motley, Boston born, Harvard educated, and internationally known as a historian, was one of the Lincoln Administration's better choices of Ministers to represent the United States abroad. He felt isolated in Vienna because it was so far from London and Paris where so much was happening that concerned his country. Some compensation, perhaps, was the fact that he had an excellent chance to observe Europe's haughtiest aristocrats, the Hapsburgs, who had been a power on the continent for more than 700 years and who had allied themselves by conquest or marriage to Spain, France, Italy, and the Netherlands.

Motley, however, remained unimpressed by the ceremonial showmanship of Austrian royalty. He had been brought up in New England at a time when town meetings flourished and intellectuals like Emerson and Thoreau were zealous advocates of the spirit of freedom that was then sweeping the western world. There is no doubt where Motley stood. In an intimate letter to his eldest daughter, written in 1864, he said:

> I like democracy. I don't say that it is pretty or genteel or jolly. But it has a reason for existing, and is a fact in America, and is founded on the immutable principle of reason and justice. Aristocracy certainly presents more brilliant social phenomena, more luxurious social enjoyments. Such a system is very cheerful for a few thousand select specimens out of the few hundred millions of the human race. It has been my lot . . . to see how much splendour, how much intellectual and physical refinement, how much enjoyment of the highest character has been created by the English aristocracy; but what a price is paid for it. Think of a human being working all day long, from six in the morning to seven at night for fifteen or twenty kreutzers a

day in Moravia or Bohemia, Ireland or Yorkshire, for forty or fifty years, to die in the workhouse at last! This is the lot of the great majority all over Europe; and yet they are of the same flesh and blood, the *natural* equals in every way of the Howards and Stanleys, Esterhazys and Liechtensteins.[1]

Motley's official duties had been relatively light because Vienna was so remote from the war in America. In 1863, when the French occupied Mexico City and Napoleon III turned to Austria to provide a genuine Hapsburg for the throne there, Motley's post suddenly became more important because the chosen member of royalty was young Ferdinand Maximilian Joseph, younger brother of the Austrian Emperor. (This family was to tie the American Civil War to the even greater conflict of 1914–18 when the Emperor's nephew was assassinated at Sarajevo while the old Emperor was still alive.)

Motley studied the situation carefully from his vantage point in Vienna and wrote about it frequently to Seward. In his letters to his mother, however, he could say whatever he wished and even indulge in speculation. On September 22, he wrote:

> The great interest just now is about the new Mexican Emperor. The Archduke Maximilian is . . . about thirty years of age. He has been a kind of Lord High Admiral, an office which, in the present condition of the Imperial Navy, may be supposed to be not a very onerous occupation. He was Governor-General of Lombardy until that kingdom was ceded to Victor Emmanuel, and he is considered a somewhat restless and ambitious youth. He has literary pretensions too, and has printed, without publishing, several volumes of travels in various parts of the world. . . .
>
> It is, I believe, unquestionable that the Archduke is most desirous to go forth on the adventure. It is equally certain that the step is exceedingly unpopular in Austria. That a Prince of the House of Hapsburg should become the satrap of the Bonaparte dynasty, and should sit on an American throne which could not exist a moment but for French bayonets and French ships is most galling to all classes of Austrians. The intrigue is a most embarrassing one to the Government. If the fatal gift is refused, Louis Napoleon, of course, takes it highly in dudgeon. If it is accepted, Austria takes a kind of millstone around her neck in the shape of gratitude for something she didn't want, and some day she will be expected to pay for it in something she had rather not give. The deputation of the so-called nota-

bles is expected here this week, and then the conditions will be laid down on which Maximilian will consent to live in the bed of roses of Montezuma and Yturbide. I still entertain a *faint* hope that the negotiations may be protracted, and that something may interrupt them before they are concluded. The matter is a very serious and menacing one to us.[2]

Motley wrote again, on March 16, 1864, to tell his mother how matters were progressing:

Next Sunday . . . the Archduke Maximilian accepts the imperial crown of Mexico, and within two or three months he will have arrived in that country. Then our difficulties in this most unfortunate matter will begin. Thus far the Austrian Government on the one side, and the United States Government on the other, have agreed to wash their hands of it entirely. But when the new "Emperor" shall notify his succession to the Washington Government, we shall perhaps be put into an embarrassing position.[3]

Motley was right that Washington was very much concerned about Maximilian becoming Emperor of Mexico. Such a move would strengthen France's position there; it was in direct defiance of the Monroe Doctrine; and a democratic country like the United States could hardly be expected to relish having a European Archduke become a monarch on the North American continent. Only the fact that Washington had an internal war on its hands kept it from taking action. Richmond, however, was inclined to favor the French in Mexico, although some Southerners had reservations about collaborating with them.

Not only Motley but Dayton was writing to Seward about the Mexican problem. On March 11, he told him that Drouyn de Lhuys had denied that France was interested in acquiring Texas. In fact the French Foreign Minister said emphatically that "France would not take Texas as a gift."

Stories about Texas and France had been planted in European newspapers. One of them said that Alexander Stephens, Vice-President of the Confederacy, had gone to Europe to conclude a treaty with France for the cession of Texas and other Southern states. But Stephens, whose health was never good, happened to be ill in his home in Georgia at this time.[4]

When Maximilian came to Paris early in March to consult with Napoleon III, Slidell vainly sought an audience with him. He told Benjamin on March 16 that he felt that the Archduke was evasive because he

considered it inexpedient to see him. He also said that the French thought
Maximilian was delaying his departure for Mexico unnecessarily. And,
he added, "it is impossible to exaggerate the unpopularity of the Mexican
expedition among all classes and parties in France. It is the only subject
upon which public opinion seems to be unanimous. I have yet to meet
the first man who approves of it, and several persons very near the Emperor have spoken to me of it in decided terms of condemnation. The
Emperor is fully aware of this feeling and is, I believe, very desirous to
get rid of the embarrassment as soon as he decently can; the Archduke
may be obliged to rely on his own resources at a much earlier day than
he expects."

Slidell told Benjamin that he had heard that Lincoln had told Mercier
at a farewell interview that "he was authorized to say to the Archduke
that his government would be recognized by Washington without difficulty on the condition . . . that no negotiations should be entered into
with the Confederate States."[5]

It was most unlikely that Lincoln would ever have made such a com-
mitment. Furthermore, Mercier had not had a farewell interview with
him. (It is possible that Chase, who was soon to resign as Secretary of
the Treasury, did give some sort of vague promise to the Minister from
France.)[6] But Slidell believed the Lincoln story and was greatly put out
by Maximilian's evasiveness. He wrote: "All this is very disgusting, and
I find it very difficult to keep my temper amidst all this double dealing.
. . . This is a rascally world, and it is most hard to say who can be
trusted."[7] Unable to reach the Archduke, Slidell persuaded a French
officer to brief him while en route to Mexico. He showed his resentment
by telling the officer to inform Maximilian about "the consequences that
will result from a refusal to be on good terms with the Confederacy."[8]

Maximilian went for a final visit to his beloved castle Miramar near
Trieste. He and his ill-starred wife Charlotte left there on April 14 to
make a ceremonial journey to the new world. When they stepped ashore
at Vera Cruz on May 29, European royalty made its last bid for a foot-
hold in America.

In the United States on April 4, Henry Winter Davis of Maryland asked
unanimous consent of the House to report from the Committee on Foreign Affairs a joint resolution, originally introduced in the Senate in
January, which declared that Congress was unwilling to let the world
think that it was indifferent to what was going on in the Republic of
Mexico and that it did "not accord with the policy of the United States to

acknowledge any monarchical government erected on the ruins of any republican government in America under the auspices of any European power." Samuel S. Cox of Ohio got up to say that the resolution was "a little late" and that he was afraid it might therefore be only "words, words, words—nothing more." Nevertheless, he was in favor of it. It should be backed up by something physical, he added, especially now that Maximilian, who was being called "the Arch Dupe" of Napoleon III, was on his way to Mexico.

After a brief debate, the resolution was passed unanimously, 109 to 0. The bill went to the Senate the next day. Many weeks later, the Speaker laid before the House letters from Lincoln and Seward together with recent correspondence between the State Department and Dayton in Paris which stressed the fact that Congress had no right to deal directly with foreign affairs, and Seward had asked Dayton to make that clear to the French Foreign Office.[9]

Drouyn de Lhuys had already heard about what Congress had done when Dayton called on him on April 22. In fact he greeted the American Minister with the words: "Do you bring us peace or bring us war?" Dayton managed to explain that the resolution was only intended to express what the North felt about France's actions in Mexico. Beyond that it had no official significance.[10]

The resolution languished in the Senate Committee on Foreign Relations for so long that on June 28 one of the Senators charged that it had lain there "as well buried as if it had been put into the Tombs of the Capulets" when it should have been printed. Sumner defended his Committee by saying that if all the papers now before it were printed they would take two large volumes. A wrangle over economy followed, and in that to-print or not-to-print argument, the joint resolution quietly expired.[11] Seward and the President, doubtless with much behind-the-scenes maneuvering, had won the day, and the embarrassing Congressional intrusion into foreign affairs was heard about no more.

An interesting comment on what may very well have been the true motive behind Congress' attempt to pass the resolution was made by Benjamin in a letter to Slidell written on April 16. According to the politically astute Confederate Cabinet member, "the resolution was offered as a party move to break down Lincoln's chance of re-election, its author, Winter Davis, being in active opposition and controlling the vote of Maryland for Mr. Chase."[12]

Slidell, reporting to Benjamin from Paris on May 3, took a serious view of the possible importance of the Congressional resolution, saying

that he believed that if it "had reached Europe a few days sooner Maximilian would still be at Miramar."[13]

Maximilian had not exactly endeared himself to the Confederates in Europe. Not only Slidell but Mann also had a poor opinion of him. Writing
to Benjamin from Brussels on April 15, just after the new Mexican Emperor had started toward his far-away throne, he said:

> If he [Maximilian] does not find . . . that he has been over-
> reached by the duplicity of Louis Napoleon, I shall be egre-
> giously mistaken. . . . Always the most extravagant of princes,
> grievously tormented by pecuniary embarrassments, his reign is
> likely to be inaugurated by reckless expenditures. A 6 per cent
> loan of 201,600,000 francs at 63 to the 100 has already been
> contracted by him in Paris. . . . Compared with the Govern-
> ment of the Confederate States (as stable as any within the
> confines of civilization), that of Maximilian scarcely deserves
> to be regarded as the skeleton of a government, and yet it will
> be generally and promptly recognized.[14]

Hotze was kinder; he merely said: "I doubt whether the new Emperor
has really a settled policy in regard to us; but it is beyond question that
he left Paris in a frame of mind so hesitating and timid that any anxiety
on our part to win his good graces would only confirm him in a cautious
reserve."[15]

Hotze had been in Paris for a short visit early in April in order to survey the chances for persuading the French press to favor the Confederacy.[16] Napoleon III's involvement with Maximilian and Mexico might
make pro-Southern propaganda more acceptable.

That the Confederacy had thought that Maximilian's being the Emperor of a neighboring country might be of great importance was shown
earlier in the year when Davis had appointed Brigadier General William
Preston of Kentucky to succeed John T. Pickett as Minister to Mexico.[17]
Pickett's career as a diplomat had been so absurd that it had hurt the
Confederacy's standing in that country. His successor's failure was even
more remarkable, for he was not even to set foot in Mexico until after
the war was over. The fault, however, was not entirely his. He was instructed not to go there until it was certain that he would be properly
received by Maximilian. He went to Havana to wait and then proceeded
to Europe in the summer of 1864. By the time he tried to get to Mexico,
the South's last ports had been closed. He went to Matamoras, joined

forces with Kirby-Smith, and became a major general. He was among
the Confederates who sought refuge in Mexico after the war.

Although the Confederate State Department was inept in its dealings
with Mexico, Seward was at his best in handling relationships with that
country. Experience had made him into a first-rate statesman. He had
handled the difficult problem of the Congressional resolution well, and
he now saw the Mexican problem very clearly. On May 21 he wrote a
confidential letter to John Bigelow in Paris in which he explained his
position:

> I regret that you think my course towards the French Govern-
> ment is too conciliatory and courteous. If our armies succeed as
> we hope, we shall have no conflict with France or with any
> foreign power. So long as our success in suppressing the slavery
> faction at home is doubted abroad, we shall be in danger of
> war with some one of the Maritime Powers upon some sudden
> provocation. If we have war with one, we may expect to have
> war with more than one. If we escape war with all, my courtesy
> to France will have done no harm. If we shall at last, through
> unavoidable delay here, fall under the calamity of a foreign war,
> it will then have come soon enough; and we shall be none the
> less able to meet it for all the prudence we practised in trying
> to delay and, if possible, to avert it. I think . . . that with our
> land and naval forces in Louisiana retreating before the rebels
> instead of marching towards Mexico, this is not the most suit-
> able time we could choose for offering idle menaces to the Em-
> peror of France. We have compromised nothing, surrendered
> nothing, and I do not propose to surrender anything. But why
> should we gasconade about Mexico when we are in a struggle
> for our own life?[18]

Chapter 40

THE SOUTH AS IT REALLY WAS
—AND AS OUTSIDERS SAW IT

Judah P. Benjamin had every reason to be a pessimist. Life had not treated him well, and despite the fame and fortune he had acquired entirely by his own efforts he had a right to wear the pain-twisted mask of tragedy. But he did not; he preferred the mask of comedy and always faced the world with a ready smile. That he covered his true feelings with a mask is certain. He had found that the best way for him to survive was to be ingratiating, and he tried to see the best side of things—or at least to act as if he did. For him, this way of life was eminently successful. Of all the Confederate civilian leaders he did best in the postwar era; he escaped to England and built a distinguished new legal career there.

Evidence of his irrepressible optimism can be seen in a letter he wrote to Slidell on April 23, 1864. On this day, the people of Richmond knew very well that Grant was massing his forces to attack them and were grateful for the heavy rains that had thus far prevented any army movements. Boys and old men were being pressed into service, and the city was to be partly evacuated so it would be easier to feed those who had to remain in it. There was no longer just a scarcity of food in Richmond; the situation was desperate. Earlier in the month J. B. Jones had written in his diary:

> I cannot afford to have more than an ounce of meat daily for each member of my family of six; and today, Custis's parrot, which has accompanied the family in all their flights, and, it seems, will *never* die, stole the cook's ounce of fat meat and gobbled it up before it could be taken from him. . . . The old cat goes staggering about from debility, although Fannie often gives him her share. We see neither rats nor mice about the

premises now. This is famine. Even the pigeons watch the
crusts in the hands of the children and follow them in the yard.
. . . Rich speculators, however, and the officers of influence
stationed here . . . get enough to eat. Potatoes sell at $1 per
quart; chickens, $35 per pair; turnip greens, $4 per peck! . . .
Every day we have accounts of robberies . . . of cows, pigs,
bacon, flour—and even the setting hens are taken from their
nests![1]

April 23, the day Benjamin wrote to Slidell, was a remarkable one in
many ways. It was the 300th anniversary of Shakespeare's birth, which
was being widely celebrated in England. At sea, Semmes was using the
captured *Rockingham* for a target and finding out that his powder was
no longer much good. In London, Russell was writing a letter to Lyons
which showed how little the head of the British Foreign Office understood the United States, for he said that it was a pity for it to go on with
the war because it could never hope to get obedience from the South. "If
they can obtain the right bank of the Mississippi and New Orleans, they
might as well leave to the Confederates Charleston and Savannah," he
suggested.[2] But he had never met Lincoln or Seward.

In Richmond, the day was warm and sunny, languorous with spring
and the perfume of flowers. Perhaps it was the fine weather that made
Benjamin so cheerful. At any rate, he wrote this optimistic prediction to
Slidell:

It had long been foreseen by us that Mr. Seward would hesitate
at no promises in order to postpone the evil day which is approaching with such giant strides when the whole structure of
the North will topple from its sandy foundation and our recognition be forced not only upon neutrals but upon the enemy by
the strength, valor, and fortitude of our people. Every hour pro-
duces fresh evidence of the early and disastrous breakdown in
Northern resources both of men and money, and our day of
happy deliverance is seen to be dawning by those even who
have hitherto been despondent. The contrast between our
armies and those of the enemy in dash, spirit, and confidence is
amazing and is displayed so strikingly as to produce marked
effect on the spirit of the people in the two countries. You can
not fail to be impressed with the wonderful change in the tone
of the public journals North and South. But Europe is still as
blind as ever and hugs with fondness the delusive promises of
the United States Secretary of State.[3]

Richmond was uninformed about Europe, while Europe was even more uninformed about Richmond. Letters like Benjamin's were giving a false impression of the city's real condition. His was intended, of course, to bolster up the courage of the Confederates stationed abroad. Jones' entries in his diary, which were addressed only to himself—and to posterity —gave a much truer picture.

When the tremendous Union spring campaign came to an end at Cold Harbor on June 3 in a final assault which was so wasteful of life that Grant himself regretted having ordered it, the Confederacy was far worse off than it had been in April. Lee's veterans had repulsed the long series of attacks, Richmond was still safe, and the North was weary of the endless bloodshed, for it had lost 50,000 men in the two-month campaign. The Confederates had lost 32,000, but these figures, like Benjamin's letter, do not tell the whole story, for the Union Army's losses were 41 per cent of its total strength while the Confederate losses were 46 per cent. The real truth was even worse. The South could no longer replace its losses; the North could because its population had been increased during the war by immigration. And Lee had lost one of his best commanders, daring young J. E. B. Stuart, who had been mortally wounded at Yellow Tavern.

But the Confederate dollar went up in June, and some misinformed —or willfully blind—people overseas still persisted in thinking that the South was in a stronger position than ever before. Actually it was a hollow shell.

One of the most significant indications of the South's economic decay was the fact that although the price of everything else had increased enormously, the cash value of slaves had declined. Seward brought this to world attention in his circular of February 4: "$150 or $200 of United States currency is the highest price which the most marketable slave commands, either in Virginia or in Georgia. The Richmond papers declare that board and clothing are a full equivalent for the hire of the best servants in that market. I need not say that this is a confession that slaves, as property, are absolutely worthless."[4]

In a letter written to Dayton a few days later, Seward pointed out that this meant "a reduction of 1000 per cent in the value of slaves since the war began." Land and not the outright ownership of labor was becoming the chief investment of wealth in the South as it was elsewhere. "When this change takes place," Seward said, "all the motives of disunion perish."[5]

Nevertheless, the Confederacy fought on, not merely because it wanted to preserve slavery, but because it was embarked on a course from which there could be no turning back. When a nation's armies are fighting in the field, it seldom seeks peace even though it knows that the object for which it started the war is lost. To surrender at such a time would require more common sense than is ordinarily given to men.

Some Europeans were becoming aware of the true situation, for they were now investing in United States bonds. Dudley was in such a good position to watch what was happening in the foreign market that Secretary Chase wrote to thank him for his reports and to assure him that the amount of bonds being purchased abroad was so large that he would not "be surprised if the surplus of exchange before long is in our favor."[6]

Dudley was trying to get information about two ships which he suspected were intended for the Confederate Navy. One of them, the *Amphion,* was a former British naval vessel; the other was the *Hawk,* a newly built Glasgow steamer which was acquired, not for the Confederacy, but for the Virginia State Navy.[7] Even this late in the war, the individual Southern states were asserting their right to have ships of their own. Both vessels quickly came to nothing. The *Hawk* succeeded in getting to Bermuda, only to remain idle there for six months and then go back to England. The *Amphion* had even less of a career, for she was soon sent to Copenhagen to be sold.[8] But these and other suspected ships had to be watched. In some cases Bulloch may have deliberately planted false leads in order to keep Dudley and his men busy running them down.

Bermuda and Nassau were thriving because they were useful way-stops where deep-draft ocean liners could discharge big loads which they had brought from Europe without risk. Smaller, faster, shallow-draft blockade-runners could then take selected cargoes of merchandise into Confederate ports. Since Nassau was near the American coast, it got most of this business during the early part of the war. Then, as Union naval ships began to watch the channels there, much of the business was transferred to Bermuda. It was farther from the coast, but that was not important.

The major ports of Charleston and Wilmington remained open in 1864, and the Union Navy could harass but not entirely stop the secret traffic that slipped in and out on dark nights. In an effort to end the trade with Europe for good, the North began to plan huge campaigns to capture these essential cities. Attempts to take Charleston from the sea never ceased; they had been going on for years but had always failed.

Wilmington was too far up the Cape Fear River for warships to get past the heavily fortified shores. Near the mouth of the river was Fort Fisher with huge defensive works on which were mounted some of England's largest and most modern cannon. The Confederates spent months still further strengthening their defenses. The Union was equally busy devising ways to get by them.

The North's hatred for the *Alabama* became greater as news of her activities was received. Gideon Welles grumbled about the money it was costing to keep ships on the lookout for her, but he never hesitated to send another one out when Semmes' most recent depredations were located.

In a propaganda effort to make people believe that Semmes was an unfeeling monster, the United States Legation in London paid for the printing of a 16-page pamphlet entitled "Narrative of the Cruise of the *Alabama* by One of Her Crew."[9] This little circular told a familiar tale, but one thing in it was new. Although it was known that Semmes had had trouble with some of his crew, his methods of dealing with them had not been publicized. According to the author of this pamphlet, a seaman who had been recaptured after deserting the *Sumter* was "frequently punished by having his hands and legs fastened to the rigging, the punishment being known as the 'Spread Eagle. . . .' He would be kept in this position for four hours . . . and this was done at least twenty times. At last they ironed his legs and arms and put him on shore on a desolate island. . . . The crew subscribed some seventeen pounds unknown to Captain Semmes, which we gave him in the hopes of its being some inducement to a vessel to take him off."

The pamphlet did not mention the fact that the man had been a constant troublemaker who had smuggled liquor on board and who, at one time, was suspected of trying to incite the crew to mutiny. There is no doubt that he bitterly hated his captain and would have killed him if he could, but Semmes never gave him the chance.

Chapter 41

CIVIL WAR IN THE ENGLISH CHANNEL

On June 3, when the Union dead were piled up in rows at Cold Harbor and Grant was about to discontinue his costly spring campaign, the *Alabama* was 500 or 600 miles from Cherbourg, moving rapidly before the western winds. If it had not been for her foul bottom she would have made even better time than usual, for Semmes had taken spars from the *Tycoon,* equipped them with sails, and put them up on the masts.[1] His primary purpose was to disguise the *Alabama's* too-well known appearance, but the extra canvas should also have increased his ship's speed.

At 12:30 P.M., June 11, the sea-worn Confederate raider dropped anchor in Cherbourg Harbor.[2] Semmes obtained leave to land his 38 prisoners and sent them ashore that day. He also telegraphed Slidell in Paris that he had arrived. His crew was at last able to get fresh food. Semmes, despite his illness, noted in the ship's log: "We are here in the midst of the strawberry season, and the strawberries are large and fine." Fine also, he added, were the beef, mutton, milk, and butter.[3] They should have been, for he was in Normandy, one of the richest agricultural regions of France, and it was late in the spring when that region's food is at its best.

Semmes surely knew that Cherbourg was a naval port with no commercial shipyards. He soon found out that he needed special permission from the Emperor to have the *Alabama* repaired there—and the French ruler was in Biarritz for at least a week. There was nothing to do but wait, for one did not disturb His Highness while he was enjoying a carefree stay at his favorite seaside resort.

While Semmes was in Cherbourg, *The Times* printed a long letter he had written at sea. In it he said that the British Queen's Proclamation of Neutrality, which had inspired other nations to take a similar stand, had made it necessary for him to destroy Yankee shipping because it prohibited him from taking captured prizes into a port where they could be sold and put to use. England could still revoke "her unjust and unnatural orders," he suggested. But all that his letter accomplished was to make the United States Government more eager than ever to collect damages from Britain for the destruction done by the Confederate raiders she had built.[4]

Two days before this letter was published, Semmes' nemesis appeared at the eastern entrance to Cherbourg Harbor. This was the U.S.S. *Kearsarge* under the command of Captain John A. Winslow. Dayton had summoned him by telegram from Flushing where his ship had been waiting for just such a chance.[5]

Semmes had expected to remain in Cherbourg for three months while the *Alabama* was being repaired. The safe and sensible thing for him to do was to stay there and have his ship put into fighting trim. The only trouble with this was that he would then be blockaded, not by one man-of-war, but by as many as the Union Navy could send in. He might be able to put the *Kearsarge* out of commission or sink her; he could not hope to conquer a whole fleet. What he would do after such a victory remains an open question. Semmes, the hitherto articulate writer, has little to say about what happened near Cherbourg in June 1864. Some of his subordinates believed that he sought combat deliberately because of "the insinuations he had been forced to listen to regarding his avoidance of armed ships of his foe."[6]

Semmes began the affair by sending a note to the Confederate agent in Cherbourg which read: "I desire to say . . . that my intention is to fight the *Kearsarge* as soon as I can make the necessary arrangements. I hope these will not detain me more than until tomorrow evening, or after the morrow morning at furthest. I beg she will not depart before I am ready to go out."[7]

Winslow did not reply to the challenge; he had no reason to because the United States Navy took the official position that Confederate ships were rebels without any national rights. It was his duty to find them and then capture or sink them. He had found the *Alabama;* now he waited grimly outside the harbor to complete the job.

The elegant British yacht *Deerhound,* owned by John Lancaster, was in Cherbourg. By coincidence, she had also been built by the Lairds as a smaller version of the *Alabama.* The Lancasters had their children with them, and it was these youngsters' eagerness to see a real naval battle that caused the *Deerhound* to be present at the engagement.

While the *Alabama* was being coaled and made ready, Semmes sent ashore all the specie he was carrying as well as the ransom bonds and the valuable chronometers he had captured. But he kept on board nearly a hundred American flags taken from the ships he had destroyed or bonded.

The *Alabama* and the *Kearsarge* were not too unevenly matched in size, armament, or original speed. But the *Kearsarge* had the advantage because she was in better condition, had anchor chains draped along her sides as a sort of makeshift armor to protect her engines, and her gunners had had plenty of practice with fresh gunpowder. Semmes' first officer, John McIntosh Kell, said that he reminded his captain that the *Alabama's* cannon powder had proved to be stale when they fired practice shots at the *Rockingham*. But a junior officer, Arthur Sinclair, claimed that Semmes had no suspicion his powder was defective.[8]

It has been said that the encounter that day was "the first decisive engagement between shipping propelled by steam and the first test of the merits of modern naval artillery," but neither of these statements is true. Any number of steam-powered ships had been fighting with recently made guns on American inland waters. Steam—and even screw propellers—had been used in the Crimean War ten years before the *Kearsarge* and the *Alabama* met. And the poorly armed U.S.S. *Hatteras,* which Semmes had sent to the bottom off the coast of Texas in January 1863, was a steamship even though she was a sidewheeler.

Nor was it true that the battle was the "first ever fought between two vessels in which horizontal shell firing was employed."[9] Shell guns had been used with devastating effect by the Russians when they attacked the Turkish fleet at Sinop in 1853 and also by the British in ship-to-shore bombardments during the Crimean War. Thousands of explosive shells had been fired in the numerous naval engagements in American waters during the past few years, and most of them came from horizontal guns —not from mortars that lobbed their missiles up almost vertically. Yet it was not "modern" rifled shell guns but old-fashioned smooth-bores shooting explosive shells that decided the *Alabama's* fate, for the *Kearsarge's* two massive 11-inch Dahlgrens (then considered obsolescent in America) did most of the damage.

The only real naval "first" in the conflict on June 19 was the fact that two propeller-driven steamships were fighting with horizontal shell guns on the open sea and not in the confined waters of a river or a bay. Semmes and Winslow were therefore able to circle around each other with the same side of their ships facing. This was a novel way of maneuvering which steampower made possible, but it was hardly revolutionary in its tactical significance.

What made the conflict between the *Kearsarge* and the *Alabama* important was the fact that the eyes of the world were watching it. And the setting—the English Channel—meant that the two European nations most involved in the war in America had the battle fought out in the narrow waters between them. The conflict in America had seemed far away and therefore unreal. Now the North and the South were shooting at each other on the doorsteps to France and England. No one was more aware of this than Semmes. He told it to his crew when he addressed them before the battle began.

A special train brought sightseers from Paris to Cherbourg. Among them was 32-year-old Edouard Manet, who went out on a French fishing boat to see the great spectacle and paint it.[10] Thus one of the innovators who had exhibited his rejected work at the Salon des Refusés the year before was recording history firsthand instead of inventing the pageantry of war in a studio.

William S. Dayton, son of the American Minister to France, had also come down from Paris. Early on Sunday morning, June 19, he stationed himself with a telescope on some high ground west of the port. In a letter to his father he wrote: "About nine o'clock the English yacht *Deerhound* . . . ran out a little toward the breakwater. After apparently observing for a few minutes, she returned and went alongside the *Alabama*. She then stood out again straight through the western pass to sea; about two miles out she headed more towards the *Kearsarge*. The *Alabama* then came out by the same pass and stood straight out to sea, the yacht running up and apparently communicating with her."[11]

What messages—if any—passed between the two vessels is unknown. Semmes, Lancaster, and the *Deerhound's* captain all later denied that there had been any communication at all, but their denial may, of course, have been an agreed-upon cover-up story. There is no doubt that the yacht came out of the harbor at 9 A.M., for her log says so.

The French warship *La Couronne* accompanied the *Alabama* to make certain that no shots were fired within the marine league. When the Confederate ship was well outside it, the French vessel returned to port. Some small local boats with spectators aboard also tagged along. The *Kearsarge*, in order to prevent Semmes from running back to seek refuge inside the marine league, stood far out to draw him away from shore. The weather was fine, but there was a light haze hanging over the surface of the sea. And the water was cold, as it always is in the deep parts of the Channel where the restless Atlantic currents surge back and forth.

Semmes was the challenger and Winslow the challenged. Both their ships were ready for combat as the *Alabama* approached her waiting adversary. Decks had been sanded so hurrying feet would not slip on blood that was still coursing through yet unwounded men's veins. And tubs of water stood on the decks for washing down the planks or putting out fires. Semmes wanted to fight at a distance because his long-range Blakeley rifle could throw a hundred-pound shell more than a mile. Winslow preferred to be closer so his two big smooth-bores could slam in their tremendous missiles.

At 10:50, when the *Kearsarge* was seven miles off shore, she turned and headed toward the *Alabama*, hoping to run her down. Seven minutes later, while the two ships were still about a mile apart, Semmes opened fire with a starboard broadside. The shots went high, cutting some of the *Kearsarge's* rigging or missing entirely and falling into the sea.[12] His gunners worked fast and had another broadside ready in a few minutes. This was followed by a third. The Confederate gunners were willing and they worked hard, but they had never had enough practice in aiming and firing at a target to make them truly expert. The limited amount of gunpowder on the *Alabama* always had to be hoarded; it was too scarce to be used except to stop ships, so practice drills had been rare. Besides, Confederate raiders were supposed to destroy commercial vessels and avoid combat.

One shot finally hit the *Kearsarge's* counter a glancing blow about 20 feet from the end of the ship, scored the planking, and lodged itself in the wooden stern-post. It was a percussion shell which should have exploded when it first hit. If it had, it would have done some damage to an area of no great importance. Much was made of the fact that it entered the stern-post and that if it had gone off there it would have torn out the afterpart of the ship, opening the *Kearsarge's* planks to the sea so she would surely have sunk. But there was no chance of its exploding once the percussion cap had proved to be defective.[13] All it did was make the rudder so hard to move that four men had to be assigned to it.

Good steering was essential at this stage of the battle because the two ships were now circling about a common center in order to keep their starboard batteries facing each other. Both were listing somewhat because so much weight had been shifted to one side. This was supposed to be an advantage because it exposed less of the hull to fire. And the *Alabama* was listing more than the *Kearsarge*.

In just 18 minutes after the firing had begun, a 68-pound, 8-inch Blakeley shell exploded on the quarter-deck of the *Kearsarge* and seriously wounded three men, one so badly that he died later. These were the only Union sailors hurt in the entire battle.[14]

The Confederate gunners loaded and fired quickly, but most of their shots were inaccurate. The *Kearsarge* gun crews took careful aim and made many hits. During the engagement, which lasted only a little more than an hour, the Union ship fired exactly 173 shots, 55 of which came from the two big Dahlgrens. No record was preserved of the number of times the *Alabama's* guns were discharged. Winslow estimated the figure at 370; Semmes did not even make a guess. All accounts agree that the Confederates fired much more rapidly than their opponents did, but even the shots that actually struck the *Kearsarge* did relatively little damage. Winslow said that 13 or 14 shots hit the lower part of the ship and 16 or 17 the masts or rigging.[15]

What really counted against the Confederates was that their aim was not good enough and that their powder had lost much of its strength. When their shells exploded, they often went off feebly. But the fact that they hit the *Kearsarge* only about 28 times, with less than half of these striking areas that mattered, shows that they were no match for their coolly efficient opponents.

When the two ships got close to each other, the heavy Dahlgrens reached their full effectiveness. Shell after shell from them smashed into the *Alabama* and literally blew her apart. Wood, iron, and human bone and flesh were torn asunder. One of her guns had to have its crew replaced four times as repeated explosions put able-bodied men out of commission by killing or wounding them. The Dahlgrens concentrated their attention on the lower part of the *Alabama's* hull, opening big holes into which sea water rushed. The smaller guns were aimed higher to clear the decks—which they did with terrifying efficiency.

Within a matter of minutes the *Alabama* was a shot-ridden wreck. Semmes, slightly wounded in the right arm, tried to head for the shore, but to do this he had to turn his crippled ship so her port side was exposed. Shots from her adversary poured in, and soon the Confederate battle flag came down. Winslow could not tell whether it had been shot or hauled down.

At this moment something happened about which accounts differ widely. Winslow said that the *Alabama* displayed a white flag of surrender, but that after fire from the *Kearsarge* had stopped, the Confederates began shooting again. Dr. J. M. Browne, the surgeon on the

Kearsarge, who had a chance to talk with some of the *Alabama's* wounded men when they were brought on board, said that they told him that two Confederate junior officers, who swore they would never surrender, rushed "in a mutinous spirit" to the two port guns and fired them.[16] Winslow's biographer said that this happened "by some chance never explained," and that the *Kearsarge's* guns then roared out again.[17] Finally a white flag did appear over the *Alabama's* stern, and all shooting ceased for good. Semmes claimed that Winslow fired "five times" after the *Alabama's* colors had been struck. Kell said that it was "five shots." Sinclair thought that the smoke of battle might have obscured the fact that the battle flag was gone.[18]

Master's Mate George T. Fullam took the *Alabama's* dinghy to the *Kearsarge* to ask that boats be sent to save the wounded. When he arrived there, he was asked if his ship had surrendered, and he said that she had. He had a chance to observe shot holes through the wooden casing over the *Kearsarge's* protective side chains. He also found out that her lifeboats had been damaged by shell fire and that only two of them were in condition to be used. A boat from the *Alabama* with twenty wounded men and an officer now reached the *Kearsarge,* while still another was on the way.

The *Deerhound* came up, and Winslow hailed her saying: "For God's sake, do what you can to save them!" The yacht then steamed toward the *Alabama* which was now ready to sink.[19]

Kell went below and found that the operating table with a patient on it had been swept away by an 11-inch shell. As the hold filled with water, huge bubbles of air rose and broke when they reached the surface. The strange noises made it seem as if the mortally wounded ship was moaning in her death agony.

When Kell reached the deck again, Semmes told him to abandon ship. Kell ordered each man to save himself and advised them "to jump overboard with a spar, an oar, or a grating, and get out of the vortex of the sinking ship."

Semmes and Kell hurled their swords into the water and removed their outer clothing so they could swim freely. When they plunged in, the sea around them was filled with men trying to stay afloat in the cold Channel water. They caught sight of the body of the assistant surgeon Llewellyn who could not swim but who had refused to go in one of the boats with the wounded. Then a boat from the *Deerhound* appeared.

When Kell was pulled into it, he saw Semmes lying in the stern sheets completely exhausted.[20]

Kell got Semmes to lie down flat on the bottom so he would not be seen, borrowed a cap with the word *Deerhound* on it, and took an oar to make it look as if he were one of the crew. Then, when a launch from the *Kearsarge* came by on a search for Semmes, Kell deliberately lied and said that he had been drowned.[21]

When the salvaged Confederates were safely aboard the *Deerhound* its owner asked Semmes where he wanted to be landed and got the reply: "I am under English colors; the sooner you land me on English soil the better." The yacht, which was very fast, then raced away to Southampton.[22]

When one of the officers on the *Kearsarge* saw the *Deerhound* moving off, he told Winslow that some of the prisoners said that she had Semmes and some of his officers on board. He suggested that a shot be fired to stop her, but Winslow replied "that no Englishman who flies the royal yacht flag would act so dishonorable a part as to run away with his prisoners when he had been asked to save them from drowning." Another officer backed up the first one, but Winslow thought that the yacht was "simply coming round." She proceeded on her course, and it was soon too late to overtake her.[23]

She was carrying 13 Confederate officers and 29 men. The *Kearsarge* had 70, of whom 17 were wounded and three were dying. A French pilot-boat rescued nine more and took them to Cherbourg. It was never determined exactly how many had been on the *Alabama,* but the number was close to 150. That meant that nearly 30 men were killed in battle or drowned.

Kell was surprised to find Fullam on the *Deerhound* because he had sent him to the *Kearsarge* to ask for help. From him he learned about the holes in the planking covering the chain armor. Semmes thought that the use of concealed protection was an outrage. "Had we been in possession of this knowledge," Kell wrote later, "the unequal battle would never have been fought."[24]

Semmes and Kell were good fighters but poor losers. Semmes carried on about the draped chains to the point where he became absurd. Winslow "did not show me a fair fight," he complained, "for . . . his ship was ironclad." And the planking over the chains, he said, made matters even worse. "The *Kearsarge,* though as effectually protected as if she had been armored with the best of iron plates, was to all appearances a wooden ship of war." And Semmes made these statements, not in a private letter or report, but in his book which was published four years after the battle.[25]

His own lieutenant, Arthur Sinclair, said bluntly that Semmes knew all about the chain armor.[26] Certainly, the use of anchor chains for protecting the sides of a wooden vessel was no secret, for it was known that this had been done on some of Farragut's ships when they captured New Orleans in 1862.

Far more important than young Sinclair's statement, however, is Bulloch's, for he was the Confederacy's best-qualified naval expert. "Captain Winslow," he wrote, "was quite right in doing whatever he could to increase the defensive power of his ship, and he was not bound to inform his adversary that he had encased her most vulnerable parts with chain cables."[27]

An examination which was made of the *Kearsarge* when she went into Cherbourg that afternoon showed that her hull had been struck only twice.[28] Since both hits were from 32-pounders and were well above the waterline, they would have done no great damage even if the protecting chains had not been there. Semmes became angry without justification, and his unfounded complaints were unworthy of an experienced naval officer.

Bulloch admitted that the *Kearsarge* had been well fought. But Winslow, whose conduct of the battle had been skillful, made several mistakes after it was over. One of them was to allow Confederate officers to return to the *Alabama* to pick up more survivors. If he had taken them prisoner and had put some of his own officers in charge of the boats, the Confederates would never have gotten away to reach the *Deerhound*. The other, and much more serious error, was to stay far away from the sinking ship until she went down. He was afraid that Semmes might be "using some ruse."[29] As a result, he sent the *Deerhound* in to do rescue work, and she then promptly made off for England with the men she had saved from drowning. That Winslow resented this can be seen in a private letter he wrote to Dudley five days after the battle: "The *Deerhound* ran off with the prisoners, which I did not believe any cur dog could have been guilty of under the circumstances."[30]

Not only Winslow but most Northern people were furious that Semmes had escaped to England on a British yacht and was made welcome when he arrived at Southampton. This, added to all he had done on the English-built *Alabama,* increased American hatred for the mother country.

After a short rest in the country, Semmes went off for a six-week holiday on the Continent. He returned to the Confederacy by way of Matamoras in time to take part in the evacuation of Richmond and the Appomattox Campaign. He was made a general as well as an admiral so he could command infantry troops.

But with the sinking of the *Alabama,* Semmes' career as a world figure came to a close. Her loss was a matter of universal interest, for she had been more than a ship—she had been a symbol of Confederate intransigency and had carried the Stars and Bars halfway around the world. When she went down, defeated by heavier Yankee arms and more powerful Yankee gunpowder, observers in Europe, who had taken far more interest in the naval battle fought near their continent than they ever had in the much more important engagements in far-off America, noted what had happened and chalked up the Union victory as one that made the South a poor investment. Why should they back an untried nation which had nothing but defective gunpowder for its fine English guns? Perhaps Southerners were aristocrats, but what good were gentlemen if they could not defend themselves from Northern vulgarians?

Chapter 42

THE CONFEDERATE NAVY
RUNS INTO MORE BAD LUCK

The *Alabama* was gone, but she immediately became the center of a controversy that was to go on for years. Seward was angry because a British yacht had rescued Semmes and some of his men and had put them safely ashore on English soil. But he was even angrier when he read British newspaper accounts of the way Semmes was being lionized. "The Government experiences much pain in reviewing these extraordinary incidents," he noted ruefully.

Adams was also concerned about the aftermath of the naval battle. For months he sent a series of letters to Russell demanding that Semmes and the others rescued by the *Deerhound* be turned over to his government. Russell's replies were consistently negative.[1] Nor were matters cleared up by an investigation which Dudley made in August when he interrogated several seamen who had been on the *Deerhound* and the *Alabama*. Some of them said there had been previous communication between the two ships; others said there had not. Dudley admitted that "all are very unreliable."[2]

But he did not let the matter drop. He went for a brief visit to the United States during the summer, and while there may have received instructions from Seward to try to solve the baffling problem of Lancaster's possible collusion with Semmes. He spent some time in France at the end of August interviewing young Dayton and the United States consul from Cherbourg, both of whom had witnessed the battle from the heights west of the city.

Dayton repeated what he had said in his letter to his father—that he had personally seen the *Deerhound* communicate twice with the *Alabama* during the morning before the battle. The consul confirmed this and went even further by saying that:

All the repairs on the *Alabama* were through and coal taken in some three or four days before the *Deerhound* arrived. Captain Semmes seemed to be waiting for something or somebody. . . . The fight took place the next morning after the arrival of Mr. Lancaster. In fact, the commander of the *Alabama,* from the time indicated in the letter when he would be ready to fight, up to the time when it came off, did nothing but drill his men. The repairs were all finished, and he merely laid at anchor, as if waiting. He could have gone out as well on one day as another. These facts made the impression on my mind that these two vessels were acting in concert, and that Captain Semmes was waiting for the arrival of Mr. Lancaster before he went out to fight.[3]

This information was conveyed to Earl Russell, but he was still unimpressed. After returning to Liverpool in September, Dudley found a seaman from the *Alabama* who was willing to testify that people from the *Deerhound* had visited the Confederate ship before the battle and that Lancaster had spent ten minutes in Semmes' cabin. This was just what Dudley wanted to hear, but the man spoiled it by insisting that there had been no communication at all between the two ships while they were at sea.[4] For him to say this was practically to nullify everything else he had said. Dudley was doubtless unhappy, but he mailed the deposition to Seward. Seward sent it to Adams, Adams sent it to Russell, and a wrangling exchange of letters went on for the rest of the year.

Russell refused to budge from his original contention that the British had not done anything wrong. And Adams stubbornly continued to ask for Semmes and his men to be surrendered even when he knew they were no longer in England.

The quarrel petered out to a futile end. To this day no one knows whether Lancaster and Semmes were in collusion or not. The available evidence can be interpreted to mean that they were—or that they were not. Unless new material comes to light, there seems to be no way of establishing the real truth.

That British readers were very much interested in Semmes and his career is evidenced by the fact that an enterprising publishing firm rushed out his *Cruise of the Alabama and Sumter* a few weeks after his ship was sunk. Moran purchased the two-volume work on August 1 and read it in such haste that he was able to say in his *Journal* the next day that it was a poor literary performance but that it contained "certain facts that will be very useful some day against G.B."

Something was going on in the Confederate Navy during the summer of 1864, which would have been of far greater concern to Seward than the *Alabama-Kearsarge* battle if the elaborate plot had succeeded. With the *Alabama* at the bottom of the ocean, the *Georgia* out of commission as a raider, and work stopped on all the other ships which had been under construction in England and France, the *Florida* seemed to be the only sea-going Confederate naval vessel left. But there was a British-built ship in Wilmington which had made two trips as a blockade-runner and which was now being armed to go out as a commerce-raider. This was the *Tallahassee,* a steamer which was to have so many names that she appropriately ended up as the *Chameleon.* She was to proceed north along the Atlantic Coast to strike a blow at shipping coming from the ports located there. This was part of Mallory's long-cherished scheme to attack New England, but by this time it had become even more ambitious.[5]

After the *Florida* left Brest on February 10, her new commander, Lieutenant C. M. Morris, stopped at Bermuda several months later. There he found a letter from Mallory dated June 2, which told him that more officers were waiting to join him, that he was authorized to draw up to $50,000 on Bulloch for funds, that his plan for cruising near the mouths of the Mississippi seemed less useful than an attack on New England, and that he should pay special attention to ships registered under the Brazilian flag because it was "generally used fraudulently to cover shipping between Brazil and the United States."[6]

Morris dutifully started for the New England coast and had successfully captured and destroyed several vessels on the way when he encountered one that was being towed by the fast steam tug *America.* The tug cast loose and ran for the shore to notify Welles that the *Florida* was near enough to be captured or sunk. Morris promptly decided to take no part in the projected coastal attack and crossed the ocean to Teneriffe in order to avoid the Union ships that would surely come out to search for him.[7]

He wrote a long letter of explanation to Mallory on July 13 and mailed it a few weeks later from the Canary Islands. The accidental escape of a fast steam tug had spoiled Mallory's carefully nurtured plot, because the *Florida* and the *Tallahassee* were expected to join forces for a combined raid on New England in which land-based forces were to come down from Canada and terrorize the State of Maine.

The *Florida's* leaving the scene of proposed action, however, was not the only thing that ruined the scheme. When four Confederates entered the border town of Calais on July 16 to hold up a bank there, they were caught, and one of them talked. Much of what he said may have been untrue, but it caused a Federal investigation to be made.[8]

Meanwhile, the *Tallahassee* had run through the blockade of Wilmington on August 6 and was going north along the coast, capturing and burning ship after ship. When she was off Sandy Hook, her captain wanted to enter New York Harbor, set fire to the shipping there, shell the Brooklyn Navy Yard, and steam up the East River to Long Island Sound. But the local pilots he captured were unwilling to show him the way, so he had to abandon the idea.[9]

He kept on going along the coast and was near Maine at the very time the Federal investigation of the Confederate plot was being conducted. The *Tallahassee's* presence there naturally lent credence to the testimony of the witnesses who were charging the Confederacy with an international conspiracy to invade American soil.

Nothing definite came of the investigation, but the *Tallahassee* was very real. She entered the port of Halifax to obtain coal and a new mast to replace one which had been damaged. Welles sent more than a dozen ships after her. Several were already lying off the western entrance to the harbor, when the *Tallahassee*, with the help of a friendly Canadian pilot, ran out one night through the shallow, seldom-used eastern channel. By making a swift return to Wilmington, she evaded pursuit and slipped past the blockade to reach her home port. She made another short cruise that autumn under the name *Olustee*, and then as the *Chameleon* went to Bermuda and Liverpool, where she arrived on April 9, 1865—the day Lee was surrendering his army at Appomattox.[10] She was sold after the war and ended up in the Japanese Navy.

Closely connected with the *Tallahassee's* second cruise as the raider *Olustee* was another British-built blockade-runner renamed the *Chickamauga*. She sailed from Wilmington, destroyed six ships along the coast, went to Bermuda for coal, and returned safely to Wilmington.[11]

Charles M. Morris followed Mallory's orders to investigate ships sailing under the Brazilian flag. After taking on coal in the Canary Islands early in August, he recrossed the Atlantic and entered the Brazilian port of Bahia at night on October 4.[12] He had an unpleasant surprise awaiting him, for the U.S.S. *Wachusett* was in the harbor although the two ships did not sight each other until morning. The Federal vessel was larger and more powerfully armed than the *Florida*; furthermore she was under the command of an exceedingly ambitious 50-year-old officer, Napoleon Collins, who had been in the Navy for 30 years and had slowly been promoted to the rank of commander although he had never done anything outstanding. When he awoke to find the notorious Confederate raider anchored only half a mile away, his ambition soared. This was a Heaven-sent chance to win the fame that had been denied him.

International law stood in his way, for it prohibited conflict in the harbor and gave the *Florida* 24 hours' clearance before Collins could start after her. The Brazilians, too, were a nuisance. They were taking no chances. One of their sloops of war brought word to the *Florida* that she could stay in port 48 hours for repair (later changed to four days). Then, for safety's sake, the Confederate ship was requested to anchor between the Brazilian vessel and the shore.

For some inconceivable reason, the *Florida's* commander gave a few of his officers shore leave on the night of October 6–7 and went to stay in a hotel himself. He was awakened at 3:30 A.M. to be told that there was some trouble in the harbor. When he reached the waterfront, he was informed that the *Wachusett* had rammed his ship, captured her, and was towing her out to sea.

The Brazilian Navy sent a steamer pulling a sailing corvette after the rapidly disappearing ships, but the clumsy pair were unable to overtake Collins. Nor did any of the shots fired from the harbor forts find a target. The *Florida* and more than 70 of her officers and men had been successfully seized by an open violation of international law. Some kind of amends and apologies would have to be made to Brazil, but meanwhile the Confederate Navy had lost one of its most effective commerce-raiders.

On his way home, Collins put in at St. Thomas and there permitted 18 of his prisoners to escape in order to get rid of them. When he arrived at Hampton Roads on November 11, he found himself to be both a hero and a villain.

Despite the public acclaim for him, the Administration was embarrassed, the Navy was embarrassed, and the State Department was embarrassed. Collins was subjected to the formality of a court-martial in which he was found guilty but was later exonerated. Seward apologized to Brazil, and there was even talk of returning the illegally captured ship to Bahia. The need for doing so, however, was nicely avoided, for the *Florida*, while moored in Hampton Roads, was struck by an army transport on November 19. She then developed a slow leak and sank gently to the bottom after being towed to Newport News. There were rumors that her sea-cocks had been deliberately opened, but there was no way of proving such a charge.[13]

Chapter 43

WAR WITH ENGLAND IS AGAIN AVOIDED

During the middle of 1864, while a good part of the Confederate Navy was being liquidated, the prospects for the success of the contending armies varied considerably from month to month. At the beginning of July, Jubal Early came out of the Shenandoah Valley with 10,000 men to launch a whirlwind attack on Harpers Ferry, Hagerstown, and Frederick. He then threatened Baltimore, and by July 11 was on the outskirts of Washington. Union troops were rushed to the city, but for a few hours it looked as if the Northern capital was in serious danger of being captured.

John Hay wrote a vivid account of what happened in the White House that day: "At three o'clock P.M., the President came in bringing the news that the enemy's advance was at Ft. Stevens. . . . He was in the fort when it was first attacked, standing upon the parapet. A soldier roughly ordered him to get down or he would have his head knocked off. I can see a couple of columns of smoke just north of the White House. It is thought to be Silver Springs in flames. . . . The President is in very good feather this evening. He seems not in the least concerned about the safety of Washington."

Lincoln went to Fort Stevens again the next day and saw a man shot by his side.[1] Then the Confederate wave rolled back, and the national capital was safe, as the President had evidently believed it would be.

The attack on Washington was merely a diversion; the main contest between the two armies was going on at Petersburg and Richmond which were now protected by heavily fortified lines. An attempt was made to break through at the end of July, when a powerful mine was exploded near Petersburg. But the operation, which had been intelligently conceived and skillfully planned up to the very moment that 8000 pounds of buried gunpowder went off, turned into a disaster for the Union forces when they tried to dash through the resultant crater. Stupid staff work sent many soldiers to their deaths in the yawning hole, and the elaborate effort came to nothing. The armies then settled down to a highly perfected system of trench warfare which was to continue until a few days before Appomattox.

It must have been difficult for diplomats trying to keep their home offices posted about the progress of the war to tell which side was winning. Less than a week after the North's unsuccessful offensive at the Petersburg crater, a Union naval force led by Farragut steamed through a thickly planted minefield and defeated the little Confederate fleet that was trying to defend the entrance to Mobile Bay. When word was received in London that Farragut had won, his victory was made to seem unimportant because he had not taken the city. The fact that Mobile was nearly 30 miles from the entrance to the harbor was ignored. So was the reality of the situation, for the loss of Mobile Bay meant that the South no longer had a major port on the Gulf with rail connections to it.

It was even more difficult for ordinary citizens in Europe to see beyond day-to-day victories and defeats to understand the true meaning of what was happening. When the attempt to blast a hole through the lines at Petersburg failed, one British journal which had generally favored the North said: "it is supposed that [Grant] will have to retire . . . to Washington, unable to arrest the threatened advance of the Confederates."

But the Confederates were not even trying to advance; they were solidly dug in and had no intention of leaving their trenches unless they were driven out. The same paper went on to say that Sherman was being held in check before Atlanta at the very time he was about to occupy that city. The editorial writer was paying more attention to gossip in the London clubs than to reports from the field when he said: "Just now the probability of a change in the character of the war, by which the Confederates will cease to be on the defensive and become the aggressors, is much discussed."[2]

What was influencing British opinion more than anything else was that after more than three years of intensive warfare, the admittedly more powerful North was still unable to subjugate the rebellious South. It was therefore felt that the Confederacy would eventually become independent, and stories of the North's war weariness confirmed this belief. But England did not know that Southern railroads were in hopelessly bad condition or that there were desperate shortages of manpower, food, clothing, and almost everything else. Grant's failure to beat Lee, vituperative attacks on the Lincoln Administration during the bitter election campaign, and lack of reliable information about conditions in the South were all helping to confirm many Englishmen's stubborn belief that the Confederacy would survive. It was ironic that this belief was still strong in the late summer of 1864 when the South was showing obvious signs of defeat.

European bankers, however, were not deceived because the Confederate dollar gave them their clue. After Christopher G. Memminger, Secretary of the Treasury, resigned in June, the always sensitive currency began to decline in value and was never to go up again. This was not because the man who succeeded him—George A. Trenholm—was any less able, or even less esteemed. The Confederate dollar now had nothing behind it, and the astounding Funding Act passed by the Congress in Richmond on February 13 had destroyed confidence in all the various kinds of financial paper issued by the government.[3]

During the last half of 1864, Confederate finances, which had been shaky even during the earlier part of the war, now entered the nightmare phase. The Confederate dollar was a myth; it had some purchasing value only because the people had nothing else for currency. Trading of one object for another naturally became more popular, for each party to such a transaction then acquired something useful.

Some of the British upper-class people's wrong-headedness about the South's chance to continue as a separate nation, undoubtedly came from their desire to see it do so. And fear was adding to this desire, for the British were concerned about what might be done with the North's vast armed forces, huge supplies of weapons, and suddenly expanded navy after the war was over. Whether the long conflict ended with a Union victory or a negotiated peace, the threat to Canada would be the same.

Lyons was very much aware of this danger and had indicated it in his letters to Russell. That Russell believed there might be an attack on Canada is shown by the fact that on July 23 he requested Lyons to go to Quebec to consult with Lord Monck and Sir James Hope about defending that country. Yet at this time Russell was still willing to deal with the South by sending "a civil or military agent or commissioner" to Richmond by way of Mexico and Texas.[4]

Lyons was glad to escape the summer heat of Washington so he remained in Canada until October. That he was not the only one to be worried about the border defenses can be seen in an analysis of the situation made by the British War Office on July 6. It was pessimistic about communications there and pointed out why they worked to Canada's disadvantage:

> Railway and telegraphic communication exist from one end of Canada to the other, but the line runs parallel to the frontier and is very much exposed at many points, while the railways of the United States strike the frontier at several places at right angles and afford great facilities for the sudden concentration of a large attacking army in a manner which, by breaking through our single line of communication, would render the drawing in of the outlying portions of our scattered forces a difficult and hazardous undertaking.[5]

The British had reason to be apprehensive about the attitude of the United States toward Canada, for it was during the end of 1864 that the Confederacy, in desperation, turned to guerrilla tactics, underground warfare, sabotage, and outright terrorism. It believed that such methods were justified because of what Sherman and Sheridan were doing in their ruthless campaigns in the South. Since Canada was the easiest place from which to operate against the Northern states, Commissioners and secret agents were sent there.

James P. Holcombe, a scholarly attorney, an ardent secessionist, and a steadfast defender of States' rights, had already gone to Canada in connection with the capture of the *Chesapeake*. Then, on April 27, Davis appointed Jacob Thompson and Clement Clay as Commissioners to carry out instructions which were never committed to writing so there is no way of knowing what they were. But what the Confederates admittedly did is fairly well covered by a long report which Thompson sent to Benjamin on December 3. It is one of the most remarkable secret-service documents of the war and certainly the most authoritative in its descriptions of actual operations.

The first was the organization of what became known as the Northwest Conspiracy. The Confederates rather naïvely believed that Illinois, Indiana, and Ohio, which had large numbers of disaffected and war-weary people, could be seized by "a bold, vigorous, and concerted movement." They also believed that Kentucky and Missouri would join these states, after which the war should end in 60 days. The original idea for a bold and vigorous movement was replaced by an attempt to influence the Presidential election. This did not work, for Union spies and detectives found out what was being planned and began to arrest the key figures. A great deal of Confederate gold—some of it sent in from Europe —was spent in trying to swing the election, but the North returned Lincoln to office. Thompson felt that the money had not been squandered, for he thought that the fear it created made it necessary to keep at least 60,000 soldiers away from the front to preserve peace at home.

Thompson also told about the underground efforts which had been made to capture the U.S.S. *Michigan,* a patrol vessel on the Great Lakes, and use it to attack Johnson's Island on Lake Erie in order to try to set free the Confederate prisoners confined there. This daring plot was put into effect on September 18 when two excursion steamers were seized. But again, "by some treachery," one of the ringleaders was arrested, and the attempt failed.[6]

Then, following a suggestion made by Benjamin, Thompson tried to induce Northerners to convert their paper money into gold, a move that would drive up the price of specie. Benjamin probably got the idea shortly after Chancellorsville when some Northern speculators planted a fraudulent newspaper report that Hooker had made a miraculous recovery from his defeat and had suddenly captured Richmond. The story was so obviously false that it was exposed before it could have much effect on the price of gold.[7] But the ingenious Benjamin may have been inspired by it.

Thompson advanced $100,000 to John Porterfield, a former Nashville banker, to buy gold in New York, export it, and then sell it in London for sterling bills of exchange which would be converted back into gold. The bad luck that seemed to haunt all the Confederate operations in Canada quickly put an end to this plot when a former partner of Porterfield was arrested for exporting the easily traced metal. After that, Porterfield himself "felt it prudent to return to Canada."

Thompson also said that he had paid several men to burn river steamers in St. Louis and "organize a corps for the purpose of incendiarism" in Cincinnati. Then, on November 25, an attempt was made to start simultaneous conflagrations in a number of New York hotels by the use of Greek fire. Even this elaborate plot fizzled out, although some damage was done.

The report also said that buildings had been set on fire in half a dozen Northern cities and hinted at a mysterious but never explained scheme to be carried out by a Dr. K. I. Stewart for $20,000 in gold. Thompson estimated that he and Clay had spent about $300,000 on these underground activities. He urged that further efforts be made to "force the enemy to keep . . . a large standing army at home, and to burn whenever it is practicable, and thus make the men of property feel their insecurity and tire them out with the war."[8]

Thompson had nothing to do, however, with the one operation from Canada which caused more trouble between that country and the United States than everything else that happened during the war. This was the raid on St. Albans, Vermont, which Clement C. Clay sponsored.

When Bennett H. Young, who had been one of Morgan's raiders, approached Clay with the idea of making a series of armed attacks across the border, the Confederate Commissioner approved the plan and advanced the money for expenses. Young then took about 20 men from Canada to St. Albans, where they lodged separately on the night of October 18. During the next day they held up the town of 5000 people and robbed its three banks of more than $200,000. When they started to set fire to several buildings, the citizens struck back by shooting at them. The Confederates then used their guns and caused several casualties. They left town and rode swiftly to the border, pursued by irate townspeople who followed them into Canada. This brought on a three-way conflict among the pursuers, the raiders, and the local authorities, after which the Confederates were taken into custody by the Canadians.[9]

The already tense situation was made worse when a telegram was delivered to hot-tempered General John A. Dix while he was attending a dinner in New York at which Lord Lyons was present.[10] Dix immediately telegraphed orders for a military force to go after "the marauders who came from Canada." And, he said, "if they cannot be found on this side, pursue them into Canada and destroy them." Dix, who was never reticent about letting people know about his dramatic gestures, informed the dinner guests of what he had done.

Lyons asked Dix if his orders were authorized by the Federal Government and was told that they were not. The British Minister then got in touch with Washington to make sure that the explosive incident was handled on a top-governmental level, for he knew that if the pugnacious general's commands were carried out they would lead to armed conflict.[11]

In Richmond, J. B. Jones commented on the affair by saying: "A war with England would be our peace."[12] But Seward promptly sent a representative to Canada, and both governments tried to handle the matter by diplomatic methods. To do so was difficult, however, because another Confederate attempt to strike at the United States from Canada was made at this time.

Thompson had put up $18,000 to purchase the steamer *Georgian* and arm her for an attack on American ports. She was cruising the Great Lakes early in November and causing great excitement when four informants told the United States consul in Toronto about her. Seward asked the Canadian authorities to investigate. They did so and then invented one excuse after another to keep the would-be raider from getting arms.[13]

The St. Albans Raid, however, was not so easily disposed of. Canada refused to let the raiders be extradited, and when they were brought to trial, they were allowed to go free. Dix boiled up again and sent another angry telegram to military commanders along the border authorizing them, in case of more raids, "to shoot down the perpetrators, if possible, while in the commission of their crimes, or . . . to pursue them wherever they may take refuge; and, in the event of their capture, they are in no circumstances to be surrendered, but are to be sent to these headquarters for trial and punishment by martial law."[14]

This was a good way of bringing on a war, but hostilities were again averted when Lincoln revoked Dix's order. Many people were furious with Canada for letting the raiders go and were aroused to new anger when the loot taken from the St. Albans banks was turned over to John Porterfield, who had engineered the Confederate gold plot. He promptly disappeared with the money.

By this time Northern people were threatening to make retaliatory raids on Canada. Seward tried to pacify the public by putting into effect new passport regulations which had never been thought necessary before.

The Canadian Government was impressed by the violence of the reaction which the release of the raiders had caused and sent out warrants for them. Five were found and arrested, Bennett Young among them. Their trial began at the end of the year and went on until a few days before Appomattox. Then four of the five prisoners were let go while Young was held in custody for several months when he too was allowed to go free.[15]

That the St. Albans Raid did not lead to an open break was due to the fact that responsible men in the United States and Canada kept the strong tides of emotion under firm control. This raid was a better reason for war than the *Trent* Affair because it struck closer to home, and the Vermonters involved in it had been innocent victims of a guerrilla attack.

Lincoln summed up the situation in his Annual Message to Congress on December 6, 1864: "The Colonial authorities of Canada are not deemed to be intentionally unjust or unfriendly toward the United

States. . . . There is every reason to expect that . . . they will take the necessary measures to prevent new incursions across the border."[16]

One thing more remains to be told about the Canadian story. After John Wilkes Booth killed Lincoln, there was found among the assassin's personal effects a bank book showing that he had deposited $455 in the Montreal branch of the Ontario Bank on October 27, 1864. At the trial of the conspirators, the teller of that bank testified that Booth had bought "a bill of exchange for £61 and some odd shillings" on the same day he made the deposit shown in the bank book. This bill of exchange was found on the assassin's body when he was killed.[17]

Booth had also been in St. Lawrence Hall, a Montreal hotel, where Jacob Thompson and other Confederate secret agents often stayed. But the trail ends there and comes to nothing as do so many of the mysterious trails the assassin left behind.

October 27 was only eight days after the St. Albans Raid, and it was then that the Confederate conspiracies in Canada were at their height. Other connections of Booth with Canada were learned about after he killed Lincoln.

Chapter 44

INTERNATIONAL AFFAIRS AND PRIVATE SCANDAL

The war weariness that swept the country after Cold Harbor manifested itself—among other ways—in efforts to bring about a negotiated peace. Lincoln was not averse to this if he could obtain the terms he wanted. And the Vice-President of the Confederacy had tried to make peace overtures soon after Gettysburg. Lincoln discussed Stephens' proposal with the Cabinet then, but his associates were cool to the idea.[1]

Now, a year later, Canada became the base from which gestures toward peace were made. A strange and somewhat irresponsible Northerner, William C. Jewett, who had made money in Colorado and liked to be identified with that Territory, started things by informing Horace Greeley on July 5 that "two ambassadors of Davis & Co." were in Canada with "full and complete powers for a peace."[2] He was speaking about James Holcombe and George Sanders, who were authorized by Richmond to make war upon the United States but not to make peace.

The comedy of errors began. Unfortunately, it was a farce played against a background of war and suffering, and the players went through their silly parts while soldiers were dying on battlefields in Virginia, Georgia, Mississippi, and Tennessee. Even the initiator, "Colorado" Jewett, was an absurd figure who was characterized by the New York *World* as "a dancing windbag of popinjay conceit."[3]

Greeley, too, was a bit on the comic side. Although he had said many sensible things, and he certainly meant well, he sometimes made non-sensical suggestions during the war. The idea of a negotiated peace was not new to him, for he had already said that Switzerland should be appointed as an arbitrator to settle the conflict.

Since Greeley was the editor of the powerful New York *Tribune*, Lincoln could not ignore him. When Greeley sent him Jewett's letter, he countered by proposing that the editor should go to Niagara Falls to meet the Confederates who were living on the Canadian side of the river.

Greeley went rather reluctantly. After he had talked with Sanders and Holcombe, he telegraphed Lincoln that he did "not find them so empowered as [he] was previously assured." However, he thought they might be able to deal with the Confederate Government and asked the President to give them a safe conduct pass to Washington and Richmond.[4]

Lincoln sent John Hay to Niagara Falls with a letter addressed "To Whom It May Concern."

> Any proposition which embraces the restoration of peace, the integrity of the whole Union, and the abandonment of slavery, and which comes by and with an authority that can control the armies now at war against the United States will be received and considered by the Executive government of the United States, and will be met by liberal terms on other substantial and collateral points; and the bearer, or bearers thereof, shall have safe conduct both ways.[5]

When Hay and Greeley met the Confederates in Canada, Hay thought that Sanders was "a seedy-looking Rebel with grizzled whiskers and a flavor of old clo'" and that Holcombe "was a tall, solemn, spare, false-looking man with false teeth, false eyes, and false hair."[6]

The interview was brief and inconclusive. Greeley then consulted hastily with Jewett and returned to New York. The Confederates released a statement saying that Lincoln could not be trusted and was responsible for the continuation of the war. But this exercise in futility did not end there.

Simultaneous with the Greeley peace mission to Canada was another that reached Richmond on July 17 when Colonel James Jaquess and John R. Gilmore arrived there from Washington to talk with Judah P. Benjamin and Jefferson Davis. This meeting turned out to be as useless as the Canadian one, but it was held on a higher level and from it came a clear-cut statement from Davis about what he wanted at this time. "We are not fighting for slavery," he said. "You may emancipate every Negro in the Confederacy; but we will be free! We will govern ourselves! We will do it if we have to see every Southern plantation sacked and every Southern city in flames."[7]

Davis' attitude was publicized by Gilmore in an article which appeared in the September *Atlantic Monthly* in time to influence the Presidential election in November. Even Greeley admitted that:

> We have always supposed that there was a general understanding arrived at between the rebel commissioners in Canada and their Democratic visitors from this side as to what should be said and done at Chicago, and that it was spoiled by Jeff Davis's preemptory declaration to Jaquess and Gilmore that he would consent to no peace that did not recognize the Southern Confederacy as henceforth independent. We believe that visit of Jaquess and Gilmore to Richmond saved the vote of this [New York] state to Lincoln, though Sherman's capture of Atlanta and Sheridan's victories in the Valley doubtless coöperated with the semi-treasonable follies of the Chicago Convention and Platform to render the general triumph of Lincoln more complete and overwhelming.[8]

Lincoln realized this even sooner than Greeley did. A week after Gilmore and Jaquess returned from Richmond, he wrote to Abram Wakeman, the New York postmaster, that the Confederates in Canada had been empowered by Richmond "to assist in selecting and arranging a candidate and a platform for the Chicago [Democratic] Convention. . . . Thus the present Presidential contest will almost certainly be no other than a contest between a Union and a Disunion candidate."[9]

But Lincoln won the Presidential contest on November 8 when his Democratic rival, George B. McClellan, got the electoral votes of only three states. In London, Moran said that "the English don't like the reelection of Mr. Lincoln and grieve over it as if it were a disaster to themselves."[10]

By this time Sherman had taken Atlanta and begun his march to the sea while Sheridan was systematically devastating the Shenandoah Valley which had supplied the Confederacy with food.

A Union campaign to cut Georgia in half had been advocated more than two years before by two political commentators and theorists who had left Germany after the revolution of 1848 to settle in England. They were Karl Marx and Frederick Engels whose names were to be far better known in the next century than they were in their own. They had been writing for the New York *Tribune* and the Vienna *Presse*. On March 27, 1862, the latter paper had printed an article in which they scoffed at General Scott's Anaconda Plan to surround the Confederacy and squeeze it like a giant boa constrictor. The thing to do was to cut across it at its most vital point, and this, they said, was Georgia, the key to Secessia. "With the loss of Georgia," the article stated, "the Confederacy would be cut into two sections which would have lost all connection with one another."[11]

This was now being done, and before the year was over, Sherman was to reach the sea and take Savannah. His march northward then isolated Charleston from the rest of the Confederacy and also eliminated the Carolinas when his armies swept across them.

Napoleon III was kept informed about the progress of the war in America in 1864 because Dr. Thomas W. Evans, the American dentist who was on good terms with highly placed people in Paris, volunteered to go to the United States and bring back a firsthand report for the Emperor. Since the French ruler knew that Evans was strongly pro-Union, he could discount any obvious bias.

Evans arrived in New York on August 23 and went on to Washington where he found Seward "gloomy and dispirited" while other Cabinet members seemed downcast. This was when the election appeared to be uncertain, and there were no military victories. He also met Lincoln who said: "Well, I guess we shall be able to pull through; it may take some time. But we shall succeed—I *think*."

The President then suggested that Evans visit Grant at City Point. After his disappointing experience in Washington, the doctor was glad to go closer to the front in the hope of picking up more encouraging news. He spent some time with the man who was in charge of the Union war effort and was rather amused to find that the great general was completely ignorant of European affairs. But Grant enjoyed hearing Evans talk about the Emperor and his court and said that he would like to visit Paris.

Evans was with Grant for five days during which he had a good opportunity to watch the enormous Union build-up for the coming spring campaign. What he saw convinced him that the Confederacy could not last much longer. He returned to Paris in November, later claiming that he then knew all about the Grant-Sherman plan for their armies to advance toward each other until they met. He said that when he informed Napoleon III about the projected juncture, the Emperor said: "This is the beginning of the end."

Evans believed that one reason why England was never willing to grant full recognition to the Confederacy was that Queen Victoria was opposed to it. He also said that the death of her beloved husband, whose last act had been to soften the truculent British demands on Washington at the time of the *Trent* Affair, had made her feel that she must preserve peace between England and America as a tribute to the late Prince Consort.[12]

Another incident which happened in Paris at this time shows how personal matters can affect international affairs. When William C. Preston, the Confederacy's appointed Minister to Mexico, came to France, Mercier told him that he should call upon the Emperor. Preston said that any such move could be made only if it was arranged by his government's regularly authorized diplomatic representative—John Slidell.

"In that case," Mercier said, "you will meet with failure, as Mr. Slidell is now *persona non grata* with his Majesty."[13]

He then told him about an odd little episode which had occurred in a private club where Slidell had been playing cards with some French noblemen. The Confederate Commissioner was indiscreet enough to speak "about a certain promise and request in high quarters" which had to do with Maximilian and Mexico. One of the French dukes at the table said that no such request had ever been made. This so infuriated Slidell that he jumped up and shouted: "By God, no man, whether duke or Emperor, shall say that John Slidell ever said what was not true." The story, of course, quickly got back to Napoleon, and, according to John Bigelow, to whom it was related by Preston several years after the war, it seriously damaged Slidell's influence at the French Court.[14]

Slidell wrote to Benjamin on September 26 that he had met the Emperor at the races in the Bois de Boulogne and was gratified to report that His Majesty had greeted him "very cordially with a shake of the hand." But this overt gesture did not help the Confederate cause in France. The war had only a few months to go, and during that terminal period there was very little the Confederacy could hope to get in the way of favors from Napoleon III.

During the latter part of 1864, the Confederate agents in Europe had to stand by and watch the six ships which had been under construction for them in France be sold off to other governments. Prussia bought one of the ironclad rams and the two Bordeaux wooden corvettes, while Peru acquired the two Nantes corvettes. The other ironclad went to Denmark.[15] By the time she arrived there she was no longer needed because the war against Prussia and Austria was over, and the Duchies of Schleswig and Holstein had been lost.

The fact that this ship might be available reached Bulloch's attention, and highly secret negotiations to purchase her were begun.

The Union's diplomatic relationship with France changed with dramatic suddenness on December 1 when the American Minister, William L. Dayton, died under circumstances so bizarre that they seem more suitable to a spy thriller than to history. Bigelow's account of the strange death in his *Retrospections* is a marvel of carefully calculated discretion intended to shield the dead man from scandal. According to him, Dayton, who "was a man of strong appetites and fond of the pleasures of the table" had eaten a very hearty dinner and partaken freely of pumpkin pie. He then joined his son William, who was on his way to the theater, and later went to the apartment of a Mrs. Sophie Eccles in the Hôtel du Louvre. When he began to feel unwell, a doctor was sent for. But by the time he arrived, Dayton was dead, apparently of apoplexy.

According to Bigelow, "the doctor at once comprehended the importance of removing the body before the police could interfere, for . . . they would insist upon holding an inquest upon the premises, which would involve many inconveniences, all of which would be avoided by placing the body within the precincts of the Legation." Dayton's son was summoned, and the Minister's body was placed in a carriage and taken to the Legation. Mrs. Eccles insisted on going along in order to tell Mrs. Dayton exactly what had happened, because, she explained, her reputation was involved.

That was Bigelow's version of the story, slightly rewritten from his diary. He also said that Mrs. Dayton asked to see him alone the next day and then told him that young Mr. W. S. Pennington, the first Secretary of the Legation, would try to get her dead husband's post, but that he did not deserve it, because "he knew nothing of the business . . . [and] had never enjoyed Mr. Dayton's confidence." She wanted Bigelow to write to Seward to that effect. He did so, perhaps wondering why she was so antagonistic to Pennington. He was careful to tell Seward that he did not want the post for himself.

Before long a much more sensational account of Dayton's sudden end began spreading through Paris when a printed brochure entitled "The True Account of the Death of Minister Dayton" was put into circulation. This pamphlet, which people who were in the know thought was "exaggerated but not improbable" was also said to have been "clearly inspired if not actually written" by Mrs. Eccles herself.[17]

According to the pamphlet, the whole episode had begun when a servant gave Dayton a letter which arrived just as he was finishing dinner. It read:

> This is to inform you that your Secretary of the Legation, Mr. Pennington, is jeopardising your prestige and the honour of the United States by his scandalous liaison with the former Sophie Bricard, now known as Mrs. Eccles, and a rebel spy. The writer knows for a fact that Pennington will be spending this evening alone with this *lady* at her apartment at the Louvre Hotel. This ought to be stopped. It is your duty, Sir, to stop it.
> An Outraged American[18]

The pamphlet went on to say that Dayton called at the lady's apartment to ask if Pennington was there. She said that he was not. The Minister then showed signs of some kind of physical attack and nearly fell to the floor. Mrs. Eccles helped him to a chair, gave him some brandy, and suggested that he wait for a while because Pennington would call on her later in the evening.

Dayton bluntly charged her with being on intimate terms with his secretary and told her that if it were known it would damage Pennington's career and perhaps his own. When Mrs. Eccles asked why, he said that she was avowedly his country's enemy.

She smiled and told him that Mr. Bigelow knew that this was not true. (Bigelow says nothing about this.) She also said that she had broken with the Confederacy because Benjamin had called her "a woman of dubious morals." She then showed Dayton several letters proving that she was in the secret service of the Union.

After this Dayton was more friendly. They had some champagne, and he asked her to sing. While she was at the piano, "she heard a groan and a dull thud on the floor. She turned and to her horror saw that the Minister had fallen out of his chair and now lay rolling on the carpet in a sort of paroxysm. She knelt beside him; his eyeballs protruded, his lips were twisted in a hideous grimace."

While she was telling her servant to go for a doctor, a key turned in the lock, and Pennington entered the room. He felt Dayton's heart, saw that he was dead, and quickly sized up the situation—they had to get the Minister's body out of the apartment in order to avoid a scandal.

The pamphlet's description of the midnight journey through the streets of Paris with the dead body of a noted man does not differ much from Bigelow's, except in one respect. It says that Pennington would not let Sophie go along, whereas Bigelow wrote: "And so she went."

Still a third version of that night's melodramatic event exists, although this one neatly circumvents even the hint of scandal. It was written by Dayton's son to Thomas Haines Dudley in reply to a letter of condolence. It is the official version and is an interesting example of the way a mid-nineteenth century middle-class American family wanted to have the story presented:

> He was apparently very well on Thursday at dinner. After din-ner I accompanied him into the city and left him in the Palais Royal about 1/4 before 8. At that time he seemed as usual. He must have gone then almost immediately to the Hôtel du Louvre and asked for Mr. Vanderpool—probably simply with the intention of calling upon him. Mr. V. was not in his room and it seems he then began to feel quite unwell and asked to [be] directed or taken to the room of a Mrs. Eckel whom he knew resided there. Upon arrival he said to her—"I can't see." He sat down however and seemed to recover. Soon he swooned away. She brought him to and they chatted together cheerfully as if nothing had occurred. He swooned soon again—and again revived and recommenced chatting. He soon again complained of feeling sick and in a short time laid back and appeared to fall first into a deep sleep and then into a quiet slumber. Mrs. E. covered him to keep him warm and allowed him, as she sup-posed, to continue his nap. In about an hour she went to him to see how he was and feeling of his hands found them cold & then first the truth flashed upon her that he was dead. He prob-ably died almost immediately after his third swoon—quietly— peacefully as if falling asleep—his eyes being closed. When I arrived at the room he had already been dead several hours, but he seemed so natural sleeping so quietly that I could scarcely be made to realize the awful fact. He was at once removed to the house.[19]

Here are three versions of what happened in Paris on that December night. Each one relates the details somewhat differently, and young Dayton's says nothing at all about the midnight ride of his father's corpse. It is also possible, of course, that the real truth about the American Min-ister's death has never been told.

Chapter 45

MORE WORLD INVOLVEMENTS

In Japan, the American Minister, Robert H. Pruyn, summed up how matters stood there when he wrote to Seward on May 26: "The two centuries in which Japan remained isolated and unchanged were centuries of unparalleled progress in Europe and America; and now that the ports are opened, the past and the present stand face to face. These two forces will only harmonize as do light and darkness. One or the other must disappear. They cannot quietly coexist when brought into contact."[1]

The move to bring light to Japan was begun not by Pruyn, but by the British Minister, Sir Rutherford Alcock, who had returned to that country after a two-year absence in England. His proposal to the men who represented other nations in Japan was "to make war to forestall war," because he was afraid the hostile Japanese might drive them all out or compel them to confine their activities to Nagasaki.[2] Part of his plan was to back the Tycoon's central government against the warring underlords, the Daimios. The first overt move would be the reopening of the Inland Sea and an attack on Choshiu who dominated the already fought-over Straits of Shimonoseki.

When Alcock sent an outline of his proposal to the Foreign Office in London, Earl Russell disapproved of it so strongly that he ordered Alcock to return home. But communication between England and Japan was so slow that the British Minister went ahead to put plans into effect without knowing that he had been recalled. On May 30, the representatives of Great Britain, France, Holland, and the United States signed an agreement which led to action, although several months passed before the international fleet was ready to sail.

Since the only American naval vessel available at this time was the

20-year-old sail ship *Jamestown,* Pruyn decided to charter a local steamer, the *Ta-Kiang* for $9500 a month with a guarantee to pay the owners $75,000 if she were lost. A lieutenant and 17 men from the *Jamestown* were placed on the chartered vessel which was armed with an American 30-pounder in addition to the three small guns already on the ship. Sending the *Ta-Kiang* along was more a gesture of solidarity with the international fleet than anything else, for her few cannon would not mean much. The fleet consisted of nine British, four Dutch, and three French warships, while the *Ta-Kiang* was to carry the American flag into battle.[3]

The 17 vessels sailed from Yokohama on August 28 and 29 and were at the entrance to the Straits of Shimonoseki in time to begin a concerted assault on the Japanese ships and forts on September 5. In this encounter the American ship fired 18 shells, "thus identifying herself . . . with the expedition." She eventually brought back 24 Englishmen who had been wounded in the fighting. During the night a British landing party spiked some of the guns in a Japanese battery. Firing continued during the second day, while men from all the ships fought on shore.[4]

The Japanese positions were knocked out by September 8, when hostilities ceased. The essential strait was open to international traffic thereafter, and the fleet returned to its base. In his report to Washington, Pruyn said "it is my belief that the result of the expedition . . . has greatly contributed to, if it has not secured altogether, our safety in Japan." When Alcock showed him Earl Russell's letter directing him "to refrain from using the forces of Her Majesty against either the government of the Tycoon or any Daimio," Pruyn noted that it had "fortunately [been] received after the sailing of the expedition."[5]

The Japanese had been taught a lesson. Peace could now be expected from a people who had learned that a feudal empire could not stand up against the more advanced nations of Europe and America, especially when they got together to stage a joint demonstration.

The failure of the Polish revolt against Russia in 1863 had sent thousands of exiles to other European countries. One of their military leaders, Colonel Valery Sulakowski, who had served in the Confederate Army, along with several other Poles who had been in the South, proposed to organize a large force of trained exiles, arm them with guns bought from Garibaldi, and have them fight for the Confederacy. They were to be rewarded with land grants after the war.

A delegation of four Polish army officers ran the blockade late in August and went to Richmond to talk to Davis and Benjamin. They were successful in persuading the Confederate officials to send £50,000 in sterling to Colin McRae in Liverpool for chartering ships to transport Polish recruits from Europe to the Confederacy by way of Matamoras. The money for this came from a fund placed by Congress at Davis' disposal for secret service. Expenditures were to be accounted for through Benjamin, who was in charge of such operations, while the Treasury did not have to be notified. Letters of introduction were given to the Polish officers who were then sent back to Europe in September to enlist their fellow countrymen.[6]

The Union learned quickly about what was going on because a Charleston newspaper was incautious enough to print an article which said that 30,000 Polish troops were expected to go to the South in a number of fast steamers that were to be built in Europe especially for the purpose.[7]

Simultaneous with this, the Richmond government sent a Scottish officer, who had been in the Confederate Army, back home to try to induce his countrymen to come to America to fight for the South.[8]

Both these schemes to add volunteers to the depleted Confederate Army came to nothing. No recruits ever arrived, perhaps because they were astute enough to see that at this late date the nation they were supposed to fight for would not be in existence very long.

The British upper classes were still supporting the Confederacy late in 1864. On October 18, a Southern Bazaar opened for a five-day run in Liverpool. Held under the sponsorship of such old faithfuls as James Spence, Charles Prioleau, James Mason, Mr. and Mrs. John Slidell, their unmarried daughter and the one who had been wedded to young Erlanger, the Bullochs, and an impressive list of marchionesses, countesses, ladies, baronesses, and even a princess, the affair was intended to raise money for the relief of Confederate prisoners in Northern prison camps. A local paper stated that the Bazaar was "pure charity that . . . had no political significance"; it also said that those in charge "transformed the cold and formal aspect" of St. George's Hall "into a scene of fairylike beauty" where each Confederate state had a stall presided over by young ladies chosen for their "youth, beauty, tact, discretion, calm temper, energy, health, and untiring limbs." Great energy was evidently needed, for the account also said that "from early morning to late at night did these noble girls ply their unwonted vocation." Their unwonted vocation was to sell articles that had been contributed. Since the pretty young salesgirls had to get as much as they could for specimens of fancy-work, bric-a-brac, and other ornate objects that would appeal to Victorian customers, they had to work hard.

It rained most of the week, but the Bazaar had been so well publicized that several thousand people attended it to donate £20,000 to the suffering prisoners in America. This was twice as much as Spence had told Mason to expect. The Confederates felt that such generosity was evidence of the sympathy of the English for the South.

After expenses were deducted, £17,000 remained for the prisoners. Lord Wharncliffe, who had been one of the sponsors of the Bazaar, wrote to Adams asking that an accredited agent be allowed to go to America to inspect the Northern military prisons and distribute the money to the Confederates held there.[9]

That this presumably charitable gesture was not going to be well received by the North was forecast by Moran's reaction to it in his *Journal*. He said that Wharncliffe expressed himself "in a canting hypocritical tone" and that "the cool insolence is charming, and the impertinence of the whole thing is just what might be expected from an English nobleman."[10]

Adams was less harsh. He forwarded the request to Seward with a copy of his own noncommittal reply to Wharncliffe. Moran had correctly predicted the result. Seward wrote to Adams, disallowing the request and saying "that it is expected that your correspondence with Lord Wharncliffe will end."

It did, but the matter did not. Wharncliffe wrote to *The Times,* charging that a pile of the bodies of Southern captives who had died of starvation had been seen in one of the Northern prison camps, and that Seward was excluding the agent from England lest he observe cruelties which the North did not want brought to light. Then Goldwyn Smith wrote to the more friendly *Daily News* to say that he had just returned from Camp Douglas near Chicago and the Prisoners' Hospital in Baltimore, and that he had seen no want of food or any cruelty.[11]

The whole truth about prison camps, Southern and Northern alike, had not yet come out although rumors of what was going on in some of them were already beginning to spread. And even though the terrible stories about conditions in Confederate Libby and Andersonville were largely correct, life in Northern prisons was very hard.

Bulloch's efforts to build ships for the Confederate Navy in Europe had been impeded by one misfortune after another, but he never gave up

trying. On September 16 he wrote to Mallory about the purchase of a
vessel that could be converted into a cruiser.[12] This was the *Sea King*
which had just returned from her first trip to the Far East. Bulloch had
seen her the year before in company with a young Confederate naval
officer.[13] He had then been so favorably impressed by her suitability for
carrying the war into the Arctic that he is supposed to have planted a
man on her to report how she behaved on her maiden voyage.

There is some evidence to believe that this was true, for on April 11,
1864, Napoleon Collins, then in command of the U.S.S. *Wachusetts*
(and who was to capture the *Florida* later in the year), sent a letter to
Gideon Welles in which he said that he had met the captain of an American whaler who had some interesting information for the Navy Department. An English merchant in Tasmania had told the captain "that
there was a steamer fitting out in England called the *Sea King*. She was
to be ready to sail from England by the middle of January [1865]. She
was to proceed to Australia, calling en route at some place on Van Die-
man's Land for coal. Her object was to prey on the whalers in that sea."[14]
This was a remarkably accurate forecast of what the *Sea King* was to do
although she went into action three months before January.

Mallory wrote on August 19 to say that the Confederate naval officer
who had been with Bulloch when he first saw the *Sea King* was now in
Richmond and was enthusiastic about the ship as a potential cruiser.
Mallory suggested that Bulloch try to purchase her for use against the
New England whalers. With his letter he enclosed a suggestion from
Commander John M. Brooke, one of the most brilliant and original-
thinking officers in the Confederate Navy, giving detailed suggestions
for operating in the Pacific.[15]

Bulloch bought the *Sea King* by having a British friend to take title
to her so she could be transferred to Confederate ownership at sea. She
sailed from London on October 8; the next day the *Laurel*, which Bulloch
had recently acquired, left Liverpool with guns, supplies, a crew, and a
captain for the intended cruiser. The two ships met at Funchal and
proceeded to their place of rendezvous, a barren rocky island near Ma-
deira, named Desertas, where the *Sea King* was rapidly armed and commissioned under the name *Shenandoah* on October 19 with Lieutenant
James I. Waddell as her commander.[16] But most of the British sailors
who had been brought along to man the ship refused to go on the long
voyage and returned home on the *Laurel*. The *Shenandoah* sailed with
only 43 officers and men—less than a third of the number needed to
operate her as a fighting ship. Waddell would have to sign on more sea-

men from the vessels he captured. This would not be difficult because most sailors did not care what flag they sailed under.

Word was given out that the *Sea King* had foundered at sea and that the men the *Laurel* brought back to Liverpool had been rescued before she sank. Dudley, however, was able to disprove this when some of the disgruntled sailors began to talk.[17]

Not until October 15, a week after the *Sea King* had sailed, did United States officials in Europe become aware of what they had missed. Moran then wrote to Dudley describing the vanished ship in detail and even telling how she had been acquired. The U.S.S. *Sacramento* and *Niagara* were alerted, and circulars were sent to American consuls in various ports, but it was too late to stop the new C.S.S. *Shenandoah.*[18]

The letter which had given advance notice from Tasmania about the *Sea King's* ultimate destiny had gone to waste, and was probably buried somewhere in the vast piles of naval paper that were accumulating in Washington. The Confederacy's last cruiser was far away at sea and would soon be carrying on her work of destruction. Mallory's often-expressed desire to strike a blow at the New England whaling fleet was becoming a reality.

Chapter 46

LINCOLN AND DAVIS INTERPRET
THE SAME FACTS DIFFERENTLY

When Lincoln sent his Annual Message to Congress on December 6, it was evident from what he said that the war was nearing its end. And the events of the next few weeks—a Union victory at Nashville, the occupation of Savannah, and an attempt to capture Fort Fisher—all helped to bring the conflict to a close. The assault on Fort Fisher failed, but it was to be renewed successfully in January.

In his speech Lincoln gave actual figures to show how rapidly the Union Navy had grown:

> Including vessels under construction [there is] . . . a total of 671 vessels carrying 4,610 guns, and of 510,396 tons, being an actual increase during the year, over and above all losses by shipwreck or in battle, of 83 vessels, 167 guns, and 42,427 tons. The total number of men at this time in the naval service, including officers, is about 51,000. There have been captured by the navy during the year 324 vessels, and the whole number of naval captures since hostilities commenced is 1,379, of which 267 are steamers.[1]

The disparity between the Union and Confederate Navies by this time had become so great that it was absurd. The Union had 671 ships; the Confederacy, even by a generous estimate which would include floating batteries and vessels so small that they carried only one gun, had fewer than fifty. The Confederate Navy, which had had 3960 enlisted men on its ships on inland waters at the end of April, now had only 3674.[2] Iron for armoring vessels under construction in the South had become so scarce that the Richmond rolling mills often had to remain idle. As to the strength of the armies, the Union forces numbered 959,-460, while the Confederates numbered only 445,203.[3]

In his Message to Congress, Lincoln discussed the proposed Amendment to the Constitution that would abolish slavery. This had passed the Senate during the previous session of Congress but had not obtained the necessary two-thirds vote in the House. Lincoln was hopeful that the House would vote favorably upon it now.[4] His own attitude toward the South's "peculiar institution" had come a long way from his cautious stand at the beginning of the war. He said forthrightly:

> I repeat the declaration made a year ago that "while I remain in my present position I shall not attempt to retract or modify the Emancipation Proclamation, nor shall I return to slavery any person who is free by the terms of that proclamation or by any of the Acts of Congress." If the people should, by whatever mode or means, make it an Executive duty to re-enslave such persons, another, and not I, must be their instrument to perform it.[5]

What Jefferson Davis had told Jaquess and Gilmore in Richmond had made an indelible impression upon the President. He alluded to it and went on to show that Davis' stubborn stand did not necessarily have to be taken by his people. The way to a peaceful settlement of the war was open to them. About this Lincoln said:

> On careful consideration of all the evidence accessible it seems to me that no attempt at negotiation with the insurgent leader could result in any good. He would accept nothing short of severance of the Union—precisely what we will not and cannot give. His declarations to this effect are explicit and oft-repeated. He does not attempt to deceive us. He affords us no excuse to deceive ourselves. He cannot voluntarily re-accept the Union; we cannot voluntarily yield it. Between him and us the issue is distinct, simple, and inflexible. It is an issue which can only be tried by war and decided by victory. If we yield, we are beaten; if the Southern people fail him, he is beaten. Either way, it would be the victory and defeat following war. What is true, however, of him who heads the insurgent cause is not necessarily true of those who follow. Although he cannot re-accept the Union, they can. Some of them, we know, already desire peace and re-union. The number of such may increase. They can, at any moment, have peace simply by laying down their arms and submitting to the national authority under the Constitution.[6]

And he summed up the North's position: "We have *more* men *now* than we had when the war began. . . . We are not exhausted, nor in the process of exhaustion . . . we are gaining strength, and may, if need be, maintain the contest indefinitely. This as to men. Material resources are now more complete and abundant than ever."

Jefferson Davis had delivered his Annual Message on November 7, the day before Lincoln was re-elected. The President of a government in rebellion that had only five months to live gave a joint session of the Confederate Congress an optimistic survey of national affairs. What he said was a masterpiece of evasion.

According to Davis, all of Texas and most of Louisiana, Arkansas, and Missouri had been freed from Federal occupation. East of the Mississippi River "nearly the whole of northern and western Mississippi, of northern Alabama, and of western Tennessee" had been recovered and only "the outer defenses of Mobile Bay" were in enemy hands. Things were fine in Virginia although Sheridan admittedly was in the Shenandoah Valley "converting a fruitful land into a desert." Sherman, it was true, had taken Atlanta but had been "unable to secure any ultimate advantage from this success." Nor had he been able to "control a single mile of territory beyond the narrow track of his march." This was like saying that a man who has had his throat cut was not seriously injured because the knife was too sharp.

The Confederacy, Davis boasted, was unconquerable. "There is no military success of the enemy which can accomplish its destruction. Not the fall of Richmond, nor Wilmington, nor Charleston, nor Savannah, nor Mobile, nor of all combined," he said, could save the North from such an expenditure of blood and treasure that it would have to realize that there could be no peace unless the South was granted its "indefeasible rights." By coincidence, Davis had listed the cities (with the exception of Mobile) in the reverse order of their eventual capture.

The section of the speech devoted to foreign relations was merely a recital of Davis' old complaint about other nations—especially England —being unreasonable in their refusal to recognize the Confederacy. On this subject he could say nothing new, but his presentation of his government's monetary problem can be studied with admiration and profit by anyone who has to draw up a pretty-looking financial statement for an organization facing bankruptcy. Even when he admitted that "the chief difficulty to be apprehended in connection with our finances results from the depreciation of the Treasury notes, which seems justly to be attributed . . . to two causes, redundancy in amount and want of confidence in ultimate redemption," he said that there were remedies which "will commend themselves to your consideration as being practical as well as efficient."

The shortage of men for the army made it necessary for the Confederate President to bring up the touchy subject of rewarding slaves employed as military laborers by eventually emancipating them. Beyond using Negroes for manual labor he did not want to go at this time. But his long discussion of the possibility of making slaves into soldiers shows that the problem would soon have to be faced.

He concluded by mentioning negotiations for peace, but on this he was as vague and repetitious as he had been on foreign relations.[7] In both cases he masked the problems with words and blamed the others involved.

Both Davis' and Lincoln's year-end summaries were, of course, carefully studied abroad. Anyone except a willfully blind person should have been able to interpret them properly. Many people did.

But if Davis did not state how matters really stood in the Confederacy at the end of 1864, that ever-observant diarist, Mrs. Chesnut, did. "The deep waters are closing over us," she wrote. "Doctor Trezevant came to tell me the dismal news. How he piled on the agony! Desolation, mismanagement, despair. General Young, with the flower of Hampton's cavalry, is in Columbia. Horses cannot be found to mount them. Neither the Governor of Georgia nor the Governor of South Carolina is moving hand or foot. They have given up. The Yankees claim another victory for Thomas. Hope it may prove like so many of their victories, brag and bluster."[8] But Thomas' victory was very real, for he had broken up Hood's army at Nashville.

J. B. Jones, the Rebel War Clerk in Richmond, expressed his discouragement many times during the last two weeks of 1864: "There is deep vexation in the city—a general apprehension that our affairs are rapidly approaching a crisis such as has not been experienced before. . . . There is a rumor on the street that the government is to be removed to Lynchburg." During the week between Christmas and New Year's Day it rained steadily with some wet snow to add to the discomfort of everyone in the besieged Confederate capital. Jones' melancholy refrain continued: "The dark and dismal weather, together with our sad reverses, have made the countenances of croakers in the streets and in the offices more gloomy and somber than ever, foreboding evil in the future. . . . Men are silent, and some dejected. It is unquestionably the darkest period we have yet experienced. Intervention on the part of European powers is the only hope of many. Failing that, no doubt a Negro army will be or-ganized—and it might be too late!" General Lee, he wrote, was supposed to be in favor of employing Negro troops. And then, on the last day of the year, Jones said that Lee had notified the administration that "Grant is concentrating (probably for an attack on Richmond), bringing in another corps from the Valley; and if the local troops are brought in, he does not know how to replace them. His army diminishes rather than increases. . . . It is a dark and dreary hour when Lee is so despondent!"[9]

Even the usually cheerful Benjamin was downcast. On December 27 he wrote a long letter to both Mason and Slidell in which he cautiously indicated that a sharp break in Confederate policy might be due. The ambiguously worded passage in which he asked his envoys to find out how France and England felt toward the Confederacy at this time read: "If . . . there be objections not made known to us which have for four years prevented the recognition of our independence . . . justice . . . demands that an opportunity be afforded us for meeting and overcoming those objections, if in our power to do so."[10]

Like the men who had drafted the United States Constitution, Benja-min did not want to come right out with the emotion-packed word "slav-ery," but that is what he meant. Would France and England recognize the Confederacy if it adopted a policy of emancipation? The defiant firing on Sumter in April 1861 now seemed far away. That symbolic fort was in ruins after being pounded by years of heavy bombardment. And the state of South Carolina, which had initiated secession, was about to be overrun by Sherman's army. If slavery was the cornerstone of the Confederate Government, that key to its foundation was now to be pulled out.

Duncan Kenner, a wealthy planter from Louisiana, who had served the Confederacy faithfully since the beginning of the war, had felt for some time that only by freeing the slaves could the South hope to win European recognition and have at least a chance to continue as an inde-pendent nation. He had persuaded Benjamin to send out this feeler, and in a few weeks Kenner would go to Europe on a secret mission to deter-mine whether or not this proposed change in national policy would be enough to gain support from France and England.

The North, which at first had only wanted to preserve the Union and ignore slavery, had been forced to take the first step toward emancipa-tion as a war measure. Now the South, which had fought to preserve slavery, was willing to consider emancipation if such a move would per-mit it to remain independent. Jones had been correct in saying that Lee favored the use of Negro soldiers in the Confederate Army. The black man, whose enslavement had been the major reason for founding the government in revolt, was about to be asked to fight in the field to save that government from collapse.

The year 1864 ended in despair in the South, in hope in the North, and in watchfulness in other nations as they waited to see which part of the once-United States would be victorious.

The value of gold, which is always a good indication of a government's stability, dropped from 38 to the Confederate dollar in December 1864 to 53 in January 1865. There were few takers, however, because it was already obvious that Confederate paper money had no real value at all.

Chapter 47

BRITISH POLICY UNDERGOES A SUDDEN CHANGE

The Confederacy was born during the period from January to April 1861; it died during those same months in 1865. As early as January 2, orders were issued for unneeded Confederate naval officers in Europe to return home.[1] And then, on January 15, when Fort Fisher fell, and Wilmington, the South's last major port, was cut off from the sea, essential war matériel stopped coming in from abroad. Charleston, which had successfully resisted heavy attacks since the beginning of the war, was occupied by Union troops on February 18 when Sherman's army swept past the city where the rebellion had started. Even before news of these events reached Europe, opinion there began to change. It was obvious now that the Confederacy could not win the war.

In less than a week, Earl Russell underwent a remarkable change. He had never favored the South because of its slavery policy, but he had thought that it would remain independent. And he had been honest but not always co-operative when Adams complained about the ships and arms which English businessmen were selling to the Confederates.

On February 8, 1865, the Earl wrote a reply to one of Adams' numerous protests, saying: "After careful consideration of these papers there appears to me to be nothing in them upon which a person can be convicted of a breach of the law. Her Majesty's government will apply the law with strictness, but they cannot go beyond it. . . . Her Majesty's government . . . cannot consider themselves bound to answer for the acts of every individual who may evade the operation of the laws by fitting out and arming vessels bought in this country, in some distant port or on the seas beyond her Majesty's jurisdiction."[2]

This had been Russell's attitude throughout the war. Ship after ship had gone to sea because of his interpretation of British neutrality. Now

things were different so far as the Confederacy's chances for survival
were concerned. All her seaports were gone, her financial credit was dubious, her armies were in no condition to fight an offensive action, while
dispatches from America showed that Grant was preparing a huge army
to overwhelm Lee's depleted forces. And the North was at last taking a
positive step to get rid of slavery. On January 31, the House passed the
Thirteenth Amendment by a vote of 119 to 56. Three-fourths of the
states then had to ratify the Amendment, but this was eventually done,
and on December 18, 1865, the United States Constitution formally
abolished slavery from the land.

On February 10, Sir John Walsh attacked the United States in the House
of Commons, charging that it was threatening to abrogate its treaty with
Canada and arm more ships on the Great Lakes in order to defend itself
from further raids across the border. Walsh insisted that England stand
behind Canada, or "the world will look on the old British oak not only
as withered in its leaves but as rotten at its heart." He accused the United
States of being hostile to both Canada and England and said that perhaps it wanted war.

At this point, Lord Palmerston, who was certainly no friend of the
North, rose and quietly said that the United States was "justly entitled
to complain" about what had been done to it from Canada. He concluded
with the words: "Let us refrain from discussions which would tend to
precipitate opinions and excite feelings which it is the interest of the
two countries to put aside."[3]

Everything said in the House of Commons was public, but Cabinet
meetings were not. During the next three days, England made a complete turnabout in national policy so far as it concerned her attitude toward the war in America. There were many reasons for this, the chief
of which that it was apparent that the long conflict was ending. Fear of
the North's vast army and expanded navy undoubtedly influenced British
thinking. References to this occur again and again in the writings of the
time. And Lord Lyons, who was in England on his way to a new post in
Constantinople, knew more about American affairs than anyone else
and could be trusted to give the Foreign Office an impartial and truthful
interpretation of them.

Adams received a note from Russell asking him to call on February 14.
When he arrived, the Foreign Secretary told him that "with regard to the
state of things in Canada . . . it was thought that enough had been done
to establish confidence there." He also said that the Cabinet had decided

to address a letter to Slidell, Mason, and Mann which he wanted to read to Adams.

The American Minister had long wanted to resign from his difficult and thankless post and had written to Seward to that effect in November.[4] As he listened to Russell, he realized that his arduous stay in England was at last being crowned with a decisive diplomatic victory. He heard Russell's voice go on with statements to the Confederates that he had never even dared hope would be spoken by a high British official: The head of the Foreign Office was telling the Confederate triumvirate that:

1. "The unwarrantable practice of building ships in this country to be used as vessels of war against a State with whom her Majesty is at peace still continues. . . . Resort is had to evasion and subtlety in order to escape the penalties of the law; that a vessel is built in one place, and that her armament is prepared in another, and that both are sent to some distant port beyond her Majesty's jurisdiction, and that thus an armed steamship is fitted out to cruise." Also that "a crew composed of British subjects is procured . . . to serve in a Confederate man-of-war."

2. "Confederate organs have published . . . a memorandum of instructions for the cruisers . . . which would, if adopted, set aside some of the most settled principles of international law and break down rules . . . established for . . . maintaining her Majesty's neutrality."

3. Operations from Canada to capture the U.S.S. *Michigan* and raid St. Albans had shown "a gross disregard of her Majesty's character as a neutral power and a desire to involve her Majesty in hostilities with a coterminus power with which Great Britain is at peace."

Russell concluded his letter to the Commissioners by saying: "I trust you will feel yourselves authorized to promise on behalf of the Confederate Government that practices so offensive and unwarrantable shall cease and shall be entirely abandoned for the future."[5] Then he asked Adams for a favor which showed that he did not trust the Commissioners and was afraid that they might suppress his letter and never let it reach Richmond. He wanted Adams to send a duplicate to Washington and request the authorities there to be sure that it was passed through the lines to reach Davis and Benjamin.

Adams was cautious. He had no objection to such an idea but could not say how his government would react to it. He would, of course, send on the letter. The Confederates in Richmond, he predicted, might refuse to receive it because of the unusual way it came. Russell told him that the original had already been delivered to the three Commissioners in Europe and that only a copy was to be forwarded through Washington.

Adams dispatched Russell's policy-making letter of February 13 to Seward together with a large collection of supporting documents. His own covering note contained only the moderately expressed statements that were characteristic of him. Nor does his diary show any undue emotions in its entries for that day. Yet this was Adams' greatest triumph, for Russell, speaking as the voice of the British Empire, had finally broken with the Confederacy. The rebellious states could hope for nothing from England now.[6]

The news from America was making such an impression on Europeans that United States securities were rising sharply on the market. Everything that was happening was helping to establish new confidence in the North.

Adams' prediction about the way Richmond would receive Russell's letter of February 13 was uncannily correct. It arrived through the lines from Washington under a flag of truce and reached its destination on March 14. J. B. Jones, the Rebel War Clerk, wrote a vivid account of its reception in the Confederate capital at a time when the government there had only a few days of existence left.

> Gen. Lee sends to the department this morning a copy of a fierce letter from Lord John Russell . . . to our commissioners abroad, demanding a discontinuance of expeditions fitted out in Canada and the building and equipping of cruisers in British ports. It says such practices must cease, for they are not only in violation of British law but calculated to foment war between Great Britain and the United States, which Lord John is very much averse to. The communication is sent to *Washington, D.C.*, and thence forwarded by Mr. Seward to Lieut-Gen. Grant, who sends it by flag of truce to Gen. Lee. Great Britain gives us a kick while the Federal generals are pounding us.[7]

The Richmond government was crumbling, and the sound of Union guns could be heard from the lines south of the city when Benjamin mulled over the letter which showed very clearly that England wanted to have nothing further to do with the Confederacy. He discussed the unpleasant document with Davis, and a week after its receipt decided how to act. Jones describes the Secretary of State's reactions with some relish, for he did not like him:

> Lord Russell's letter, forwarded from Washington some days ago, after much consultation here, was sent back to Gen. Lee by the Secretary of State, declining to receive a communication from a neutral power through a hostile one and expressing doubts of its *authenticity*. Gen. Lee returns the papers today, suggesting that the expression of doubts of the *authenticity* be omitted—but will . . . have it delivered to Gen. Grant. Mr. Benjamin thinks there is some occult diplomatic danger in the papers—at least he is idle, and wants some diplomatic work on his hands in the regular way. How to avoid doing anything whatever, diplomatically, with this matter before him is the very quintessence of diplomacy! He can look at it, read it, handle it, and return it to Lord John, and then diplomatically prove that this government never had any knowledge of its existence![8]

Even at this impossibly late date the Confederates, knowing that they could expect nothing from England, were still hoping for assistance from France. Duncan F. Kenner had finally arrived in Paris and was there while Mason, Slidell, and Mann were trying to agree on the phrasing of a reply to Russell's letter of February 13, a document which Slidell thought was "extremely insolent and offensive."[9]

Their reply, drafted on February 28, stated that they were transmitting Russell's letter to Richmond as requested; that they protested the general tone of it; that no more ships of war were being built in England for the Confederacy; and that all of Russell's complaints could be satisfactorily explained. Their reply was purposely evasive, for the Commissioners had to tone down what they really wanted to say because Kenner had brought them a new problem. This was Benjamin's ambiguously worded paragraph which instructed them to try to find out whether France or England would recognize the Confederacy if it agreed to free its slaves. The Commissioners could not afford to antagonize Russell by a harsh reply to his letter if they still had to deal with him.[10]

Getting anywhere with England was going to be difficult. On the very day that Russell had written his disturbing letter, the previously friendly *Times* had printed an editorial advising the Confederacy that it was too late to attempt to influence British policy by an offer of emancipation.

Tied in to the Kenner mission was the move on foot in the Confederacy to use Negroes in the army. Mason's reaction to this, when he first heard of it in January, was one of mixed feelings. He realized that it was a desperate gesture, but he could not publicly admit that. He also knew that it was a first step toward emancipation, something he had never favored. When he wrote to Benjamin, he said he had told the British that he did not "doubt that our slaves would make better soldiers in the ranks than those [sic] of the North." Then he predicted that if Negroes were given their freedom for serving in the army, "great mischief and inconvenience would result from any increase in the number of free blacks amongst us" after the war.[11]

When Benjamin's ambiguously phrased message was deciphered, Mason was so angry that he refused to carry out the instructions. Only when told that he would be removed from office if he did not obey them, did he reluctantly agree to do what his government asked.[12]

Mason went to London to see Palmerston while Slidell remained in France to seek an audience with Napoleon III. On March 5 the Emperor gave him the depressingly familiar excuse that France was "willing and anxious" to act with England so far as recognizing the Confederacy was concerned but would not move without her. Nor did the offer to free the slaves make any impression.[13] The South had held back her trump card for so long that it had become worthless.

Sherman's advance up the coast was convincing Europeans that the North was going to win the war. To them, Sherman was far more effective than Grant. They saw the top Union commander only as a remote figure from the West who had failed to conquer Lee's smaller army in the spring of 1864 and had then failed again at Petersburg and in minor battles during the autumn and winter. Sherman, on the other hand, was sweeping all resistance aside as he cut a path through the Confederacy. Atlanta, Savannah, Columbia, Charleston, and Wilmington were all well-known cities, and their fall was closely associated with Sherman, while Grant remained at City Point, preparing but not fighting, planning but not doing, so far as they could see. They were soon to learn more about Grant.

Mason's interview with Palmerston on March 14 was as unsatisfactory as Slidell's had been with the French Emperor. Mason hemmed and hawed about stating the offer to end slavery if such a move would gain recognition for the Confederacy, but he thought that he finally made himself clear enough for it to be impossible for Palmerston to misunderstand just what his carefully guarded words meant. When he reported the interview to Benjamin, he said he had long believed that the real impediment to recognition was that England feared a war with the

United States and also that the longer the conflict in America lasted the better it was for them. Rumors had been going around "that a war with England or France would follow a peace in America and that a war with either would involve both." With all this in mind, Mason tried to make Palmerston believe that immediate recognition of the Confederacy would prevent such a war. But the Prime Minister was not going to bargain with a government that was about to collapse.[14]

And on March 31, when Mason was writing his report, Grant's armies already were on the march. On that day Mrs. Davis and her four children left Richmond on a special train that was also carrying the more important Confederate records.[15] That night lights burned late in the government offices as still more records were being packed, or—in many cases —destroyed. Benjamin's secret service documents certainly had to be burned, for they involved too many people to let them fall into enemy hands.

Chapter 48

THE BITTER-ENDERS

The numerous attempts to end the Civil War by a negotiated peace reached a climax in February 1865, when Lincoln personally took part in a conference on board the *River Queen* at Hampton Roads. This, like the meeting at Niagara Falls, began with Horace Greeley, although he did not take part in it. He started it by writing to Francis Preston Blair, Senior, on December 15, 1864, suggesting that the 74-year-old statesman go to Richmond to see Davis and try to bring the war to a close.

The elder Blair was delighted with the idea. He was in a position to deal directly with Lincoln, for his son Montgomery was Postmaster General and a Cabinet Member. And the old gentleman was not only a power in his own right but a Southerner with many friends in Richmond. Equipped with a Presidential pass he arrived at the Confederate capital on January 12 and had no trouble in arranging a meeting with Jefferson Davis.[1]

Blair began by saying that "his views . . . were to be regarded merely as his own and . . . perhaps merely the dreams of an old man." His proposal was certainly farfetched enough to belong to the reveries of the senile. He wanted the North and the South to join together to implement the Monroe Doctrine by driving the French and Maximilian from Mexico. The armies would fraternize as fellow-Americans, peace would be restored, North America would be freed from French influence, and Davis would be a hero fit to rank with Washington and Jefferson. Blair also intimated that part or all of Mexico would then be absorbed into the reunited country.[2]

Davis listened solemnly and made a memorandum of the conversation. According to Blair, the Confederate President favored his proposal, but Davis' coolly considered account gives no indication of this.[3] The Hampton Roads Conference, however, did result from the meeting. Like all the preceding ones, it turned out to be useless, for Lincoln insisted on there being only one country while Davis demanded that there be two. Alexander H. Stephens was one of the three Confederate Commissioners sent to meet Lincoln on the *River Queen* on February 3. It was his last act as a government official. After the failure of the mission, he retired to his home in Georgia and remained there until he was arrested by Federal authorities after the war was over.

The one thing that came out of the conference turned out to be as unsuccessful as the conference itself. This was Lincoln's proposed joint resolution to Congress to compensate the slaveholders with $400,000,000 for emancipating their Negroes. When the President read this to his Cabinet on February 5, it met with such determined opposition that he had to table it.[4]

Benjamin and Davis spoke to a large audience at the old African Church in Richmond on February 9. The two irreconcilables wanted to keep fighting. Benjamin was for nationalizing cotton, tobacco, and bacon; he also advocated arming the slaves. These were desperate notions that would have been called treasonable earlier in the war. Now the audience listened without showing any signs of shock.[5]

Davis delivered an impassioned address which many people thought was the best he had ever made. In it he promised victory when no victory was in sight. By June 21, he said rashly, "the authorities at Washington would be suing those at Richmond for peace on their own terms as their masters."

The disgruntled Stephens remembered that prophecy when he was in a Northern prison on June 21. Davis' speech, he admitted grudgingly, had been a brilliant one, but even then he had "looked upon it as not much short of dementation."[6]

Not only was the Vice-President of the Confederacy calling its President demented, but one of its members of Congress, after resigning and trying to flee to the North, charged that the peace mission at Hampton Roads, so far as the South's part in it was concerned, was a deliberate ruse made by Davis as a meaningless concession to Southerners who were demanding peace.[7]

When an organization begins to fall apart, its leaders quarrel, and each one tries to fix the blame on the others. This was now happening in the Confederacy. Stephens was openly opposed to Davis; Benjamin was exceedingly unpopular; only Lee escaped the general charges of incompetence. On February 6, he was made the head of all the Confederate armies. On March 13, one of the last acts of the Confederate Congress was to authorize the use of Negro slaves as soldiers.

The Confederacy was in desperate straits in Richmond, but it was still active on two oceans. At the end of January, the *Shenandoah* was in Melbourne to get a much-needed recaulking of her seams and have a damaged propeller repaired. Waddell was pleased to see that the Australians seemed friendly and that many of them openly favored the South.

And on January 26, Bigelow who had been appointed Minister to France only two weeks before, heard that an ironclad of nationality unknown was anchored in Quiberon Bay on the southern coast of Brittany. He telegraphed the American consul at Nantes and got a quick reply. The ironclad was the one named the *Sphinx,* which Arman had built in Bordeaux for the Confederates and which had then been sold to Denmark.[8] Her Danish name had been *Stoerkodder;* she was now called *Olinde* and was soon to be christened the C.S.S. *Stonewall.* A British steamer was on hand with supplies, ammunition, and a crew to replace the Danes who had brought the new ironclad from Copenhagen. At this moment she was busy taking on coal from another ship.[9]

Bigelow went to the French Foreign office to try to prevent this once-exorcised ghost from coming to life again. But before anything could be done, she left Quiberon Bay and went to Spain for repairs which she was evidently reluctant to apply for in France. What Bigelow did not know was that she had been ordered to attack Port Royal, South Carolina, in an effort to damage the Union fleet there and destroy supply vessels for Sherman's army. Then she was to go on to bombard Northern ports.[10]

Nor did Bigelow know just how powerful the mysterious ironclad was. Adequately armored against most of the missiles that might strike her, she carried an enormous Armstrong rifle which could hurl a 300-pound shell; she also had two others that could fire projectiles of half that weight.[11] There would be no withstanding such weapons if the *Stonewall* succeeded in crossing the Atlantic.

Bigelow, who never lost his interest in the war even after it was over, in 1888 obtained a long account of the *Stonewall's* origin from Caleb Huse, the Confederate agent whose primary assignment was to purchase weapons and munitions for the army. In London, Huse had encountered De Rivière, the French entrepreneur who was trying to get the ship away from the Danes. In his postwar letter to Bigelow, Huse called the roving

Frenchman "one of the most accomplished and unscrupulous men I have
ever met."[12]

De Rivière told him that he had been on the ironclad's trial run near
Copenhagen and that in order to have the Danes reject her, he had secretly gone below to open up a bilge-cock in order to flood one of the
compartments and slow down the ship. His trick was successful, and
the former *Sphinx* was now for sale.

De Rivière persuaded Huse to go to Paris to talk Slidell into buying
her. Bulloch had already refused to deal with the French agent because
he knew he was the unmitigated scoundrel that Huse had called him.
But Bulloch was always practical; he finally consented to pay De Rivière
the huge commission he demanded.

Huse went to Copenhagen and while there met Captain Thomas J.
Page, who was to command the new ironclad. Huse was unfavorably
impressed with Page's "foggy slowness," and wanted faster action. "My
plan," he wrote, "was simply to sail the ship to Charleston or Wilmington, and I have no doubt one or two things would have happened—
either we should have gone to the bottom or got there. . . . My ignorance of the danger of taking a direct course would have caused me to
take it, and as I had one single idea of getting the ship into a C.S. port,
I think I should have succeeded."

But Page and other navy officers who were authorized to take the
Stonewall out got possession of her, so Huse's desperate scheme was
never put into effect. Page was slow-moving, unenthusiastic about his
ship, and far too cautious to be of any use at a time when boldness was
needed. He took the *Stonewall* to Quiberon Bay, from there to Spain,
and early in February found himself blockaded by the *Sacramento* and
the *Niagara* in the sheltered waters between Corunna and Ferrol.[13]

While Page waited there, he got word that Fort Fisher had fallen and
that the war was going against the Confederacy. He went to Paris to
consult with the Commissioners and was told to go to Bermuda for more
men, munitions, and coal. While he was in Paris, the temporary commander of the *Stonewall,* who was afraid of a sudden attack by the two
American warships waiting outside the harbor, had the fires under the
ship's boilers started up so as to be prepared for a fast run under steam.
This brought out two Spanish guard boats and a warning not to attempt
to break the peace.

Page was not ready to take his ship to sea until March 24. Yet the
Stonewall was armored, while his Union adversaries were wooden ships
with far less powerful guns. When he finally sailed out in broad day-

light, the commanders of the *Sacramento* and the *Niagara,* knowing full well that to give battle was hopeless, remained quietly at anchor. (This brought on a court-martial, but the proceedings were set aside.)[14]

The *Stonewall* entered the harbor of Lisbon where the Portuguese authorities made it plain that she was not welcome. When the *Niagara* arrived in port, she got into trouble with the commander of the ancient Moorish fort called Torre de Belem. Portuguese guns fired several shots at the American ship, five of which struck her, but her captain again very sensibly did not shoot back.[15]

The *Stonewall* got away to sea, stopping for coal at Teneriffe, Bermuda, and Nassau. Communication with those ports was so slow that it was not until Page reached Havana on May 11 that he heard the war was over. With no government to advise him, he sold the costly warship to Spain for $16,000 in order to pay off his crew.

The Confederacy's only ironclad that got to sea never fired a shot. Her commander's procrastination and lack of confidence in his ship canceled her possible effectiveness.[16]

While Page was wasting time in the Atlantic, Waddell was preparing to carry the war into the farthest reaches of the Pacific. He had had to remain in Melbourne for nearly a month until repairs were completed. During this time some of his men deserted, but when he left that port on February 18, he found 42 stowaways who had hidden themselves on board so they could enlist as crew members.

Waddell's instructions from Richmond ordered him to stop at Ascension Island, which he did on April 1. He captured and burned four New England whaling ships there and also invited one of the native kings to visit his ship. A South Sea Island feast on shore gave Waddell and his men a chance to see how primitive people lived. After leaving 130 prisoners behind, he started north again on April 13—after Lee had surrendered—ran through the Sea of Okhotsk and reached the Bering Sea on June 16. This put him far ahead of the Richmond schedule which had called for him to wait near Honolulu until September so he could intercept the whalers as they came down from the north. By taking this bold action he was able to begin his attack on the whaling fleet at the beginning of summer. It also gave him a chance to capture the ships by surprise because their captains naturally did not expect to see a Confederate raider among the Arctic ice floes.

In the six days between June 22 and 28, Waddell burned 20 ships and put his prisoners aboard four other whalers. One of the captains taken on the first day told him that the war had ended, but he could not prove it. Then Waddell got some newspapers from a ship which had recently been in San Francisco. They said that Lee had surrendered, but they also printed a statement from Jefferson Davis that the war was to be continued. Waddell felt justified in going on with his work of destruction. When he had completed it, he turned southward, brooding over a mad scheme to run into San Francisco Bay and attack the city. He had the sense not to try this and sailed on until he met the British ship *Baracouta* on August 2. She had San Francisco newspapers on board which finally convinced Waddell that the war really was over. He had the *Shenandoah's* guns dismounted and then began the 17,000-mile run to Liverpool.

Some of the officers wanted him to put in at Cape Town because they believed they would be treated better there than in England. For a short while there was a threat of mutiny, but enough harmony was restored to continue the long voyage to its original destination. Along the way Waddell carefully avoided coming within hail of another ship. All through September and October, the last Confederate raider kept going under sail until she sighted the British Isles early in November. Waddell then headed for the entrance to the Mersey River, uncertain of the kind of reception his nationless ship would get when she reached Liverpool.[17]

Chapter 49

THE YEARS BEYOND

On March 27, Lincoln met with Grant, Sherman, and Admiral David Dixon Porter on board the *River Queen* at City Point. At this conference, final arrangements for the great spring drive on Petersburg and Richmond were agreed upon, and the Union forces in Virginia began moving out of their long-held trenches that night.

After that, events succeeded one another so quickly that the Appomattox Campaign was over before news of its running battles could reach Europe. Consequently, what was happening came as a series of stunning surprises to the people there. When word of the fall of Petersburg and Richmond—at the start of the campaign—arrived in London on April 15, Moran said that it "staggered the English rebel sympathizers." From Britain, the news was sent by telegraph to all sections of Europe and was carried by British ships to the ports of the world.

By April 19, London heard that Lee's Army of Northern Virginia was disintegrating rapidly as Grant drove it toward Appomattox. Following fast upon this came word that Seward had been seriously injured in a carriage accident in Washington. Lord Lyons called at the American Legation to ask for further information about the health of the man he had so often opposed. He expressed his satisfaction to Adams at the evacuation of Richmond and also said that he had long ago predicted it as well as the eventual success of the Union cause. Moran wrote spitefully in his *Journal* that he would like to see the dated dispatch containing that prediction. His comment, however, did Lyons an injustice because he had never favored the South.[1]

On Sunday, April 23, just two weeks after it had taken place, London received the news of the end of Lee's army. Lord Acton, who wanted to write a history of liberty but never did, wrote to Mary Gladstone: "I broke my heart over the surrender of Lee."

And then, three days later, the assassination of President Lincoln and the simultaneous attempt to kill Seward were announced. Appomattox had been a surprise; this was a terrible shock to the entire world.

The next day, while it was still believed that Seward was dead, *The Times*, which had always vilified Lincoln, made honorable amends by running an editorial about him which was not only a tribute but an understanding one:

> The Confederate cause will not escape the dishonor cast upon it by the wanton murders of Mr. Lincoln and the Secretary. The admiration won by the long and gallant defence of Richmond will be lessened; the memory of Lee's lofty bearing and Jackson's deep religious feeling will be obscured by the atrocities committed in the name and on behalf of the South. Arson in New York; theft, under the pretence of war, in Vermont, and assassination in the capital, dim the lustre of a four years' resistance to superior forces and of many a well-fought field in Virginia. . . .
>
> Mr. Lincoln was a man who could not, under any circumstances, have been easily replaced. Starting from a humble position to one of the greatest eminence, and adopted by the Republican Party as a makeshift simply because Mr. Seward and their other prominent leaders were obnoxious to different sections of the party, it was natural that his career should be watched with jealous suspicion. The office cast upon him was great, its duties most onerous, and the obscurity of his past career afforded no guarantee of his ability to discharge them. His shortcomings, moreover, were on the surface. The education of a man whose early years had been spent in earning bread by manual labor had necessarily been defective, and faults of manner and errors of taste repelled the observer at the outset.
>
> In spite of these drawbacks Mr. Lincoln slowly won for himself the respect and confidence of all. His perfect honesty speedily became apparent, and . . . he was [never] betrayed into any intemperance of language towards his opponents or towards neutrals. His utterances were apparently careless, but his tongue was always under command. The quality of Mr. Lincoln's administration which served . . . to enlist the sympathy of bystanders, was its conservative progress. He felt his way gradually to his conclusions; and . . . his mind was growing. . . . The *naiveté* with which he once suggested to the Negroes

that they should take themselves off to Central America because their presence in the states was inconvenient to the white population, soon disappeared. The gradual change of his language and of his policy was most remarkable. Englishmen learned to respect a man who showed the best characteristics of their race in his respect for what was good in the past, acting in unison with a recognition of what was made necessary by the events of passing history. But the growth of Mr. Lincoln's mind was subject to a singular modification. It would seem that he felt himself of late a mere instrument engaged in working out a great cause which he could partly recognize, but which he was powerless to control. . . .

What may be the actual destiny of the United States deprived of the guiding hand of Mr. Lincoln and of the experience of Mr. Seward no one would venture to foretell. . . . The fate of a nation hangs in the balance, and we wait with anxiety to see which way it will turn.[2]

And the humorous magazine *Punch*, which had often cruelly caricatured Lincoln and his Administration, printed a long poem by Tom Taylor to make up for all the harsh things it had said. Taylor, by a strange coincidence, was the author of *Our American Cousin*, the comedy which had been playing at Ford's Theatre on the night the President was shot there. This poem, which began by chiding *Punch* and the British for having made fun of Lincoln's "shambling limb, his furrowed face" and "his garb uncouth, his bearing ill at ease," went on to praise the man who had battled for liberty and been cut down by an assassin's bullet "just as . . . triumph came."[3]

The news of Lincoln's death hit London only a few weeks after another stanch advocate of the Northern cause had died. This was Richard Cobden, who had worked with John Bright to try to convince their fellow countrymen that Washington and not Richmond deserved their support.

The reaction to the Lincoln assassination was so great that hundreds upon hundreds of letters of condolence poured in to Washington from all parts of the world. Many of these, together with newspaper editorials from foreign newspapers, were printed in a 700-page volume issued by the State Department as an appendix to the Diplomatic Correspondence of 1865. The widespread extent of their origin is impressive. They came from Argentina, Austria, Belgium, Brazil, Bolivia, Chile, China, Colombia, Costa Rica, Denmark, Ecuador, Egypt, France, Great Britain, Greece, Guatemala, Hawaii, Haiti, Honduras, Italy, Japan, Liberia, Mexico, Morocco, the Netherlands, Nicaragua, Peru, Portugal, Prussia and other German states, Russia, Spain, Sweden and Norway, Switzerland, Tunis, Turkey, Uruguay, and Venezuela. Those from England, France, and Switzerland filled many pages.

More than Appomattox, more than the surrenders of other Confederate armies that followed it, and even more than the flight of the Confederate Government and the arrest of several of its leaders, the assassination of Abraham Lincoln convinced the civilized world that the war in America was at last over and that the rebellious South was about to be re-absorbed into the United States. And the fact that the now much-praised President had been slain by an assassin who shouted the motto of Virginia after he fired the fatal shot did more to damage the South than anything that had happened during the long war.

A curious bit of information came to light at this time which again connected Booth with Canada. It was now learned that he had shipped his theatrical costumes and prompt books from Montreal to Nassau on a schooner which was supposed to go down the St. Lawrence River. When it was stopped on the way by a lawsuit (which had nothing to do with the assassin), his effects were seized and sent to Washington for examination, but no incriminating material was found. It was evident that Booth had intended to flee the country. His long stay on the shores of the Potomac before crossing into Virginia to meet his death there may have been to await a boat that would take him out to sea to meet a blockade-runner.[4]

The conspirators who had been in the plot with Booth were all Southerners. Charged with them at their trial were Jefferson Davis, Jacob Thompson, Clement C. Clay, Beverly Tucker, George N. Sanders, William C. Cleary "and other rebels and traitors against the government of the United States."[5] Lincoln had advocated a generous peace, but his assassination brought on a wave of fierce resentment that negated everything he had sought.

Since there were no more Confederate newspapers or people of official standing to speak for the South, the world heard only what the embittered North wanted it to hear. For years the tides of venom engulfed the former Confederate states; for years they had to pay for what an insane and irresponsible Southern actor had done. And even though the Thirteenth Amendment abolished slavery, it did nothing to help the Negro after it set him free. The Johnson administration began well, but it soon ran into so much trouble that it was not able to accomplish much in improving conditions in the impoverished South.

The Civil War did not end at Appomattox, nor did it end when the *Shenandoah* reached Liverpool on November 6 and was turned over to the British authorities there. It did not even end on March 22, 1866, when this last Confederate raider was put up at auction and sold for £15,750.[6] It ended officially on April 2, 1866, the first anniversary of the fall of Petersburg and Richmond, when President Andrew Johnson proclaimed the supposedly united nation to be at peace. But echoes of the war rolled on, and its effects are still felt today.

Thomas Haines Dudley remained at his post in Liverpool, where he got possession of the *Tallahassee,* the *Rappahannock,* and the *Sumter,* and had them sold. He spent a great deal of time tracking down other Confederate assets, but he found that in many cases large sums had disappeared. He kept at this work until 1871 when he wanted to resign and return home. But he was persuaded to stay on in Europe to help prepare evidence for the United States in the arbitration of the *Alabama* Claims. He had had more direct experience than anyone else in keeping a watchful eye on the building of Confederate ships in England, and his files of information were to be of prime importance in documenting the American case.[7]

The British had long been hostile to the idea of paying anything for the damage done by the Confederate cruisers built in their shipyards. The war had been profitable to them, for it had practically eliminated the United States as their most important rival in carrying the ocean traffic of the world. Semmes and his fellow captains had done their work so well by destroying 110,000 tons of commercial shipping that most American vessels had been driven off the high seas.[8]

But now something happened that made the British change their minds about this former colony which was rapidly becoming a great power. Napoleon III and the French Army were routed by the Germans at Sedan in September 1870; then Paris withstood a four-month siege, and after its surrender the Commune took over the city until it was violently suppressed. England had good reason to fear the growing might of Germany and the threat of international socialism. In 1871 she needed an ally. Any sum she might have to pay to the United States as compensation for damage done by the ships she had built for the Confederates was small compared with the good will that might result from such a settlement.

The elaborately documented case began in Geneva late in 1871 and dragged on for nearly a year. The printed evidence fills many volumes in which the acts of the Confederate commerce-destroyers are described in minute detail. In them the *Alabama,* the *Florida,* the *Shenandoah,* and other ships sail again, cruising the oceans of the world to leave behind a trail of flames, smoke, and sunken wrecks. England took the position that she was responsible only for the damage done by these three cruisers. They had been the most destructive, but there had been plenty of others as well.

Despite the fact that the British Empire badly needed the United States as a friend at this time, her men of law fought the claims with every legal device they could command. The case lasted until September 14, 1872, when it was settled by an award of $15,500,000 in gold.[9]

No actual metal was ever shipped, for both countries were afraid that the transfer of 28½ tons of gold might upset the market. By a complicated series of transactions, $15,500,000 worth of United States bonds belonging to European investors were purchased as they matured, and the cash proceeds were then deposited in London. On September 9, 1873, a single hand-engrossed certificate for the full amount was presented to the Treasury in Washington, thus completing payment.[10]

During this period and for more than a decade afterward, the American Navy remained in a state of obsolescence and decay. Isolated from the other major powers of the world by oceans which were falsely believed to be sufficient protection, the men in charge of the destiny of the United States did not even keep themselves technically informed about progress in naval design. Not until nearly a generation after 1865 was the American Navy given a chance to replace some of its out-of-date ships.

And American diplomacy, which had seemed exciting and important in wartime, became a petty occupation about which Henry Adams said: "Anyone who had held, during the four most difficult years of American diplomacy, a position at the centre of action, with his hands actually touching the lever of power, could not beg a post of Secretary at Vienna or Madrid in order to bore himself doing nothing until the next President should do him the honor to turn him out."[11]

Many of the Confederate officials who had been stationed abroad felt that it was inadvisable for them to return home. Maury went to Mexico where he played a prominent part in the effort to start a colony of ex-Confederates. It failed even before Maximilian was executed by a firing squad at Querétaro in 1867. Mason settled in Canada, which became a temporary refuge for former Confederates. He stayed there for three years and then returned to his native Virginia to die. Slidell and Mann remained in France for the rest of their lives, while Bulloch went into business in Liverpool, and died and was buried there. Kenner, who had brought Benjamin's desperate but vaguely worded offer of emancipation to Europe, was among the first to give up and try to return home. Although he had been closely associated with Slidell early in his life, he was not openly identified with Confederate activities abroad. He asked Bigelow to let him take the oath of amnesty on June 20, 1865, admitted that "the late rebellion . . . was a mistake," and was allowed to go back to his native state. Like Benjamin in London, Kenner's career in Louisiana after the war was even more successful than it had been before. Few of the better-known Confederates were as lucky—or as shrewd and able—as these two. Most of them had their lives scarred by failure—failure in war, and failure in the peace that followed.

Jefferson Davis, after a long stay in jail, spent the rest of his life trying to convince the world that every move he had made was correct and that the fall of his government was not his fault. His Secretary of the Navy returned to Key West and re-opened his law office there. Mallory felt that he had wasted his time during the war, for he said that "his greatest regret was that he had spent four years of his life in working for a people unfit for independence."[12]

The long enmity between Britain and the United States, which was the natural heritage of the Revolution and the War of 1812, had been dangerously aggravated during the sectional conflict of the 1860s and was not easily forgotten. But peace had been preserved. Behind the scenes in the British Government was the Queen, who remembered that her beloved husband's last act had been to tone down the originally provocative note to the United States at the time of the *Trent* Affair. That this discreet womanly figure had more to do in preventing war than appears in the record was testified to by Seward in a letter written to Adams on March 1, 1865: "I think the Queen of England is as popular in the United States today as she is among her own subjects. . . . Why cannot British statesmen be as generous to the United States as their sovereign?"[13]

Earl Russell also deserves credit for maintaining peace. He undoubtedly would have preferred to see the United States permanently divided into two nations in order to reduce its power as an economic rival, but he was no war-monger as Palmerston was. The supposedly intelligent Gladstone had showed a notable lack of mental power during the first part of the conflict. Disraeli, who might have been an important factor,

THE YEARS BEYOND

was not in the Cabinet in the early sixties, nor had the most brilliant part of his career yet begun.

As a result of maintaining a peaceful relationship during the Civil War, the United States and Great Britain slowly grew closer together in the decades that followed, although it took a long time for the ancient breach to be healed. And when Napoleon III lost his throne in the Franco-Prussian War, normal relationships between France and the United States could be restored. Except for that petty tyrant's 19-year reign, they had always been good. The enmity between France and England during the American Revolution and the Napoleonic Era had made France an early friend of the United States. That long-continued friendship was to be important in 1917 and again in 1941.

The American Civil War has many meanings, many consequences, and is open to many interpretations. Most important is the fact that a reactionary government pledged to support slavery went down in defeat while a liberal government went from victory in the field to a series of later victories in the improvement of living conditions at home. The heavy weight of the past was thrown off in April 1865. The re-united nation had to go through many serious setbacks after that, but it grew and still continues to grow.

Chapter 50

YESTERDAY AND TOMORROW

The downfall of the Confederacy was of small concern to other governments. To them it merely meant that the United States had successfully compelled its rebellious Southern states to return to the Union. Rebellions had been put down so often that people seldom paid much attention to such measures so long as they were not directly involved. The nineteenth-century conception of States' rights was that a state had the right to exist if it had the power to do so. If it did not, it was quickly taken over by a stronger state. That subdivisions of a nation—provinces, shires, cantons, or *départements*—should have rights on major external issues was unthinkable, especially if they ran counter to the well-being of the entire country. (Scotland, Wales, and some small European states had a fair amount of autonomy, but it meant little because they were ordinarily not powerful enough to act independently.)

People in other nations who bothered to think about the matter at all simply felt that the Confederacy had been an unsuccessful experiment. For four years, its government had tried to maintain a separate agricultural economy operated by slave labor in a part of the world that was becoming increasingly industrialized and that paid its workmen wages. The experiment had failed, and the United States, somewhat shaken by all the bloodletting, was again in command.

Although it fought well on the battlefield, the Confederacy's chances for ultimate survival were ruined because it had insisted upon perpetuating slavery at the very time the Western World was turning against the cruel ways of the past. There were plenty of Southerners who had realized this, and as the war dragged on toward obvious defeat, even more of them began to see that slavery was doomed. But the hard core of hard men who controlled the country and its Congress refused to admit that they could be wrong. The South had always been somewhat isolated from the rest of the world; during the war practically all connection was cut off. Southern squires set their faces grimly against the opinions of other nations and were willing to lose all rather than surrender any part of their feudal holdings. Buried in their own provincialism, blind to what was going on elsewhere, and determined to keep their way of life intact, they dominated Confederate policy and dragged their people down with them. Only ten thousand families owned more than 50 slaves, but this small group and the men associated with it ruled the nine million people of the South.[1]

Even the comparable power groups in England and France were unwilling to accept slavery as a positive good. And vast numbers of ordinary men there, who were becoming more important in influencing government policy, were outspokenly opposed to slavery. Again and again, when attempts were made to get England or France to recognize the Confederacy, organized protest—and the knowledge that an even greater body of unorganized protest existed—prevented such moves. Lincoln and the North had a host of supporters in Europe. Many of them were silent, but their presence was felt by politicians who can sense where the public stands even when it does not speak up.

Looming above the four-year squabble over American affairs was the dark figure of a Negro in chains. He was the symbol around which the contending parties fought. No one could forget that he was there, for he represented the conscience of mankind.

At an earlier time in history the Confederacy would easily have found allies. But 1861 was too late. Nations with advanced industry that could manufacture powerful weapons were unwilling to come to the aid of a slave country which had only one thing they needed—cotton. But cotton was not enough. For four years the world struggled on without it, and the workmen whose livelihood depended on the mills that made it into cloth went hungry. But they, too, were unwilling to support slavery. Without England, without France, the Confederacy could not win its independence. The slave nation went down, and millions of people throughout the world were glad to see it go.

Obviously, there was much more to the American Civil War than slavery. There were many other causes for the conflict, and they have been brought forth, one after another, in an effort to present the Confederacy in a more favorable light. Economic differences, the South's fear of losing power in the national government, the desire to control the newly opened West, and the resort to emotion rather than to plain common sense were all contributing factors in bringing on the war. In fact, slavery had been pushed into the background of public thinking by 1861. The active controversy at that time was more concerned with stopping its spread into the new Territories. But slavery dominated the South, and its dark and terrible presence haunted all America.

Four million black slaves could not be forgotten. There were many causes for the war, but if those four million human beings had not been owned like farm animals, the South would not have seceded to protect its investment in them, and the North would not have used force to restore the Union. If there had been no slavery, there would have been no war.

This was freely admitted by Southerners at the beginning of the conflict, but when they found out that Europe despised their "peculiar institution" and was withholding aid because of it, they learned to speak softly of something which they had never bothered to conceal before. Then, in later years, they built up an elaborate case to prove that slavery had had nothing to do with the war. Such misrepresentation of the truth has helped to perpetuate the myth of white superiority, the rituals of segregation, the repressive measures to limit the freedom of millions of American Negroes, and the sinister hold which reactionary Southern politicians have upon the national government. The Confederacy is dead, but some of its worst qualities live on, and its flag still flies defiantly in the forefront of actions fought over civil rights.

Since most Americans now know very little about what slavery was really like, there has been a deliberate attempt to tell them that it was not so bad and that many Negroes actually thrived under it. Popular fiction, motion pictures, and television have ignored the realities of the slave trade, the auction block, the iron shackles, and the lash. The truth about the festering sore that was the single most destructive element in American life has been suppressed in most accounts about the antebellum South, and the facts are usually to be found only in scholarly books or in libraries where contemporary records are kept. Even the modern Negro wants to forget the agony his ancestors went through. Forgotten also is the most dreadful thing about slavery—that it bound master and slave together in a relationship which brutalized them both. The tragedy of the Civil War was that tens of thousands of non-slaveholding Southerners fought and died to defend an economy which had no use for them, for the poor white had little to gain from a Confederate victory.

It is true, of course, that Southerners were no more responsible for

American slavery than Northerners were. (Many New England shipping merchants had grown rich by bringing in Negroes from Africa.)
But Southerners resorted to arms to keep their black servants in bondage,
and South Carolina had begun the hostilities when she fired on the
Federal Government at Fort Sumter.

Lincoln said forthrightly that the North and the South were equally
guilty in foisting the slave system upon the land.[2] He temporized for a
long while before he attacked slavery directly, but he knew how evil it
was. At Alton, Illinois, on October 15, 1858, during his seventh and
final debate with Stephen A. Douglas, he defined its meaning in words
that ring down the years:

> That is the real issue. That is the issue that will continue in this
> country when these poor tongues of Judge Douglas and myself
> shall be silent. It is the eternal struggle between these two prin-
> ciples—right and wrong—throughout the world. They are the
> two principles that have stood face to face from the beginning
> of time; and will ever continue to struggle. The one is the com-
> mon right of humanity, and the other the divine right of kings.
> It is the same principle in whatever shape it develops itself. It
> is the same spirit that says, "You toil and work and earn bread,
> and I'll eat it." No matter in what shape it comes, whether from
> the mouth of a king who seeks to bestride the people of his own
> nation and live by the fruit of their labor, or from one race of
> men as an apology for enslaving another race, it is the same
> tyrannical principle.[3]

And that same tyrannical principle, which Southern plantation owners wanted to preserve at any cost, still rules a great part of mankind.
The struggle for the common right of humanity to live peacefully, free
from fear and want, still continues, as Lincoln predicted it would. In
his day, hundreds of thousands of men died in the American phase of
that contest. In our century, millions more have perished in the same
struggle when the entire world became involved.

Perhaps the ultimate weapons, which can annihilate us all, may im-
pose an uneasy peace upon antagonistic factions of class, nation, and
race. But even under the dreadful threat of those weapons the endless
battle will go on. Man, in his brief transit from dust to dust, is made of
the stuff from which he came. In him are mingled mud and dung and
much that is foul—but also clean air, water from the high mountains,
and the good sustenance that grows under the warm light of the sun. All
these factors—and more—determine his actions, so he is at once brother

to the beast and a little akin to the angels. Sometimes he behaves so well that he transcends his earthly origin and reaches toward the stars.

He will need to aspire to new heights if he is to survive. The old patterns of life have become inadequate. Only a keen sense of moral justice and quick intelligence can save him now. In the past he could afford to indulge in the idiot luxury of war and count the cost, no matter how great, in a finite number of grave-markers. He can no longer do that. War on a big scale has become so massively destructive that the very idea of it is a madman's thought. Peace is not merely desirable but imperative. Only by learning to live with others, no matter how strange or different they may seem, can man hope to endure. He has no other choice. Only by improving his world can he hope to retain it; only by dedicating himself to life can he avoid sudden death and the end of all human things.

NOTES

Chapter 1. THE UNHAPPY NEW YEAR

1. Ms. weather diary in possession of the author.
2. New York *Herald*, Jan. 1, 1861.
3. *Ibid*, Jan. 3, 1861.
4. *The Diary of Orville Browning*, ed. by T. C. Pease and James G. Randall, Springfield, Ill., 1925. (Hereafter Browning *Diary*).
5. *Lincoln Day by Day, a Chronology, 1809–1865*, Wash., D.C., 1960. (Hereafter *Lincoln Day by Day*).
6. *Diary of Gideon Welles*, ed. by H. K. Beale, N.Y., 1960. Entry for Dec. 3, 1865. (Hereafter Welles *Diary*).
7. Hudson Strode, *Jefferson Davis*, N.Y., 1955, I, 38 ff.
8. *Autobiography of Thurlow Weed*, ed. by Harriet A. Weed, Boston, 1883, I, 639. (Hereafter Weed *Autobiography*).
9. Communications in 1861: Roy West Howard, *Hoofbeats of Destiny*, N.Y., 1960; Roy S. Bloss, *The Pony Express*, Berkeley, Cal., 1959; Robert L. Thompson, *Wiring a Continent*, Princeton, 1947; James Dugan, *The Great Iron Ship*, N.Y., 1953; *Illustrated London News*, May 25, 1861. (Hereafter ILN).
10. M. L. Bonham, Jr., *The British Consuls in the Confederacy*, N.Y., 1911. (Hereafter Bonham). Also FO5 (Foreign Office) documents in the Public Record Office, London.

Chapter 2. THE HOUSE DIVIDING

1. *The Diary of George Templeton Strong, 1860–65*, ed. by Allan Nevins and Melton H. Thomas, N.Y., 1952.
2. New York *Herald*, Feb. 9, 1861.
3. *Lincoln Day by Day*.
4. C.F.A., ms. *Diary* in possession of the Adams Manuscript Trust, Boston.
5. Charles Hamilton and Lloyd Ostendorf, *Lincoln in Photographs*, Norman, Okla., 1963, pp. 374–75.
6. *Lincoln Day by Day*.
7. *New England Magazine*, Feb. 1908.
8. *The Collected Works of Abraham Lincoln*, ed. by Roy Basler, New Brunswick, N.J., 1953, IV., 271. (Hereafter CWAL).

Chapter 3. A NEW NATION, NOT CONCEIVED IN LIBERTY

1. Raphael Semmes, *Memoirs of Service Afloat During the War between the States*, London and Baltimore, 1869. (Hereafter Semmes).
2. Joseph T. Durkin, *Stephen R. Mallory: Confederate Navy Chief*, Chapel Hill, N.C., 1954.
3. J. W. Du Bose, *The Life and Times of William Lowndes Yancey*, Birmingham, Ala., 1892.
4. ORN, II, 3. See correspondence listed in the index. (ORN stands for *Official Records of the Union and Confederate Navies*, 30 vols.)
5. FO5/780, 147–153.
6. ORN, II, 3, p. 195.
7. *A Compilation of the Messages and Papers of the Confederacy*, ed. by James D. Richardson, Nashville, 1906. Also Charles Edward Lee, Jr., *The Confederate Constitutions*, Chapel Hill, 1963.

8. Frank Moore, *Rebellion Records,* N.Y., 1861, Vol. 1, document section, p. 45.
9. Robert H. Smith, "An Address to the Citizens of Alabama on the Constitution and Laws of the Confederate States of America," Mobile, 1861.

Chapter 4. AS ENGLAND SAW IT
1. C. M. MacInnes, *England and Slavery.* Bristol, 1934, pp. 200 ff.
2. Dictionary of American Biography, N.Y., 1936. (Hereafter DAB).
3. Donaldson Jordan and Edwin J. Pratt, *Europe and the American Civil War,* Boston, 1931, Chapter 4.
4. Lionel Stevenson, *The Showman of Vanity Fair,* N.Y., 1947, pp. 385–86.
5. Dickens' *Letters,* N.Y., 1879, II, 167.
6. Jordan and Pratt, supra.
7. Philip Guedalla, *Palmerston,* London, 1926, p. 431.
8. A. Wyatt Tilby, *Lord John Russell,* London, 1930, p. 197. (Hereafter Tilby, *Russell*).
9. Bertrand Russell, *Portraits from Memory,* London, 1958, pp. 112–16.
10. FO5/762, Lyons to Russell, Mar. 30, 1861.
11. ILN, Sept. 23, 1863.
12. Appleton's Cyclopaedia, 1861. Article on Great Britain. Also ILN, June 15, 1861.
13. Encyclopaedia Britannica, eleventh edition, 1911. Article on Ireland.
14. G. K. C. Clark, *The Making of Victorian England,* London, 1962, pp. 59–60.
15. William Kent, *An Encyclopaedia of London,* London, 1937.

Chapter 5. THE NEW PRESIDENT AND THE STATE DEPARTMENT
1. Frederick W. Seward, *Reminiscences of a Wartime Statesman and Diplomat,* N.Y., 1916, pp. 140 ff. (Hereafter F. W. Seward *Reminiscences*).
2. William Howard Russell, *My Diary North and South,* Boston, 1863, p. 118. (Hereafter W. H. Russell *Diary*).
3. *The Lincoln Papers,* ed. by David C. Mearns, N.Y., 1948, II, 478.
4. David L. Smiley, *Lion of White Hall, the Life of Cassius M. Clay,* Madison, Wisc., 1962.
5. James Ford Rhodes, *History of the U.S. from the Compromise of 1850,* N.Y., 1892. I, 300.
6. W. H. Russell *Diary,* pp. 36–39.
7. Charles Francis Adams, Jr., *Charles Francis Adams, by His Son,* Boston, 1900, p. 146. (Hereafter CFA, Jr.).

Chapter 6. THE IRREPRESSIBLE SEWARD MEETS HIS MATCH
1. CWAL, V, 317n.
2. *Ibid, IV,* 317.
3. T. W. Newton, *Lord Lyons,* London, 1913, I, 30. (Hereafter LL).
4. Richard Cobden to William Slagg, Dec. 19, 1861. Cobden ms. British Museum.
5. *Confidential Correspondence of Gustavas Vasa Fox,* ed. by R. M. Thompson and R. Wainright, N.Y., 1918, I, 21 ff., also CWAL, IV, 315.
6. *The Writings of Thomas Jefferson,* ed. by Paul Leicester Ford, N.Y., 1899. X, 158. Jefferson to John Holmes, Apr. 22, 1820.

Chapter 7. THE LINEUP IN LONDON
1. *The Journal of Benjamin Moran,* ed. by Sarah A. Wallace and Frances E. Gillespie, Chicago, 1949, II, 815. (Hereafter Moran *Journal*).

2. CFA *Diary*, June 22, 1868.

3. E. D. Adams, *Great Britain and the American Civil War*, London, 1925, II, 23 n. (Hereafter E. D. Adams).

4. FO5/754/79. Apr. 6, 1861.

5. ORN, III, 2, 215.

6. *Ibid*, 216.

7. *London Gazette*, May 14, 1861.

8. Moran *Journal*, I, 810.

9. *Diary and Letters of John Hay*, ed. by Tyler Dennett. N.Y., 1939, p. 8, (Apr. 22, 1861).

10. *Inns and Taverns of Old London*, Henry C. Shelley, London, 1909; *London in the Nineteenth Century*, Sir Walter Besant, London, 1905; Black's *New Guide to London*, Edinburgh, 1863.

11. *My Life in Many States and Foreign Lands*, George Francis Train, N.Y., 1902, pp. 263 ff., also ILN, Apr. 20, 1861.

12. ILN, Feb. 9, 1861; Dec. 17, 1864.

Chapter 8. MR. ADAMS BEGINS HIS WORK

1. Moran *Journal*, I, 814.

2. CFA *Diary*, Oct. 16, 1871.

3. Moran *Journal*, II, 825.

4. *The Works of William H. Seward*, ed. by George Baker, Boston, 1884, V, 192 ff.

5. CFA, Jr. pp. 175–76.

6. Moran *Journal*, II, 816.

7. *The Letters of Henry Adams*, ed. by Worthington Chauncey Ford, Boston, 1930, I, 91–92.

8. CWAL, IV, 376 ff.

9. Henry Adams *Letters*, *supra*, I, 93.

10. CFA, Jr., p. 196 ff.

11. ORN, II, 221 ff.

12. FO5/763. Lyons to Russell, May 6, 1861.

Chapter 9. EFFORTS TO WIN FRIENDS

1. Appleton's Cyclopaedia, 1861, pp. 625 ff.

2. ORN, II, 3, 315 ff.

3. Beckles Willson, *American Ambassadors to France*, N.Y., 1928, pp. 262–63.

4. Thomas W. Evans, *The Second French Empire*, N.Y., 1905, pp. 119–20.

5. Frank L. Owsley, *King Cotton Diplomacy*, Chicago, 1931, p. 98. (Hereafter Owsley).

6. John M. Callahan, *The Diplomatic History of the Southern Confederacy*, Baltimore, 1901, p. 74.

7. New York *Herald*, May 28, 1861.

8. CWAL, IV, 360.

Chapter 10. ERRORS AND BLUNDERS

1. Robert Carter, "Gurowski," *Atlantic Monthly*, Nov. 1866, pp. 625–33.

2. Welles *Diary*, June 8, 1863.

3. Adam Gurowski, *Diary*, Boston, 1862, pp. 52–53.

4. *Ibid*, p. 24–25.

5. *Ibid*, pp. 27–28.

6. *Ibid*, p. 56.

7. James A. B. Scherer, *Cotton as a World Power*, N.Y., 1916, p. 47.
8. Louis B. Schmitt, "The Influence of Wheat and Cotton on Anglo-American Relations during the Civil War," *Iowa Journal of History and Politics*, July 1918.
9. William M. Robinson, Jr., *The Confederate Privateers*, New Haven, 1929, ch. IV.

Chapter 11. CONFEDERATE AGENTS ABROAD
1. George W. Dalzell, *The Flight from the Flag*, Chapel Hill, N.C., 1940, p. 75.
2. DAB
3. OR, IV, 1, 220.
4. *Ibid*, p. 343 ff.
5. *Ibid*, p. 540.
6. Caleb Huse, "Supplies for the Confederate Army," Boston, 1904.
7. James Dunwoody Bulloch, *The Secret Service of the Confederate States in Europe*, London, 1883, chapters II, IV, and V. (Hereafter Bulloch).
8. *Ibid*, ch. III.
9. ORN, I, 5, 735.
10. *Ibid*, II, 2, 98.
11. CWAL, IV, pp. 426, 438–39.

Chapter 12. NEWS OF FIRST MANASSAS
1. John Bigelow, *Retrospections of an Active Life*, N.Y., 1909, I, 585–89. (Hereafter Bigelow *Retrospections*).
2. W. H. Russell *Diary*, p. 499.
3. *Ibid*, p. 515.
4. Moran *Journal*, II, 855.
5. LL, I, 48.
6. ORN, II, 3, 236 ff.
7. *Ibid*, 247.
8. Moran *Journal*, II, 832–33.
9. *The Reminiscences of Carl Schurz*, N.Y., 1907, II, 221–22.
10. *Ibid*, II, 245–46.
11. Moran *Journal*, II, 850.
12. *The Correspondence of John Lothrop Motley*, Boston, 1889, II, 35–36. (Hereafter Motley *Corresp.*).
13. Moran *Journal*, II, 875.
14. Bigelow *Retrospections*, I, 336–37.
15. Bigelow *Diary*, Sept. 10, 1861; Oct. 12, 1861; Apr. 1862. Manuscript in possession of the New York Public Library.
16. Arthur F. Beringause, *Brooks Adams*, N.Y., 1955, p. 30.
17. Moran *Journal*, II, 866.
18. E. D. Adams, II, 186.
19. Moran *Journal*, II, 873.
20. *Ibid*, II, 878.
21. *Ibid*, II, 907; Bonham, 45.

Chapter 13. THE WAR REACHES OUT
1. New York *Herald*, Aug. 18, 1861.
2. Sir Leslie Stephen, *The "Times" on the American War; a Historical Study*, London, 1865.

3. Comte A. E. de Gasparin, *America Before Europe*, N.Y., 1862, p. 106.
4. New York *Herald*, Aug. 18, 1861.
5. ILN, Sept. 28, 1861.
6. Moran *Journal*, II, 883.
7. *Ibid*, II, 881–82.
8. Bigelow *Retrospections*, I, 371–72.
9. Letter dated Sept. 14, 1862, in possession of Carnegie Book Shop, N.Y.
10. ORN, II, 3, 332–33.
11. Moran *Journal*, II, 868.
12. ORN, II, 3, 104–5.
13. Frank E. Vandiver, *Confederate Blockade Running Through Bermuda*, Austin, 1947.
14. New York *Herald*, Aug. 21, 1861.
15. James Duggan, *The Great Iron Ship*, N.Y., 1953, p. 97.
16. Robin Winks, *Canada and The United States, The Civil War Years*, Baltimore, 1960, p. 54. (Hereafter Winks *Canada and The U.S.*).
17. Rembert W. Patrick, *Jefferson Davis and His Cabinet*, Baton Rouge, 1944, p. 93 n.
18. ORN, II, 3, 257–74.

Chapter 14. THE TRENT AFFAIR

1. ORN, II, 3, 280.
2. Bigelow *Retrospections*, I, 378.
3. *The Public Life of James Murray Mason*, ed. by Virginia Mason, N.Y., and Wash., 1906. (Hereafter *Public Life of Mason*).
4. Mary Boykin Chesnut, *A Diary from Dixie*, Boston, 1949, p. 92. (Hereafter Chesnut *Diary*).
5. *Ibid*, pp. 123–24; 343–44.
6. Moncure Daniel Conway, *Autobiography*, London, 1904, I, 76.
7. Murat Halstead, *Caucuses of 1860*, Columbus, Ohio, 1860, pp. 12–13.
8. Jim Dan Hill, *Sea Dogs of the Sixties*, Minneapolis, 1935, p. 92.
9. Thomas Le Grand Harris, *The Trent Affair*, Indianapolis, 1896, p. 99.
10. ORN, I, 1, 130, Wilkes Report.
11. *Public Life of Mason*, pp. 205 ff.
12. LL, I, 58.
13. Moran *Journal*, 913–14.
14. *Ibid*, II, 917.
15. Tilby, *Russell*, p. 208.
16. Brian Connell, *Regina and Palmerston*, London, 1961, p. 346–48.
17. Weed *Autobiography*, I, 644–46.
18. Bigelow *Retrospections*, I, 385–408.
19. Winks *Canada and the U.S.*, p. 78.
20. MS. summary from the Duke of Somerset to Palmerston, Broadlands Archives, Dec. 6, 1861.
21. LL, I, 60.
22. F. W. Seward *Reminiscences*, pp. 187–88.
23. Benson J. Lossing, *Pictorial Field Book of the Civil War*, N.Y., 1868, II, 156–57.
24. F. W. Seward *Reminiscences*, pp. 189–90.
25. CWAL, V, 62.
26. *Public Life of Mason*, pp. 235–46.

Chapter 15. THE YEAR 1861

1. CWAL, V, 52–53. Dunbar Rowland, *Jefferson Davis, Constitutionalist,* Jackson, Miss., 1923, V, 166–73. (Hereafter Rowland's *Davis*).
2. *Prologue to Sumter,* ed. by P. V. D. Stern, Bloomington, Ind., 1961, p. 18.
3. Thompson, *Wiring a Continent, supra,* p. 368.
4. Appleton's Cyclopaedia, 1861, p. 27.
5. *Annual Report* of the Secretary of the Navy, Washington, 1862, pp. 26 and 43.
6. J. B. Jones, *A Rebel War Clerk's Diary,* ed. by Howard Swiggett, N.Y., 1935, I, 92 and 104. (Hereafter Jones *Diary*).
7. Frank E. Vandiver, *Ploughshares into Swords: Josiah Gorgas and Confederate Ordnance,* Austin, 1952, p. 75.
8. Appleton's Cyclopaedia, 1862, p. 239.
9. T. L. Livermore, *Numbers and Losses in the Civil War,* Boston, 1901, p. 47. (Hereafter Livermore).

Chapter 16. SEEDS OF CONFLICT

1. LL, I, 76.
2. Moran *Journal,* II, 939.
3. Winks *Canada and the U.S.,* p. 106 ff.
4. ILN, Jan. 11, 18, 25; Feb. 22; Mar. 1, 28; Apr. 5, 12, 26; June 21, etc.
5. *Proceedings* of the American Philosophical Society, Philadelphia, XXXIV, 147, May 20, 1895, pp. 102–28.
6. George Trevelyan, *The Life of John Bright,* Boston, 1913, pp. 312–13.
7. DU-314, Brown to Dudley, Dec. 9, 1861. DU stands for ms. number in the Dudley Papers, Huntington Library, San Marino, Cal.
8. A. C. Rogers, *Our Representatives Abroad,* N.Y., 1874, article on T. H. Dudley.
9. DU-2714, Maguire to Dudley, bill rendered, Dec. 1861.
10. DU-1176, Dudley's financial report for quarter ending Dec. 31, 1861. Dated Jan. 24, 1862.
11. Moran *Journal,* II, 942–43.
12. ORN, I, 1, 747.
13. *Ibid,* p. 299.
14. Semmes, pp. 315–16.
15. *Ibid,* 333–34, ORN, I, 1, 310 ff.
16. *Diplomatic Correspondence,* Wash., D.C., 1862, pt. 2, p. 861. (Hereafter *Diplo. Corresp.*).
17. ORN, I, 1, 319.
18. *Diplo. Corresp.,* 1862, pt. 2, 859 ff.

Chapter 17. CONFEDERATE PROPAGANDA IN EUROPE

1. ORN, II, 3, 325.
2. *Ibid,* 328.
3. *Ibid,* 331.
4. James Spence, *The American Union,* London, 1861, p. 326.
5. Henry Hotze, "Three Months in the Confederate Army," ed. by Richard Harwell, University, Ala., 1952.
6. ORN, II, 3, 280; 399–400.
7. J. F. Jameson, "The London Expenditures of the Confederate Secret Serv-

ice," *Amer. Historical Rev.*, XXXV, July 1930. Also Hotze Papers, Library of Congress.
8. Appleton's Cyclopaedia, 1862, p. 254.
9. John Bigelow, "The Confederate Diplomatists," *Century*, XLII, May 1891, pp. 113–26.
10. John W. Du Bose, *The Life and Times of William Lowndes Yancey*, Birmingham, Ala., 1892, II, 735.
11. ORN, II, 3, 324–25.
12. *The Index*, London, May 1, 1862, Vol. 1, No. 1.
13. Lincoln had urged Congress to appropriate funds for an American exhibit. It did—for $2000. CWAL, IV, 450–51.
14. ILN. Issue after issue in 1862 covered the Exhibition in pictures and text.

Chapter *18*. LINCOLN DEALS WITH INTERNATIONAL AFFAIRS

1. CWAL, V, 125–26.
2. Carl Sandburg, *Abraham Lincoln, The War Years*, N.Y., 1939, II, 301.
3. *Journals of Ralph Waldo Emerson*, ed. by E. W. Emerson and W. E. Forbes, Boston, 1913, IX, 375.
4. CWAL, V, 128.
5. New York *Herald*, Feb. 22, 1862.
6. U. S. Navy Dept., *Civil War Naval Chronology*, Pt. 2, 1862, Wash., 1962, Feb. 19, 1862.
7. Warren S. Howard, *American Slavers and the Federal Law*, Berkeley, 1963, pp. 59 ff.
8. CWAL, V, 144.
9. *Ibid*, p. 145.

Chapter *19*. CONFEDERATE AFFAIRS

1. Jones *Diary*, I, 111 n.
2. U. S. Navy Dept., *Civil War Naval Chronology*, 1862, Feb. 26, 1862.
3. Jones *Diary*, I, 114.
4. Chesnut *Diary*, p. 204.
5. *Ibid*, p. 222.
6. Benjamin F. Butler, *Butler's Book*, Boston, 1892, p. 418.
7. CFA, Jr., pp. 248–49.
8. Moran *Journal*, II, 1027–29.
9. Butler's *Book*, p. 419.
10. Henry Adams, *The Education of Henry Adams; an Autobiography*, Boston, 1918, p. 123. (Hereafter *Education of Henry Adams*).
11. Moran *Journal*, II, 1125–26.

Chapter *20*. THE FRENCH MINISTER VISITS RICHMOND

1. Owsley, 283.
2. New York *Herald*, Apr. 17, 1862.
3. Pierce Butler, *Judah P. Benjamin*, Phila., 1907, p. 286.
4. Simon I. Neiman, *Judah P. Benjamin*, Indianapolis, 1963, p. 33.
5. Robert D. Meade, *Judah P. Benjamin, Confederate Statesman*, N.Y., 1943, pp. 34 and 125. (Hereafter Meade's *Benjamin*).
6. ORN, II, 3, 463.
7. LL, I, 82–83.
8. F. W. Seward *Reminiscences*, p. 173.

9. E. D. Adams, I, 287 ff.
10. LL, I, 88.

Chapter 21. THE UNION CONSOLIDATES ITS POSITION

1. Albert A. Woldman, *Lincoln and the Russians,* Cleveland, 1952, p. 116.
2. David L. Smiley, *Lion of White Hall,* Madison, Wisc., Ch. 13.
3. Bigelow *Retrospections,* I, 492–93.
4. *Ibid,* pp. 498–500.
5. *Ibid,* pp. 500 ff.
6. *Ibid,* p. 502.
7. *Ibid,* p. 505.
8. Theodore Roscoe, *Web of Conspiracy,* N.Y., 1959, pp. 14 and 84–85.
9. Moran *Journal,* II, 918–19.
10. *Education of Henry Adams,* pp. 136–37.
11. DU-3362, Parry to Wilding.

Chapter 22. THE *FLORIDA* AND *ALABAMA* START

1. Bulloch, I, 65–66.
2. *Diplo. Corresp.,* 1862, I, 66–67.
3. Bulloch, I, 152–74.
4. ORN, I, 1, 763 ff.
5. DU-1422, Edwards to Squarey, July 23, 1862.
6. *Diplo. Corresp.,* 1862, July 12.
7. DU-4213, Wilding to Dudley, June 19, 1862.
8. Douglas H. Maynard, "Union Efforts to Prevent the Escape of the *Alabama*."
    The Mississippi Valley Historical Review, XLI, 1954, pp. 41–60. Also
    the Dudley Papers in HEH, and *Diplo. Corresp.,* 1862.
9. Copy of M. Maguire papers in possession of Mrs. Helen Roosevelt Robinson
    of New York.
10. Brooks Adams, "The Seizure of the Laird Rams," Mass. Hist. Soc. *Proceedings,*
    1911–1912, vol. 45, p. 260 note. (Hereafter Brooks Adams, "Seizure
    of the Laird Rams").
11. Bulloch, I, 238, also pp. 260–62.
12. DU-1368, Squarey to F. G. Gardner, July 28, 1862; DU-1773, Gardner's
    reply of same date.
13. Bulloch, I, p. 239.
14. *Ibid,* 240 ff.
15. DU-2913, Moran to Dudley, Sept. 3, 1862.
16. DU-3964 A and B, Jan. 24, 1872.
17. DU-4110, Aug. 8, 1871.

Chapter 23. GLADSTONE SPEAKS OUT OF TURN

1. Spencer Walpole, *Life of Lord John Russell,* London, 1891, II, 360. (Here-
    after Walpole's *Russell*).
2. John Morley, *The Life of William Ewart Gladstone,* London, 1903, I, 23.
    (Hereafter Morley's *Gladstone*).
3. *Ibid,* II, 79.
4. Moran *Journal,* II, 1078.
5. *Diplo. Corresp.,* 1862, No. 243, Oct. 17.
6. ORN, II, 3, p. 551.
7. DU-315, Oct. 18, 1862.

8. Morley's *Gladstone*, II, 80, Oct. 20, 1862.
9. *Ibid*, 81–82.
10. *Education of Henry Adams*, pp. 152–66.
11. Brooks Adams, "Seizure of the Laird Rams," p. 265.
12. CWAL, V, 388.
13. John Hope Franklin, *The Emancipation Proclamation*, N.Y., 1963, pp. 46 ff. (Hereafter Franklin).
14. London *Post*, Oct. 8, 1862.
15. London *Times*, Oct. 7, 1862.
16. Franklin, pp. 76 ff.
17. *Ibid*, p. 78.
18. Geo. M. Trevelyan, *A Life of John Bright*, N.Y., 1913, p. 306.
19. *The Diaries of J. Bright*, ed. by R. A. J. Walling, N.Y., 1930, p. 264 and 264 n. Trevelyan, *supra*, 309 n.

Chapter 24. MORE COUNTRIES BECOME INVOLVED
1. Payson J. Treat, *Japan and the United States*, N.Y., 1921.
2. *Diplo. Corresp.*, 1862, p. 797 ff., June 7 to Nov. 27, 1861.
3. ILN, Dec. 6, 1862.
4. *Diplo. Corresp.*, 1863, p. 967. Sept. 8, 1862.
5. *Ibid*, p. 970.
6. Payson J. Treat, *Diplomatic Relations between the United States and Japan*, 1853–1895, I, 131.
7. *Ibid*, p. 149.
8. *Diplo. Corresp.*, 1862, p. 172.
9. Moran *Journal*, II, 1092–93.
10. Ella Lonn, *Foreigners in the Confederacy*, Chapel Hill, N.C., 1940, Ch. IV.

Chapter 25. BUILDING THE CONFEDERATE NAVY IN EUROPE
1. ORN, I, 1, 785 (Semmes' *Journal*).
2. Dudley Collection: Clippings, 1860–62.
3. Francis Leigh Williams, *Matthew Fontaine Maury, Scientist of the Sea*. New Brunswick, N.J., 1963.
4. James Morris Morgan, *Reminiscences of a Rebel Reefer*. Boston, 1917, p. 98.
5. ORN, II, 2, 70.
6. *Ibid*, 193 ff.
7. DU-4490–93, n.d., (Sept. 1863?).
8. ORN, II, 2, 213–14.
9. *Ibid*, 3, 898.
10. *Ibid*, 551, 560–61, and 572–78.
11. *Ibid*, 547.
12. *Ibid*, 572 and 576.
13. *Ibid*, 577.
14. *Ibid*, 569 ff. Bulloch, I, 391–97.
15. *Ibid*, 2, 292, also 584.

Chapter 26. THE UNION HAS ITS TROUBLES TOO
1. Forrest Wilson, *Crusader in Crinoline*, Phila., 1941, pp. 482 ff.; also 342.
2. CWAL, V, 518–37.
3. Browning *Diary*, I, 600.
4. Welles *Diary*, I, 201.

5. CWAL, VI, 11–12.
6. Bigelow *Retrospections,* I, 583.
7. E. D. Adams, II, 72.
8. Bright *Diaries, supra,* p. 262.
9. *Diplo. Corresp.,* 1862, pp. 625–44.
10. *Ibid,* p. 645 ff.
11. *The Private and Official Correspondence of Gen. Benjamin F. Butler,* Norwood, Mass., 1917, II, 559–61.
12. *Butler's Book,* Boston, 1892, p. 547.
13. LL, I, 94–95.
14. CWAL, VI, 64.

Chapter 27. THE YEAR 1862
1. E. Merton Coulter, *The Confederate States of America,* Baton Rouge, La., 1950, pp. 141–42. (Hereafter Coulter).
2. Benjamin Quarles, *The Sable Arm,* N.Y., 1956, pp. 17 ff.
3. Livermore, p. 47. OR, III, 1, 775.
4. *Report of the Secretary of the Navy,* Washington, 1862, pp. 26 and 43; ORN, II, 3, 528 and 545.
5. Welles *Diary,* I, 211.

Chapter 28. THE CONFEDERATE SEESAW
1. Franklin, pp. 69 and 122 ff.
2. *Magazine of History,* Tarrytown, N.Y., 1925. Special No. 113, pp. 67–69.
3. Rowland's *Davis,* V, 396–415.
4. George T. Fullam, "Our Cruise on the Confederate States War Steamer *Alabama,*" London, 1863. Fullam's complete manuscript is in the Mobile Public Library.
5. ORN, II, 1, 100.
6. *Ibid,* I, 2, 18–21.
7. *Ibid,* 667 ff. Maffitt's *Journal.*
8. CFA, Jr., p. 312.
9. *Diplo. Corresp.,* 1863, I, 59 ff.
10. Moran *Journal,* II, 1119.
11. ORN, II, 3, 798; LL, I, 97 ff. *Diplo. Corresp.,* 1863, I, 59 ff.
12. Moran *Journal,* II, 1124.
13. *Diplo. Corresp.,* 1863, I, 83–97.
14. Moran *Journal,* II, 1108.
15. ORN, I, 13, 769–75.

Chapter 29. THE ERLANGER COTTON LOAN
1. DU-4386, Wilson to Dudley, Feb. 19, 1863.
2. DU-3892, R. M. Thomas to Dudley, Feb. 2, 1863.
3. ILN, Feb. 7, 1863.
4. Moran *Journal,* II, 1115.
5. DU-1088, Dudley to Cooper, Feb. 23, 1863; DU-773, Cooper to Dudley, Mar. 13, 1863.
6. ILN, Mar. 7, 1863.
7. *Ibid,* Mar. 7, 1863.
8. DU-773, Cooper to Dudley, Mar. 13, 1863.
9. DU-4133, Mar. 16, 1863 and DU-4134, Mar. 19, 1863.

10. DU-3164, Mar. 18, 1863.
11. ORN, II, 3, 655.
12. *Ibid*, 617.
13. *Ibid*, p. 714.
14. Beckles Willson, *John Slidell*, N.Y., 1932, p. 125. (Hereafter Willson).
15. ORN, II, 3, 736.
16. *Ibid*, 737.
17. Owsley, pp. 403–4.
18. John C. Schwab, *The Confederate States of America: a Financial . . . History*, N.Y., 1901, p. 42. (Hereafter *Schwab*).

Chapter 30. THE FORBES-ASPINWALL MISSION
1. Douglas Maynard, "The Forbes-Aspinwall Mission," *The Mississippi Valley Historical Review*, June 1958, p. 67–89, XLV, No. 1.
2. DAB; Robert B. Forbes, *Personal Reminiscences*. Boston, 1876.
3. *John Murray Forbes, a Memoir*, ed. by Sarah Forbes Hughes, Boston, 1905, II, 4 ff. (Hereafter *Forbes*).
4. *Ibid*, II, 9.
5. Moran *Journal*, II, 1141.
6. Hansard's *Parliamentary Debates*, Third Series, London, 1863, CLXX, 71; (Hereafter Hansard). Also *Alabama* Claims, I, 585.
7. DU-604, Chapman to Dudley, Apr. 1, 1863.
8. DU-1650, Forbes to Dudley, Mar. 30, 1863.
9. Forbes, II, 8 ff.
10. Maynard, p. 73.
11. ORN, II, 3, p. 732; Forbes, II, 45.
12. Welles *Diary*, I, 298, May 12, 1863.
13. *Diplo. Corresp.*, 1863, I, 207.
14. Bulloch, I, 331.
15. ORN, II, 3, 768.
16. DU-88, Lloyd Aspinwall to Dudley, Apr. 9, 1863.
17. Maynard, *supra*, p. 74.
18. Forbes, II, 40.
19. *Ibid*, 41. Also Maynard, p. 76.
20. Moran, *Journal*, II, 1148.
21. *Ibid*, 1149.
22. ORN, II, 3, 750–51.
23. A. E. Taylor, "Walker's Financial Mission to London," *Journal of Economic and Business History*, Boston, Feb. 1931.
24. CFA, Jr., p. 355.
25. Moran *Journal*, II, 1155.
26. DU-1653 and 1654, Apr. 17 and 19, 1863.
27. DU-319, Apr. 22, 1863.
28. Maynard, p. 80 n.
29. Forbes, II, 31.
30. *Ibid*, p. 34.
31. *Ibid*, p. 48.

Chapter 31. MR. ADAMS THREATENS WAR
1. Bigelow *Retrospections*, I, 9, 23–24.
2. Chester L. Barrows, *William M. Evarts*, Chapel Hill, N.C., 1941, p. 118.

3. *A Cycle of Adams Letters*, edited by Worthington Chauncey Ford, Boston, 1920, II, 40.
4. Hansard, Third Series, CLXXI, p. 1779; CLXXII, p. 67, 177, 252, 554 ff.
5. CFA, Jr., 333.
6. Jones *Diary*, I, 382.
7. *Diplo. Corresp.*, I, 310.
8. *Ibid*, 309.
9. DU-1099, 1139, and 1371.
10. Bulloch, I, 410 ff.
11. Brooks Adams, "Seizure of the Laird Rams," p. 291.
12. *Ibid*, p. 291.
13. *Ibid*, 292.
14. DU-1138, Aug. 28, 1863.
15. DU-1140, Sept. 1, 1863; 1141, Sept. 3, etc.
16. ORN, I, 2, 660.
17. ILN, July 18, 1863.
18. *Diplo. Corresp.*, 1863, I, 325.
19. W. D. Jones, *Confederate Rams at Birkenhead, supra*, pp. 69–72.
20. *Diplo. Corresp.*, 1863, I, 363.
21. Walpole's *Russell*, II, 359 n.
22. *Diplo. Corresp.*, 1863, I, 357.
23. *Ibid*, p. 365.
24. *Ibid*, p. 361. See Brooks Adams, "Seizure of the Laird Rams," 294–95 note, for a summary of the order in which these letters were received.
25. *Education of Henry Adams*, p. 178.
26. Sir Thomas Brassey, *The British Navy*, London, 1882, I, 68.
27. Willson, p. 163 ff.
28. DU-1143 and DU-4434.
29. Bulloch, I, 420.

Chapter 32. THE CONFEDERATES ORDER SHIPS
1. Bulloch, II, 21 ff.
2. ORN, II, 2, 351–52.
3. Willson, p. 129.
4. Bulloch, II, 23–35.
5. Bigelow *Diary*, May 14, July 19, Aug. 24, and Sept. 1, 1963.
6. John Bigelow, *France and the Confederate Navy*, N.Y., 1888, pp. 1–4.
7. Bigelow *Retrospections*, II, 56 ff.
8. Margaret Clapp, *Forgotten First Citizen, John Bigelow*, Boston, 1947. p. 204.
9. Bigelow *Retrospections*, II, 58–64.
10. ORN, II, 2, 813.
11. *Ibid*, 501.
12. *Ibid*, 510.
13. ORN, II, 3, 960.
14. *Ibid*, 2, 525.
15. *Ibid*, 527.
16. Henri Moreau, *La Politique Française en Amérique; 1861–1864*, Paris, 1864.
17. Bigelow *Retrospections*, II, 144.

Chapter 33. THE *ALABAMA* GOES TO THE FAR EAST

1. ORN, I, 2, 754, Semmes *Journal.*
2. *Ibid,* 759 and 762. Also DU-67, H. W. Allcot's affidavit, Nov. 24, 1871.
3. ORN, I, 2, 720–807, Semmes *Journal.*
4. *Ibid,* 58 and 261.
5. Treat, *Diplomatic Relations Between the United States and Japan, supra,* I, 171.
6. ORN, I, 2, 397–98, Log of the *Wyoming.*
7. *Ibid,* 777, Semmes *Journal.*
8. *Ibid,* 784 ff.
9. *Ibid,* 791.
10. DU-67, Nov. 24, 1871.
11. ORN, I, 2, 794.

Chapter 34. THE INTERNATIONAL CHESS GAME

1. Frederick W. Seward, *Seward at Washington, 1861–72.* N.Y., 1891, p. 184.
2. LL, I, 117–19.
3. Benjamin P. Thomas, *Russo-American Relations, 1815–67,* Johns Hopkins University Studies, Series 48, No. 2, Baltimore, 1930, p. 126.
4. ORN, II, 3, 848–49.
5. Harper's *Weekly,* Oct. 17 and Nov. 21, 1863.
6. F. A. Golder, "The Russian Fleet and the Civil War," *Amer. Hist. Rev.,* vol. 20, July 1915, pp. 809–10.
7. E. A. Adamov, "Russia and the United States at the Time of the Civil War," *The Journal for Modern History,* II, No. 4, Dec. 1930, pp. 586–611.
8. ORN, II, 3, 559–60.
9. *Ibid,* 910–11. Sept. 23, 1863.
10. *Ibid,* 949–50.
11. Owsley, p. 518.
12. ORN, II, 3, 952–55.
13. *Ibid,* 954–55.
14. *Ibid,* 975.
15. *Ibid,* 973–74.
16. *Ibid,* 1000.
17. *Ibid,* 1015.

Chapter 35. THE SOUTH BREAKS WITH ENGLAND

1. Rowland's *Davis,* VI, 93–128.
2. Coulter, p. 192.
3. Bonham, ch. XII.
4. Owsley, pp. 504 ff.
5. ORN, II, 3, 928.
6. *Ibid,* 929; Meade's *Benjamin,* p. 294.
7. *Public Life of Mason,* p. 457.
8. ORN, II, 2, 567.
9. *Ibid,* 524–27.
10. ILN, Dec. 26, 1863.
11. Jones *Diary,* II, 123.
12. ORN, II, 2, 640; Livermore, p. 47.
13. CWAL, VII, pp. 36–56.

14. F. W. Seward, *Seward in Washington*, p. 202.
15. William M. Robinson, Jr., *The Confederate Privateers*, New Haven, 1928, ch. XXII.
16. CWAL, VII, 71; *Diaries of John Bright*, 266–67.
17. ORN, I, 2, 513–60.
18. *Ibid*, 556.

Chapter 36. THE CONFEDERACY RUNS INTO TROUBLE
1. Bigelow *Retrospections*, II, 120–21.
2. Willson, pp. 150 ff.
3. ORN, II, 3, 354, 301, and 424.
4. *Ibid*, 962.
5. Bigelow *Retrospections*, II, 126.
6. James Spence, *The American Union*, London, 1861, pp. 131–32. American edition, pp. 90–91.
7. E. D. Adams, II, 195.
8. *The Index*, Feb. 18, 1864.
9. Schwab, chart in Appendix I.
10. ORN, II, 2, pp. 581–91.
11. *Ibid*, 2, 618 ff.
12. OR (Army), III, 4, 78. Feb. 6, 1864.
13. *Ibid*, IV, 2, 585.
14. Bulloch, II, 237 ff.

Chapter 37. "THE CONFEDERACY'S ONLY FOREIGN WAR"
1. ORN, II, 1, 104.
2. ORN, I, 15, 327 ff.
3. Semmes, 723.
4. *Ibid*, 730.
5. *Ibid*, 737; ORN, I, 2, 808.
6. Semmes, 747.
7. ORN, I, 3, 9–10.
8. J. M. Morgan, *Rebel Reefer, supra*, p. 175.
9. *Ibid*, 180–82.
10. Thomas J. Scharf, *History of the Confederate Navy*, N.Y., 1887, p. 818.
11. *Alabama Claims*, I, 410.
12. ORN, I, 3, 644–45.
13. *Ibid*, 671 ff; Semmes, 749 ff.
14. *Ibid*, 681; Semmes, 749.
15. *Ibid*, 674 ff.

Chapter 38. THE LAIRD RAMS BECOME AN ISSUE
1. *Diplo. Corresp.*, 1863, I, 308–10.
2. Dictionary of National Biography.
3. Hansard, vol. 173, p. 40.
4. *Ibid*, 310.
5. *Ibid*, 427 ff.
6. *Ibid*, 432–33.
7. *Ibid*, 439.
8. *Ibid*, 942 ff.
9. *Ibid*, 955 ff.

10. *Ibid*, 971–72.
11. *Ibid*, 995.
12. ORN, II, 597.
13. *Diplo. Corresp.*, 1864, pt. 3, p. 31.
14. *Ibid*, pp. 43–44.
15. ORN, II, 2, 596–602.
16. *Diplo. Corresp.*, 1864, pt. 3, pp. 55–56.
17. *Alabama Claims*, I, 585; Hansard, vol. 173, p. 989.
18. *Ibid*, 996.
19. *Ibid*, 1018.
20. *Ibid*, 1021.
21. Brooks Adams, "Seizure of the Laird Rams," pp. 324 and 326.
22. Jones, *Confederate Rams at Birkenhead*, p. 110.

Chapter 39. FRANCE MAKES MAXIMILIAN EMPEROR OF MEXICO
1. *Motley Corresp.*, II, 192–93.
2. *Ibid*, II, 138.
3. *Ibid*, II, 3, 154.
4. ORN, II, 3, 1059.
5. *Ibid*, 1063 ff.
6. Bigelow *Retrospections*, II, 163–65.
7. Louis Martin Sears, *John Slidell*, Durham, N.C., 1925, p. 221.
8. Willson, p. 217.
9. *The Congressional Globe*, 1st Session, 38th Congress, pp. 1408 and 1416.
10. *Ibid*, 2475.
11. *Ibid*, 3339.
12. ORN, II, 3, 1093.
13. *Ibid*, 1108.
14. *Ibid*, 1086.
15. *Ibid*, 1088.
16. *Ibid*, 1090.
17. *Ibid*, 154 ff.
18. Bigelow *Retrospections*, II, 188.

Chapter 40. THE SOUTH AS IT REALLY WAS
1. Jones *Diary*, II, 183–85.
2. E. D. Adams, II, 199.
3. ORN, II, 3, 1100.
4. F. W. Seward, *Seward in Washington*, p. 209.
5. *Diplo. Corresp.*, 1863, pt. 3, 38.
6. DU-2885, Feb. 26, 1864, and DU-618, Mar. 11, 1864.
7. ORN, II, 2, 671.
8. *Alabama Claims*, II, 152 ff.
9. DU-4420, Jan. 30, 1864.

Chapter 41. CIVIL WAR IN THE ENGLISH CHANNEL
1. DU-67, H. W. Allcot affidavit.
2. Semmes, 750.
3. ORN, I, 3, 676.
4. *The Times*, June 16, 1864.
5. ORN, I, 3, 52.

6. John McIntosh Kell, *Recollections of a Naval Life*, Washington, D.C., 1900, p. 245. (Hereafter Kell).
7. ORN, I, 3, 648.
8. Kell, p. 245; Arthur Sinclair, *Two Years on the Alabama*, Boston, 1896, p. 259. (Hereafter Sinclair).
9. Francis B. C. Bradlee, "The *Kearsarge-Alabama* Battle," Essex Institute Historical Collections, Essex, Mass., LXVII, July 1921, p. 225.
   Frederick W. Edge, "The *Alabama* and the *Kearsarge*," London, 1868, p. 3.
10. The Manet painting is now in the John G. Johnson Collection in Philadelphia.
11. From a transcript of this letter in possession of Thomas Green, Esq., of Southampton, England.
12. ORN, I, 3, 64–65. Log of the *Kearsarge*, June 19, 1864. Winslow's Supplementary Report, 79–81.
13. F. M. Bennett, *The Steam Navy of the United States*, Pittsburgh, 1896, p. 435.
14. ORN, I, 3, 59–83.
15. *Ibid*, 80 ff.
16. J.M. Browne, "The Story of the *Kearsarge* and the *Alabama*," San Francisco, 1868, p. 13.
17. John M. Ellicott, *John A. Winslow*, N.Y., 1902, p. 205.
18. ORN, I, 3, 650; Semmes, 757; Kell, p. 1248; Sinclair, 270.
19. Browne, *supra*, p. 15.
20. Kell, p. 249.
21. Sinclair, Capt. Jones' statement, p. 289.
22. Kell, p. 251.
23. Browne, pp. 16–17.
24. Kell, p. 251.
25. Semmes, p. 753–54.
26. Sinclair, p. 274.
27. Bulloch, I, 287.
28. J. R. Soley, *The Blockade and the Cruisers*, N.Y., 1883, p. 212.
29. ORN, I, 3, 60.
30. DU-4456, June 24, 1864.

Chapter 42. THE CONFEDERATE NAVY RUNS INTO MORE BAD LUCK

1. Moran *Journal*, II, 1320 and 1332.
2. *Alabama Claims*, III, 281–90.
3. *Ibid*, 293.
4. *Ibid*, 302.
5. ORN, I, 2, 664.
6. *Ibid*, 3, 612–13.
7. *Ibid*, 623–25.
8. Winks, *Canada and the U.S.*, pp. 284–85.
9. John Taylor Wood, "The *Tallahassee's* Dash into New York Waters," *Century*, LVI, No. 3, July 1898, pp. 408–17.
10. Moran *Journal*, II, 1408.
11. ORN, I, 3, 710–14.
12. *Ibid*, 646.
13. ORN, I, 3, 255–94 and 631–42.

Chapter 43. WAR WITH ENGLAND IS AGAIN AVOIDED
1. *Lincoln and the Civil War in the Diaries and Letters of John Hay,* ed. by Tyler Dennett, N.Y., 1939, pp. 208–9.
2. ILN, Aug. 20, 1864, p. 182.
3. Schwab, p. 69.
4. LL, I, 132–33.
5. Gladstone Papers, British Museum, Hartington in the War Office to T. F. Elliot, July 6, 1864.
6. ORN, I, 3, 714–19. Also OR, I, 43, 933.
7. J. C. Andrews, *The North Reports the Civil War,* Pittsburgh, 1955, p. 371.
8. ORN, I, 3, 719.
9. *The St. Albans Raid,* compiled by L. N. Benjamin, Montreal, 1865; also Winks, *Canada and the U.S.,* Ch. 14.
10. LL, I, 135.
11. Oscar A. Kinchen, *Daredevils of the Confederate Army; the Story of the St. Albans Raid,* Boston, 1959, p. 36; *Alabama Claims,* II, 26; *Memoirs of John Adams Dix,* N.Y., 1883, II, 111. Dix misdates the incident.
12. Jones *Diary,* II, 359.
13. ORN, I, 3, 718. Also 349, 352, 371 ff; *Alabama Claims,* II, 28 ff., also 58 ff.
14. Dix *Memoirs, supra,* II, 112. *Alabama Claims,* II, 75.
15. Kinchen, *supra,* p. 73 ff.
16. CWAL, VIII, 141.
17. *The Conspiracy Trial of the Murder of the President,* ed. by Ben: Perley Poore, Boston, 1865, I, 65 and II, 87.

Chapter 44. INTERNATIONAL AFFAIRS AND PRIVATE SCANDAL
1. Welles' *Diary,* I, 359.
2. Edward C. Kirkland, *The Peacemakers of 1864,* N.Y., 1927, p. 68.
3. New York *World,* July 22, 1864.
4. CWAL, VII, 451 n.
5. *Ibid,* 451.
6. William R. Thayer, *The Life of John Hay,* Boston, 1915, I, 180.
7. ORN, II, 3, 1190–94; James R. Gilmore, *Personal Recollections of Abraham Lincoln and the Civil War,* Boston, 1898, p. 271. These are Gilmore's re-creation of Davis's words. Davis himself had a very poor opinion of the two emissaries and said he had "no disposition to discuss questions of state with such persons." Davis, *Rise and Fall,* II, 611.
8. Gilmore, 291.
9. CWAL, VIII, 461.
10. Moran *Journal,* II, 1351.
11. Karl Marx and Frederick Engels, *The Civil War in the United States,* N.Y., 1937, p. 175.
12. *The Memoirs of Dr. Thomas W. Evans,* London, 1905, I, 156 ff.
13. Willson, pp. 223 and 212.
14. Bigelow *Retrospections,* II, 197–201; and 211.
15. *Diplo. Corresp.,* 1865–66, pt. 2, 205.
16. Bigelow *Retrospections,* II, 234–38.
17. Willson, pp. 242–52.
18. The spelling of the lady's name changes from account to account.
19. DU-925, Dec. 7, 1864.

Chapter 45. MORE WORLD INVOLVEMENTS

1. *Diplo. Corresp.*, 1864, Washington, 1865, pt. 3, p. 494.
2. *Ibid*, 495–99.
3. *Ibid*, 579.
4. ORN, I, 3, 202 ff.
5. *Diplo. Corresp.*, 1864, pt. 3, p. 553–58.
6. ORN, II, 3, 1196–1204 and 1229–30.
7. *Diplo. Corresp.*,1864, pt. 4, p. 113.
8. Lonn, *Foreigners in the Confederacy*, p. 228; ORN, II, 3, 1202–03.
9. Dudley Papers, *Newspaper Scrapbook*, 1862–65; ORN, II, 3, 1220.
10. Moran *Journal*, II, 1348.
11. Joseph H. Barrett, *Life of Abraham Lincoln*, N.Y., 1888, pp. 688–91.
12. ORN, II, 2, 723–25.
13. Bulloch, II, 125.
14. ORN, I, 3, 10–11.
15. ORN, II, 2, 708–9.
16. *Ibid*, 2, 731–34, also 736–37; C.S.S. *Shenandoah; The Memoirs of . . . James I. Waddell*, ed. by James D. Horan, N.Y., 1960, p. 93.
17. DU-853, C. W. Dabney to Dudley, Nov. 15, 1864. Dudley persuaded two of the seamen to make affidavits for him. DU-2240A, Nov. 12; DU-4436A, Nov. 14; and DU-3032, Nov. 12, 1864.
18. DU-3026, Moran to Dudley, Oct. 15, 1864.

Chapter 46. INTERPRETING THE SAME FACTS DIFFERENTLY

1. CWAL, VIII, 144.
2. ORN, II, 2, 640, 754, 753, and 534. Mallory's reports.
3. Livermore, p. 47.
4. *Ibid*, 149.
5. *Ibid*, 152.
6. CWAL, VIII, 151.
7. Rowland's *Davis*, Nov. 7, 1864.
8. Chesnut *Diary*, pp. 339–40.
9. Jones *Diary*, II, 359–71.
10. ORN, II, 3, 1253–56.
11. Schwab, chart facing p. 312.

Chapter 47. BRITISH POLICY UNDERGOES CHANGE

1. ORN, II, 3, 785–97.
2. *Diplo. Corresp.*, 1865, pt. 1, 171–72.
3. Hansard, Third Series, CLXXVII, 147–50.
4. *Diplo. Corresp.*, 1865, pt. 3, 165–68.
5. ORN, II, 3, 1267–69.
6. *Diplo. Corresp.*, 1865, pt. 3, 165–68.
7. Jones *Diary*, II, 449.
8. *Ibid*, 455–56; ORN, II, 3, 1265.
9. *Ibid*, 1264. Feb. 24, 1865.
10. *Ibid*, 1266.
11. ORN, II, 3, 1259, Jan. 21, 1865.
12. C. S. Henry, "Kenner's Mission to Europe." William and Mary *Quarterly*,

XXV, July 1916, pp. 9–12. A transcript of a conversation with Kenner shortly before his death in 1887.

13. ORN, II, 3, 1270–77.
14. *Ibid*, 1270–77.
15. A. J. Hanna, *Flight into Oblivion*, Richmond, 1938, pp. 3–4.

Chapter 48. THE BITTER-ENDERS

1. William E. Smith, *The Francis Preston Blair Family in Politics*, N.Y., 1933, II, 301 ff.
2. Jefferson Davis, *The Rise and Fall of the Confederate Government*, N.Y., 1881, II, 612 ff.
3. John G. Nicolay and John Hay, *Abraham Lincoln, a History*, N.Y., 1890, X, Chapter V, "Blair's Mexican Project."
4. CWAL, VIII, 260–61.
5. Meade's *Benjamin*, p. 307.
6. *Recollections of Alexander H. Stephens*, ed. by Myarta L. Avary, N.Y., 1910, p. 241.
7. New York *Times*, Feb. 14, 1865. Letter from H. S. Foote.
8. ORN, I, 3, 809.
9. L. H. Bolander, "The CSS *Stonewall*; Ship of Many Names and Many Flags." American Neptune, vol. 1, 1941, pp. 241–54.
10. ORN, I, 3, 731.
11. ORN, II, 1, 267.
12. Bigelow *Retrospections*, II, 452–55.
13. ORN, I, 3, 735–46.
14. *Ibid*, 470.
15. *Ibid*, 743; J. N. Hyde, "Two Stone Walls," Illinois Commandery. *Military Essays and Recollections*, Chicago, 1891, pp. 458–59. The author's dates are incorrect.
16. Bulloch's account of the *Stonewall's* career—especially the part about her acquisition in Denmark—is evasive, probably because he did not play a major part in it. See Bulloch II, 45–105. Also Bigelow, *France and the Confederate Navy*, pp. 56–89.
17. Waddell *Memoirs*, p. 83; ORN, II, 2, 708.

Chapter 49. THE YEARS BEYOND

1. Moran *Journal*, II, 1410–15.
2. *The Times*, Apr. 27, 1865.
3. William S. Walsh, *Abraham Lincoln and the London Punch*, N.Y., 1909, pp. 98–112.
4. National Archives, Old Army Records, JAG, Exhibits Box.
5. *The Assassination of President Lincoln and the Trial of the Conspirators*, compiled by Benn Pitman, Washington, D.C., 1865, p. 19.
6. DU-Box 61.
7. Brainerd Dyer, "Thomas H. Dudley," *Civil War History*, I, 4, 401–13, Dec. 1955.
8. For an excellent discussion of the disappearance of American shipping during and after the Civil War see George W. Dalzell, *The Flight from the Flag*, Chapel Hill, 1940, Ch. XII.
9. Thomas W. Balch, *The Alabama Arbitration*, Phila., 1900.
10. Francis W. Hackett, *The Geneva Award Acts*, Boston, 1882.

11. *Education of Henry Adams*, p. 210.
12. Coulter, p. 567 n.
13. *Diplo. Corresp.*, 1865, pt. 1, 192.

Chapter 50. YESTERDAY AND TOMORROW
1. Kenneth M. Stampp, *The Peculiar Institution*, N.Y., 1956, p. 30.
2. CWAL, II, 255. Speech at Peoria, Ill., Oct. 16, 1854.
3. *Ibid*, III, 315.

INDEX

Acton, Lord, his pro-Southern attitude, 21

Adamov, E. A., reveals purpose for visit of Russian fleet to America, 234

Adams, Brooks, 49; tours London with his father, 77; calls Oct. 1862 a turning point in Anglo-American affairs, 155–56; on the Laird rams, 265

Adams, Charles Francis, United States Congressman, 9; Seward suggests that he be Minister to England, 32; meets Lincoln, 35–36; arrives in England, 44; his ancestors, 45; presented to the Queen, 49; his family, 49–50; calls on Russell, 50–54; described by Schurz, 75; by Bigelow, 76; activities in London, 77; has to deal with Confederates' letters forwarded by Bunch, 77–79; learns about the *Trent* Affair, 90; controversy with Palmerston over Butler's "Woman Order," 126–29; his reaction to Gladstone's Newcastle speech, 154; and the Forbes-Aspinwall mission, 200–1; and the Laird rams, 210–13; demands that Russell surrender Semmes, 291–92; and Lord Wharncliffe, 316; and Russell's change of attitude toward the Union, 325–28

Adams, Henry, 50; on English society, 52; on Seward's dispatch of May 21, 1861, 53; regrets his father's break with Palmerston over Butler's "Woman Order," 128–29; his opinion of Thurlow Weed, 140–41; his long study of Gladstone's Newcastle speech, 155; characterizes Roebuck, 208; on postwar diplomacy as a career, 344

Alabama, C.S.S., (former 290 and *Enrica*), the building of, 143; her escape from Liverpool, 146–51; commissioned at sea, 163; at end of 1862, 180; reaction of crew to the Emancipation Proclamation, 186; sinks the U.S.S. *Hatteras*, 186–87; Russell calls her escape a scandal, 200, 264; in Bahia, then South Africa, 223; and the *Wyoming*, 224; in Singapore, 225–27; in the Indian Ocean, 254; Cape Town to Brazil, 254–55; enters Cherbourg, 257; pamphlet written by one of her crew, 279;

battle with the *Kearsarge*, 281–90; controversy afterwards, 291–92

Alabama Claims, 343–44

Albert, Prince, Victoria's Consort, 24; in *Trent* Affair, 91–92; his death, 92

Alcock, Sir Rutherford, British Minister to Japan, his plans for attack on Shimonoseki disapproved by Russell, 313

Alexander II, Emperor of Russia, 83

Alexandra, C.S.S., built by Fraser, Trenholm, 192; seized by the British, 199; the court rules against the seizure, 207, 210

America, the yacht, used as blockade-runner, 68

Amphion, C.S.S., 278

Anderson, Major Robert, moves garrison to Fort Sumter, 1; informs Lincoln that Sumter cannot be held, 29

Antietam, battle of, 153

Antonelli, Cardinal Giacomo, introduces Mann to the Pope, 235; praises Davis and the C.S.A., 235

Appomattox Campaign, 339

Arman, M. L., French shipbuilder, offers to construct Confederate ships, 215–16

Army, Confederate (1861), 100; (1862), 180; (1863), 243

Army, Union, (1861), 98; (1862), 180; (1863), 243

Arnold, Matthew, pro-Southern, 20

Aspinwall, William Henry, American shipping magnate, goes to Europe on secret mission, 197–206

Atlanta, Ga., 307, 321, 330

Atlantic cable, goes out of service, 5; Lincoln wants it restored, 172

Atlantic Monthly, prints Mrs. Stowe's article on slavery, 172; and Gilmore's on his visit to Richmond, 307

Australia, 291

Bahia, Brazil, Semmes there, 223; Morris takes the *Florida* there, 294; she is captured there, 295–96

Baring, Thomas, ends debate in Parliament on Laird rams, 264

Baring Brothers and the Forbes-Aspinwall mission, 198, 201, 202

378INDEX

Holcombe, James P., Confederate agent in
Canada, 300, 305–6
Homer, Winslow, illustrates Russian Ball
for Harper's *Weekly*, 232
Hotze, Henry, Confederate propagandist,
111–12; proposes publication of *The
Index*, 113–14; denounces Spence, 246;
defends slavery, 247; on Maximilian,
272
Housatonic, U.S.S., sunk by submarine
H. L. *Hunley*, 253
Hunley, H. L., Confederate submarine,
sinks U.S.S. *Housatonic*, 253
Hunter, Robert M. T., replaces Toombs
as Confederate Secretary of State, 86
Hunter, William, and Gurowski, 62
Huse, Caleb, goes to Europe to buy mu-
nitions for the Confederates, 67–68; and
the *Stonewall*, 335–36
Huxley, T. H., attitude toward American
Civil War, 20

Illustrated London News, prints arma-
ment pictures, 101; attitude toward the
United States, 102; reports Exeter Hall
meeting, 191–92; praises American re-
lief ships, 192; prints picture of the
Laird rams, 214
Index, The, Confederate newspaper in
England, 114, 247
International Exhibition, London, 1862,
114–15

Jamestown, U.S.S., in Nagasaki, 225; and
the attack on Shimonoseki, 314
Japan and the United States, 159–60; possibility of outfitting privateers there,
209; the *Pembroke* fired on, *Wyoming*
retaliates, 224–25; Straits of Shimonoseki attacked by an international fleet,
313–14
Japan. See C.S.S. *Georgia*
Jaquess, Colonel James, goes to Richmond
on peace mission, 306–7, 320
Jefferson, Thomas, predicts that slavery
will destroy the Union, 40
Jewett, William C. and Greeley's peace
negotiations, 305–6
Johnson, President Andrew, proclaims end
of the war, 343
Johnson's Island, Lake Erie, attempts to

set free the Confederate prisoners there,
301
Jones, J. B., the Rebel War Clerk, diary
entries, 123, 124, 125, 176, 208–9,
275–76, 302, 322–23, 328
Juavez, Benito, President of Mexico, 58;
resists the French, 207

Kearsarge, U.S.S., appears off Cherbourg,
281; compared with the *Alabama*, 283;
sinks the *Alabama*, 284–87
Kell, James McIntosh, first officer on the
Alabama, reports on the battle with the
Kearsarge, 283–88
Kenner, Duncan F., on secret mission to
Paris, 323, 329; postwar career, 345

Laird, John, and the C.S.S. *Alabama*,
148; defends her in Parliament, 191
Laird rams, 163, 164, 168, 187, 192, 197;
ownership of, 168, 210, 213, 219; and
the Forbes-Aspinwall mission, 197, 202;
first one launched, 210; *Illustrated London News* prints pictures of them, 214;
to be sold, 248; dispute in Parliament,
259–66; bought by British Government,
265; Brooks Adams on, 265
Laird yards in Birkenhead, 144, 163
Lancashire cotton workers, starvation
among, 158, 242
Lancaster, John, owner of the yacht *Deerhound*, 282
Lee, General Robert E., replaces Johnston,
135, 138; makes army into fighting
force, 179; defeats Burnside at Fredericksburg, 173; and Hooker at Chancellorsville, 205, 207; defeated at Gettysburg, 208; his poor health, 239; the
Lynchburg *Virginian* suggests that he
be made a dictator, 243; compared with
Bulloch, 249–50; and Russell's letter to
Davis, 328
Lhuys, Drouyn De, becomes French Foreign Minister in Oct. 1862, 167; stops
work on Confederate ships being built
in France, 220; denies that France
wants to acquire Texas, 269; and Congressional resolution on Mexico, 268,
271
Lincoln, Abraham, elected 1860, 1; in
Springfield, 3; goes to Washington, 9;
inaugurated, 10; warned that Fort Sum-

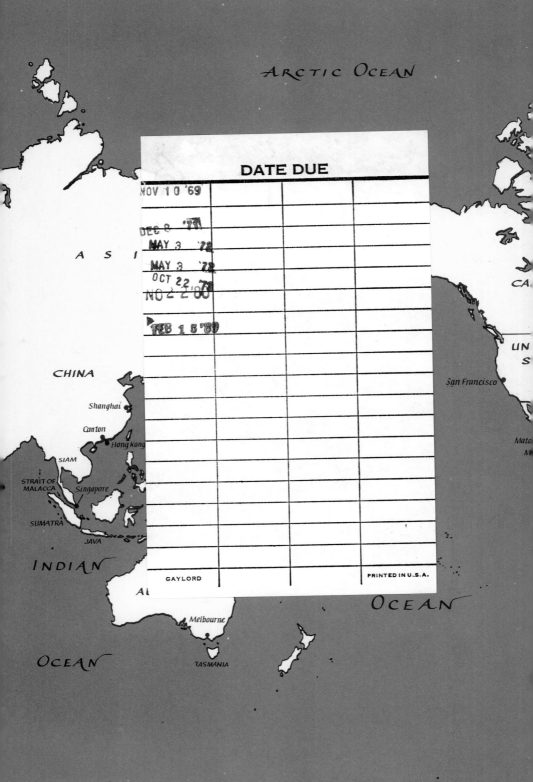